1536 – Anne Boleyn beheaded • Hen
  • the Ten Articles promulgated
  William Tyndale burnt at the st
  First edition of Calvin's *Institut*
1537 – Jane Seymour bears future Edw
  "Matthews' Bible" published •
  Man published
1538 – English Bibles ordered placed in every church
1539 – "the Great Bible" published • the Six Articles passed
1540 – Systematic dissolution of all English monasteries completed
1542 – Roman Inquisition officially sanctioned by Pope Paul III
1543 – *A Necessary Doctrine and Erudition for Any Christian Man*
  published
1545 – Council of Trent assembles
1546 – Martin Luther dies

1547 – **Edward VI crowned**
  Parliament repeals: Six Articles • all restrictions on printing
  and circulation of the Scriptures • laws under which *heretics*
  were burnt • marriage of priests legalized • laity allowed
  communion • all images removed from churches
1552 – Second Prayer Book of Edward VI sanctioned • altar called
  a *table* • priest a *minister* • minister's vestments limited to
  surplice
1553 – Forty-two Articles of Religion issued
  Edward VI dies • Lady Jane Grey crowned for nine days

1553 – **Mary I becomes first Queen to rule England**
  all religious laws of Edward VI repealed • all laws against
  heresy revived • all Bibles removed from churches • Bible-
  printing ceases • Bible-reading forbidden • communion
  for laity forbidden • Prayer Book banished • ministers
  forbidden marriage
1554 – Lady Jane Grey beheaded • Cardinal Pole returns to
  England • England officially returns to Popery
1555 – Marian persecution begins • 71 Protestants burnt at stake
1556 – 89 Protestants burnt at the stake
  Mary I and Phillip II (King of Spain) joined in marriage
1557 – 88 Protestants burnt at the stake
1558 – 40 Protestants burnt at the stake
  Bloody Mary dies • Cardinal Pole dies 12 hours later

Light From Old Times

"If the trumpet give an uncertain sound,
who shall prepare himself to the battle?"

1 Corinthians 14:8

LIGHT FROM OLD TIMES

or

PROTESTANT FACTS AND MEN

with an

INTRODUCTION

For Our Own Days

BISHOP JOHN CHARLES RYLE, D.D.

CHARLES NOLAN PUBLISHERS
MOSCOW, IDAHO

First published in 1890
This volume is re-typeset from
Light From Old Times
Fifth edition, illustrated
Charles J. Thynne & Jarvis, Ltd.
London, England, 1924
First Charles Nolan Publishers edition 2000

Frontispiece courtesy of Mr. Jim Wilson.

ISBN
0-9677603-0-5

CHARLES NOLAN PUBLISHERS
MOSCOW, IDAHO
UNITED STATES OF AMERICA

PUBLISHER'S NOTE

THOUGH fallen on hard times of late, *books* have played an essential role in Church history. Witness these martyrs, whose lives composed portions of that history: the Apostle Paul, chained in a filthy dungeon beneath the streets of Rome, had three simple requests prior to staring down the block: a winter blanket, *books*, and writing parchments (2 Tim. 4:13); William Tyndale, facing death by fire, echoed Paul's list when he beseeched winter garments, a Hebrew *Bible*, and a Hebrew *dictionary*; John Bradford, himself only days away from being bound to the stake, offered a petition that was short and to the point—that he might "have his *books*, and time enough to peruse them" (page 182). Yes, some men maintain well-focused priorities to the end.

J.C. Ryle was a man of like passion. Within these pages his affection for the printed word is made manifest. No doubt the Reformers were first and foremost in his mind, nevertheless, *few things* eclipsed his appreciation of *books*. While documenting William Gurnall's last will and testament, Ryle lamented, "The end to which good men's libraries finally come is a melancholy subject. Few things are so much loved by some, and despised and neglected by others as books, and specially theological books" (page 341). We second that motion.

Indeed, the volume now in the reader's hands has been reprinted with that lamentation in mind. It is our decided conviction that the works of J.C. Ryle belong in all "good men's libraries." To that end we have made this work available. Moreover, we have endeavored to craft a book, both in style and appearance, that is as much a tribute to J.C. Ryle, as *Light From Old Times* is to the Puritans and Reformers. And since he wrote "to our children's children" (page 39), we have intentionally bound this book with the hope that it will endure for generations to come.

As the first American edition of *Light From Old Times*, a few notes are in order. (1) Slight modifications have been made to the punctuation, though no text has been removed. (2) Outlines inconsistent with themselves, such as subsets (*a*) and (*b*) directly following subset (*c*), have been changed to (i) and (ii), and some points have been accentuated with a bold font. (3) Parenthetical source notes have been changed to footnotes. (4) Supplemental footnotes, a glossary, and a chronological timeline have been inserted. Symbols have been used to identify J.C. Ryle's footnotes, and Arabic numerals for the publisher's.

CONTENTS

ILLUSTRATIONS

FOREWORD

THAT this book is coming into print again is a matter for great rejoicing. For many reasons, few of them any good, contemporary mainstream Christian book publishers do not usually publish the kinds of books they ought to be publishing. And so those who are hungry for substance in what they read are forced to turn to those specialty publishers who are willing to bring us *light from old times*. Thank God that more and more of these publishers are coming forward to fill this shameful vacuum. Perhaps when we have reprinted enough books, our generation will grow to have the maturity to contribute something of our own to the grand Puritan heritage.

This first volume from a new publishing house promises to bring many more behind it, and those who want to encourage this process may do so by taking this book over to the cash register right now. But encouraging the process and encouraging your soul are two different things. The latter should be done by sitting down as soon as you have the book and some hours to spend with it. Once the reader has well begun, stopping will be extremely difficult. The lessons Ryle draws, and the stories he tells, have the ability to grip the mind and hold the reader down in his seat. In these pages, we see Hooper and Ridley and Latimer and Baxter and Gurnall.

Who said these words, with fire approaching? "Be of good comfort, brother Ridley, and play the man; we shall this day light such a candle, by God's grace, in England, as I trust never shall be put out." Some were tied to stakes, some were imprisoned, some were hounded by the law, and a few were given an entire lifetime of preaching in relative peace. But fidelity in any circumstance is to be honored, not forgotten. The fact that we have forgotten these stories, and have not told them to our children *once*, is astounding. Only the last day will completely reveal the glorious nature of the martyrdoms under Bloody Mary. But a significant portion of that glory can be read, here. And the concluding story about James II and the trial of the Seven Bishops is worth the price of the whole book. Some of our fathers went through cruel mockings and scourgings, while others overthrew kingdoms (Heb. 11:33–38). But whether we are considering godly, dying defiance in the face of crushing authority, or godly triumph over tyranny, the fact that we do not love to tell these stories is inexplicable.

After this book is finished, the reader will have learned a great deal about the English Reformation. But I trust he will also have learned about the man who has wonderfully reminded us of these things.

Honest Ryle. Despite all the names that fly around us during any controversy, the world can basically be divided into two parties— the honest party and the dishonest party. Any acquaintance with the work of J.C. Ryle immediately reveals him to be a lover of the truth. His honest face peers out from every page. The reader always knows what he is getting, and is confident that nothing is being slipped by him. Circumstances will change, and the names of factions will change, but men who love the truth always recognize one another. Throughout this book, time after time, Ryle shows how those who were undermining the doctrinal integrity of the Church of England in his day, and who were doing so in the name of "High Churchmanship," were actually misrepresenting their own history, their own standards, and the very nature of the Church of England. The evangelical party in the Church of England was readily dismissed by them with a wave of the hand and a taunt of "low churchmanship." But as Ryle shows repeatedly, the Church of England is Reformed in its standards and Reformed in its founding. Those who have sought to make it into something else, from Laud to the Tractarians, from the Tractarians to the modernists, have declared their allegiance to the dishonest party.

Protestant Ryle. To modern ears, any polemic against the Roman Catholic Church grates on us. Unhappily for such modern ears, such a polemic will be found in this book. Ryle has no love for "Popery," and I am afraid he is completely out of step with our modern zeal to murmur peace, peace when there is no peace.

Ryle is a thorough-going Christian, and this means he has a high view of the importance of *history*. To the modern evangelical, this is all a jangling of words, a throwing of theological dust in the air while we all shout, "Great is Diana of the Ephesians!" We are momentary men, and so we have no answer to those who say the Reformation was so long ago and so far away, and why are we still making a fuss over ancient history? But Ryle is connected with the history of the Church, and he has an admirable loyalty to our fathers in the faith who sealed their testimony in blood and fire. Classical Protestants and Roman Catholics do have one thing in common, and this is an understanding of the importance of historical continuity. This leaves many modern evangelicals baffled about the whole dispute. But we are speaking to a church that claims to remember. We also remember, and we have to say to the Roman Church, as Ryle does in this book, very effectively, "There still remains a controversy between us. Centuries ago you embraced some deadly errors, and, to compound your guilt, you have slaughtered many thousands of white-robed martyrs who dared to identify that sin, separating themselves from it. This controversy still stands between us, and time will not erase it. The blood of the Lord Jesus is offered to the repentant, not the ancient."

Holy Ryle. Despite the controversy, the Protestantism exhibited by Ryle throughout this book cannot be dismissed as an unholy "love of party." He was vigorous in his defense of the truth of God, but he was no bigot. He was an Anglican churchman, a man who loved and understood his church, and yet his sympathies were with the Dissenters when the truth was with them. And when he differed with the Puritans in their stand over the Act of Uniformity, he still admired their constancy, and knew them to be honest, conscientious men. Consistently, he writes against dishonesty and error, and not against those who simply happen to belong to a different party.

He was able to do this because he was a holy man. Ryle is probably best known for the book he wrote on holiness, and in the book you hold, it is possible to see that holy demeanor displayed. He was a warrior, but not a cranky fighter. He was a shepherd of souls, and never tired of pointing the way to green pastures. He fought wolves, not because he loved conflict, but because he loved sheep. This man was a true minister of the gospel, one who delighted to turn to a declaration of that gospel whenever possible. His fundamental stance, always, was that of a man who loved.

Ryle was a man of God. Those who complete this book will certainly come away better informed. But that is just a part of what they will receive.

DOUGLAS WILSON

Christ Church
Moscow, Idaho

INTRODUCTION

THE volume now in the reader's hands requires a few words of prefatory explanation. It is partly *historical*, and partly *biographical*. It is about facts and men.

Under the *historical* head, the reader will find some account of the three most remarkable events in the history of the Reformed Church of England. The first of these events is the ferocious attempt which was made by Queen Mary, of unhappy memory, to destroy the work of religious Reformation which was begun in the reign of Edward VI. The second event is the blind and abortive effort of Archbishop Laud to un-Protestantize the Church of England, which resulted in his own execution and well-nigh ruined the Church and the Monarchy for ever. The third event is the daring attack on English Protestantism which was made by James II when he prosecuted the Seven Bishops, and under the specious name of *toleration*, endeavoured to reestablish the power of the Bishop of Rome in the land. These three events ought to be familiar to every Englishman. In the second, tenth, and last papers in this volume, I have tried to supply some condensed information about them. We live in an age when they cannot be known too well and ought to be continually kept before the public eye.

Under the *biographical* head, the reader will find in this volume some account of the lives and opinions of eleven remarkable men. At the head of the eleven I have placed John Wycliffe, "the Morning Star of the Reformation." He lived before the invention of printing and consequently is far less known than he ought to be. But I believe that English Christianity owes him a great debt which has never been fully paid. Among the eleven I have placed Archbishop Laud. He is a man who did such indelible harm to the Church of England, and yet is so generally overvalued and misunderstood that I have felt it a plain duty to place him before my readers in his true colours. I believe the wounds he inflicted on our church will never be healed. Of the remaining nine, six were Reformers, who were burned alive in Queen Mary's days because they would not abjure their Protestant principles and believe in the sacrifice of the Mass. Three of the nine were Puritan divines, who lived in the seventeenth century and made a deep mark in their day and generation. One common remark applies both to Reformers and Puritans: They are far less known and understood in these latter times than they ought to be. Of course, I have chosen the six Reformers as subjects of biographies, deliberately, purposely, and with special reasons. What those reasons are I will proceed to explain.

(1) I hold, then, first of all, that the lives, deaths, and opinions of the leading English Reformers demand special investigation in the present day. The Church of England, as it now is, was in great measure the work of their hands. To them, with a few trifling exceptions, we owe our present articles, liturgy, and homilies. That great ecclesiastical machinery, whose centre is at Lambeth Palace and whose influence is more or less felt throughout the world wherever the British flag waves, was purified, remoulded, and recast in its present form by their instrumentality. Can anyone doubt that it is of the utmost importance to ascertain what they thought and did, and in defence of what opinions they lived and died? Surely common sense points out that if we want to know who is a *true* "churchman," we should find out what manner of men the *first* "churchmen" were! The natural way to ascertain what *views* of religion are "church views" is to inquire what kind of *views* were held by our church Reformers in the sixteenth century. In matters of doctrine, are we of one mind with Cranmer, Ridley, Hooper, and Latimer? If not, our "churchmanship" is of a somewhat peculiar and equivocal kind.

Holding these opinions, I have endeavoured to produce a correct sketch of six of the leading champions of the English Reformation. Those whom I have chosen, undoubtedly, with the exception of Ridley, were not equal to Cranmer in point of learning. In popular talent, however, and general influence with their countrymen, they were probably second to none. I venture the conjecture that the middle classes and lower orders of Englishmen in the sixteenth century were more familiar with the names of two of them, *viz.,*

Bishop Hooper and Bishop Latimer, than of any of the Reformers. None, I suspect, made such a deep impression on the minds of their generation, none were so often talked of round English firesides, as the two whose lives are fully given in this volume. None, I am firmly persuaded, so thoroughly deserve to be had in honour. They were men of whom the Church of England may well be proud. She may reckon among her sons some perhaps who were their equals, but none, I am sure, who were their superiors. For abounding usefulness in life and noble courage in death, Hooper and Latimer have never been surpassed.

Certain modern churchmen, I am well aware, have tried hard to depreciate the value of the English Reformation and to vilify the character of the English Reformers. One writer in particular, who occupied no mean position among the champions of the extreme ritualistic or Catholic school, did not scruple to put in print the following extraordinary sentences:

> Robespierre, Danton, Marat, St. Just, Couthon,[1] and the like, merit quite as much admiration and respect as Cranmer, Ridley, Latimer, Hooper, and the others, who happened to have the ill luck to be worsted in a struggle wherein they meant to serve their adversaries as they were served themselves. . . .

It has been brought as a serious charge against men of my school, that we should have been safe under Queen Mary. But we should have been burnt for refusing a new and immoral creed, if that young tiger-cub Edward VI had lived, and Cranmer had not been arrested in his wicked career by Divine vengeance. Of the depth of infamy into which this wretched man descended, as the unscrupulous tool of the tyrant Henry and his minion, Thomas Cromwell,[2] I have no leisure to speak now. . . .

If history were honestly written, Latimer would change places with Bonner, and appear in true colours as the coarse, profane, unscrupulous, persecuting bully which the other prelate is usually called, and with the special brand of cowardice besides, of which no man can accuse Bonner. . . .

---

[1] All five men were radical leaders during the French Revolution.

[2] Cromwell (c. 1485–1540) was Henry the Eighth's chief advisor during England's Reformation. At the instigation of his enemies, he was arrested for heresy and treason, then executed.

Latimer was a coward. . . .

Latimer was perjured and unscrupulous. . . .

Latimer's coarseness and profanity are not left to conjecture, nor to the bias of partisans. He has given ample proof of them under his own hand in his still extant sermons. . . . *

Violent language like this injures nobody but the man who uses it. It utterly defeats its own object. It proves far too much, if it proves anything at all. How any set of men so bad as the Reformers are painted by the writer I have just quoted could have obtained the influence they undoubtedly obtained, and swayed public opinion as they undoubtedly swayed it, is a *little difficulty* which he did not think fit to explain. If our ancestors allowed the Reformation to be carried on by men of such wretched characters as he attributes to the English Reformers, the Englishmen of that day must have been idiots and fools. It is clear as daylight to my mind, even if there were no historical evidence on the subject, that the generation which really knew Cranmer, Ridley, Latimer, and Hooper, thought far more highly of them than Dr. Littledale did. If they had been the bad, worthless men that he represents them, they would never have left such a deep mark on the religious character of England as they certainly did.

But, after all, what historical proof did Dr. Littledale give that his low estimate of the English Reformers is correct? I answer unhesitatingly, "*None* that will satisfy any impartial judge of evidence." The testimony of a contemporary historian, the well-known John Fox, the martyrologist, stands in the way; and how did he get over it? He simply abused him, or, in plain English, called him a *liar.* He said that he was "a mendacious partisan." He styled the *Acts and Monuments* of Fox "a magazine of lying bigotry: a book which no educated man now living, possessed of any self-respect or honesty, does otherwise than repudiate with contempt and aversion."†

Attacks on Fox such as these are very ancient things. From the day that the good old *Book of Martyrs* first appeared, it has been assailed and abused more violently by the advocates of Popery than

---

* See *Innovations*, a lecture by Dr. Littledale, priest of the Church of England. Delivered at Liverpool, April 23, 1868. Pages 15, 16, 17, 44, 45.

† See lecture on *Innovations*, already quoted.

any uninspired book that ever was printed. Dr. Littledale was only walking in the steps of Harpsfield, Parsons, Laud, Heylin, Dr. John Milner (the Roman Catholic), and others. The objections of these writers will be found fully examined in the preface to Canon Townsend's edition of Fox. That preface is a document which is far too little known. It deserves an attentive perusal.

My own opinion of Fox's great work differs widely from that of Dr. Littledale. That he never erred I do not pretend to say. He was no more infallible than the Pope. But that he is generally accurate in his statement of facts and generally trustworthy in his estimate of character, I am thoroughly persuaded. In this opinion, the following extracts from the prospectus or preface of Canon Townsend's edition of Fox's *Acts and Monuments* will prove that I do not stand alone:

The three Archbishops of Canterbury of Fox's own day bore the strongest testimony to his integrity. Archbishop Parker, in the Canons of 1571, ordered all bishops and other dignitaries to have in their hall or public dining room the Bible and Fox's great work. Archbishop Grindall was Fox's main assistant in the compilation; and Archbishop Whitgift speaks of Fox as "that worthy man who hath deserved so well of the Church of England."

Leaving his own times, we come to Fuller, the Church historian, who says of Fox: "His industry hath starved the endeavours of such as shall succeed him, leaving nothing for their pains to feed upon. For what can the man do that cometh after the king." Strype styles him "A most painstaking searcher into records and archives; and one who, as he hath been found most diligent, so most strictly true and faithful." And Bishop Burnet adds, "Having compared Fox's book with the records, I have never been able to discover any errors or prevarications in them, but the utmost fidelity and exactness."

Coming down to our own times, we find every competent judge agreeing, both as to the great value of Fox's collection and as to its entire faithfulness. Foremost among these is the late Prebendary Soames, himself an historian of no mean rank, who says, "The first portion of this important work which is principally an historical exposure of the Papacy, was originally printed in Latin on the Continent, whither the author had fled from the Marian prosecution. Having arrived at home soon after Elizabeth's accession, Fox was encouraged by various members of the hierarchy to crown his former labours, by adding to them copious accounts of those who had perished as religious delinquents under the late Queen. Every facility was afforded to him for the completion of this task in the most satisfactory manner; and he shows himself fully worthy of the confidence reposed in him. Invariable accuracy is not to be expected in any historical work of such extent; but it may be truly said of England's venerable martyrologist, that his relations are more than ordinarily worthy of reliance. His principal object being, indeed, to leave behind him a mass of authentic information relating to those miserable times which it had been his lot to witness, he printed a vast mass of original letters, records of judicial processes, and other documentary evidence. The result of this judicious policy was a work which has highly gratified the friends of Protestantism, and successfully defied its enemies. Numerous attacks have been levelled at the honest chronicles of Rome's intolerance, but they have ever fallen harmless from the assailant's hand."

The late Dr. Wordsworth (Master of Trinity College, Cambridge) says, "I am not ignorant of what has been said by Milner, and by his predecessors, Harpsfield, Parsons, and others. But neither his writings nor theirs have proved, and it never will be proved, that John Fox is not one of the most faithful and authentic of all historians. We know too much of the strength of Fox's book, and of the weakness of those of his adversaries, to be further moved by Dr. John Milner's censures than to charge them with falsehood. All the many researches and discoveries of later times, in regard to historical documents, have only contributed to place the general fidelity and truth of Fox's narrative on a rock which cannot be shaken."

Dr. Jenkyns (the Editor of *Archbishop Cranmer's Remains*) says, "I had occasion to compare several of the papers printed by Fox with the original documents, and I had good reason to be satisfied with the martyrologist's fidelity and accuracy."

Mr. Froude, who has carefully gone over the whole Tudor period, in his history of the times, adds, "I trust Fox when he produces documentary evidence, because I have invariably found his documents accurate."

Dr. Southey wrote, "I have always intended to write the life of John Fox for the *Quarterly Review*, wherein I might render due honour to a man for whom I have a great veneration."

Archbishop Howley wrote, "I am glad you intend to republish the great work of the martyrology, and willingly consent to its being dedicated to myself."

After all, the *animus* of most modern attacks on the English Reformers is too transparently clear to be mistaken. The writers who make them appear to dislike Protestantism most cordially and to want the Church of England to be Romanized once more. The writings and opinions of the Reformers stand sadly in their way! How can they possibly get over this barrier? They try to damage their character, and so to impair the value of their testimony. I predict that they will not succeed. I believe that, like the viper biting the file, they are only labouring in vain and hurting themselves. I am not afraid of the result of any amount of examination that can be applied to such men as Hooper and Latimer. Let men turn on them all the light they please, so long as it is fairly and honestly turned on. They will stand any properly conducted investigation. They will come out unscathed from the ordeal of any just inquiry. In a word, their names will live and be honoured when their assailants are clean forgotten.

(2) With regard to the *Puritans*, of whom I have brought forward three specimens in this volume, I believe that they deserve almost as much attention in the present day as the Reformers. I want to promote acquaintance with them in the minds of all students of English Church history. Never, I believe, were men so little understood and so absurdly maligned as the Puritans. On no subject, perhaps, are English churchmen so much in the dark and require such thorough enlightening. If the biographies of Ward, Baxter, and Gurnall only help to make my readers understand what a Puritan really was, I shall feel I have done the cause of truth some service.

The common impression of most English churchmen about the Puritans is that they were ignorant, fanatical dissenters, who troubled England in the seventeenth century—that they hated the monarchical form of government and cut off Charles the First's head—that they hated the Church of England and caused its destruction—and that they were unlearned enthusiasts who despised knowledge and study, and regarded all forms of worship as Popery. There are some ecclesiastical orators of high rank and brilliant reputation who are never weary of flinging the epithet *Puritanical* at evangelical churchmen as the hardest word of scorn that they can employ. Let no churchman's heart fail when he hears himself stigmatised as a *Puritan*. The man who tells the world that there is any disgrace in being a Puritan is only exposing his own ignorance of plain facts, or shamefully presuming on that widespread ignorance of English Church history which marks the nineteenth century.

The Puritans were not faultless, I freely admit. They said, did, and wrote many things which cannot be commended. Some of them, no doubt, were violent, fierce, narrow-minded sectarians. Yet, even then, great allowance ought to be made for the trying circumstances in which they are placed and the incessant irritating persecution to which they were exposed. It is written that "oppression maketh a wise man mad" (Eccles. 7:7). With all their faults, the leaders of the party were great and good men. With all their defects, the Puritans, as a body, were not the men that certain writers and orators in the present day are fond of representing them to have been.

(*a*) The Puritans were *not enemies to the Monarchy*. It is simply false to say that they were. The great majority of them protested strongly against the execution of Charles I, and were active agents in bringing back Charles II to England and placing the crown on his head after Oliver Cromwell's death. The base ingratitude with which they were afterwards treated in 1662 by the very monarch whom they helped to restore is one of the most shameful pages in the history of the Stuarts.

(*b*) The Puritans were *not enemies to the Church of England*. They would gladly have seen her government and ceremonial improved, and more liberty allowed to her ministers in the conduct of public worship. And they were quite right! But the bulk of them were originally ordained by bishops, and had no special objection either to episcopacy or a liturgy. Baxter, one of their leaders, expressly testifies that a very few concessions in 1662 would have retained in the Church of England *sixteen hundred* out of the two thousand who were driven out by the Act of Uniformity on St. Bartholomew's Day!

(c) The Puritans were *not unlearned and ignorant men*. The great majority of them were Oxford and Cambridge graduates, many of them fellows of colleges, some of them heads and principals of the best houses in the two Universities. In knowledge of Hebrew, Greek, and Latin—in power as preachers, expositors, writers, and critics—the Puritans, in their day, were second to none. Their works still speak for them on the shelves of every well-furnished theological library. Those who hold them up to scorn in the present day, as "shallow, illiterate men," are only exhibiting their own lamentable shallowness, their own ignorance of historical facts, and the extremely superficial character of their own reading.

The Puritans, as a body, have done more to elevate the national character than any class of Englishmen that ever lived. Mighty at the council board and no less mighty in the battlefield—feared abroad throughout Europe and invincible at home while united—great with their pens and great with their swords—they were a generation of men who have never received from their countrymen the honour that they deserve. The body of which Milton, Selden, Blake, Cromwell, Owen, Manton, Baxter, and Charnock were members, is a body of which no well-informed Englishman should ever speak with disrespect. Lord Macaulay, no mean authority in matters of history, might well say, in his essay on Milton, "We do not hesitate to pronounce the Puritans a brave, a wise, an honest, and an useful body." Unhappily, when they passed away, they were followed by a generation of profligates, triflers, and sceptics, and their reputations have suffered accordingly, in passing through prejudiced hands. But, judged with "righteous judgment,"[1] they will be found men "of whom the world was not worthy."[2] The more they are really known, the more they will be esteemed.

For myself, I can only say that the very reason why many in this day dislike the Puritans is the very reason why I love them, and delight to do honour to their names. They deserve honour, in my opinion, on account of their bold and outspoken *Protestantism*.

---

[1] John 7:24.
[2] Hebrews 11:38.

They deserve honour on account of their clear, sharply-cut, distinct *evangelicalism*. I want to see their writings more widely read, and their conduct more fairly judged and duly appreciated by English churchmen. If a perusal of the three biographies I have compiled helps to make them better known and better understood, I shall feel that this volume has not been issued in vain.

For the length of the attempt I have made in this introduction to defend the Reformers and Puritans, I have no apology to make. I have defended them because they have numerous enemies and few friends in this day, and many Englishmen seem to know nothing about them. In fact, the tide of unreasoning prejudice runs strongly against them, and for many years it has been the fashion to vilify them in the pulpit, on the platform, and in the press. As long as I live, I hope I shall never be ashamed to stand up for them, and to vindicate their claim to respect. They were only human, and of course they had their faults and infirmities. But the men of this age, who are fond of abusing them, are often grossly ignorant of the writings of those whom they abuse and "know not what they say nor whereof they affirm."[1]

(3) The English Reformers, in particular, appear to me to deserve far better treatment than they receive in these latter days. I have already said that people seem to forget that to these very Reformers of Edward the Sixth's and Elizabeth's reigns we owe the Articles and Prayer Book, which are the glory of the Church of England, and which most churchmen delight to honour. But, unhappily, this is not all. People forget that these same Reformers are the genuine prototypes and predecessors of a "school of thought" which, however lightly esteemed by some, is certainly not the least useful and influential within the pale of the Establishment—I mean the *evangelical school*. This, however, is a point which I shall take occasion to handle at some length.

(*a*) I begin by saying that of all the schools, sections, or parties into which the Church of England is unhappily divided, there is none which is so thoroughly misunderstood, and so frequently misrepresented, as that which is commonly called *evangelical*. There is no school which, from the days of Archbishop Laud to the

---

[1] 1 Timothy 1:7.

present time, has had to endure such hard usage, such unfair treatment, and such petty persecution, as the evangelical school. That its distinctive opinions have long been regarded with scorn and contempt by many English people is such a notorious fact that I need hardly stop to prove it. But I will mention a few facts.

(i) It is matter of history that in the year 1662, nearly two thousand clergymen were driven out of the Church of England by the unhappy Act of Uniformity. Many of them were the ablest preachers and the most learned, holy ministers of the time. Such were Owen, Manton, Baxter, Bates, Calamy, Philip Henry, Poole, Brooks, and Watson. Not a few of them might have been kept within our pale by some reasonable concessions. But the ruling party showed no desire to keep them—they were all of them evangelical men! We reap the consequence of their expulsion at this day. It laid the foundation of English Nonconformity.

(ii) It is certain that in the middle of last century, the maintenance of evangelical opinions was the true cause why Daniel Rowlands, the great Welsh preacher, George Whitefield, John and Charles Wesley, and many others, were practically driven out of the Church of England. Their lives were blameless. They were faithful to the Liturgy and Prayer Book. But they were evangelical, and therefore the Church shut her doors on them and obliged them to work outside! The result is to be seen in the hundreds of Methodist chapels all over the land and in the undeniable strength of Nonconformity in Wales.

(iii) It is equally certain that during the same century, evangelical clergymen like Romaine, Venn, Grimshaw, and Berridge retained their position in our communion with much difficulty, were regarded with coldness and distrust by ecclesiastical rulers, and were treated as little better than *tolerated heretics*. Romaine was dismissed from the morning preachership at St. George's, Hanover Square, because his sermons filled and overcrowded the church! Berridge would have been expelled from Everton by the Bishop of Ely if the elder Pitt had not interfered in his behalf. Grimshaw, of Haworth, was on the brink of secession in consequence of the harsh treatment of the Archbishop of York, and narrowly escaped.

(iv) Even at this day evangelical churchmen are continually told "that they are unlearned and ignorant men—that they do not interpret the formularies honestly and naturally—that they are more like Dissenters than churchmen—that they are narrow Calvinists—that they despise the sacraments and are Zwinglians—that they do not understand catholic views and corporate privileges—that they are *not*, in a word, *true* churchmen, and are out of their proper place!" All this, and much more similar language, evangelical churchmen have long had to bear. But, after all, there remains one great fact which can never be denied. If agreement with the English Reformers is to be the measure of true churchmanship, there are no truer churchmen than those who are called *evangelical*! Their title is one which cannot be overthrown. If they are wrong, the Reformers were wrong. You cannot condemn and unchurch the *evangelicals* without condemning and unchurching the *Reformers* at the same time.

In saying these things, I ask my readers not to misunderstand me. I willingly admit that there are other honest schools of thought within our pale besides the evangelical, and I disclaim all sympathy with those who would exclude them. From the time of Charles I, there have always been high, and broad, as well as low church-men, and probably there always will be till the Lord comes. The inherent imperfection of language, and the consequent impossibility of making all men put the same meaning on words, are the explanation of this condition of things. There have been at one and the same time within our camp, for 250 years and more, divines like Davenant and Andrews and Whichcote in the seventeenth century, and bishops like Sumner and Whately and Blomfield in our own day. I have not the slightest desire to narrow our limits, to unchurch and ostracise any of the men I have named, or to confine honest and loyal churchmanship to any one of the three schools I have just mentioned. I do not pretend to claim any exclusive possession of learning zeal, or devoutness for any of them. But when people tell me that "evangelicals are *not* true churchmen," I reply unhesitatingly that the charge is not true and shows gross and culpable ignorance, to say the least, in those who make it.

(*b*) I maintain firmly that the distinctive views of those who are called *evangelical churchmen* are neither more nor less than the views of the Reformers! He who would drive out of the Church of England all evangelicals, would drive out Ridley, Latimer, Hooper,

Bradford, Jewell, and all their companions. The leading opinions of the two bodies, after an interval of three centuries, are one and the same. Whether those opinions are sound or unsound, scriptural or unscriptural, is not the point on which I insist at present. All I assert is that the doctrinal views of the two parties are identical. He that says "evangelical churchmen are *not* sound churchmen," is in the same breath condemning the very men who reformed the Church of England and placed it on its present basis! There is no escape from this conclusion. The views of the two parties are in complete harmony, and they stand or fall together. A few instances will show what I mean.

(i) Do evangelical churchmen hold and teach that the Bible is the only rule of faith and practice? Do they maintain that it is able *alone* to make a man wise unto salvation, and that even the Creeds are only to be received and believed because they may be proved by most certain warrant of Holy Scripture? So did the Reformers!

(ii) Do evangelical churchmen hold and teach that we are accounted righteous before God only for the merit of our Lord Jesus Christ, by faith, and not for our own works and deservings? Do they maintain that in the matter of our *justification*, our own goodness and holiness have nothing whatever to do? So did the Reformers!

(iii) Do evangelical churchmen hold and teach that good works, which follow after justification, spring necessarily out of a true and lively faith? Do they maintain that a living faith may be as evidently discerned by the good works which spring from it as a tree is discerned by its fruit; and that, consequently, the man in whom no good works and holiness can be seen is not yet a believer and not a converted man? So did the Reformers!

(iv) Do evangelical churchmen hold and teach that Christ's sacraments do not convey and confer grace, *ex opere operato*,[1] and that they only do good to those who rightly, worthily, and with faith receive them? Do they maintain that a man may be duly baptized with water in his infancy, and yet give plain proof by his life, when he has come to man's estate, that he has not the grace of the Holy Ghost in his heart? So did the Reformers!

---

[1] "by the act performed."

(v) Do evangelical churchmen hold and teach that there is no *corporal* presence of Christ's natural flesh and blood in the consecrated elements of bread and wine in the Lord's Supper? Do they maintain that the body of Christ is given, taken, and eaten at the Lord's Supper only after a heavenly and spiritual manner, and that the only *real presence* of Christ in that sacrament is in the hearts of believing communicants? So did the Reformers!

(vi) Do evangelical churchmen hold and teach that the Lord's Supper is a sacrament, and not a sacrifice, and that in it there is no sacrifice, excepting that of praise and thanksgiving? Do they maintain that a clergyman is only a minister of God's Word, and not a sacrificing priest? Do they maintain that the sacrifice of the Mass, which many seem anxious to reintroduce into the Church of England, is one of the cardinal errors of the Church of Rome? So did the Reformers!

(vii) Do evangelical churchmen object strongly to the Lord's Table being called an *altar* and maintain firmly that this is an improper name, and that when there is no sacrifice and no sacrificing priest, there can be no altar? So did the Reformers!

(viii) Do evangelical churchmen thoroughly disapprove of lighted candles during the day on communion tables, and object to crucifixes, processions, incense-burning, gaudy sacrificial vestments, superstitious gestures and postures at the celebration of the Lord's Supper, and a close imitation of Romish ceremonial? So did the Reformers!

(ix) Do evangelical churchmen hold and teach that the practice of habitual private *confession* to a minister is nowhere taught or recommended in Scripture? Do they maintain that it is a practice to be strongly deprecated and avoided, having been proved by history to lead to most immoral and soul-ruining consequences? So did the Reformers!

(x) Do evangelical churchmen hold and teach that episcopacy is not absolutely necessary to the *being* of a church, however useful and desirable for its *well-being*, when properly administered? Do they maintain that we have no right to unchurch non-episcopal churches, and to hand them over to the uncovenanted mercies of God? So did the Reformers!

(xi) Do evangelical churchmen hold and teach that the Church of Rome has erred, not only in ceremonies, but also in matters of faith? Do they maintain that *separation* from the Church of Rome was a positive duty three centuries ago, and that no one ought to think of *reunion* with her in this day until Rome has renounced her errors and been reconciled to Christ? So did the Reformers!

(xii) Do evangelical churchmen hold and teach that repentance, faith, holiness of heart and life, justification, conversion, union with Christ, and the indwelling of the Holy Ghost are the primary and principal things in religion? Do they maintain that church-membership, reception of Christ's sacraments, and attendance on ordinances, however important and valuable in their due place, are by comparison things of *secondary* importance? So did the Reformers!

I commend these twelve points to the calm consideration of all my readers. I do not for a moment say that no man is a sound churchman unless he holds exactly all distinctive evangelical views about them. But I do say that they are precisely the *kind of points* about which evangelical churchmen are continually taunted, sneered at, ridiculed, and held up to scorn, as "unsound church-men," "low churchmen," "Puritans," "half-Dissenters," and the like. Yet on these very points they are entirely in harmony with the men who first reformed the Church of England, the Edwardian and Elizabethan Reformers! If those who dislike evangelical views, and look coldly on all who hold them, would undertake to prove that the distinctive opinions of the evangelical school are a mere modern invention, and unknown to the Reformers, I could understand their position. But until they do this, I shall firmly maintain that the treatment which evangelical churchmen too often receive in these latter days is neither fair, nor reasonable, nor wise. They have a right to demand juster balances and more "righteous judgment."[1] Whatever good there may be in other schools of thought, it is certain that no men can show a better title to be called "Successors of the Reformers" than the members of the evangelical school.

In reply to these things, I am aware that many regard the divines of the Caroline age and the Restoration as better and truer

---

[1] John 7:24.

representatives of the Church of England than the Reformers. They coolly tell us that the true doctrinal standard of churchmanship is that of 1662, when the Act of Uniformity was passed, and the Puritans rejected from our pale. This is simply untrue. It is an ignorant assertion, which will not bear investigation for a moment. The Thirty-nine Articles are the only doctrinal standard which the Church of England recognises, and to which she requires all her clergy to declare solemnly their assent.

Nor is this all. She requires every clergyman who is appointed to a living to "read publicly and openly, to his congregation, the whole of the Thirty-nine Articles, and after reading to declare his assent to them." Now these very articles were drawn up by the Edwardian and Elizabethan Reformers, and finally settled in their present shape in 1571. From that time to this, a period of over 300 years, they have never been altered! The revisers of the Liturgy, in 1662, thought it prudent to leave the Articles untouched! In the face of these facts, it is rather too much to tell us that the doctrine of the divines of 1662 is the true doctrinal standard of the Church of England. It is nothing of the kind. The true standard is that of the Reformers. To that standard evangelical churchmen appeal with confidence, and defy anyone to show that their views are not fully in agreement with it. If the Reformers were sound and loyal churchmen, so also are the members of the evangelical body.

(c) I will close this paper with one bold assertion. I commend it to the attention of all who want to know the real claim of the evangelical school to respect. I assert, then, that as evangelical churchmen have no cause to be ashamed of their distinctive *doctrinal* views, so also they have no cause to be ashamed of their distinctive plans of *church work.* Which of these plans has not been borrowed by other schools of thought in the last thirty-five years, and too often borrowed without the slightest acknowledgment? Who first employed *laymen* in Christ's work, in the face of a torrent of obloquy? The evangelical body! Who first called *women* forward, and gave them an office and position among church workers, though not a uniform? The evangelical body! Who first revived a due reverence for the Lord's Supper, and first crowded communion rails with devout communicants? The evangelical body! It would be hard to name any church at this day, where there

are so many regular communicants as there were at Grimshaw's
Church at Haworth, a hundred years ago, or at St. John's, Bedford
Row, within the present century. Who first introduced hearty
and congregational singing? The evangelical body! Charles Wesley,
and Toplady, and John Newton composed hymns which myriads
sang, long before the compilers of *Hymns Ancient and Modern* were
born. Who first commenced special short services for the working
classes? The evangelical body! Exeter Hall was opened on Sunday
evenings before Westminster Abbey or St. Paul's. Who first
attempted what are now called *"mission* services"? The evangelical
body! Thirty-five years ago they had preaching for six nights in
succession at Birmingham, Ipswich, and Islington parish churches.
Who first tried prayer-meetings and short services in uncon-
secrated places and were denounced as fanatical and disorderly for
holding them? The evangelical body!

Do I ask these questions in a taunting, boastful spirit? God forbid
I should do so. I think I know and see the many weaknesses and
defects of the evangelical body as clearly as anyone, and am always
ready to acknowledge them. As a bishop, I hold out my hand to
every loyal churchman and am ready to welcome him and work
with him, to whatever school he may belong. I honour a zealous,
honest, loyal, working churchman whenever I see him, though he
may not work exactly on what I think the best lines. All I say is that
evangelical churchmen have no more cause to be ashamed of their
plans of *working* than they have of their doctrinal views. Their
modes of working, as well as their principles, will bear any amount
of fair investigation.

I know well that the body for which I have tried to plead in
these pages is only a small minority among the clergy of the Church
of England. Yes! evangelical clergymen are a minority in every
diocese, in every convocation, in every diocesan conference, in
every congress; and they must not be surprised to find it so. But I
charge them, and especially the younger men, to remember that
majorities possess no more monopoly of truth and wisdom today
than they did in the days of Athanasius.[1] I beseech them, for the

---

[1] Renowned church father (*c.* 293–373) who was the chief defender of
Christian orthodoxy in the battle against Arianism, the heresy that the Son
of God was of *like*, but not of the *same*, substance as God the Father.

sake of Christ and their country, to stand firm, to stand together, never to compromise, and never to sacrifice a single vital principle under the vain pretence of obtaining unity and peace. Like gold, peace and unity may be bought too dear. Why should they be afraid, and faint-hearted, and weak-kneed, and give way by little and little? The Lord God of Ridley and Latimer and Jewell is not dead, but alive. The laity will stand by them if they are bold, decided, and true to the principles of the Reformation. So long as the Articles and Prayer Book remain unaltered, evangelical churchmen cannot justly, honestly, and legally be expelled from the Church of England.

What saith the Scripture? "Watch ye, stand fast in the faith, quit you like men, be strong. Let all your things be done with charity" (1 Cor. 16:13, 14). My own sentence is clear and distinct. If we cannot maintain the Established Church of England without giving up Protestantism and admitting Romanism, we had better have no Establishment at all. Time will show, in a few years, who is right. But if the Established Church of England tolerates and sanctions the Romish Mass and the confessional among her clergy, it is my firm conviction that the people of this country will not long tolerate the Established Church of England.

I now send forth this volume with an earnest prayer that God may be pleased to use it for His own glory and for the good of souls.

J. C. LIVERPOOL

November 1890

John Wycliffe (*c.* 1324–1384)
"the Morning Star of the Reformation"

I

JOHN WYCLIFFE

It is an old and true saying that nations sometimes know little about some of their greatest benefactors. If there ever was a man to whom this saying applies, it is John Wycliffe, the forerunner and first beginner of the Protestant Reformation in this country. To Wycliffe England owes an enormous debt—yet Wycliffe is a man of whom most Englishmen know little or nothing.

In drawing up a few pages about this great and good man, the words of the Apostle St. Peter, rise up before my mind. He says, "I think it meet to stir you up by putting you in remembrance" (2 Pet. 1:13). This is exactly what I want to do in this paper. I wish to stir up my readers and try to make them remember and never forget the man who has been justly called "the Morning Star of the English Reformation."

I. England's Religious Condition

First and foremost, I shall ask you to *remember the religious condition of England in the age when Wycliffe lived.* I shall make no apology for dwelling briefly on this point. A right understanding of it lies at the very root of my whole subject. Without this it is impossible to form a correct estimate of the man about whom I am writing; of the enormous difficulties he had to contend with; and of the greatness of the work which he did.

John Wycliffe was born in the north of Yorkshire, on the banks of the Tees, about the year 1324 in the reign of Edward II, and died in 1384 in the reign of Richard II, more than 500 years ago. So you will remember that he was born at least 100 years before the invention of printing,[1] and died about 100 years before the great

---

[1] 1450.

German Reformer, Martin Luther, was born.[1] These two facts alone should never be forgotten.

The three centuries immediately preceding our English Reformation, in the middle of which Wycliffe lived, were probably the darkest period in the history of English Christianity. It was a period when the Church of this land was thoroughly, entirely, and completely Roman Catholic—when the Bishop of Rome was the spiritual head of the Church—when Romanism reigned supreme from the Isle of Wight to Berwick-on-Tweed, and from the Land's End to the North Foreland, and ministers and people were all alike Papists. It is no exaggeration to say that for these three centuries before the Reformation, Christianity in England seems to have been buried under a mass of ignorance, superstition, priestcraft, and immorality. The likeness between the religion of this period and that of the apostolic age was so small, that if St. Paul had risen from the dead he would hardly have called it Christianity at all!

Such were the days when Wycliffe lived. Such were the difficulties which he had to encounter. I charge my readers not to forget them. The man who could do the work he did, and leave the mark that he left on his generation, must have been no common man. I go further: he must have been a servant of Christ, of rare grace and gifts, and singularly filled with the Holy Ghost. I say he is a man worthy of all honour, and we do well to keep him in remembrance.

II. Wycliffe's Work

Let me now turn from Wycliffe's time to *Wycliffe's work*. That Wycliffe did a great work in a very dark day—that he made a deep impression on his generation—that he was felt and acknowledged to be a *power* in England both by church and Parliament for some twenty-five years, is simple matter of history which no well-read person can deny.

But there is much obscurity about his early life. We know nothing of his first schools and schoolmasters, and can only guess that he may have picked up the first rudiments of his education at Eggleston Priory, on the Tees. But we do know that he went to

---

[1] Martin Luther, 1483–1546.

Oxford between 1335 and 1340, and profited so much by the instruction he got there that he obtained a very high reputation as one of the most learned men of his day. He was made Master of Balliol in 1361, and was afterwards connected with Queen's, Merton, and Canterbury Hall. From that date for about twenty years, when he retired to Lutterworth, Oxford seems to have been his headquarters, though he evidently was often in London. Lecturing, preaching, writing both for learned and unlearned, arguing, controversy appear to have been the diet of his life. But we have no minute and systematic account of his life from the pen of any contemporary biographer. How he first obtained his sound theological views—whether he learned anything from Archbishop Bradwardin, who preceded him—whether he was intimate with Fitzralph of Armagh, Chancellor of Oxford, or the famous Grostète, Bishop of Lincoln—who, in short, were his helpers and fellow-labourers, or whether he had none and stood alone—on all these points we know little or nothing. It is useless, however, to complain, as there was no printing in Wycliffe's day and few could read or write. I shall not waste time in guessing, but shall content myself with mentioning four facts which are beyond controversy, and pointing out four reasons why Wycliffe's name should always be honoured in England.

(a) For one thing, we should gratefully remember that Wycliffe *was one of the first Englishmen who maintained the sufficiency and supremacy* of Holy Scripture as the only rule of faith and practice. The proof of this is to be seen so continually in his writings, that I shall not attempt to supply quotations. The Bible comes to the front in all his remains. The importance of this great principle can never be overrated. It lies at the very foundation of Protestant Christianity. It is the backbone of the Articles of the Church of England and of every sound church in Christendom.

The true Christian was intended by Christ to prove all things by the Word of God, all churches, all ministers, all teaching, all preaching, all doctrines, all sermons, all writings, all opinions, all practices. These are his marching orders. Prove all by the Word of God; measure all by the measure of the Bible; compare all with the standard of the Bible; weigh all in the balances of the Bible; examine all by the light of the Bible; test all in the crucible of the

Bible. That which can abide the fire of the Bible, receive, hold, believe, and obey. That which cannot abide the fire of the Bible, reject, refuse, repudiate, and cast away. This is the standard which Wycliffe raised in England. This is the flag which he nailed to the mast. May it never be lowered!

All this sounds so familiar to our ears that we do not realize its value. Five hundred years ago, the man who took up this ground was a bold man, and stood alone. Let us never forget that one of the first to set down his foot upon this principle was John Wycliffe.

(b) For another thing, let us gratefully remember that Wycliffe *was one of the first Englishmen who attacked and denounced the errors of the Church of Rome.* The sacrifice of the Mass and transubstantiation, the ignorance and immorality of the priesthood, the tyranny of the See of Rome, the uselessness of trusting to other mediators than Christ, the dangerous tendency of the confessional —all these and other kindred doctrines will be found unsparingly exposed in his writings. On all these points he was a thorough Protestant Reformer a century and a half before the Reformation.

Well would it be for England if men saw this subject in the present day as clearly as Wycliffe did. Unhappily, nowadays, the edge of the old British feeling about Protestantism seems blunted and dull. Some profess to be tired of all religious controversy, and are ready to sacrifice God's truth for the sake of peace. Some look on Romanism as simply one among many English forms of religion, and neither worse nor better than others. Some try to persuade us that Romanism is changed, and is not nearly so bad as it used to be. Some boldly point to the faults of Protestants, and loudly cry that Romanists are quite as good as ourselves. Some think it fine and liberal to maintain that we have no right to think anyone wrong who is in earnest about his creed. And yet the two great historical facts, (i) that ignorance, immorality, and superstition reigned supreme in England 400 years ago under Popery; (ii) that the Reformation was the greatest blessing God ever gave to this land—both these are facts which no one but a Papist ever thought of disputing fifty years ago! In the present day, alas, it is convenient and fashionable to forget them!

In short, at the rate we are going, I shall not be surprised if it is soon proposed to repeal the Act of Settlement, and to allow the crown of England to be worn by a Papist.[1] If we are to put the clock back and get behind the Reformation, as some coolly propose, I trust we shall not stop at Henry VIII or VII or VI, but go back to consult Wycliffe.

(c) For another thing, let us gratefully remember that Wycliffe *was one of the first, if not the very first, Englishmen who revived the apostolic ordinance of preaching.* The "poor priests," as they were called, whom he sent about the country to teach, were one of the greatest benefits which he conferred on his generation. They sowed the seed of thoughts among the people which were never entirely forgotten, and, I believe, paved the way for the Reformation. If Wycliffe had never done anything but this for England, I believe that this alone would entitle him to our deep thankfulness.

I maintain firmly that the first, foremost, and principal work of the minister is to be a preacher of God's Word. I say this emphatically, because of the time in which we live, and the peculiar dangers of the Christian warfare in our own land. I believe that the pretended *sacerdotalism* of ministers is one of the oldest and most mischievous errors which has ever plagued Christendom. Partly from an ignorant hankering after the priesthood of the Mosaic dispensation, which passed away when Christ died; partly from the love of power and dignity, which is natural to ministers, as much as to other men; partly from the preference of unconverted worshippers for a supposed priest and mediator whom they can see, rather than one in heaven whom they cannot see; partly from the general ignorance of mankind before the Bible was printed and circulated; partly from one cause and partly from another, there has been an incessant tendency throughout the last eighteen centuries to exalt ministers to an unscriptural position, and to regard them as priests and mediators between God and man, rather than as preachers of God's Word.

I charge my readers to remember this. Stand fast on old principles. Do not forsake the old paths. Let nothing tempt you to believe that multiplication of forms and ceremonies, constant reading of liturgical services, or frequent communions, will ever do

---

[1] The Act of Settlement was passed in 1701, frustrating any hopes that exiled James II had of returning to the throne. The Act decreed that only a Protestant could inherit the Crown.

so much good to souls as the powerful, fiery, fervent preaching of God's Word. Daily services without sermons may gratify and edify a few handfuls of believers, but they will never reach, draw, attract, or arrest the great mass of mankind. If men want to do good to the multitude, if they want to reach their hearts and consciences, they must walk in the steps of Wycliffe, Latimer, Luther, Chrysostom, and St. Paul. They must attack them through their ears; they must blow the trumpet of the everlasting Gospel loud and long; they must preach the Word.

(*d*) Last in order, but first in importance, *let us ever gratefully remember that Wycliffe was the first Englishman who translated the Bible into the English language* and thus enabled it to be understood by the people. The difficulty of this work was probably something of which we can form no conception at this day. There were probably few, very few, that could help the translator in any way. There was no printing, and the whole book had to be laboriously written in manuscript, and by written manuscript alone could copies be multiplied. To inspect the machinery and apparatus of our blessed Bible Society in Blackfriars, and then to think of the stupendous toil which Wycliffe must have gone through, is enough to take one's breath away. But with God's help nothing is impossible. The work was done, and hundreds of copies were circulated. In spite of every effort to suppress the book, and the destruction of it by time, fire, and unfavourable hands, no less than 170 complete copies were found extant when it was reprinted at Oxford some 40 years ago, and no doubt many more are in existence.

The good that was done by the translation of the Bible will probably never be known till the last day, and I shall not attempt to form any conjecture about it. But I shall never hesitate to assert that if there is any one fact more incontrovertibly proved than another it is this: that the possession by a people of the Bible in their own language is the greatest possible national blessing. Five hundred years have passed away since the first translator of the English Bible was laid in his grave. I ask anyone this day to look at the map of the world and see what a tale it tells about the value of a free and widely circulated Bible.

Which are the countries where the greatest amount of ignorance, superstition, immorality, and tyranny is to be found at this very moment? The countries in which the Bible is a forbidden or neglected book—such countries as Italy and Spain, and the South American States. Which are the countries where liberty and public and private morality have attained the highest pitch? The countries where the Bible is free to all, like England, Scotland, and the United States. Yes! when you know how a nation deals with the Bible, you may generally know what a nation is. O that the rulers of some nations did but know that a free Bible is the grand secret of national prosperity, and that the surest way to make subjects orderly and obedient is to allow a free passage to the living waters of God's Word! O that the people of some countries did but see that a free Bible is the beginning of all real freedom, and that the first liberty they should seek after is liberty for the apostles and prophets— liberty to have a Bible in every house, and a Bible in every hand! Well said Bishop Hooper, "God in heaven and king on earth have no greater friend than the Bible." It is a striking fact that when British sovereigns are crowned, they are publicly presented with the Bible and told, "This book is the most valuable thing the world affords."

This is the book on which the well-being of nations has always hinged, and with which the best interests of every nation in Christendom at this moment are inseparably bound up. Just in proportion as the Bible is honoured or not, light or darkness, morality or immorality, true religion or superstition, liberty or despotism, good laws or bad, will be found in a land. Come with me and open the pages of history, and you will read the proof of these assertions in time past. Read it in the history of Israel under the kings. How great was the wickedness that then prevailed! But who can wonder? The law of the Lord had been completely lost sight of and was found in the days of Josiah in a corner of the temple. Read it in the history of the Jews in our Lord Jesus Christ's time. How awful the picture of scribes and Pharisees and their religion! But who can wonder? The Scripture was "made void"[1] by man's traditions. Read it in the history of the Church of Christ in the Middle Ages. What can be worse than the accounts we have of ignorance and superstition? But who can wonder? The times might

---

[1] Mark 7:13.

well be dark, when men had not the light of the Bible. The plain truth is this: the Bible is the parent of free thought and mental activity. It is a curious fact that the British and Foreign Bible House and the *British Times* offices are almost side by side!

Which are the churches on earth which are producing the greatest effect on mankind? The churches in which the Bible is exalted. Which are the parishes in England and Scotland where religion and morality have the strongest hold? The parishes in which the Bible is most circulated and read. Who are the ministers in England who have the most real influence over the minds of the people? Not those who are ever crying "Church! Church!" but those who are faithfully preaching the Word.

A church which does not honour the Bible is as useless as a body without life, or a steam engine without fire. A minister who does not honour the Bible is as useless as a soldier without arms, a builder without tools, a pilot without compass, or a messenger without tidings. It is cheap and easy work for Roman Catholics, Neologians, and friends of secular education to sneer at those who love the Bible; but the Romanist, the Neologian, and the friends of mere secular education have never yet shown us one New Zealand, one Tinnevelly, one Sierra Leone as the fruit of their principles.[1] They only can do that who honour the Bible. These are the works of the Word and the proofs of its power.

This is the book to which the civilized world is indebted for many of its best and most praiseworthy institutions. Few probably are aware how many are the good things that men have adopted for the public benefit, of which the origin may be clearly traced up to the Bible. It has left lasting marks wherever it has been received. From the Bible are drawn many of the best laws by which society is kept in order. From the Bible has been obtained the standard of morality about truth, honesty, and the relations of man and wife, which prevails among Christian nations, and which—however feebly respected in many cases—makes so great a difference between Christians and heathen. To the Bible we are indebted for that most merciful provision for the poor man, the Sabbath day. To

---

[1] Three remote missionary colonies founded by evangelicals—New Zealand in the South Pacific, Tinnevelly in southeastern India, and Sierra Leone in western Africa.

the influence of the Bible we owe nearly every humane and charitable institution in existence. The sick, the poor, the aged, the orphan, the lunatic, the idiot, the blind were seldom or never thought of before the Bible leavened the world. You may search in vain for any record of institutions for their aid in the histories of Athens or of Rome.

Alas, many sneer at the Bible and say the world would get on well enough without it, who little think how great are their own obligations to the Bible. Little does the infidel think, as he lies sick in some of our great hospitals, that he owes all his present comforts to the very book he affects to despise. Had it not been for the Bible, he might have died in misery, uncared for, unnoticed, and alone. Verily, the world we live in is fearfully unconscious of its debts. The last day alone, I believe, will tell the full amount of benefit conferred upon it by the Bible. This is the book which John Wycliffe was the first to translate and give to Englishmen in their own mother tongue. I repeat, that if he had done nothing else he would deserve to be gratefully remembered by every English Christian, every English patriot, and every English churchman. Such are the four leading reasons for which the memory of John Wycliffe ought to be had in honour.

I do not tell you that this great man had no weak points, and held no disputable opinions, and was sound on every theological doctrine. I say nothing of the kind. He lived in a twilight age and had to work out many a problem in divinity without the slightest help from man. He wrote much, and wrote perhaps hastily; and I do not pretend to endorse all that he wrote. Like Luther and Cranmer, at the beginning he was not clear on all points. But when I consider his solitary, isolated, difficult position, I only wonder that he was as free from error as he was. One fact far outweighs all his alleged defects. That fact is that he was the *first* translator of the Bible into the English tongue.

How he escaped without a violent death, and finally died quietly in his bed at Lutterworth, is a miracle indeed. But it is evident to my mind that God protected him in a miraculous way. "The earth helped the woman."[1] It was God who raised up John of Gaunt and

---

[1] Revelation 12:16.

the Princess of Wales to favour him.[1] It was God who sent the earthquake which broke up a London synod when it was about to condemn him.[2] It was God who inclined the University of Oxford to give him support. The Council of Constance had not yet set the example of burning heretics.[3] The Council of Trent had not yet crystallised and formulated all Popish doctrine.[4] But above all, I see the hand of God over Wycliffe—the hand of Him who said, "When a man's ways please the LORD, He makes his enemies to be at peace with him."[5] Yes! the hand over Wycliffe was the crucified hand of Him who said to the apostles, "I am with you always;"[6] the hand of Him who said to Paul at Corinth, "Speak, and hold not thy peace; I am with thee. No man shall set on thee to hurt thee."[7] He was immortal till his work was done.

Let me now bring this paper to a conclusion by pointing out some practical conclusions to which the whole subject ought to lead us.

(1) Let us then resolve to rally round Wycliffe's first principles and grasp them more firmly than we have done of late years. The supremacy and sufficiency of Scripture, the absolute necessity of watching and resisting the dangerous pretensions of the Church of Rome, the immense importance of preaching God's Word—these are a basis on which all Protestant Englishmen ought to unite and work heartily.

---

1 John of Gaunt was the son of King Edward III.

2 Known as "the Earthquake synod" (1382), Wycliffe applied the remarkable providence to his judges asserting that "the friars had put heresy upon Christ in the matter of the sacrament, and the earth trembled as it did when Christ was damned to bodily death."

3 In 1415, thirty years after the death of Wycliffe, the Council of Constance condemned him on 260 counts, decreed him "to have been a notorious heretic," ordered his writings to be burned, and directed that his bones be exhumed and cast out of consecrated ground. Thirteen years later in 1428, by Papal command, Wycliffe's remains were dug up, burned, and thrown into a nearby stream.

4 Condemning all Protestants as *heretics* and pronouncing a *double anathema* upon them, the Council of Trent (1545–63) is Rome's official response to the Reformation.

5 Proverbs 16:7.

6 Matthew 28:20.

7 Acts 18:9, 10.

(2) Let us learn the astonishing power and influence which one man possesses if he comes forward boldly for Christ, and has the courage of his opinions. One Moses, one Elijah, one John the Baptist, one Paul at Corinth, one Savonarola at Florence, one Luther in Germany, one Zwingle, one Wesley, one Whitefield, one Romaine in London set thousands thinking and shook a sleeping world. We want more boldness among the friends of truth. There is far too much tendency to sit still and wait for committees and number our adherents. We want more men who are not afraid to stand alone, as Wycliffe did.

(3) Finally, let us not forget that the Lord God of John Wycliffe is not dead but alive. Men change. Something new is the cry of the day. Freer handling of Scripture! Broader and looser theology! This is what many long to see. But we want nothing better than the old Gospel if we wish to do good. Jesus Christ never changes. At the end of five hundred years He is still the same. He did not fail the Rector of Lutterworth, and He will not fail us if we walk in His steps.

The Place of Execution in Smithfield

2

WHY WERE OUR REFORMERS BURNED?

THERE are certain facts in history which the world tries hard to forget and ignore. These facts get in the way of some of the world's favourite theories and are highly inconvenient. The consequence is that the world shuts its eyes against them. They are either cut dead as vulgar intruders, or passed by as tiresome bores. Little by little they sink out of sight of the students of history, like ships in a distant horizon, or are left behind like a luggage train in a siding. Of such facts the subject of this paper is a vivid example: "The Burning of our English Reformers; and the Reason why they were Burned."

It is fashionable in some quarters to deny that there is any such thing as certainty about religious truth, or any opinions for which it is worth while to be burned. Yet, 300 years ago, there were men who were certain they had found out truth, and were content to die for their opinions. It is fashionable in other quarters to leave out all the unpleasant things in history and to paint everything with a rose-coloured hue. A very popular history of our English Queens hardly mentions the martyrdoms of Queen Mary's days! Yet Mary was not called "Bloody Mary" without reason, and scores of Protestants were burned in her reign. Last, but not least, it is thought very bad taste in many quarters to say anything which throws discredit on the Church of Rome.

Yet it is as certain that the Romish church burned our English Reformers as it is that William the Conqueror won the Battle of Hastings.[1] These difficulties meet me face to face as I walk up to the

---

[1] In 1066, William the Conqueror (the Duke of Normandy) defeated Harold II, the last Anglo-Saxon King of England, establishing the Normans as rulers of England.

subject which I wish to unfold in this paper. I know their magnitude, and I cannot evade them. I only ask my readers to give me a patient and indulgent hearing.

After all, I have great confidence in the honesty of Englishmen's minds. Truth is truth, however long it may be neglected. Facts are facts, however long they may lie buried. I only want to dig up some old facts which the sands of time have covered over, to bring to the light of day some old English monuments which have been long neglected, to unstop some old wells which the prince of this world has been diligently filling with earth. I ask my readers to give me their attention for a few minutes, and I trust to be able to show them that it is good to examine the question, "Why were our Reformers burned?"

I. The Broad Facts

The *broad facts* of the martyrdom of our Reformers are a story well known and soon told. But it may be useful to give a brief outline of these facts, in order to supply a framework to our subject.

Edward VI, "that incomparable young prince," as Bishop Burnet justly calls him, died on the 6th July, 1553. Never, perhaps, did any royal personage in this land die more truly lamented, or leave behind him a fairer reputation. Never, perhaps, to man's poor fallible judgment, did the cause of God's truth in England receive a heavier blow. His last prayer before death ought not to be forgotten, "O Lord God, defend this realm from Papistry, and maintain Thy true religion." It was a prayer, I believe, not offered in vain.

After a foolish and deplorable effort to obtain the crown for Lady Jane Grey,[1] Edward was succeeded by his eldest sister, Mary, daughter of Henry VIII and his first Queen, Catherine of Aragon, and best known in English history by the ill-omened name of "Bloody Mary." Mary had been brought up from her infancy as a rigid adherent of the Romish church. She was, in fact, a very Papist of Papists, conscientious, zealous, bigoted, and narrow-minded in the extreme. She began at once to pull down her brother's work in

---

[1] In 1553, unscrupulous politicians forced the Crown upon Lady Jane Grey (1537–54), the fifteen year old great-granddaughter of Henry VII. After nine days she abdicated the throne to Mary Tudor, who then had her beheaded.

every possible way and to restore Popery in its worst and most offensive forms. Step by step she and her councillors marched back to Rome, trampling down one by one every obstacle, and as *thorough* as Lord Strafford in going straight forward to their mark.[1] The Mass was restored; the English service was taken away; the works of Luther, Zwingle, Calvin, Tyndale, Bucer, Latimer, Hooper, and Cranmer were proscribed. Cardinal Pole was invited to England.[2] The foreign Protestants resident in England were banished. The leading divines of the Protestant Church of England were deprived of their offices, and while some escaped to the Continent, many were put in prison. The old statutes against heresy were once more brought forward, primed and loaded. And thus by the beginning of 1555 the stage was cleared, and that bloody tragedy, in which bishops Bonner and Gardiner played so prominent a part, was ready to begin.

For, unhappily for the credit of human nature, Mary's advisers were not content with depriving and imprisoning the leading English Reformers. It was resolved to make them abjure their principles—or to put them to death. One by one they were called before special commissions, examined about their religious opinions, and called upon to recant, on pain of death if they refused. No third course, no alternative was left to them. They were either to give up Protestantism and receive Popery, or else they were to be burned alive. Refusing to recant, they were one by one handed over to the secular power, publicly brought out and chained to stakes, publicly surrounded with faggots, and publicly sent out of the world by that most cruel and painful of deaths—the

[1] Known for his maxim, *thorough*, Lord Strafford was the ruthless First Minister to Charles I. Accused of *treason*, he was beheaded in 1641.

[2] Reginald Pole (1500–58) had a remarkable career in Papistry: When Henry VIII sought to annul his marriage with Catherine of Aragon, Pole, an English prelate, broke with Henry and left England. In exile he became a cardinal, served as the presiding legate at the Council of Trent, and was nearly elected Pope. After Mary Tudor's accession, Pole was appointed legate for England, formally received the country back into Popery, was made Archbishop of Canterbury, and virtually ran Mary's government— he *never* opposed the burning of Protestants. For political reasons the Pope condemned Pole as a heretic and cancelled his legatine authority. Pole died 12 hours after the death of Queen Mary.

death by fire. All these are broad facts which all the apologists of
Rome can never gainsay or deny.

It is a broad fact that during the four last years of Queen Mary's
reign no less than 288 persons were burnt at the stake for their
adhesion to the Protestant faith.

In	1555	there were burnt	71
"	1556	"	89
"	1557	"	88
"	1558	"	40
			288*

Indeed, the faggots never ceased to blaze whilst Mary was alive, and
5 martyrs were burnt in Canterbury only a week before her death.
Out of these 288 sufferers, be it remembered, 1 was an archbishop,
4 were bishops, 21 were clergymen, 55 were women, and 4 were
children.

It is a broad fact that these 288 sufferers were not put to death for
any offence against property or person. They were not rebels against
the Queen's authority, caught red-handed in arms. They were not
thieves or murderers or drunkards or unbelievers or men and
women of immoral lives. On the contrary, they were, with barely
an exception, some of the holiest, purest, and best Christians in
England, and several of them the most learned men of their day.

I might say much about the gross injustice and unfairness with
which they were treated at their various examinations. Their trials,
if indeed they can be called trials, were a mere mockery of justice.
I might say much about the abominable cruelty with which most
of them were treated, both in prison and at the stake. But you must
read *Fox's Martyrs* on these points. I make no comment on the
stupid impolicy of the whole persecution. Never did Rome do
herself such irreparable damage as she did in Mary's reign. Even
unlearned people, who could not argue much, saw clearly that
a church which committed such horrible bloodshed could hardly
be the one true Church of Christ!† But I have no time for all this.

---

* These numbers are given by Soames, in his *History of the Reformation*
(vol. 4, p. 587), and are taken from Strype. Other historians give higher
numbers.

† A lady in high position told Bonner in a letter, after Philpot's death,

I must conclude this general sketch of this part of my subject with two short remarks:

(*a*) For one thing, I ask my readers never to forget that for the burning of our Reformers the Church of Rome is wholly and entirely responsible. The attempt to transfer the responsibility from the Church to the secular power is a miserable and dishonest subterfuge. The men of Judah did not slay Samson, but they delivered him bound into the hands of the Philistines! The Church of Rome did not slay the Reformers, but she condemned them, and the secular power executed the condemnation! The precise measure of responsibility which ought to be meted out to each of Rome's agents in the matter is a point that I do not care to settle. Miss Strickland, in her *Lives of the Queens of England*, has tried in vain to shift the blame from unhappy Mary. With all the zeal of a woman, she has laboured hard to whitewash her character. The reader of her biography will find little about martyrdoms. But it will not do. Mr. Froude's volume tells a very different tale. The Queen and her Council and the Parliament and the Popish bishops and Cardinal Pole must be content to share the responsibility among them. One thing alone is very certain: They will never succeed in shifting the responsibility off the shoulders of the Church of Rome. Like the Jews and Pontius Pilate when our Lord was crucified, all parties must bear the blame. THE BLOOD is upon them all.

(*b*) For another thing, I wish my readers to remember that the burning of the Marian martyrs is an act that the Church of Rome has never repudiated, apologized for, or repented of, down to the present day. There stands the huge blot in her escutcheon; and there stands the huge fact side by side that she has never made any attempt to wipe it away. Never has she repented of her treatment of the Vaudois and the Albigenses;[1] never has she repented

---

that his cruelty had lost the hearts of 20,000 Papists in twelve months.

[1] Both groups were twelfth-century, proto-Protestants of southern France. The *Vaudois* (also known as the *Waldenses*) endured more than five centuries of persecution from the hands of Rome. Despite Pope Innocent the Eighth's bull in 1487 calling for them to be crushed out "as venomous serpents," they survive to this day.

The *Albigenses* are remembered more for their anti-sacerdotalism than for their orthodoxy. Indeed, many of their views were heretical. Between the Crusades and the Inquisition, they were stamped out of existence by

of the wholesale murders of the Spanish Inquisition;[1] never has she repented of the massacre of St. Bartholomew;[2] never has she repented of the burning of the English Reformers. We should make a note of that fact, and let it sink down into our minds, Rome never changes. Rome will never admit that she has made mistakes. She burned our English Reformers 300 years ago. She tried hard to stamp out by violence the Protestantism which she could not prevent spreading by arguments. If Rome had only the power, I am not sure that she would not attempt to play the whole game over again.

II. Who Were the Leading Reformers that Were Burned?

The question may now arise in our minds, *Who were the leading English Reformers* that were burned? What were their names, and what were the circumstances attending their deaths? These are questions which may very properly be asked, and questions to which I proceed at once to give an answer. In this part of my paper I am very sensible that I shall seem to many to go over old ground. But I am bold to say that it is ground which ought often to be gone over. I, for one, want the names of our martyred Reformers to be *household words* in every Protestant family throughout the land. I shall, therefore, make no apology for giving the names of the nine principal English martyrs in the chronological order of their deaths, and for supplying you with a few facts about each of them. Never, I believe, since Christ left the world, did Christian men ever meet a cruel death with such glorious faith and hope and patience, as these Marian martyrs. Never did dying men leave behind them such a rich store of noble sayings, sayings which deserve to be written in

---

the end of the fourteenth century.

[1] From 1478 until 1524, the Spanish Inquisition (authorized by Pope Sixtus IV) burned 14,344 people at the stake, 9,372 in effigy, and condemned 195,937 to other penalties or released as penitents (Philip Schaff, *History of the Christian Church*, vol. 6, p. 553). These numbers do not account for the unspeakably cruel tortures employed during inquiry.

[2] On August 24, 1572, Charles IX of France set out to completely exterminate the Huguenots—the bloodletting did not cease until October, leaving the death-toll somewhere between twenty and one hundred thousand. Pope Gregory XIII struck a medal *and* appointed a jubilee celebrating the massacre.

golden letters in our histories and handed down to our children's children.

(1) John Rogers

The first leading English Reformer who broke the ice and crossed the river as a martyr in Mary's reign was John Rogers, a London minister, Vicar of St. Sepulchre's, and Prebendary and Reader of Divinity at St. Paul's. He was burned in Smithfield on Monday, the 4th of February, 1555. Rogers was born at Deritend, in the parish of Aston, near Birmingham. He was a man who, in one respect, had done more for the cause of Protestantism than any of his fellow-sufferers. In saying this I refer to the fact that he had assisted Tyndale and Coverdale in bringing out a most important version of the English Bible, a version commonly known as "Matthews' Bible." Indeed, he was condemned as "Rogers, *alias* Matthews." This circumstance, in all human probability, made him a marked man, and was one cause why he was the first who was brought to the stake.

Rogers' examination before Gardiner gives us the idea of his being a bold, thorough Protestant, who had fully made up his mind on all points of the Romish controversy and was able to give a reason for his opinions. At any rate, he seems to have silenced and abashed his examiners even more than most of the martyrs did. But arguments, of course, went for nothing. "Woe to the conquered!"[1] If he had the word, his enemies had the sword.[*]

On the morning of his martyrdom he was roused hastily in his cell in Newgate and hardly allowed time to dress himself. He was

---

[1] Quoted from *Pseudolus*, a play by Plautus (*c*. 254–184 B.C.). A proverbial saying since the day when Brennus (*c*. 390 B.C.), leader of the Gauls, entered Rome and consented to depart upon payment of 2,000 talents, but when reproached with deceit, threw his sword into the scale with the cry of "Væ victis," (*Woe to the vanquished*).

[*] Rogers' prophetical words in prison, addressed to Day, printer of Fox's *Acts and Monuments*, are well worth quoting: "Thou shalt live to see the alteration of this religion, and the Gospel freely preached again. Therefore, have me commended to my brethren, as well in exile as here, and bid them be circumspect in displacing the Papists and putting good ministers into churches or else their end will be worse than ours." Fox, 3, p. 309.

then led forth to Smithfield on foot, within sight of the Church of St. Sepulchre, where he had preached, and through the streets of the parish where he had done the work of a pastor. By the wayside stood his wife and ten children (one a baby) whom the diabolical cruelty of Bishop Bonner had flatly refused him leave to see in prison. He just saw them, but was hardly allowed to stop, and then walked on calmly to the stake, repeating the 51st Psalm. An immense crowd lined the street and filled every available spot in Smithfield. Up to that day men could not tell how English Reformers would behave in the face of death, and could hardly believe that prebendaries and dignitaries would actually give their bodies to be burned for their religion. But when they saw John Rogers, the first martyr, walking steadily and unflinchingly into a fiery grave, the enthusiasm of the crowd knew no bounds. They rent the air with thunders of applause. Even Noailles, the French Ambassador, wrote home a description of the scene and said that Rogers went to death "as if he was walking to his wedding." By God's great mercy he died with comparative ease. And so the first Marian martyr passed away.

(2) John Hooper

The second leading Reformer who died for Christ's truth in Mary's reign was John Hooper, Bishop of Gloucester. He was burned at Gloucester on Friday, the 9th of February, 1555.

Hooper was a Somersetshire man by birth. In many respects he was, perhaps, the noblest martyr of them all. Of all Edward the Sixth's bishops, none has left behind him a higher reputation for personal holiness and diligent preaching and working in his diocese. None, judging from his literary remains, had clearer and more scriptural views on all points in theology. Some might say that Edward the Sixth's Bishop of Gloucester was too Calvinistic; but he was not more so than the Thirty-nine Articles. Hooper was a far-sighted man and saw the danger of leaving nest-eggs for Romanism in the Church of England. In his famous dispute with Cranmer and the other bishops about wearing Romish vestments at his consecration, it has been, I know, the fashion to condemn him as too stiff and unbending. I say boldly that the subsequent history of our church makes it doubtful whether we ought not to reverse our verdict. The plain truth is that in principle Hooper was right, and his opponents were wrong.

A man like Hooper, firm, stern, not naturally genial, unbending and unsparing in his denunciation of sin, was sure to have many enemies. He was one of the first marked for destruction as soon as Popery was restored. He was summoned to London at a very early stage of the Marian persecution, and, after lingering eighteen months in prison and going through the form of examination by Bonner, Gardiner, Tunstall,[1] and Day, was degraded from his office and sentenced to be burned as a heretic.

At first it was fully expected that he would suffer in Smithfield with Rogers. This plan, for some unknown reason, was given up, and to his great satisfaction Hooper was sent down to Gloucester and burnt in his own diocese and in sight of his own cathedral. On his arrival there, he was received with every sign of sorrow and respect by a vast multitude, who went out on the Cirencester Road to meet him, and was lodged for the night in the house of a Mr. Ingram, which is still standing and probably not much altered. There Sir Anthony Kingston, whom the good Bishop had been the means of converting from a sinful life, entreated him, with many tears, to spare himself and urged him to remember that "Life was sweet, and death was bitter." To this the noble martyr returned this memorable reply, that "Eternal life was more sweet, and eternal death was more bitter."

On the morning of his martyrdom he was led forth, walking, to the place of execution, where an immense crowd awaited him. It was market-day; and it was reckoned that nearly seven thousand people were present. The stake was planted directly in front of the western gate of the cathedral-close and within one hundred yards of the deanery and the east front of the cathedral. The exact spot is marked now by a beautiful memorial at the east end of the church-yard of St. Mary-de-Lode. The window over the gate, where Popish friars watched the Bishop's dying agonies, stands unaltered to this day.

---

[1] Condemning the English translation of the Scriptures as "strange learning," Bishop Tunstall (1474–1559) bears the unique, historical distinction of being the *first* man to publicly burn William Tyndale's New Testament.

When Hooper arrived at this spot, he was allowed to pray, though strictly forbidden to speak to the people. And there he knelt down and prayed a prayer which has been preserved and recorded by Fox and is of exquisitely touching character. Even then a box was put before him containing a full pardon, if he would only recant. His only answer was, "Away with it; if you love my soul, away with it!" He was then fastened to the stake by an iron round his waist and fought his last fight with the king of terrors. Of all the martyrs, none perhaps, except Ridley, suffered more than Hooper did. Three times the faggots had to be lighted, because they would not burn properly. Three quarters of an hour the noble sufferer endured the mortal agony, as Fox says, "neither moving backward, forward, nor to any side," but only praying, "Lord Jesus, have mercy on me; Lord Jesus, receive my spirit;" and beating his breast with one hand till it was burned to a stump. And so the good Bishop of Gloucester passed away.

(3) Rowland Taylor

The third leading Reformer who suffered in Mary's reign was Rowland Taylor, Rector of Hadleigh, in Suffolk. He was burned on Aldham Common, close to his own parish, the same day that Hooper died at Gloucester, on Friday, the 9th February, 1555. Rowland Taylor is one of whom we know little, except that he was a great friend of Cranmer, and a Doctor of Divinity and Canon Law. But that he was a man of high standing among the Reformers is evident from his being ranked by his enemies with Hooper, Rogers, and Bradford; and that he was an exceedingly able and ready divine is clear from his examination, recorded by Fox. Indeed, there is hardly any of the sufferers about whom the old martyrologist has gathered together so many touching and striking things. One might think he was a personal friend. Striking was the reply which he made to his friends at Hadleigh, who urged him to flee, as he might have done, when he was first summoned to appear in London before Gardiner:

> What will ye have me to do? I am old, and have already lived too long to see these terrible and most wicked days. Fly you, and do as your conscience leadeth you. I am fully determined, with God's grace, to go to this Bishop and tell him to his beard that he doth

naught. I believe before God that I shall never be able to do for my God such good service as I may do now.*

Striking were the replies which he made to Gardiner and his other examiners. None spoke more pithily, weightily, and powerfully than did this Suffolk incumbent. Striking and deeply affecting was his last testament and legacy of advice to his wife, his family, and parishioners, though far too long to be inserted here, excepting the last sentence: "For God's sake beware of Popery: for though it appear to have in it unity, yet the same is vanity and Antichristianity, and not in Christ's faith and verity."†

He was sent down from London to Hadleigh, to his great delight, to be burned before the eyes of his parishioners. When he got within two miles of Hadleigh, the sheriff of Suffolk asked him how he felt. "God be praised, Master Sheriff," was his reply, "never better. For now I am almost at home. I lack but just two stiles to go over, and I am even at my Father's house."

As he rode through the streets of the little town of Hadleigh, he found them lined with crowds of his parishioners, who had heard of his approach and came out of their houses to greet him with many tears and lamentations. To them he only made one constant address, "I have preached to you God's Word and truth, and am come this day to seal it with my blood."

On coming to Aldham Common, where he was to suffer, they told him where he was. Then said he, "Thank God, I am even at home." When he was stripped to his shirt and ready for the stake, he said with a loud voice, "Good people, I have taught you nothing but God's Holy Word, and those lessons that I have taken out of the Bible; and I am come hither to seal it with my blood." He would probably have said more, but like all the other martyrs, he was strictly forbidden to speak, and even now was struck violently on the head for saying these few words. He then knelt down and prayed, a poor woman of the parish insisting, in spite of every effort to prevent her, in kneeling down with him. After this, he was chained to the stake, and repeating the 51st Psalm and crying to God, "Merciful Father, for Jesus Christ's sake, receive my soul into

---

* Fox's *Acts and Monuments*, vol. 3, p. 138.
† Fox's *Acts and Monuments*, vol. 3, p. 144.

Thy hands," stood quietly amidst the flames without crying or moving, till one of the guards dashed out his brains with a halberd. And so this good old Suffolk incumbent passed away.

(4) Robert Ferrar

The fourth leading Reformer who suffered in Mary's reign was Robert Ferrar, Bishop of St. David's, in Wales. He was burned at Carmarthen on Friday, the 30th March, 1555. Little is known of this good man beyond the fact that he was born at Halifax and was the last Prior of Nostel, in Yorkshire, an office which he surrendered in 1540. He was also Chaplain to Archbishop Cranmer and to the Protector Somerset, and to this influence he owed his elevation to the episcopal bench.

He was first imprisoned for various trivial and ridiculous charges on temporal matters in the latter days of Edward VI, after the fall of the Protector Somerset, and afterwards was brought before Gardiner, with Hooper, Rogers, and Bradford, on the far more serious matter of his doctrine. The articles exhibited against him clearly show that in all questions of faith he was of one mind with his fellow-martyrs. Like Hooper and Taylor, he was condemned to be burned in the place where he was best known and was sent down from London to Carmarthen.

What happened there at his execution is related very briefly by Fox, partly, no doubt, because of the great distance of Carmarthen from London in those pre-railways days; partly, perhaps, because most of those who saw Ferrar burned could speak nothing but Welsh. One single fact is recorded which shows the good Bishop's courage and constancy in a striking light. He had told a friend before the day of execution that if he saw him once stir in the fire from the pain of his burning, he need not believe the doctrines he had taught. When the awful time came, he did not forget his promise, and by God's grace, he kept it well. He stood in the flames holding out his hands till they were burned to stumps, until a bystander in mercy struck him on the head and put an end to his sufferings. And so the Welsh Bishop passed away.

(5) John Bradford

The fifth leading Reformer who suffered in Mary's reign was John Bradford, Prebendary of St. Paul's, and Chaplain to Bishop

Ridley. He was burned in Smithfield on Monday, July the 1st, 1555, at the early age of thirty-five. Few of the English martyrs, perhaps, are better known than Bradford, and none certainly deserve better their reputation. Strype calls Bradford, Cranmer, Ridley, and Latimer the "four prime pillars" of the Reformed Church of England. He was by birth a Manchester man and to the end of his life retained a strong interest in the district with which he was connected.

At an early age his high talents commended him to the notice of men in high quarters, and he was appointed one of the six royal chaplains who were sent about England to preach up the doctrines of the Reformation. Bradford's commission was to preach in Lancashire and Cheshire and he seems to have performed his duty with singular ability and success. He preached constantly in Manchester, Liverpool, Bolton, Bury, Wigan, Ashton, Stockport, Prestwich, Middleton, and Chester with great benefit to the cause of Protestantism, and with great effect on men's souls. The consequence was what might have been expected. Within a month of Queen Mary's accession Bradford was in prison and never left it until he was burned. His youth, his holiness, and his extraordinary reputation as a preacher made him an object of great interest during his imprisonment, and immense efforts were made to pervert him from the Protestant faith. All these efforts, however, were in vain. As he lived, so he died.*

On the day of his execution he was led out from Newgate to Smithfield about nine o'clock in the morning, amid such a crowd of people as was never seen either before or after. A Mrs. Honeywood, who lived to the age of ninety-six and died about 1620, remembered going to see him burned, and her shoes being trodden off by the crowd. Indeed, when he came to the stake, the sheriffs of London were so alarmed at the press that they would not allow him and his fellow-sufferer, Leaf, to pray as long as they

---

* Bradford seems to have had a very strong feeling about the causes for which God permitted the Marian persecution. Writing to his mother from prison, he says: "Ye all know there never was more knowledge of God, and less godly living and true serving of God—God, therefore, is now come, and because He will not damn us with the world He punisheth us." Fox, 3, p. 255.

wished. "Arise," they said, "and make an end; for the press of the people is great."

"At that word," says Fox, "they both stood up, upon their feet, and then Master Bradford took a faggot in his hands and kissed it, and so likewise the stake." When he came to the stake he held up his hands, and looking up to heaven, said, "O England, England, repent thee of thy sins! Beware of idolatry; beware of false Antichrists! Take heed they do not deceive you!" After that he turned to the young man Leaf, who suffered with him, and said, "Be of good comfort, brother; for we shall have a merry supper with the Lord this night." After that he spoke no more that man could hear, excepting that he embraced the reeds, and said, "Strait is the gate, and narrow is the way, that leadeth to eternal life, and few there be that find it." "He embraced the flames," says Fuller, "as a fresh gale of wind in a hot summer day." And so, in the prime of life, he passed away.

(6 & 7) Nicholas Ridley & Hugh Latimer

The sixth and seventh leading Reformers who suffered in Mary's reign were two whose names are familiar to every Englishman—Nicholas Ridley, Bishop of London, and Hugh Latimer, once Bishop of Worcester. They were both burned at Oxford, back to back, at one stake, on the 16th of October, 1555. Ridley was born at Willimondswike, in Northumberland, on the borders. Latimer was born at Thurcaston, in Leicestershire. The history of these two great English Protestants is so well known to most people that I need not say much about it. Next to Cranmer, there can be little doubt that no two men did so much to bring about the establishment of the principles of the Reformation in England. Latimer, as an extraordinary popular preacher, and Ridley, as a learned man and an admirable manager of the metropolitan diocese of London, have left behind them reputations which never have been surpassed. As a matter of course, they were among the first that Bonner and Gardiner struck at when Mary came to the throne and were persecuted with relentless severity until their deaths.

How they were examined again and again by commissioners about the great points in controversy between Protestants and Rome—how they were shamefully baited, teased, and tortured by every kind of unfair and unreasonable dealing—how they gallantly fought a good fight, to the end, and never gave way for a moment to their adversaries—all these are matters with which I need not trouble my readers. Are they not all fairly chronicled in the pages of good old Fox? I will only mention a few circumstances connected with their deaths.

On the day of their martyrdom they were brought separately to the place of execution, which was at the end of Broad Street, Oxford, close to Balliol College. Ridley arrived on the ground first, and seeing Latimer come afterwards, ran to him and kissed him, saying, "Be of good heart, brother; for God will either assuage the fury of the flames, or else strengthen us to abide it." They then prayed earnestly and talked with one another, though no one could hear what they said. After this they had to listen to a sermon by a wretched renegade divine named Smith, and being forbidden to make any answer, were commanded to make ready for death.

Ridley's last words before the fire was lighted were these: "Heavenly Father, I give Thee most hearty thanks that Thou hast called me to a profession of Thee even unto death. I beseech Thee, Lord God, have mercy on this realm of England, and deliver the same from all her enemies." Latimer's last words were like the blast of a trumpet, which rings even to this day: "Be of good comfort, Master Ridley, and play the man; we shall this day, by God's grace, light such a candle in England as I trust shall never be put out."

When the flames began to rise, Ridley cried out with a loud voice in Latin, "Into thy hands, O Lord, I commend my spirit: Lord, receive my spirit," and afterwards repeated these last words in English. Latimer cried as vehemently on the other side of the stake, "Father of heaven, receive my soul."

Latimer soon died. An old man, above eighty years of age, it took but little to set his spirit free from its earthly tenement. Ridley suffered long and painfully from the bad management of the fire by those who attended the execution. At length, however, the flames reached a vital part of him, and he fell at Latimer's feet and was at rest. And so the two great Protestant bishops passed away. "They were lovely and beautiful in their lives, and in death they were not divided."[1]

---

[1] 2 Samuel 1:23.

(8) John Philpot

The eighth leading English Reformer who suffered in Mary's reign was John Philpot, Archdeacon of Winchester. He was burned in Smithfield on Wednesday, December the 18th, 1555. Philpot is one of the martyrs of whom we know little comparatively, except that he was born at Compton, in Hampshire, was of good family and well connected, and had a very high reputation for learning. The mere fact that at the beginning of Mary's reign he was one of the leading champions of Protestantism in the mock discussions which were held in Convocation is sufficient to show that he was no common man. The relentless virulence with which he was persecuted by Gardiner is easily accounted for when we remember that Gardiner, when he was deposed from his see in Edward the Sixth's time, was Bishop of Winchester and would naturally regard his successor, Bishop Ponet, and all his officials, with intense hatred. A Popish bishop was not likely to spare a Protestant archdeacon.

The thirteen examinations of Philpot before the Popish bishops are given by Fox at great length and fill no less than 140 pages of one of the Parker Society volumes. The length to which they were protracted shows plainly how anxious his judges were to turn him from his principles. The skill with which the Archdeacon maintained his ground, alone and unaided, gives a most favourable impression of his learning, no less than of his courage and patience.

The night before his execution he received a message, while at supper in Newgate, to the effect that he was to be burned next day. He answered at once, "I am ready: God grant me strength and a joyful resurrection." He then went into his bedroom and thanked God that he was counted worthy to suffer for His truth.

The next morning, at eight o'clock, the sheriffs called for him and conducted him to Smithfield. The road was foul and muddy, as it was the depth of winter, and the officers took him up in their arms to carry him to the stake. Then he said, merrily, alluding to what he had probably seen at Rome when traveling in his early days, "What, will you make me a Pope? I am content to go to my journey's end on foot."

When he came into Smithfield, he kneeled down and said, "I will pay my vows in thee, O Smithfield." He then kissed the stake and said, "Shall I disdain to suffer at this stake, seeing my Redeemer

The Martyrdom of John Philpot
"I will pay my vows in thee O Smithfield."

Thomas Cranmer (1489–1556)

did not refuse to suffer a most vile death on the cross for me?" After that, he meekly repeated the 106th, 107th, and 108th Psalms, and being chained to the stake, died very quietly. And so the good Archdeacon passed away.

(9) Thomas Cranmer

The ninth and last leading Reformer who suffered in Mary's reign was Thomas Cranmer, Archbishop of Canterbury. He was burned at Oxford, on the 21st of March, 1556. Cranmer was born at Aslacton, in Nottinghamshire. There is no name among the English martyrs so well known in history as his. There is none certainly in the list of our Reformers to whom the Church of England, on the whole, is so much indebted. He was only a mortal man and had his weaknesses and infirmities, it must be admitted; but still, he was a great man and a good man.

Cranmer, we must always remember, was brought prominently forward at a comparatively early period in the English Reformation and was made Archbishop of Canterbury at a time when his views of religion were confessedly half-formed and imperfect. Whenever quotations from Cranmer's writings are brought forward by the advocates of semi-Romanism in the Church of England, you should always ask carefully to what period of his life those quotations belong. In forming your estimate of Cranmer, do not forget his antecedents. He was a man who had the honesty to grope his way into fuller light and to cast aside his early opinions and confess that he had changed his mind on many subjects. How few men have the courage to do this!

Cranmer maintained an unblemished reputation throughout the reigns of Henry VIII and Edward VI, although frequently placed in most delicate and difficult positions. Not a single man can be named in those days who passed through so much dirt and yet came out of it so thoroughly undefiled.

Cranmer, beyond all doubt, laid the foundation of our present Prayer Book and articles. Though not perhaps a brilliant man, he was a learned one and a lover of learned men, and one who was always trying to improve everything around him. When I consider the immense difficulties he had to contend with, I often wonder that he accomplished what he did. Nothing, in fact, but his steady perseverance would have laid the foundation of our formularies.

I say all these things in order to break the force of the great and undeniable fact that he was the only English Reformer who for a time showed the white feather and for a time shrank from dying for the truth! I admit that he fell sadly. I do not pretend to extenuate his fall. It stands forth as an everlasting proof that the best of men are only men at the best. I only want my readers to remember that if Cranmer failed as no other Reformer in England failed, he also had done what certainly no other Reformer had done.

From the moment that Mary came to the English throne, Cranmer was marked for destruction. It is probable that there was no English divine whom the unhappy Queen regarded with such rancour and hatred. She never forgot that her mother's divorce was brought about by Cranmer's advice, and she never rested till he was burned. Cranmer was imprisoned and examined just like Ridley and Latimer. Like them, he stood his ground firmly before the commissioners. Like them, he had clearly the best of the argument in all points that were disputed. But, like them, of course, he was pronounced guilty of heresy, condemned, deposed, and sentenced to be burned.

And now comes the painful fact that in the last month of Cranmer's life his courage failed him, and he was persuaded to sign a recantation of his Protestant opinions. Flattered and cajoled by subtle kindness, frightened at the prospect of so dreadful a death as burning, tempted and led away by the devil, Thomas Cranmer fell and put his hand to a paper, in which he repudiated and renounced the principles of the Reformation, for which he had laboured so long.

Great was the sorrow of all true Protestants on hearing these tidings! Great was the triumphing and exultation of all Papists! Had they stopped here and set their noble victim at liberty, the name of Cranmer would probably have sunk and never risen again. But the Romish party, as God would have it, outwitted themselves. With fiendish cruelty they resolved to burn Cranmer—even after he had recanted. This, by God's providence, was just the turning point for Cranmer's reputation. Through the abounding grace of God, he repented of his fall and found mercy. Through the same abounding grace, he resolved to die in the faith of the Reformation. And at last, through abounding grace, he witnessed such a bold confession in St. Mary's, Oxford, that he confounded his enemies, filled his friends with thankfulness and praise, and left the world a triumphant martyr for Christ's truth.

I need hardly remind you how, on the 21st March, the unhappy Archbishop was brought out, like Samson in the hands of the Philistines, to make sport for his enemies, and to be a gazingstock to the world in St. Mary's Church, at Oxford. I need hardly remind you how, after Dr. Cole's sermon, he was invited to declare his faith, and was fully expected to acknowledge publicly his alteration of religion and his adhesion to the Church of Rome. I need hardly remind you how, with intense mental suffering, the Archbishop addressed the assembly at great length, and at the close, suddenly astounded his enemies by renouncing all his former recantations, declaring the Pope to be Antichrist, and rejecting the Popish doctrine of the *real presence.* Such a sight was certainly never seen by mortal eyes since the world began!

But then came the time of Cranmer's triumph. With a light heart and a clear conscience, he cheerfully allowed himself to be hurried to the stake amidst the frenzied outcries of his disappointed enemies. Boldly and undauntedly he stood up at the stake while the flames curled around him, steadily holding out his right hand in the fire and saying, with reference to his having signed a recantation, "This unworthy right hand," and steadily holding up his left hand towards heaven.* Of all the martyrs, strange to say, none at the last moment showed more *physical* courage than Cranmer did. Nothing, in short, in all his life became him so well as the manner of his leaving it. Greatly he had sinned, but greatly he had repented. Like Peter he fell, but like Peter he rose again. And so passed away the first Protestant Archbishop of Canterbury.

---

* Soames is my authority for this statement about Cranmer's left hand. I can find it nowhere else. He also mentions what other historians record, that when the fire had burned down to ashes, Cranmer's heart was found unconsumed and uninjured. Soames' *History of the Reformation*, vol. 4, p. 544.

[Sheldon (*History of the Christian Church*, vol. 3, p. 299) and Latourette (*A History of Christianity*, vol. 2, p. 810) also confirm Soames' account. Sheldon quotes Cranmer as saying, "And forasmuch as my hand has offended in writing contrary to my heart, my hand shall first be punished; for when I come to the fire it shall be first burned."—Ed.]

I will not trust myself to make any comment on these painful and interesting histories. I have not time. I only wish my readers to believe that the half of these men's stories have not been told them, and that the stories of scores of men and women less distinguished by position might easily be added to them, quite as painful and quite as interesting.* But I will say boldly, that the men who were burned in this way were not men whose memories ought to be lightly passed over, or whose opinions ought to be lightly esteemed. Opinions for which an "army of martyrs"[1] died ought not to be dismissed with scorn. To their faithfulness we owe the existence of the Reformed Church of England. Her foundations were cemented with their blood. To their courage we owe, in a great measure, our English liberty. They taught the land that it was worth while to die for free thought. Happy is the land which has had such citizens! Happy is the Church which has had such Reformers! Honour be to those who at Smithfield, Oxford, Gloucester, Carmarthen, and Hadleigh have raised stones of remembrance and memorials to the martyrs!

III. The Reason Why Our Reformers Were Burned

But I pass on to a point which I hold to be one of cardinal importance in the present day. The point I refer to is *the special reason why our Reformers were burned*. Great indeed would be our mistake if we supposed that they suffered for the vague charge of refusing submission to the Pope, or desiring to maintain the independence of the Church of England. Nothing of the kind! The principal reason why they were burned was because they refused one of the peculiar doctrines of the Romish church. On that doctrine, in almost every case, hinged their life or death. If they admitted it, they might live; if they refused it, they must die.

---

* The following martyrdoms are recommended to the special notice of all who possess *Fox's Book of Martyrs*: Laurence Saunders, burned at Coventry; William Hunter, at Brentwood; Rawlins White, at Cardiff; George Marsh, at Chester; Thomas Hawkes, at Coggeshall; John Bland, at Canterbury; Alice Driver, at Ipswich; Rose Allen, at Colchester; Joan Waste, at Derby; Richard Woodman, at Lewes; Agnes Prest, at Exeter; Julius Palmer, at Newbury; John Noyes, at Laxfield, in Suffolk.

[1] Quoted from the *Te Deum* (Latin: *God, We Praise You*), a fourth-century hymn.

The doctrine in question was the *real presence* of the body and blood of Christ in the consecrated elements of bread and wine in the Lord's Supper. Did they, or did they not believe that the body and blood of Christ were really, that is, corporally, literally, locally, and materially, present under the forms of bread and wine after the words of consecration were pronounced? Did they or did they not believe that the real body of Christ, which was born of the Virgin Mary, was present on the so-called altar so soon as the mystical words had passed the lips of the priest? Did they or did they not? That was the simple question. If they did not believe and admit it, they were burned.*

There is a wonderful and striking unity in the stories of our martyrs on this subject. Some of them, no doubt, were attacked about the marriage of priests. Some of them were assaulted about the nature of the Catholic Church. Some of them were assailed on other points. But all, without an exception, were called to special account about the *real presence*, and in every case their refusal to admit the doctrine formed one principal cause of their condemnation

(1) Hear what Rogers said:

> I was asked whether I believed in the sacrament to be the very body and blood of our Saviour Christ that was born of the Virgin Mary, and hanged on the cross, really and substantially? I answered, "I think it to be false. I cannot understand really and substantially to signify otherwise than corporally. But corporally Christ is only in heaven, and so Christ cannot be corporally in your sacrament."†

And therefore he was condemned and burned.

(2) Hear what Bishop Hooper said:

> Tunstall asked him to say, "whether he believed the corporal

---

* "The Mass was one of the principal causes why so much turmoil was made in the Church, with the bloodshed of so many godly men." Fox's Preface to vol. 3 of *Acts and Monuments*.

"The sacrament of the altar was the main touchstone to discover the poor Protestants. This point of the real, corporal presence of Christ in the sacrament, the same body that was crucified, was the compendious way to discover those of the opposite opinion." Fuller, *Church History*, vol. 3, p. 399, Tegg's edition.

† Fox *in loco*, vol. 3, p. 101, edition, 1684.

presence in the sacrament," and Master Hooper said plainly "that there was none such, neither did he believe any such thing." Whereupon they bade the notaries write that he was married and would not go from his wife, and that he believed not the corporal presence in the sacrament; wherefore he was worthy to be deprived of his bishopric.*

And so he was condemned and burned.

(3) Hear what Rowland Taylor said:

The second cause why I was condemned as a heretic was that I denied transubstantiation, and concomitation, two juggling words whereby the Papists believe that Christ's natural body is made of bread, and the Godhead by and by to be joined thereto, so that immediately after the words of consecration, there is no more bread and wine in the sacrament, but the substance only of the body and blood of Christ. Because I denied the aforesaid Papistical doctrine (yea, rather plain, wicked idolatry, blasphemy, and heresy) I am judged a heretic.†

And therefore he was condemned and burned.

(4) Hear what was done with Bishop Ferrar: He was summoned to "grant the natural presence of Christ in the sacrament under the form of bread and wine," and because he refused to subscribe this article as well as others, he was condemned. And in the sentence of condemnation it is finally charged against him that he maintained that "the sacrament of the altar ought not to be ministered on an altar, or to be elevated, or to be adored in any way."‡ And so he was burned.

(5) Hear what holy John Bradford wrote to the men of Lancashire and Cheshire when he was in prison:

The chief thing which I am condemned for as an heretic is because I deny in the sacrament of the altar (which is not Christ's Supper, but a plain perversion as the Papists now use it) to be a real, natural, and corporal presence of Christ's body and blood under the forms and accidents of bread and wine: that is, because

---

* Fox *in loco*, vol. 3, p. 123
† Fox *in loco*, vol. 3, p. 141.
‡ Fox *in loco*, vol. 3, p. 178.

I deny transubstantiation, which is the darling of the devil, and daughter and heir to Antichrist's religion.*

And so he was condemned and burned.

(6) Hear what were the words of the sentence of condemnation against Bishop Ridley:

> The said Nicholas Ridley affirms, maintains, and stubbornly defends certain opinions, assertions, and heresies, contrary to the Word of God and the received faith of the Church, as in denying the true and natural body and blood of Christ to be in the sacrament of the altar, and secondarily, in affirming the substance of bread and wine to remain after the words of consecration.†

And so he was condemned and burned.

(7) Hear the articles exhibited against Bishop Latimer:

> That thou hast openly affirmed, defended, and maintained that the true and natural body of Christ after the consecration of the priest, is not really present in the sacrament of the altar, and that in the sacrament of the altar remaineth still the substance of bread and wine.

And to this article the good old man replied:

> After a corporal being, which the Romish church furnisheth, Christ's body and blood is not in the sacrament under the forms of bread and wine.‡

And so he was condemned and burned.

(8) Hear the address made by Bishop Bonner to Archdeacon Philpot:

> You have offended and trespassed against the sacrament of the altar, denying the real presence of Christ's body and blood to be there, affirming also material bread and material wine to be in the sacrament, and not the substance of the body and blood of Christ.§

And because the good man stoutly adhered to this opinion he was condemned and burned.

---

* Fox *in loco*, vol. 3, p. 260.
† Fox *in loco*, vol. 3, p. 426.
‡ Fox *in loco*, vol. 3, p. 426.
§ Fox *in loco*, vol. 3, p. 495.

(9)   Hear, lastly, what Cranmer said with almost his last breath, in
St. Mary's Church, Oxford:

> As for the sacrament, I believe, as I have taught in my book against
> the Bishop of Winchester, the which my book teacheth so true a
> doctrine, that it shall stand at the last day before the judgment of
> God when the Papist's doctrine contrary thereto shall be ashamed
> to show her face.*

If anyone wants to know what Cranmer had said in this book, let
him take the following sentence as a specimen:

> They (the Papists) say that Christ is corporally under or in the
> form of bread and wine. We say that Christ is not there, *neither
> corporally nor spiritually*; but in them that worthily eat and drink the
> bread and wine He is spiritually, and corporally in heaven.†

And so he was burned.

Now, were the English Reformers right in being so stiff and
unbending on this question of the *real presence*? Was it a point of
such vital importance that they were justified in dying before they
would receive it? These are questions, I suspect, which are very
puzzling to many unreflecting minds. Such minds, I fear, can see in
the whole controversy about the *real presence* nothing but a logo-
machy, or strife of words. But they are questions, I am bold to say,
on which no well-instructed Bible reader can hesitate for a moment
in giving his answer. Such an one will say at once that the Romish
doctrine of the *real presence* strikes at the very root of the Gospel,
and is the very citadel and keep of Popery. Men may not see this at
first, but it is a point that ought to be carefully remembered. It
throws a clear and broad light on the line which the Reformers
took, and the unflinching firmness with which they died.

Whatever men please to think or say, the Romish doctrine of the
real presence, if pursued to its legitimate consequences, obscures
every leading doctrine of the Gospel and damages and interferes
with the whole system of Christ's truth. Grant for a moment that
the Lord's Supper is a sacrifice, and not a sacrament—grant that
every time the words of consecration are used the natural body and
blood of Christ are present on the communion table under the

---

* Fox *in loco*, vol. 3, p. 562.
† *Cranmer on the Lord's Supper*, Parker Society edition, p. 54.

forms of bread and wine—grant that every one who eats that consecrated bread and drinks that consecrated wine does really eat and drink the natural body and blood of Christ—grant for a moment these things, and then see what momentous consequences result from these premises. You spoil the blessed doctrine of *Christ's finished work* when He died on the cross. A sacrifice that needs to be repeated is not a perfect and complete thing. You spoil the *priestly office* of Christ. If there are priests that can offer an acceptable sacrifice to God besides Him, the great High Priest is robbed of His glory. You spoil the scriptural doctrine of the *Christian ministry.* You exalt sinful men into the position of mediators between God and man. You give to the sacramental elements of bread and wine an honour and veneration they were never meant to receive and produce an *idolatry* to be abhorred of faithful Christians. Last, but not least, you overthrow the true doctrine of *Christ's human nature.* If the body born of the Virgin Mary can be in more places than one at the same time, it is not a body like our own, and Jesus was not "the last Adam"[1] in the truth of our nature. I cannot doubt for a moment that our martyred Reformers saw and felt these things even more clearly than we do, and seeing and feeling them, chose to die rather than admit the doctrine of the real presence. Feeling them, they would not give way by subjection for a moment and cheerfully laid down their lives. Let this fact be deeply graven in our minds. Wherever the English language is spoken on the face of the globe this fact ought to be clearly understood by every Englishman who reads history. Rather than admit the doctrine of the real presence of Christ's natural body and blood under the forms of bread and wine, the Reformers of the Church of England were content to be burned.

IV. Bearing of the Whole Subject

And now I must ask the special attention of my readers while I try to show the *bearing of the whole subject on our own position and on our own times.* I must ask you to turn from the dead to the living, to look away from England in 1555 to England in this present enlightened and advanced age, and to consider seriously the light

---

[1] 1 Corinthians 15:45.

which the burning of our Reformers throws on the Church of England at the present day.

We live in momentous times. The ecclesiastical horizon on every side is dark and lowering. The steady rise and progress of extreme ritualism and ritualists are shaking the Church of England to its very centre. It is of the very first importance to understand clearly what it all means. A right diagnosis of disease is the very first element of successful treatment. The physician who does not see what is the matter is never likely to work any cures.

Now, I say there can be no greater mistake than to suppose that the great controversy of our times is a mere question of vestments and ornaments—of chasubles and copes—of more or less church decorations—of more or less candles and flowers—of more or less bowings and turnings and crossings—of more or less gestures and postures—of more or less show and form. The man who fancies that the whole dispute is a mere æsthetic one, a question of taste, like one of fashion and millinery, must allow me to tell him that he is under a complete delusion. He may sit on the shore, like the Epicurean philosopher, smiling at theological storms, and flatter himself that we are only squabbling about trifles; but I take leave to tell him that his philosophy is very shallow, and his knowledge of the controversy of the day very superficial indeed.

The things I have spoken of are *trifles*, I fully concede. But they are pernicious trifles, because they are the outward expression of an inward doctrine. They are the skin disease which is the symptom of an unsound constitution. They are the plague spot which tells of internal poison. They are the curling smoke which arises from a hidden volcano of mischief. I, for one, would never make any stir about church millinery or incense or candles, if I thought they meant nothing beneath the surface. But I believe they mean a great deal of error and false doctrine, and therefore I publicly protest against them and say that those who support them are to be blamed.

I give it as my deliberate opinion that the root of the whole ritualistic system is the dangerous doctrine of the *real presence* of Christ's natural body and blood in the Lord's Supper under the forms of the consecrated bread and wine. If words mean anything, this *real presence* is the foundation principle of ritualism. This *real presence* is what the extreme members of the ritualistic party want to bring back into the Church of England. And just as our martyred Reformers went to the stake rather than admit the *real presence*, so I hold that we should make any sacrifice and contend to the bitter end, rather than allow a materialistic doctrine about Christ's presence in the Lord's Supper to come back in any shape into our communion.

I will not weary my readers with quotations in proof of what I affirm. They have heard enough, perhaps too much, of them. But I must ask permission to give two short extracts. Observe what Dr. Pusey says, in a sermon called *Will ye also go away?*:

> While repudiating any materialistic conceptions of the mode of the presence of our Lord in the Holy Eucharist, such as I believe is condemned in the term "corporal presence of our Lord's flesh and blood," *i.e.*, as though His precious body and blood were present in any gross or carnal way, and not rather sacramentally, really, spiritually—I believe that in the Holy Eucharist the body and blood of Christ are sacramentally, supernaturally, ineffably, but verily and indeed present, "under the forms of bread and wine"; and that "where His body is, there is Christ."*

Observe what Dr. Littledale says, in a tract called *The Real Presence*:

> I. The Christian Church teaches, and has always taught, that in the Holy Communion, after consecration, the body and blood of the Lord Jesus Christ are "verily and indeed" present on the altar under the forms of bread and wine.
> II. The Church also teaches that this presence depends on God's will, not on man's belief, and therefore that bad and good people receive the very same thing in communicating, the good for their benefit, the bad for their condemnation.
> III. Further, that as Christ is both God and Man, and as these two natures are forever joined in His one person, His Godhead must be wherever His body is, and therefore He is to be worshipped in His sacrament.
> IV. The body and blood present are that same body and blood which were conceived by the Holy Ghost, born of the Virgin

---

* Parker's, 1867.

Mary, suffered under Pontius Pilate, ascended into heaven, but they are not present in the *same manner* as they were when Christ walked on earth. He, as Man, is now *naturally* in heaven, there to be till the last day, yet He *is supernaturally*, and just as truly, present in the Holy Communion, in some way which we cannot explain, but only believe.

In both these quotations, we may observe, there is an attempt to evade the charge of maintaining a "gross and carnal presence." The attempt, however, is not successful. It is a very curious fact that the Romish controversialist Mr. Harding, Bishop Jewell's opponent, said just as much 300 years ago. He said, "Christ's body is present not after a corporal, or carnal, or naturally wise, but invisibly, un-speakably, miraculously, supernaturally, spiritually, Divinely, and in a manner by Him known."[*]

In both cases we can hardly fail to observe that the very expressions which our martyrs steadily refused is employed, "present under the forms of bread and wine." It is clear, to my mind, that if Dr. Pusey and Dr. Littledale had been brought before Gardiner and Bonner 300 years ago, they would have left the court with flying colours, and at any rate, would not have been burned.

I might refer my readers to other published sermons on the Lord's Supper by men of high position in our church. I might refer them to several ritualistic manuals for the use of communicants. I might refer them to the famous book *Directorium Anglicanum*. I simply give it as my opinion that no plain man in his senses can read the writings of extreme ritualists about the Lord's Supper and see any real distinction between the doctrine they hold and downright Popery. It is a distinction without a difference, and one that any jury of twelve honest men would say at once could not be proved.

I turn from books and sermons to churches, and I ask any reflecting mind to mark, consider, and digest what may be seen in any thorough-going ritualistic place of worship. I ask him to mark the superstitious veneration and idolatrous honour with which everything within the chancel, and around and upon the Lord's table, is regarded. I boldly ask any jury of twelve honest and unprejudiced men to look at that chancel and communion table,

---

[*] *Harding's Reply to Jewell*, p. 434. Parker Society edit.

and tell me what they think all this means. I ask them whether the whole thing does not savour of the Romish doctrine of the *real presence*, and the sacrifice of the Mass? I believe that if Bonner and Gardiner had seen the chancels and communion tables of some of the churches of this day, they would have lifted up their hands and rejoiced; while Ridley, Bishop of London, and Hooper, Bishop of Gloucester, would have turned away with righteous indignation and said, "This communion table is not meant for the Lord's Supper on the Lord's board, but for counterfeiting the idolatrous Popish Mass."

I do not for a moment deny the zeal, earnestness, and sincerity of the extreme ritualists, though as much might be said for the Pharisees or the Jesuits. I do not deny that we live in a singularly free country, and that Englishmen, nowadays, have liberty to commit any folly short of *felo de se*.[1] But I do deny that any clergyman, however zealous and earnest, has a right to reintroduce Popery into the Church of England. And above all, I deny that he has any right to maintain the very principle of the *real presence*, for opposing which the Reformers of his church were burned.

The plain truth is that the doctrine of the extreme ritualistic school about the Lord's Supper can never be reconciled with the dying opinions of our martyred Reformers. The members of this school may protest loudly that they are sound churchmen, but they certainly are not churchmen of the same opinions as the Marian martyrs. If words mean anything, Hooper and Rogers and Ridley and Bradford and their companions held one view of the *real presence*, and the ultra-ritualists hold quite another. If they were right, the ritualists are wrong. There is a gulf that cannot be crossed between the two parties. There is a thorough difference that cannot be reconciled or explained away. If we hold with one side, we cannot possibly hold with the other. For my part, I say, unhesitatingly, that I have more faith in Ridley, and Hooper, and Bradford than I have in all the leaders of the ultra-ritualistic party.

But what are we going to do? The danger is very great, far greater, I fear, than most people suppose. A conspiracy has been long at work for *un-Protestantizing* the Church of England, and all

---

[1] "Felon of himself"; a person who commits suicide.

the energies of Rome are concentrated on this little island. A sapping and mining process has been long going on under our feet, of which we are beginning at last to see a little. We shall see a good deal more by and by. At the rate we are going, it would never surprise me if within fifty years the crown of England were no longer on a Protestant head, and High Mass were once more celebrated in Westminster Abbey and St. Paul's. The danger, in plain words, is neither more nor less than that of our church being un-Protestantized and going back to Babylon and Egypt. We are in imminent peril of reunion with Rome.

Men may call me an alarmist, if they like, for using such language. But, I reply, there is a cause. The upper classes in this land are widely infected with a taste for a sensuous, histrionic, formal religion. The lower orders are becoming sadly familiarized with all the ceremonialism which is the steppingstone to Popery. The middle classes are becoming disgusted with the Church of England and asking what is the use of it. The intellectual classes are finding out that all religions are either equally good or equally bad. The House of Commons will do nothing unless pressed by public opinion. We have no Pyms or Hampdens there now. And all this time ritualism grows and spreads. The ship is among breakers— breakers ahead and breakers astern—breakers on the right hand and breakers on the left. Something needs to be done, if we are to escape shipwreck.

The very life of the Church of England is at stake, and nothing less. Take away the Gospel from a church and that church is not worth preserving. A well without water, a scabbard without a sword, a steam engine without a fire, a ship without compass and rudder, a watch without a mainspring, a stuffed carcase without life—all these are useless things. But there is nothing so useless as a church without the Gospel. And this is the very question that stares us in the face. Is the Church of England to retain the Gospel or not? Without it, in vain shall we turn to our archbishops and bishops; in vain shall we glory in our cathedrals and parish churches. "Ichabod"[1] will soon be written on our walls. The ark of God will not be with us. Surely something ought to be done.

---

[1] 1 Samuel 4:21.

One thing, however, is very clear to my mind. We ought not lightly to forsake the Church of England. No! So long as her articles and formularies remain unaltered, unrepealed, and unchanged, so long we ought not to forsake her. Cowardly and base is that seaman who launches the boat and forsakes the ship so long as there is a chance of saving her. Cowardly, I say, is that Protestant churchman who talks of seceding because things on board our church are at present out of order. What, though some of the crew are traitors, and some are asleep! What, though the old ship has some leaks, and her rigging has given way in some places! Still I maintain there is much to be done. There is life in the old ship yet. The great Pilot has not yet forsaken her. The compass of the Bible is still on deck. There are yet left on board some faithful and able seamen. So long as the Articles and Formularies are not Romanized, let us stick by the ship. So long as she has Christ and the Bible, let us stand by her to the last plank, nail our colours to the mast, and never haul them down. Once more, I say, let us not be wheedled or bullied or frightened or cajoled or provoked into forsaking the Church of England.

In the name of the Lord let us set up our banners. If ever we would meet Ridley and Latimer and Hooper in another world without shame, let us "contend earnestly"[1] for the truths which they died to preserve. The Church of England expects every Protestant churchman to do his duty. Let us not talk only, but act. Let us not act only, but pray. "He that hath no sword, let him sell his garment and buy one."[2]

There is a voice in the blood of the martyrs. What does that voice say? It cries aloud from Oxford, Smithfield, and Gloucester: "Resist to the death the Popish doctrine of the *real presence*, under the forms of the consecrated bread and wine in the Lord's Supper!"

---

[1] Jude 3.
[2] Luke 22:36.

Note

The following quotations about the doctrine of the *real presence* are commended to the special attention of all churchmen in the present day:

1. Whereas it is ordained in this Office for the Administration of the Lord's Supper, that the Communicants should receive the same kneeling; (which order is well meant, for a signification of our humble and grateful acknowledgment of the benefits of Christ therein given to all worthy Receivers, and for the avoiding of such profanation and disorder in the Holy Communion, as might otherwise ensue;) yet, lest the same kneeling should by any persons, either out of ignorance and infirmity, or out of malice and obstinacy, be misconstrued and depraved; It is hereby declared, That thereby no adoration is intended, or ought to be done, either unto the Sacramental Bread or Wine thereby bodily received, or unto any corporal presence of Christ's natural Flesh and Blood. For the Sacramental Bread and Wine remain still in their very natural substances, and therefore may not be adored; (for that were Idolatry, to be abhorred of all faithful Christians;) and the natural Body and Blood of our Saviour Christ are in Heaven, and not here; it being against the truth of Christ's natural Body to be at one time in more places than one.*

2. As concerning the form of doctrine used in this Church of England in the Holy Communion, that the Body and Blood of Christ be under the forms of bread and wine, when you shall show the place where this form of words is expressed, then shall you purge yourself from that which in the meantime I take to be a *plain untruth*.†

3. The real presence of Christ's most blessed Body and Blood is not to be sought for in the sacrament, but in the worthy receiver of the sacrament.‡

---

* Rubric at the end of the Communion Service in the *Book of Common Prayer*.

† Cranmer's *Answer to Gardiner*, pp. 52, 53, Parker edition.

‡ Hooker's *Eccles. Pol.*, bk. 5, p. 67.

4. The Church of England has wisely forborne to use the term of *Real Presence* in all the books set forth by her authority. We neither find it recommended in the Liturgy, nor the Articles, nor the Homilies, nor the Church Catechism, nor Nowell's Catechism. For though it be one in the Liturgy, and once more in the Articles of 1552, it is mentioned in both places as a phrase of the Papists, and rejected for their abuse of it. So that if any Church of England man use it, he does more than the Church directs him; if any reject it, he has the Church's example to warrant him.*

---

* Dean Aldrich's *Reply*, p. 13, 1684. See Goode on *Eucharist*, p. 38.

John Rogers (*c.* 1500–1555)

3

JOHN ROGERS: MARTYR

JOHN ROGERS, who was burned at Smithfield in 1555, is a man who deserves to be held in peculiar honour by all English Protestants for one simple reason: He was the *first* of that noble band of Christian heroes who suffered martyrdom for God's truth in Queen Mary's reign. By his courage and constancy at the stake he supplied a glorious example to all who followed him and mightily helped forward the English Reformation. Some account of this good man can hardly fail to be interesting to all loyal churchmen. In the noble army of English martyrs, he was eminently a standard-bearer.

Rogers was born about the year A.D. 1500, at Deritend, a hamlet in the parish of Aston, and now within the present borough of Birmingham.* Little or nothing is known about his father's family, rank, or position; and just as little about his own early history and the first thirty years of his life. It is only certain that he was educated at Pembroke Hall, Cambridge, and took his degree as B.A. in 1525. Pembroke Hall, we should remember, was the college at which both Ridley and Bradford were members, and in all human

---

* By far the fullest account of Rogers will be found in a biography of him published by Mr. Chester, an American, in the year 1861. Two defects unhappily impair the value of this book very much. For one thing, the author goes out of his way to depreciate such men as Ridley and Cranmer, and praises Rogers so extravagantly that he overshoots his mark and wearies the reader. For another thing, the author speaks far too harshly of John Fox, the historian, and accuses him most unfairly of underrating Rogers. This charge, I must plainly say, I think he fails to prove. My own estimate of Rogers has always been extremely high, and it has been based on the testimony of Fox! Barring these two defects, however, Mr. Chester's book is very useful and interesting.

probability Rogers was a contemporary and acquaintance of these good men. This circumstance, and the preaching of Latimer, which began to make a stir in Cambridge about the same time, could hardly fail to exercise considerable influence on the mind of Rogers at a later period.

At Pembroke Hall, Rogers seems to have read hard and done well. Fox merely says, in one edition of his history, that he "profitably travailed in good learning": and in another, that he resided long at Cambridge, "attentively and diligently engaged in the honourable pursuit of learning." It is evident, however, that he established a reputation as a good scholar and a learned man, according to the standard of the age. This is abundantly shown by the work that he subsequently did in translating the Scriptures, and by the preferments conferred on him by Bishop Ridley, who was no mean judge of men. The best proof of his character, however, as a scholar, was his selection to be a junior canon of Cardinal's College, better known as Christ Church, Oxford, when that noble foundation was commenced by Cardinal Wolsey. Wolsey was naturally anxious to fill his new college with the best men that he could persuade to join it in either university and held out every inducement to men of promise to become members. The mere fact that he selected Rogers among the first men whom he made canons is a clear proof that the young B.A. of Pembroke Hall had the reputation of being a ripe scholar.

The next twenty-two years of John Rogers' life are a period of his history which is involved in much obscurity, chiefly because the greater part of the time was spent on the Continent. The doings and sayings of a man who lives among foreigners are never likely to be so accurately described as those of one who lives under the eyes of his countrymen and friends. Out of a rather tangled skein, the following facts are probably a correct account of his proceedings.

Rogers was ordained soon after his appointment to the canonry which he held in Cardinal's College, Oxford, but does not appear to have held any cure of souls until the year 1532. He was then presented to the living of Trinity the Less, in the city of London, a parish united to St. Michael's, Queenhithe, after the Great Fire, and held it for two years, resigning in 1534. After this he became for a short time chaplain to the company of English residents at Antwerp and was absent from England for about thirteen years. It was at this period of his life that he became intimately acquainted with the famous William Tyndale, embraced the doctrines of Protestantism, and became a fellow-labourer with him in the great work of translating the Holy Scriptures.

In 1537, not long after Tyndale's martyrdom,[1] Rogers married a lady of Antwerp named Adriana de Weyden, and shortly afterwards removed to Wittenberg, in Saxony, where he ministered to a German congregation for at least ten years. It is highly probable that this move was absolutely necessary to escape persecution, and that Rogers' life would not have been safe if he had remained in Belgium. The mere fact that he was a friend of such a man as Tyndale, and that, although a priest, he had contracted marriage, would make him a marked man. It is only fair, however, to say that these are only conjectures. In all human probability these quiet ten years at Wittenberg were a period of immense benefit to Rogers' soul. He became established in the principles of the Reformation, learned to know his own heart, grew in faith and knowledge and holiness, and became fitted for the heavy work he had afterwards to do, and the fiery death he had to die.

The exact amount of Rogers' connection with the English translation of the Bible, commonly known as "Matthews' Bible," is a point that will, perhaps, never be thoroughly cleared up. There is considerable reason to believe that he had far more to do with the translation than most people are aware, and that he deserves to take rank with Tyndale and Coverdale as one of its authors. Certain it is that he is responsible for the marginal notes and tables of "common places"[2] which accompanied the version. Equally certain is it that when Rogers was condemned to be burned, he was called "Rogers, *alias* Matthews"; while the title page of the famous Bible put forth by authority in the time of Henry VIII contains the words, "The Old and New Testaments, truly and freely translated into English,

---

[1] William Tyndale (*c.* 1494–1536) was the first man to oversee the translation, printing, and distribution of the entire English New Testament. Nine-tenths of our Authorized Version's N.T. and the first half of the O.T. are the direct result of his labours. Burnt at the stake in 1536, his last words were "Lord, open the King of England's eyes."

[2] Cross-references to other books of the Bible.

by Thomas Matthews." Whether the judge who condemned Rogers exaggerated his share in the work of translation in order to justify his condemnation, it is of course impossible to say. But on the whole, it seems most probable that Rogers may fairly be regarded as one among the earliest labourers in the great work of translating our English Bible. The sum of the whole matter, in my own judgment, is this: Tyndale has received the credit that he justly deserves, Coverdale[1] rather more than he deserves, and Rogers much less.

In 1547 Edward VI succeeded to the throne of England, and Rogers, not long after, returned to his own land. As might be reasonably expected, he was soon brought forward and placed in a prominent position. A man of his gifts and graces was just the man whom the leaders of the English Reformation were only too glad to employ. In 1550 he became vicar of St. Margaret Moyses and also of St. Sepulchre, both parishes in the City of London. In 1551 he was appointed to the Prebendal stall of St. Pancras, in the Cathedral of St. Paul, and also to the rectory of Chigwell, in Essex. In 1553 he was made Divinity Lecturer of St. Paul's. It is only fair to Bishop Ridley to state that Rogers owns to have been much indebted to him for these preferments, and that the good Bishop of London does not appear to have forgotten his old fellow-collegian. In fact he speaks of Grindall, Bradford, and Rogers in a letter addressed to Sir W. Cecil as "men so necessary to be abroad in the Commonwealth, that I can keep none of them in my house." This language shows pretty clearly that Rogers was one of his chaplains.

The death of Edward VI in 1553 and the accession of Queen Mary to the throne cut short the active usefulness of Rogers; and before the end of the year 1553 he was a prisoner, first in his own house, and afterwards in Newgate, where he was finally placed in January 1554. Of his condition in prison we know but little, except that his wife was not allowed to see him and that his treatment seems to have been very severe. He was brought before a commission presided over by Bishop Gardiner in January 1555, together

---

[1] Miles Coverdale (1488–1569) was primarily responsible for the "Great Bible" (so-called because of its *large size*), a revision of the "Matthews' Bible."

with Hooper and Cardmaker, as an obstinate heretic, partly because he denied the doctrine of the *real presence*, and partly because, being a priest, he had contracted marriage.

Of his conduct during his imprisonment, and on the day when he was burnt, no better account can be given than that which John Fox supplies. I shall, therefore, give it in the martyrologist's own words:

Amongst other words and sayings which may seem prophetically to be spoken of him, this also may be added, and is notoriously to be marked, that he spake, being then in prison, to the printer of this present book, John Day, who then also was laid up for like cause of religion: "Thou," said he, "shalt live to see the alteration of this religion, and the Gospel to be freely preached again; and, therefore, have me commended to my brethren, as well in exile as others, and bid them be circumspect in displacing the Papists, and putting good ministers into churches, or else their end will be worse than ours." And for lack of good ministers to furnish churches, his device was (Master Hooper also agreeing to the same) that for every ten churches some one good and learned superintendent should be appointed, which should have under him faithful readers such as might well be got; so that Popish priests should clean be put out, and the bishop once a year to oversee the profiting of the parishes. And if the minister did not his duty, as well in profiting himself in his book, and his parishioners in good instructions, so that they may be trained by little and little to give a reckoning how they do profit, then he to be expelled, and another put in his place, and the bishop to do the like with the superintendent. This was his counsel and request: showing, moreover, and protesting in his commendations to his brethren by the printer aforesaid, that if they would not so do, their end, he said, would be worse than theirs.

Over and besides divers things touching Master Rogers, this is not to be forgotten, how in the days of King Edward VI there was a controversy among the bishops and clergy, for wearing of priests' caps and other attire belonging to that order. Master Rogers, being one of that number which never went otherwise than in a round cap, during all the time of King Edward, affirmed that he would not agree to that decreement of uniformity, but upon this condition: that if they would needs have such a uniformity of wearing the cap, tippet, etc., then it should also be decreed withal, that the Papist, for a difference betwixt them and others, should be constrained to wear upon their sleeves a chalice with a host upon it. Whereupon if they would consent, he would agree to the other: otherwise he would not, he said, consent to the setting forth of the same, nor even wear the cap; as indeed he never did.

The Sunday before he suffered, he drank to Master Hooper, being then underneath him, and bade them commend him unto him, and tell him, "There was never little fellow better would stick to a man than he would stick to him"; presupposing they should both be burned together, although it happened otherwise, for Master Rogers was burnt alone.

Now when the time came that he, being delivered to the sheriffs, should be brought out of Newgate to Smithfield, the place of his execution, first came to him Master Woodroofe, one of the aforesaid sheriffs, and calling Master Rogers unto him, asked him if he would revoke his abominable doctrine, and his evil opinion of the sacrament of the altar. Master Rogers answered and said, "That which I have preached I will seal with my blood." "Then," quoth Master Woodroofe, "thou art a heretic." "That shall be known," quoth Rogers, "at the day of judgment." "Well," quoth Master Woodroofe, "I will never pray for thee." "But I will pray for *you*," quoth Master Rogers; and so was brought the same day, which was Monday, the 4th, of February, by the sheriffs toward Smithfield, saying the psalm *Miserere* by the way, all the people wonderfully rejoicing at his constancy, with great praises and thanks to God for the same. And there, in the presence of Master Rochester, Comptroller of the Queen's Household, Sir Richard Southwell, both the sheriffs, and a wonderful number of people, the fire was put unto him; and when it had taken hold both upon his legs and shoulders, he, as one feeling no smart, washed his hands in the flame, as though it had been in cold water. And, after lifting up his hands unto heaven, not removing the same until such time as the devouring fire had consumed them, most mildly this happy martyr yielded up his spirit into the hands of his heavenly Father. A little before his burning at the stake, his pardon was brought, if he would have recanted, but he utterly refused. He was the first martyr of all the

The Burning of John Rogers

blessed company that suffered in Queen Mary's time, that gave the first adventure upon the fire. His wife and children being eleven in number, and ten able to go, and one sucking on her breast, met him by the way as he went towards Smithfield. This sorrowful sight of his own flesh and blood could nothing move him; but that he constantly and cheerfully took his death with wonderful patience, in the defence and quarrel of Christ's Gospel.

It must always be remembered that John Rogers was the *first* who was burned in Queen Mary's reign, and that before he died at the stake, there was no example of a Protestant of the Reformed Church of England enduring death rather than recant his opinions. It is to the eternal credit of Rogers that he was the first to break the ice and to supply proof that the grace of God was sufficient to sustain a believer even in the fire. The very day that he was burned, Noailles, the French Ambassador, wrote to Montmorency the following words:

> This day was performed the confirmation of the alliance between the Pope and this kingdom, by a public and solemn sacrifice of a preaching doctor, named Rogers, who has been burned alive for being a Lutheran; but he died persisting in his opinion. At this conduct, the greatest part of the people took such pleasure, that they were not afraid to make him many exclamations to strengthen his courage. Even his children assisted at it, comforting him in such a manner that it seemed as if he had been led to a wedding.

Like Rowland Taylor, Rogers left behind him no literary remains, unless we accept his contribution to the famous "Matthews' Bible." But he left behind him a name which ought to be held in honour by all Protestant churchmen as long as the world stands.

Specimens of Translations from the Matthews' Bible

GENESIS ¶ *The fyrst Chapter*

In the beginnyng[†] God created heauen and erth. The erth was voyde and emptye, and darcknesse was vpon the depe, & the spirite of God[‡] moued vpon the water. Then God sayde: Let there be lyght: & there was lyght. And God sawe the lyght that it was good: & deuyded ye lyght from the darcknesse, & called the lyght the daye, & the darcknesse the nyght: and so of the euenying and mornyng was made the fyrst daye.

JOHN ¶ *The fyrst Chapter*

In the beginnynge was the worde, & the worde was wyth God: and the worde was God. The same was in the beginnynge wyth God. All thinges were made by it, and wythout it, was made nothynge that was made. In it was lyfe, & the lyfe was the lyght of men, &[§] the lyght shyneth in ye darcknes, but the darcknes comprehended it not.

[†] iiij. Esd. vi. d. Eccli. xviij. a. Jeremye x. b. Hebr. i. c. xi. a. Psa. ci. d. & cxxxv. a. Esaye. xliiij. d.

[‡] brethed or styred.

[§] By the light is vnderstande Chryst & by the darcknes vngodly & vnbeleuinge mē amōg whome Chryst came & they receaued him not as Ephe. iiij. d.

Present Authorized Version

GENESIS 1 : 1-5

In the beginning God created the heaven and the earth. And the earth was without form and void; and darkness was upon the face of the deep. And the Spirit of God moved upon the face of the waters.

And God said, Let there be light: and there was light. And God saw the light, that it was good: and God divided the light from the darkness. And God called the light Day, and the darkness He called Night. And the evening and the morning were the first day.

JOHN 1:1-5

In the beginning was the Word, and the Word was with God, and the Word was God. The same was in the beginning with God. All things were made by Him; and without Him was not any thing made that was made. In Him was life; and the life was the light of men. And the light shineth in darkness; and the darkness comprehended it not.

It may be interesting to some readers to add the same passage so rendered in the New Revised Version.

In the beginning was the Word, and the Word was with God, and the Word was God. The same was in the beginning with God. All things were made by Him; and without Him was not anything made that hath been made. In Him was life; and the life was the light of men. And the light shineth in the darkness; and the darkness apprehended it not.

John Hooper (1495–1555)

4

JOHN HOOPER: BISHOP AND MARTYR

IN a day of religious controversy, no one is so useful to his generation as the man who contributes a little *light*. Amidst the din and strife of ecclesiastical warfare, amidst the fog and dust stirred up by excited disputants, amidst assertions and counter-assertions, a thinking man will often cry with the dying philosopher, "I want more light: give me more light."[1] He that can make two ears of corn grow where only one grew before has been rightly called a benefactor to mankind. He that can throw a few rays of fresh light on the theological questions of the day is surely doing a service to the Church and the world.

Thoughts such as these came across my mind when I chose the subject of this biographical paper: "John Hooper, the martyred Bishop of Gloucester: his times, life, death, and opinions." I chose it with a meaning. I have long felt that the lives and opinions of the English Reformers deserve attentive study in the present day. I think that a picture of John Hooper will throw useful light on points of deep interest in our times.

We live in days when the Romish church is making gigantic efforts to regain her lost power in England, and thousands of English people are helping her. None are doing the work of Rome so thoroughly as that singular body of English churchmen, the extreme ritualists. Consciously or unconsciously, they are paving the way for her advance and laying down the rails for her trains. They are familiarizing the minds of thousands with Romish ceremonial—its millinery, its processions, its gestures, its postures, its theatrical, sensuous style of worship. They are boldly preaching

---
[1] Johann von Goethe (1749–1832).

and publishing downright Romish doctrine—the *real presence*, the priestly character of the ministry, the necessity of auricular confession and sacerdotal absolution. They are loudly proclaiming their desire for reunion with the Church of Rome. In short, it seems as if the battle of the Reformation must be fought over again. Now before we go back to Rome, let us thoroughly understand what English Romanism was. Let us bring in the light. Let us not take a "leap in the dark."[1]

We live in times when many churchmen openly sneer at our Reformation, and scoff at our Reformers. The martyrs, whose blood was the seed of our church, are abused and vilified and declared to be no martyrs at all. Cranmer is called "a cowardly traitor," and Latimer, "a coarse, illiterate bully!" The Reformation is said to have been "an unmitigated disaster," and a "change taken in hand by a conspiracy of adulterers, murderers, and thieves!"[*] Let us study one of our leading Reformers today and see what the man was like. Let us pass under review one who was a friend and contemporary of Cranmer, Ridley, and Latimer, and a leading fellow-labourer in the work of the Reformation. Let us find out how he lived, and how he preached, and what he thought, and how he died. Once more I say, let us bring in the light.

We live in times when the strangest misrepresentations prevail about the true character of the Church of England. Scores of people all over the country are not ashamed to denounce the very name of *Protestantism* and to tell people that "*evangelical* churchmen are not churchmen at all! Forsooth, they are 'Calvinists,' 'Puritans,' 'Dissenters,' 'Methodists,' 'Fanatics,' and the like, and ought to leave the Church of England and go to their own place!"

Let us bring these assertions to the test of a few plain facts. Let us examine the recorded sentiments, the written opinions, of one of the very divines to whom we owe our articles and Prayer Book, with very few alterations. Let us hear what Bishop Hooper wrote and thought and taught. Let us not hastily concede that ritualists and high churchmen are the true representatives of the Church of England. "He that is first in his own cause seemeth just, but his

---

[1] Last words of English philosopher, Thomas Hobbes (1588–1679).
[*] See *Church Times* of March 14, 1867.

neighbour that cometh after searcheth him" (Prov. 18:17). Once more, I say, let us turn on the light.

I. Bishop Hooper's Times

I will begin by giving some account of *Bishop Hooper's times.* What kind of times were they in a religious point of view? Out of the pages of Fox, Strype, Burnet, Soames, and Blunt, let me try to supply a few historical gleanings. John Hooper was born in 1495 and died in 1555. He first saw the light in the reign of Henry VII and was burned in the reign of Queen Mary. He lived through the whole reigns of Henry VIII and Edward VI and was an eyewitness of all that took place under the government of those two kings. The sixty years of his life take in one of the most eventful periods of English history. It would be impossible to exaggerate the difference there was between England in 1495 and the same England in 1555. In a religious and moral view, the whole country was turned upside down. When Hooper was born, the English Reformation had not begun, and the Church of Rome ruled England undisturbed. When he died, the Reformation had struck such deep root that neither argument nor persecution could overthrow it.

What were the leading characteristics of English religion before the Reformation? In what state did the mighty change which Hooper witnessed and helped forward, find our forefathers? In one word, what does England owe to that subversion of Popery and that introduction of Protestantism, in which Hooper was a leading instrument? Let me try to supply a short answer to these questions. They are subjects, I am sorry to say, on which most people seem to know nothing at all. The minds of the vast majority of my countrymen appear to be a total blank about the history of 300 years ago. With all the stir made about education, the ignorance of our own country's history is something lamentable and appalling and depressing. I never can believe that extreme ritualism would have obtained so many adherents, if English people only knew the extent of our debt to the Protestant Reformation. They would never trifle and tamper and dabble with Popery, if they only knew what Popery was.

(*a*) Before the Reformation, one leading feature of English religion was *dense ignorance.* There was among all classes a conspicuous absence of all knowledge of true Christianity. A gross darkness overspread the land, a darkness that might be felt. Not one in a hundred could have told you as much about the Gospel of Christ as we could now learn from any intelligent Sunday school child.

We need not wonder at this ignorance. The people had neither schools nor Bibles. Wycliffe's New Testament, the only translation extant till Henry the Eighth's Bible was printed, cost £2 16s. 3d. of our money. The prayers of the Church were in Latin, and of course the people could not understand them. Preaching there was scarcely any. Quarterly sermons indeed were prescribed to the clergy, but not insisted on. Latimer says that while mass was never to be left unsaid for a single Sunday, sermons might be omitted for twenty Sundays, and nobody was blamed. After all, when there were sermons, they were utterly unprofitable—and latterly to be a preacher was to be suspected of being a heretic.

To cap all, the return that Hooper got from the diocese of Gloucester, when he was first appointed bishop in 1551, will give a pretty clear idea of the ignorance of pre-Reformation times. Out of 311 clergy of his diocese, 168 were unable to repeat the Ten Commandments; 31 of the 168 could not state in what part of Scripture they were to be found; 40 could not tell where the Lord's Prayer was written; and 31 of the 40 were ignorant who was the author of the Lord's Prayer! If this is not ignorance, I know not what is. If such were the pastors, what must the people have been! If this was the degree of knowledge among the parsons, what must it have been among the people!

(b) But this is not all. Before the Reformation, another leading feature of English religion was *superstition of the lowest and most degrading description.* Of the extent to which this was carried few, I suspect, have the smallest idea. Men and women in those days had uneasy consciences sometimes and wanted relief. They had sorrow and sickness and death to pass through, just like ourselves. What could they do? Whither could they turn? There was none to tell them of the love of God and the mediation of Christ, of the glad tidings of free, full, and complete salvation, of justification by faith, of grace and faith and hope and repentance. They could only turn to the priests, who knew nothing themselves and could tell nothing to others. "The blind led the blind, and both fell into the ditch."[1] In a word, the religion of our ancestors, before Hooper's time, was little better than organized system of Virgin Mary worship, saint worship, image worship, relic worship, pilgrimages, almsgivings, formalism, ceremonialism, processions, prostrations, bowings, crossings, fastings, confessions, absolutions, masses, penances, and blind obedience to the priests. It was a grand higgledy-piggledy of ignorance and idolatry and service done to an unknown God by deputy. The only practical result was that the priests took the people's money and undertook to ensure their salvation, and the people flattered themselves that the more they gave to the priests, the more sure they were of going to heaven. The catalogue of gross and ridiculous impostures which the priests practised on the people would fill a volume, and I cannot, of course, do more than supply a few specimens.

(i) At the Abbey of Hales, in Gloucestershire, a vial was shown by the priests to those who offered alms, which was said to contain the blood of Christ. On examination, in King Henry the Eighth's time, this notable vial was found to contain neither more nor less than the blood of a duck, which was renewed every week.

(ii) At Bexley, in Kent, a crucifix was exhibited, which received peculiar honour and large offerings, because of a continual miracle which was said to attend its exhibition. When people offered copper, the face of the figure looked grave; when they offered silver, it relaxed its severity; when they offered gold, it openly smiled. In Henry the Eighth's time this famous crucifix was examined, and wires were found within it by which the priests could move the face of the image and make it assume any expression that they pleased.

(iii) At Reading Abbey, in Berkshire, the following relics, among many others, were most religiously worshipped: an angel with one wing, the spearhead that pierced our Saviour's side, two pieces of the holy cross, St. James' hand, St. Philip's stole, and a bone of Mary Magdalen.

(iv) At Bury St. Edmund's, in Suffolk, the priests exhibited the coals that roasted St. Lawrence, the parings of St. Edmund's

---

[1] Matthew 15:14.

toenails, Thomas à Becket's penknife and boots, and as many pieces of our Saviour's cross as would have made, if joined together, one large whole cross.

(v) At Maiden Bradley Priory, in Somersetshire, the worshippers were privileged to see the Virgin Mary's smock, part of the bread used at the original Lord's Supper, and a piece of the stone manger in which our Lord was laid at Bethlehem.

(vi) At Bruton Priory, in Somersetshire, was kept a girdle of the Virgin Mary, made of red silk. This solemn relic was sent as a special favour to women in childbirth, to insure them a safe delivery. The like was done with a white girdle of Mary Magdalen, kept at Farley Abbey, in Wiltshire. In neither case, we may be sure, was the relic sent without a pecuniary consideration.*

Records like these are so silly and melancholy that one hardly knows whether to laugh or to cry. But it is positively necessary to bring them forward, in order that men may know what was the religion of our forefathers before the Reformation. Wonderful as these things may sound in our ears, we must never forget that Englishmen in those times knew no better. A famishing man, in sieges and blockades, has been known to eat mice and rats rather than die of hunger. A soul famishing for lack of God's Word must not be judged too harshly if it struggles to find comfort in the most grovelling superstition.

(c) One thing more yet remains behind. Before the Reformation, another leading feature of English religion *was widespread unholiness and immorality.* The lives of the clergy, as a general rule, were simply scandalous, and the moral tone of the laity was naturally at the lowest ebb. Of course grapes will never grow on thorns, nor figs on thistles. To expect the huge roots of ignorance and superstition, which filled our land, to bear any but corrupt fruit would be unreasonable and absurd. But a more thoroughly corrupt set than the English clergy were, in the palmy days of undisturbed Romanism, it would be impossible to imagine.

(i) I might tell you of the habits of gluttony, drunkenness, and gambling, for which the parochial priesthood became unhappily notorious.

---

* Strype and Burnet are my authority for the above mentioned facts.

Too often [says Professor J. J. Blunt, in his excellent history of the Reformation] they were persons taken from the lowest of the people, with all the gross habits of the class from which they sprang—loiterers on the alehouse bench, dicers, scarce able to read by rote their paternoster, often unable to repeat the Ten Commandments—mass-priests, who could just read their breviaries, and no more—men often dubbed by the uncomplimentary names of Sir John Lack-Latin, Sir John Mumble-Matins, or babbling and blind Sir John. In fact, the carnal living, fat bellies, and general secularity of ministers of religion were proverbial before the Reformation.

(ii) I might tell you of the shameless covetousness which marked the pre-Reformation priesthood. So long as a man gave liberal offerings at the shrine of such saints as Thomas à Becket, the clergy would absolve him of almost any sin. So long as a felon or malefactor paid the monks well, he might claim sanctuary within the precincts of religious houses, after any crime, and hardly any law could reach him. Yet all this time for Lollards and Wycliffites there was no mercy at all![1] The very carvings still extant in some old ecclesiastical buildings tell a story in stone and wood, which speaks volumes to this day. Friars were often represented as foxes preaching, with the neck of a stolen goose peeping out of the hood behind—as wolves giving absolution, with a sheep muffled up in their cloaks—as apes sitting by a sick man's bed, with a crucifix in one hand and with the other in the sufferer's pocket. Things must indeed have been at a low ebb, when the faults of ordained ministers were so publicly held up to scorn.

(iii) But the blackest spot on the character of our pre-Reformation clergy in England is one of which it is painful to speak. I mean the impurity of their lives and their horrible contempt of the Seventh Commandment. The results of auricular

---

[1] The followers of John Wycliffe were called *Wycliffites* or *Lollards*. In many respects Lollardy anticipated the Reformation—Lollards denied the material presence of Christ in the elements; condemned pilgrimages, the worship of images, and auricular confession; and maintained the right to read the Scriptures in English. The first English statute for *the burning of heretics*, *De Hæretico Comburendo*, targeted the Lollards, and was passed in 1401; it was not repealed until 1547.

confession, carried on by men bound by their vow never to marry, were such that I dare not enter into them. The consequences of shutting up herds of men and women, in the prime of life, in monasteries and nunneries, were such that I will not defile my readers' minds by dwelling upon them. Suffice it to say that the discoveries made by Henry the Eighth's commissioners, of the state of things in many of the so-called "religious" houses, were such as it is impossible to describe. Anything less "holy" than the practice of many of the "holy" men and women in these professedly "holy" retreats from sin and the world, the imagination cannot conceive!

If ever there was a plausible theory weighed in the balance and found utterly wanting, it is the favourite theory that celibacy and monasticism promote holiness. Romantic young men and sentimental young ladies may mourn over the ruins of such abbeys as Battle, and Glastonbury, and Bolton, and Kirkstall, and Furness, and Croyland, and Bury, and Tintern. But I venture boldly to say that too many of these religious houses were sinks of iniquity, and that too often monks and nuns were the scandal of Christianity.

I grant freely that all monasteries and nunneries were not equally bad. I admit that there were some religious houses like Godstow Nunnery, near Oxford, which had a stainless reputation. But I fear that these were bright exceptions which only prove the truth of the rule. The preamble of the Act for Dissolution of Religious Houses, founded on the report of Henry the Eighth's commissioners, contains broad, general statements that cannot be got over. It declares:

> that manifest sin, vicious, carnal, and abominable living is daily used and committed in abbeys, priories, and other religious houses of monks, canons, and nuns, and that albeit many continual visitations have been had, by the space of two hundred years and more, for an honest and charitable reformation of such unthrifty, carnal, and abominable living, yet that nevertheless little or none amendment was hitherto had, but that their vicious living shamefully increased and augmented.

After all, there is no surer receipt for promoting immorality than "fulness of bread and abundance of idleness" (Ezek. 16:49). Take any number of men and women, of any nation, rank, or class— bind them by a vow of celibacy—shut them up in houses by themselves—give them plenty to eat and drink, and give them nothing to do—and above all, give them no Bible-reading, no true religion, no preaching of the Gospel, no inspection, and no check from public opinion—if the result of all this be not abominable and abundant breach of the Seventh Commandment, I can only say that I have read human nature in vain.

I make no apology for dwelling on these things. Painful and humbling as the picture is, it is one that in these times ought to be carefully looked at, and not thrown aside. Before we join in the vulgar outcry which some modern churchmen are making against the Reformation, I want English people to understand from what the Reformation delivered us. Before we make up our minds to give up Protestantism and receive back Popery and monasticism, let us thoroughly understand what was the state of England when Popery had its own way. My own belief is that never was a change so loudly demanded as the Reformation, and that never did men do such good service to England as Hooper and his fellow-labourers, the Reformers. In short, unless a man can disprove the plain historical facts recorded in the pages of Fox, Fuller, Strype, Burnet, Soames, and Blunt, he must either admit that the pre-Reformation times were bad times, or be content to be regarded as a lunatic. To no class of men does England owe such a debt as to our Protestant Reformers, and it is a burning shame if we are ungrateful and refuse to pay that debt.

Of course, it is easy and cheap work to pick holes in the character of some of the agents whom God was pleased to use at the Reformation. No doubt Henry VIII—who had the Bible translated, and made Cranmer and Latimer bishops, and suppressed the monasteries—was a brutal and bad man. I am not concerned to defend him. But God has often done good work with very bad tools; and the grand result is what we must chiefly look at. And, after all, bad as Henry VIII was, the less our Romanizing friends dwell on that point the better. His moral character at any rate will bear a favourable comparison with that of many of the Popes. At any rate he was a married man!

It is easy, on the other hand, to say that Hooper and his brother Reformers did their work badly, countenanced many abuses, left many things imperfect and incomplete. All this may be very true.

But in common fairness men should remember the numerous difficulties they had to contend with, and the mountains of rubbish they had to shovel away. To my mind the wonder is not so much that they did so little, but rather that they succeeded in doing anything at all.

After all, when all has been said and every objection raised, there remain some great plain facts which cannot well be got over. Let men say what they will or pick holes where they may, they will never succeed in disproving these facts. To the Reformation Englishmen owe an English Bible and liberty for every man to read it. To the Reformation they owe the knowledge of the way of peace with God, and of the right of every sinner to go straight to Christ by faith, without bishop, priest, or minister standing in his way. To the Reformation they owe a scriptural standard of morality and holiness, such as our ancestors never dreamed of. Forever let us be thankful for these inestimable mercies! Forever let us grasp them firmly and refuse to let them go! For my part, I hold that he who would rob us of these privileges and draw us back to pre-Reformation ignorance, superstition, and unholiness, is an enemy to England and ought to be firmly opposed.

II. Hooper Himself

I turn from Hooper's times to *Hooper himself.* For dwelling so long on his times I think it needless to make any apology. We cannot rightly estimate a public man, unless we know the times in which he lived. We cannot duly appreciate an English Reformer, unless we understand the state of England before the Reformation. We have seen the state of things that Hooper and his companions had to deal with. Now let us find out something about Hooper himself.

John Hooper was born in the county of Somerset, in the year 1495, in the reign of Henry VII. The parish in which he was born is not known, and not even a tradition has survived about it. In this respect Hooper and Rowland Taylor stand alone among the English martyrs. The birthplaces of Cranmer, Ridley, Latimer, Rogers, Bradford, Philpot, and Ferrar have all been ascertained. The position which his family occupied in the county is alike unknown. There is, however, good reason for believing that his father was not a mere yeoman, but a man of considerable wealth.

The early history of this great Reformer is wrapped in much obscurity. He entered Merton College, Oxford, in 1514, at the age of nineteen, under the tuition of an uncle who was then fellow of that college. He took his degree as B.A. in 1518 at the age of twenty-three and never afterwards proceeded to a higher degree. These are literally the only facts that have been discovered about the first twenty-three years of Hooper's life. From 1518 to 1539—a period of no less than twenty-one years—we are again left almost entirely in the dark about Hooper's history. There can be little doubt, however, that it was a most momentous crisis in his life and gave a colour and bias to the whole man for the rest of his days. Tradition says that after taking his degree at Oxford, he became a monk—first at the Cistercian Monastery of Old Cleve, near Watchet, in Somersetshire, and afterwards in another Cistercian house at Gloucester. Tradition adds that he became wearied and disgusted with a monastic life and withdrew from it in order to reside at Oxford, though at what precise date is not known. It is some corroboration of these traditions that when he was sentenced to death afterwards by Gardiner, he was described as "formerly a monk of the Monastery of Cleve, of the Cistercian order." Yet it must be admitted that there is a conspicuous absence in his literary remains of any reference to his experience as a monk.

One thing, at any rate, is very certain about Hooper at this stage of his life. It was during these twenty-one years, between 1518 and 1539, that his eyes were opened to the false doctrines and unscriptural practices of Popery, though when and where we cannot exactly tell. He says himself, in a letter to Bullinger, the Swiss Reformer, that "when he was a courtier, and living too much of a court life in the palace of the King," he met with certain writings of Zwingle, and certain commentaries of Bullinger on St. Paul's Epistles, and that to the study of these books he owed his deliverance from Papacy and the conversion of his soul. This deeply interesting letter will be found in the *Original Letters from Zürich*, published by the Parker Society. To the meaning, however, of the allusion to "a court life," and "the palace of the King," the letter, unfortunately, supplies no clue.

Another fact about Hooper at this period of his history is no less certain. He was obliged to leave Oxford in 1539, when the semi-Popish statute of the Six Articles, which made Latimer resign his bishopric, was put in operation. Fox, the martyrologist, distinctly asserts that his known attachment to the principles of the Reformation attracted the notice of the Oxford authorities, and specially of Dr. Smith, the Professor of Divinity. The consequence was that he was compelled to retire from the University and appears to have never resided there again.

On leaving Oxford, in 1539, Hooper became, for a short time, steward and chaplain in the household of Sir Thomas Arundel. Here also again his Protestant principles got him into trouble. His master liked him, but did not like his opinions. The consequence was that he sent him to Bishop Gardiner with a private letter, in which he requested him to "do his chaplain some good." Gardiner, however, after four or five days conference, could make nothing of the sturdy Reformer, and utterly failed to shake his opinions. The end of the matter was, says Fox, "that he sent Sir Thomas his servant again, right well commending his learning and wit, but bearing in his heart a grudge against Master Hooper." This grudge, unhappily, was not forgotten, and bore bitter fruit after many days.

The connection between Hooper and Sir Thomas Arundel did not last long after this. The Protestant chaplain found that his life was not safe in England, and like many of the good men of his day, withdrew to the Continent. There he appears to have lived for at least nine years—first at Strasburgh, afterwards at Bâle, and finally at Zürich. It was at this period of his life, no doubt, that he became established in those clear, distinct views of doctrinal truth, which he afterwards so nobly maintained in his own country. At this period, too, he formed friendships with Bullinger, Bucer, à Lasco, and other Continental Reformers, who ever afterwards regarded him with deep affection. At this period, too, about the year 1546, he married a noble Burgundian lady named Anna de Tzerclas, who seems to have been in every way a helpmeet for him.

In 1547 Henry VIII died, and Edward VI commenced his short but glorious reign. Soon after this Hooper began to feel it his bounden duty to give his aid to the work of the Protestant

Reformation in his own country, and after taking an affectionate leave of his Zürich friends, set out on his return to England. His parting words were painfully prophetic and deeply touching. They told him they fully expected that he would rise to a high position in his native land; they hoped he would not forget his old friends; they begged him to write to them sometimes. In reply, Hooper assured them that he should never forget their many kindnesses; promised to write to them from time to time and concluded with the following memorable words:

> The last news of all, Master Bullinger, I shall not be able to write. For there, where I shall take most pains, there shall ye hear of me to be burnt to ashes. That shall be the last news, which I shall not be able to write to you. But you shall hear it of me.

Hooper arrived in London in May 1549 and was gladly received by the friends of the Reformation, which in the face of immense difficulties, Cranmer and Ridley were slowly pressing forward. He came like a welcome reinforcement in the midst of an arduous campaign and mightily strengthened the cause of Protestantism. His reputation as a man of soundness, learning, and power had evidently gone before him. He was very soon appointed Chaplain to the Protector, the Duke of Somerset. With characteristic zeal he devoted himself at once to the work of teaching and generally preached twice a day, and this with such marked acceptance that the churches could not contain the crowds that flocked to hear him. Even Dr. Smith, his enemy, confessed that "he was so much admired by the people that they held him for a prophet: nay, they looked upon him as a deity." Fox, the martyrologist, who evidently knew Hooper well, bears the following testimony to his high character at this time, both for gifts and graces:

> In his doctrine he was earnest, in tongue eloquent, in the Scriptures perfect, in pains indefatigable. His life was so pure and good that no breath of slander could fasten any fault upon him. He was of body strong, his health whole and sound, his wit very pregnant, his invincible patience able to sustain whatsoever sinister fortune and adversity could do. He was constant of judgment, spare of diet, sparer of words, and sparest of time. In housekeeping he was very liberal, and sometimes more free than

his living would extend unto. Briefly, of all those virtues and qualities required of St. Paul in a good bishop, in his Epistle to Timothy, I know not one that was lacking in Master Hooper.

A man of this mould and stamp was rightly esteemed the very man to make a bishop in Edward the Sixth's days. Within a year of his landing in England the prophecies of his Zürich friends were fulfilled. After preaching a course of Lent sermons before the King in 1550, John Hooper, the friend of Bullinger, the exile of Zürich, the most popular preacher of the day, was nominated to fill the vacant bishopric of Gloucester. A wiser choice could not have been made. Rarely, too rarely, in the annals of the Church of England, has there been such an instance of the right man being put in the right place.

Hooper's nomination, however, brought him into a most un-happy collision with Cranmer and Ridley on a very awkward subject. He steadily refused to take the oath which had been taken hitherto by bishops at their consecration and to wear the episcopal vestments which had hitherto been worn. The oath he objected to as flatly unscriptural, because it referred to the saints as well as God. The vestments he objected to as remnants of Popery, which ought to be clean put away.

A controversy arose at once between Hooper and his two great fellow-labourers, which delayed his consecration almost a whole year and did immense harm. The more trifling and unimportant the original cause of dispute appeared to be, the more heated and obstinate the disputants became. In vain did Ridley confer and correspond with his recusant brother. In vain did Edward VI and his privy council write to Cranmer and offer to discharge him from all risk of penalties if he would "let pass certain rites and ceremonies" offensive to the bishop-designate. In vain did foreign Reformers write long letters and entreat both parties to concede something and give way. The contention grew so sharp that the Privy Council became weary of Hooper's obstinacy and actually committed him to the Fleet prison! At length a compromise was effected. Hooper gave way on some points, for peace sake. He consented to wear the obnoxious vestments on certain public occasions—at his consecration, before the King, and in his own cathedral. The objectionable words in the Episcopal Oath were struck out by the King's own hand. The prison gates were then thrown open, and to the great joy of all true Protestants, Hooper was consecrated Bishop of Gloucester on the 8th of March 1551.

This miserable controversy between Hooper and his two great opponents, like all the disputes of good men, is a sorrowful subject. Of course it need not surprise us. The best of men are only men at their best. If Paul and Barnabas quarreled until they parted company, and Peter and Paul came into open collision at Antioch, we must not judge our English Reformers too harshly if they did not always agree. But it is vain to deny that this famous quarrel did great harm at the time and sowed seeds which are bearing mischievous fruit down to this very day.

At the distance of more than 300 years, I freely admit, we are poor judges of the whole case. Both parties undoubtedly were more or less in the wrong, and the only question is as to the side which was most to blame. The general verdict of mankind, I am quite aware, has been against Hooper. To this verdict, however, I must honestly say, I cannot altogether subscribe. It is my deliberate conviction, after carefully weighing the whole affair, that Hooper was most likely in the right, and Cranmer and Ridley were most likely in the wrong.

I believe the plain truth to be that Hooper was much more farsighted than his excellent fellow-labourers. He looked further ahead than they did and saw the possibility of evils arising in the Church of England, of which they in their charity never dreamed. He foresaw, with prophetic eye, the immense peril of leaving nest-eggs for future Romanism within our pale. He foresaw a time when the Pope's friends would take advantage of the least crevice left in the walls of our Zion; and he would fain have had every crack stopped up. He would not have left a single peg on which Romanizing churchmen could have rehung the abominable doctrine of the Mass. It is my decided opinion that he was quite right. Events have supplied abundant proof that his conscientious scruples were well founded. I believe if Cranmer and Ridley had calmly listened to his objections and seized the opportunity of settling the whole question of *vestments* in a thoroughly Protestant way, it would have been a blessing to the Church of England! In a word, if Hooper's

views had been allowed to prevail, one half of the ritualistic controversy of our own day would never have existed at all.*

Once delivered from this miserable controversy, Hooper commenced his episcopal duties without a moment's delay. Though
only consecrated on the 8th of March 1551, he began at once to
preach throughout the diocese of Gloucester with such diligence as
to cause fears about his health. His wife, writing to Bullinger in the
month of April, says, "I entreat you to recommend Master Hooper
to be more moderate in his labours. He preaches four, or at least
three, times every day, and I am afraid lest these overabundant
exertions should cause a premature decay." Of all the Edwardian
bishops, none seem to have made such full proof of his episcopal
ministry as he did. Cranmer was naturally absorbed in working out
the great scheme of Reformation, of which he was the principal
architect. Ridley, from his position in London, within reach of
the Court and of Lambeth Palace, was necessarily often drawn aside
to advise the King and the Primate. For really working a diocese,
and giving a splendid pattern of what an English Protestant bishop
should be, the man of the times was John Hooper. We need not
wonder that the Government soon gave him the charge of
Worcester as well as the diocese of Gloucester. The willing horse is
always worked, and the more a man does, the more he is always
asked to do.

The state of Hooper's clergy evidently gave him great trouble.
We have already seen that many clergymen in the diocese of
Gloucester were unable to repeat the Ten Commandments and
could not tell who was the author of the Lord's Prayer. Moreover,

---

* It is a pleasing fact that at a later date there seems to have been a
complete reconciliation between Hooper and Ridley, if indeed there ever
was a real breach. When Ridley was in prison, in Queen Mary's reign, he
wrote as follows to Hooper:

"My dear brother, we thoroughly agree and wholly consent together in
those things which are the grounds and substantial points of our religion,
against which the world so furiously rageth in these days. In time past, by
certain by-matters and circumstances of religion, your wisdom and my
simplicity hath a little jarred, each of us following the abundance of his
own sense and judgment. But now I say, be you assured, that with my
whole heart, God is my witness, I love you in the truth, and for the truth's
sake!"

they were not only ignorant, but generally hostile to the doctrines of the Reformation. However, they were ready to conform to anything and subscribe anything, so long as they were allowed to keep their livings! Hooper therefore drew up for them a body of fifty articles of an admirable character, and required every incumbent to subscribe them. He also supplied them with a set of excellent injunctions about their duties. Besides this he appointed some of the better sort to be superintendents of the rest, with a commission to watch over their brethren. It is difficult to see what more he could have done, however painful and unsatisfactory the state of things may have been. The best bishops, with all their zeal, cannot give grace or change clerical hearts.

The state of the laity in the diocese of Gloucester was just as unsatisfactory as that of the clergy. This, of course, was only natural. "Like pastors, like people." With them he could of necessity do little, except reprove immorality and check it when possible to do so. Of his firm and impartial conduct in this way, a remarkable example is given by John ab Ulmis in one of the Zürich letters. He says that Sir Anthony Kingston, a man of rank in Gloucestershire, was cited by the bishop to appear before him on a charge of adultery and was severely reprimanded. He replied with abusive language and even forgot himself so far as to use violence and blows in the court. But Hooper was unmoved. He reported the whole case to the Privy Council in London, and the result was that the Gloucestershire Knight was severely punished for his contumacy, and fined no less than £500, a very large sum in those days.

The state of the two cathedrals of Gloucester and Worcester appears to have been as great a trial to Hooper as the state of the parochial clergy and laity. Curiously enough, even 300 years ago, cathedral bodies seem to have been anything but helps to the Church of England. He says, in a letter upon this subject to Sir William Cecil, the King's Secretary of State,

> Ah! Mr. Secretary, if there were good men in the Cathedral churches! God should then have much more honour than He hath now, the King's majesty more obedience, and the poor people more knowledge. But the realm wanteth light in the very churches where of right it ought most to be.

He then concludes his letter with these touching words:

> God give us wisdom and strength wisely and strongly to serve in
> our vocations. There is none eateth their bread in the sweat of
> their face, but such as serve in public vocations. Yours, Mr.
> Secretary, is wonderful, but mine passeth. Now I perceive private
> labours be but play, and private work but ease and quietness. God
> be our help!

After all, the best account of Hooper's discharge of his episcopal
duties is to be found in that good old book well known by the title
of *Fox's Martyrs*. Fox was evidently a friend and admirer of Hooper
and writes about him with a very loving pen. But Fox may always
be depended on for general accuracy. Bitterly as his many enemies
have tried to vilify his great book, they have never succeeded in
disproving his facts. They may have scratched the good man's face,
but they have never broken his bones. Froude, a thoroughly dis-
interested witness, has voluntarily declared his confidence in Fox's
trustworthiness. Townsend, in a lengthy preface to his excellent and
complete edition of the *Acts and Monuments*, has answered *seriatim*
the attacks of Fox's enemies. In short, we may rest satisfied that
those flippant modern writers who call Fox a "liar" are only
exposing their own ignorance, or their hatred of genuine Protestantism. Let us now hear how Fox describes Hooper's ways as a
bishop, so long as his episcopate lasted. He says:

> Master Hooper, after all these tumults and vexations sustained
> about his investing and princely vestures, at length entering into
> his diocese, did there employ his time, which the Lord lent him
> under King Edward's reign, with such diligence as may be a
> spectacle to all bishops which shall ever hereafter succeed him, not
> only in that place, but in whatsoever diocese through the whole
> realm of England. So careful was he in his cure, that he left neither
> pains untaken, nor ways unsought, how to train up the flock of
> Christ in the true Word of Salvation, continually labouring in the
> same. Other men commonly are wont, for lucre or promotion's
> sake, to aspire to bishoprics, some hunting for them, and some
> purchasing or buying them, as men used to purchase lordships; and
> when they have them, are loth to leave them, and thereupon are
> loth to commit that thing by worldly laws whereby to lose them.

To this sort of men Master Hooper was clean contrary; who abhorred nothing more than gain, labouring always to save and preserve the souls of his flock. Who, being bishop of two dioceses, so ruled and guided either of them, and both together, as though he had in charge but one family. No father in his household, no gardener in his garden, no husbandman in his vineyard, was more or better occupied than he in his diocese amongst his flock, going about his towns and villages in teaching and preaching to the people there.

That time that he had to spare from preaching, he bestowed either in hearing public causes, or else in private study, prayer, and visiting of schools. With his continual doctrine he adjoined due and discreet correction, not so much severe to any as to them which for abundance of riches and wealthy state thought they might do what they listed. And doubtless he spared no kind of people, but was indifferent to all men, as well rich as poor, to the great shame of no small number of men nowadays. Whereas many we see so addicted to the pleasing of great and rich men, that in the meantime they have no regard to the meaner sort of poor people, whom Christ hath bought as dearly as the other.

But now again we will return our talk to Master Hooper, all whose life, in fine, was such, that to the Church and all church-men it might be a light and example to the rest, a perpetual lesson and sermon. Finally, how virtuous and good a bishop he was, ye may conceive and know evidently by this, that, even as he was hated of none but of them which were evil, so yet the worst of them all could not reprove his life in any one jot.

I have now declared his usage and behaviour abroad in the public affairs of the Church: and certainly there appeared in him at home no less example of a worthy prelate's life. For though he bestowed and converted the most part of his care upon the public flock and congregation of Christ, for the which also he spent his blood; yet nevertheless there lacked no provision in him to bring up his own children in learning and good manners; insomuch that ye could not discern whether he deserved more praise for his fatherly usage at home, or for his bishop-like doings abroad. For everywhere he kept one religion in one uniform doctrine and integrity. So that if you entered into the Bishop's palace, you would suppose yourself to have entered into some church or temple. In every corner thereof there was some smell of virtue, good example, honest conversation, and reading of holy Scriptures. There was not to be seen in his house any courtly rioting or idleness: no pomp at all, no dishonest word, no swearing could there be heard!

As for the revenues of both his bishoprics, although they did not greatly exceed, as the matter was handled, yet if anything surmounted thereof, he pursed nothing, but bestowed it in hospitality. Twice I was, as I remember, in his house in Worcester, where, in his common hall, I saw a table spread with a good store of meat, and beset full of beggars and poor folk. And I asking his servants what this meant, they told me that every day their lord and master's manner was to have customably to dinner a certain number of the poor folk of the said city, by course, who were served by four at a mess, with whole and wholesome meats. And when they were served (being before examined by him or his deputies, of the Lord's Prayer, the Articles of their faith, and the Ten Commandments), then he himself sat down to dinner, and not before.*

After this sort and manner Master Hooper executed the office of a most careful and vigilant pastor, by the space of two years and more, so long as the state of religion in King Edward's time did safely flourish and take place. And would God that all other bishops would use the like diligence, care, and observance in their function.

III. Hooper's End

Hooper's most useful episcopal labours were brought completely to an end by Queen Mary's accession to the throne in 1555. They did not last, we may observe, longer than two years. Perhaps it is not too much to say that no bishop of the Church of England ever did so much for his church and diocese in two years, and left so deep a mark on men's minds in a short period as John Hooper.

Edward VI died in July 1553; and as soon as his Popish sister Mary was fairly seated on her throne, John Hooper's troubles began. The sword of persecution having been once unsheathed, the famous Protestant Bishop of Gloucester was almost the first person who

---

* It must be remembered that there was no Poor Law in those days.

was struck at. He was personally obnoxious both to Bonner and Gardiner, with both of whom he had come into collision. He was renowned all over England as one of the boldest champions of the Reformation and most thorough opponents of Popery. His friends warned him that danger was impending, but he calmly replied, "Once I did flee and took me to my feet. But now, because I am called to this place and vocation, I am thoroughly persuaded to tarry, and to live and die with my sheep." The threatening storm soon broke. On the 29th of August he appeared before Queen Mary's Council at Richmond; and on the 1st of September he was sent as a prisoner to the Fleet. From that day till the 9th February 1555—a period of more than seventeen months—he was kept in close confinement. On that day, at last, death set him at liberty, and the noble Protestant prisoner was free.

The history of these sorrowful seventeen months in Hooper's life would occupy far more space than I have at my disposal. Those who wish to know the particulars of it must study *Fox's Martyrs*. How the good Bishop of Gloucester and Worcester was cruelly immured in a filthy prison, to the great injury of his health, for nearly a year and a half—how he was three times examined before such judges as Gardiner, Bonner, Day, Heath, and their companions —how he was by turns insulted, browbeaten, reviled, entreated and begged to recant—how gallantly he stood firm by his Protestant principles and refused to give up a hair's breadth of Christ's truth— how he was finally condemned for holding the right of priests to marry, and for denying the doctrine of transubstantiation—all these are matters which are fully recorded by the old martyrologist. But they are far too long to describe in a biographical paper like that which is now in the reader's hands.

The end came at last. On Monday, the 4th of February 1555, Hooper was formally degraded by Bishop Bonner, in the chapel of Newgate prison, and handed over to the tender mercies of the secular power. In the evening of that day, to his great delight, he was informed that he was to be sent to Gloucester, and to be publicly burned in his own cathedral city. On Tuesday, the 5th, he commenced his journey on horseback, at four o'clock in the morning, in the charge of six guards. On the afternoon of Thursday, the 7th of February, he arrived safe at Gloucester, amidst the tears and lamentations of a great crowd of people, who came out to meet him on the Cirencester Road.

At Gloucester he was lodged in the house of one Ingram, opposite to St. Nicholas' Church. The house is still standing and to all appearance not much altered. The city sheriffs, two men named Jenkins and Bond, would fain have put him in the Northgate prison, but gave up this intention at the earnest intercession of the guards who had brought him from London. One day only was allowed to elapse between the saintly prisoner's arrival and his execution. The greater part of this short interval he spent in prayer. There were, however, some interviews of no small interest, of which Fox has preserved a record.

Sir Anthony Kingston, whom he had once offended by rebuking his sins, came to see him and entreated him, with much affection and many tears, to consult his safety and recant. "Consider," he said, "that life is sweet, and death is bitter. Life hereafter may do good." To this the noble soldier of Christ returned the ever memorable answer: "The life to come is more sweet, and the death to come is more bitter." Seeing him immovable, Kingston left him with bitter tears, telling him, "I thank God that ever I knew you, seeing God did appoint you to call me to be His child. By your good instruction, when I was before a fornicator and adulterer, God hath taught me to detest and forsake the same." Hooper afterwards said that this interview had drawn from him more tears than he had shed throughout the seventeen months of his imprisonment.

Last of all, as evening drew on, the mayor, Mr. Loveday, the aldermen, and sheriffs of Gloucester came to his lodging and courteously saluted him. To them he spoke cheerfully, thanking them for their kindness, requesting that there might be a quick fire at his burning, and protesting that he should die a true, obedient subject to the Queen, but "willing to give up his life rather than consent to the wicked papistical religion of the Bishop of Rome."

These interviews got over, the saintly Bishop began to prepare for his wrestle with the last enemy, death. He retired to bed very early, saying that he had many things to remember, and slept one sleep soundly. The rest of the night he spent in prayer. After he got up, he desired that no man should be allowed to come into the chamber, and that he might be left alone till the hour of execution.

What his meditations and reflections were at that awful crisis, God alone knows. Tradition says that he wrote the following piece of poetry with a coal, on the wall of his chamber:

> Content thyself with patience
>> With Christ to bear the cup of pain:
> Who can and will thee recompense
>> A thousand-fold, with joys again.
> Let nothing cause thy heart to fail:
> Launch out thy boat, hoist up the sail,
>> Put from the shore;
> And be thou sure thou shalt attain
> Unto the port, that shall remain
>> For evermore.
>
> Fear not death, pass not for bands,
>> Only in God put thy whole trust;
> For He will require thy blood at their hands,
>> And thou dost know that once die thou must,
> Only for that, thy life if thou give,
> Death is no death, but ever for to live.
>> Do not despair:
> Of no worldly tyrant be thou in dread;
> Thy compass, which is God's Word, shall thee lead,
>> And the wind is fair.

These lines were printed in 1559, in a volume of miscellaneous pieces by the Reformers. I give them for what they are worth.

The closing scene of Hooper's life had now come. It is so beautifully and simply described by John Fox that I think it best to give it in its entirety, with trifling omissions, just as the worthy old martyrologist wrote it. He says:

On the morning of Saturday, the 9th of February, about eight of the clock, came Sir John Bridges, Lord Chandos, with a great band of men, Sir Anthony Kingston, Sir Edmund Bridges, and other commissioners appointed to see execution done. At nine of the clock, Mr. Hooper was willed to prepare himself to be in a readiness, for the time was at hand. Immediately he was brought down from his chamber by the sheriffs, who were accompanied with bills and weapons. When he saw the multitude of weapons, he spake to the sheriffs on this wise: "Mr. sheriffs," said he, "I am no traitor, neither needed you to have made such a business to bring me to the place where I must suffer; for if ye had willed me, I would have gone alone to the stake, and have troubled none of you." Afterward, looking upon the multitude of people that were assembled, being by estimation to the number of 7,000 (for it was market-day, and many also came to see his behaviour towards death), he spake unto those that were about him, saying, "Alas! Why be these people assembled and come together? Peradventure they think to hear something of me now, as they have in times past; but, alas! speech is prohibited me. Notwithstanding, the cause of my death is well known unto them. When I was appointed here to be their pastor, I preached unto them true and sincere doctrine, and that out of the Word of God. Because I will not now account the same to be heresy and untruth, this kind of death is prepared for me."

So he went forward, led between the two sheriffs (as it were a lamb to the place of slaughter), in a gown of his host's, his hat upon his head, and a staff in his hand, to stay himself withal; for the grief of the sciatica, which he had taken in prison, caused him somewhat to halt. All the way, being strictly charged not to speak, he could not be perceived once to open his mouth; but beholding the people all the way, which mourned bitterly for him, he would sometimes lift up his eyes towards heaven, and looked very cheerfully upon such as he knew; and he was never known, during the time of his being amongst them to look with so cheerful and ruddy a countenance as he did at that present. When he came to the place appointed where he should die, smilingly he beheld the stake and preparations made for him, which was near unto the great elm-tree over against the college of priests, where he was wont to preach. The place round about, the houses, and the boughs of the trees, were replenished with people: and in the chamber over the college gate stood the priests of the college.*
Then kneeled he down (forasmuch as he could not be suffered to speak unto the people) to prayer, and beckoned six or seven times

---

* This gateway and the window are still standing exactly as they were when Hooper was burned.

unto one whom he knew well, to hear the said prayer, to make report thereof in time to come (pouring tears upon his shoulders and in his bosom), who gave attentive ear unto the same; the which prayer he made upon the whole Creed, wherein he continued the space of half-an-hour. Now, after he was somewhat entered into his prayer, a box was brought and laid before him upon a stool, with his pardon (or at leastwise, it was feigned to be his pardon) from the Queen, if he would turn. At the sight whereof he cried, "If you love my soul, away with it! If you love my soul, away with it!" The box being taken away, the Lord Chandos said, "Seeing there is no remedy, dispatch him quickly!" Master Hooper said, "Good, my lord: I trust your lordship will give me leave to make an end of my prayers."

Then said the Lord Chandos to Sir Edmund Bridges' son, which gave ear before to Master Hooper's prayer, at his request: "Edmund, take heed that he do nothing else but pray; if he do, tell me, and I shall quickly dispatch him." While this talk was going on, there stepped one or two uncalled, which heard him speak these words following:

"Lord," said he, "I am hell, but Thou art heaven; I am a swill and sink of sin, but Thou art a gracious God and a merciful Redeemer. Have mercy, therefore, upon me, most miserable and wretched offender, after Thy great mercy, and according to Thine inestimable goodness. Thou art ascended into heaven; receive me, hell, to be partaker of Thy joys, where Thou sittest in equal glory with Thy Father. For well knowest Thou, Lord, wherefore I am come hither to suffer, and why the wicked do persecute this Thy poor servant: not for my sins and transgressions committed against Thee, but because I will not allow their wicked doings to the contaminating of Thy blood, and to the denial of the knowledge of Thy truth, wherewith it did please Thee by Thy Holy Spirit to instruct me; the which with as much diligence as a poor wretch might (being thereto called), I have set forth to Thy glory. And well seest Thou, my Lord and God, what terrible pains and cruel torments be prepared for Thy creature; such, Lord, as without Thy strength none is able to bear, or patiently to pass. But all things that are impossible with man are possible with Thee. Therefore, strengthen me of Thy goodness, that in the fire I break not the rules of patience; or else assuage the terror of the pains, as shall seem most to Thy glory."

As soon as the Mayor had espied these men which made report of the former words, they were commanded away, and could not be suffered to hear any more. Prayer being done, he prepared himself to the stake, and put off his host's gown, and delivered it to the sheriffs, requiring them to see it restored unto the owner, and put off the rest of his gear, unto his doublet and hose, wherein he would have been burned. But the sheriffs would not permit that (such was their greediness),* unto whose pleasures (good man) he very obediently submitted himself; and his doublet, hose, and waistcoat were taken off. Then, being in his shirt, and desiring the people to say the Lord's Prayer with him, and to pray for him, (who performed it with tears, during the time of his pains), he went up to the stake. Now, when he was at the stake, three irons, made to bind him to the stake, were brought: one for his neck, another for his middle, and the third for his legs. But he, refusing them, said, "Ye have no need thus to trouble yourselves, for I doubt not but God will give me strength sufficient to abide the extremity of the fire, without bands; not-withstanding, suspecting the frailty and weakness of the flesh, but having assured confidence in God's strength, I am content ye do as ye shall think good." So the hoop of iron prepared for his middle was brought, and when they offered to have bound his neck and legs with the other two hoops of iron, he utterly refused them, and would have none, saying, "I am well assured I shall not trouble you."

Thus, being ready, he looked upon the people, of whom he might well be seen (for he was both tall and stood also on an high stool), and beheld round about him: and in every corner there was nothing to be seen but weeping and sorrowful people. Then, lifting up his eyes and hands unto heaven, he prayed to himself. By and by, he that was appointed to make the fire came to him, and did ask his forgiveness. Of whom he asked why he should forgive him; saying, that he knew never any offence he had committed against him. "O sir," said the man, "I am appointed to make the fire." "Therein," said Mr. Hooper, "thou dost nothing

---

* The clothes of those who were burned seemed to have been the perquisite of the sheriffs.

offend me: God forgive thee thy sins, and do thine office, I pray thee." Then the reeds were cast up, and he received two bundles of them in his own hands, embraced them, kissed them, and put under either arm one of them, and showed with his hand how the rest should be bestowed, and pointed to the place where any did lack.

Anon commandment was given that the fire should be set to, and so it was. But because there were put to no fewer green faggots than two horses could carry upon their backs, it kindled not by and by, and was a pretty while also before it took the reeds upon the faggots. At length it burned about him, but the wind having full strength in that place (it was a lowering and cold morning), it blew the flame from him, so that he was in a manner no more, but touched by the fire.

Within a space after, a few dry faggots were brought, and a new fire kindled with faggots (for there were no more reeds), and that burned at his nether parts, but had small power above, because of the wind, saving that it did burn his hair, and scorch his skin a little. In the time of which fire, even as at the first flame, he prayed, saying mildly, and not very loud (but as one without pains), "O Jesus, the Son of David, have mercy upon me, and receive my soul!" After the second fire was spent, he did wipe both his eyes with his hands, and beholding the people, he said with an indifferent loud voice, "For God's love, good people, let me have more fire!" And all this while his nether parts did burn, for the faggots were so few that the flame did not burn strongly at his upper parts.

The third fire was kindled within a while after, where was more extreme than the other two; and then the bladders of gunpowder brake, which did him small good, they were so placed, and the wind had such power. In the which fire he prayed with somewhat a loud voice, "Lord Jesus, have mercy upon me! Lord Jesus, have mercy upon me! Lord Jesus, receive my spirit!" And these were the last words he was heard to utter. But when he was black in the mouth, and his tongue swollen that he could not speak, yet his lips went till they were shrunk to the gums; and he knocked his breast with his hands until one of his arms fell off, and then knocked still with the other, what time the fat, water, and blood dropped out at his fingers' ends, until by renewing of the fire his strength was gone, and his hand did cleave fast in knocking to the iron upon his breast. So immediately, bowing forwards, he yielded up his spirit.*

Thus was he three quarters of an hour or more in the fire. Even as a lamb, patiently he abode the extremity thereof, neither moving forwards, backwards, or to any side; but having his nether parts burned, and his bowels fallen out, he died as quietly as a child in his bed, and he now reigneth as a blessed martyr in the joys of heaven, prepared for the faithful in Christ before the foundations of the world, for whose constancy all Christians are bound to praise God.†

*   *   *

I leave the story of the martyr of Gloucester at this point, having traced his life from his cradle to his fiery grave. He died as he had long lived, true to his colours; and his death was every way worthy of his life.

Something I might say about the hideous cruelty with which he and his fellow-sufferers in Mary's reign were put to death. Nothing can excuse it. The times, no doubt, were rough and coarse. Capital punishment was fearfully common. Killing people for alleged heresy was unhappily no strange thing. But these are poor defences of a huge crime. The blood of the English martyrs is an indelible stain on the Church of Rome. It was a judicial murder that can never be explained away.

Something I might say about the glorious patience and courage which Hooper exhibited throughout his sufferings. As long as the

---

* The stump of a very large oaken post, blackened and charred with fire, was dug up a few years ago on the very place where Hooper was burned. It is supposed by many to be the lower end of the stake to which the martyr was chained when he met his fiery death. Of course no positive proof can be given that this supposition is correct; but there is no improbability or impossibility in the idea. A well-seasoned charred piece of oak timber might easily last undecayed in the ground for three centuries. I saw this stump with my own eyes under a glass case, in a house near Gloucester, where it was carefully preserved.

† Fox's *Acts and Monuments, in loco.*

The Burning of Bishop Hooper
"Lord Jesus receive my soul!"

world lasts, he will be a pattern of what Christ can do for His people in the hour of need. Never may we forget that He who strengthened Hooper never changes. He is "the same yesterday, and today, and forever."[1]

Something, not least, I might say about the extreme impolicy of the Church of Rome in making martyrs of Hooper and his companions. Never, I believe, did Popery do herself such damage as when she burnt our Reformers. Their blood was the seed of the Church. The good that they did by their deaths was more than they did all their lives. Their martyrdoms made thousands think who were never reached by their sermons. Myriads, we may depend, came to the conclusion that a church which could act so abominably and cruelly as Rome did could never be the one true Church of God; and that a cause which could produce such patient and unflinching sufferers must surely be the cause of Christ and of truth. But I pass away from these points, however interesting. I only hope that they may be seeds of thought which may bear fruit in men's minds after many days.

IV. Hooper's Opinions

The last point which I wish to bring under the notice of my readers is one which I feel to be of deep importance. I have supplied some information about Hooper's life and death. I will now ask my readers to give me their attention a little longer, while I say something about *Hooper's opinions*. I have shown you how he lived and died; let me now show you exactly what he thought, and what he taught, and what he preached. I have set before you the man; let me now set before you his doctrine.

If I left my readers under the vague impression that Hooper was a good man and a zealous man and an earnest man, but told them nothing more, I should think I had not done my duty. I want men to understand what theological views the martyred Bishop of Gloucester held. I want men to see clearly what kind of doctrine was taught by the English Reformers. What kind of things did Hooper say and preach and publish and write? What kind of religion was a churchman's religion at the Reformation?

---

[1] Hebrews 13:8.

The answer to these inquiries is, happily, not difficult to find. The two volumes of Hooper's writings published by the Parker Society make the matter plain as the sun at noonday. There men may read in unmistakable language the theological opinions of one of the leading bishops of the time of the Reformation. From two documents in these two volumes I will select fair specimens.

(a) The first document I will quote from is entitled *Articles concerning Christian religion, given by the reverend father in Christ, John Hooper, Bishop of Gloucester, unto all and singular deans, parsons, prebends, vicars, curates, and other ecclesiastical ministers within the diocese of Gloucester, to be had, held, and retained of them for unity and agreement, as well for the doctrine of God's Word, as also for the uniformity of the ceremonies agreeing with God's Word.* A more authoritative and weighty declaration of Hooper's opinions it is impossible to conceive.*

The first article enjoins,

> that none of the above-named clergy do teach or preach any manner of thing to be necessary for the salvation of men, other than that which is contained in the Book of God's Holy Word, called the Old and New Testament; and that they beware to establish and confirm any manner of doctrine concerning the old superstitious and papistical doctrines, which cannot be duly and justly approved by the authority of God's Word.

The fourth article enjoins,

> that they and every one of them do diligently teach and preach that the Church of God is the congregation of the faithful, wherein the Word of God is truly preached, and the sacraments justly administered, according to the institution of Christ, and His doctrine taught unto us by His Holy Word; and that the Church of God is not by God's Word taken for the multitude, or company of bishops, priests, and such others; but that it is the company of all men hearing God's Word and obeying the same, lest any man should be seduced, believing himself to be bound to any ordinary succession of bishops and priests, but only to the Word of God and the right use of the sacraments.

---

* It is worth noticing that Ridley published many of the same articles about the same time, for the clergy of the diocese of London.

The seventh article enjoins,

that they and every one of them do diligently teach and preach the justification only by faith of Jesus Christ, and not by the merit of any man's good works, albeit that good works do necessarily follow justification, which before justification are of no value or estimation before God.

In the ninth article, he enjoins them,

that the doctrine of purgatory, pardons, prayer for them that are departed out of this world, the veneration, invocation, and worshipping of saints or images, is contrary and injurious to the honour of Christ, our only Mediator and Redeemer, and also against the doctrine of the First and Second Commandments of God.

In the tenth article, he enjoins,

that in the sacrament of the body and blood of Christ there is no transubstantiation of the bread and wine into the body and blood of Christ, or any manner of corporal or local presence of Christ, in, under, or with the bread and wine, but spiritually, by faith.

In the eleventh article, he enjoins,

that they which do unworthily come to baptism or the Supper of the Lord, do not receive the virtue and true effect of the same sacraments, although they receive the natural sign and elements.

In the twenty-fourth article, he enjoins,

that the sacraments are not of any force by virtue or strength of any internal work of the same, which of superstition is called *opus operatum*,[1] but only by the virtue and means of the Holy Ghost working in the hearts of the doers and receivers by faith.

In the forty-first article, he enjoins,

that none of you do counterfeit the Popish Mass, by blessing the Lord's board, washing your hands or fingers after the Gospel, or receipt of the Holy Communion—shifting the Book from one place to another, laying down and licking the chalice after the Communion, showing the sacrament openly before the distribution of the same, or making any elevation thereof—ringing of the sacring bell, or setting any light on the Lord's board.

---

[1] "By the work working."

In the forty-third article, he enjoins,

> Whereas in divine places some use the Lord's board after the form
> of a table, and some of an altar, whereby disunion is perceived to
> arise among the unlearned, therefore, wishing a godly unity to be
> observed in all our dioceses, and for that the form of a table may
> move more, and turn the simple from the old superstitious
> opinions of the Popish Mass, and to the right use of the Lord's
> Supper, we exhort you to erect and set up the Lord's board after
> the form of an honest table, decently covered, in such place as
> shall be thought most meet, so that the minister and com-
> municants may be seen, heard, and understood of all the people
> there present, and that you do take down and abolish all altars.
> Further, that the minister, in the use of the communion and
> prayers thereof, turn his face toward the people.

Such were the visitation articles and injunctions of a bishop of
the time of the Reformation. I turn away from them with one
single remark. There have been many dioceses in England in the last
300 years in which it might have done great good if the injunctions
of good Bishop Hooper had been distributed among the clergy and
urged on their attention.

(*b*) The only other document that I shall quote from is called *A
Brief and Clear Confession of the Christian Faith*. It deserves special
attention, because it was published in 1550, the very year in which
the writer was made Bishop of Gloucester. From the *Confession of
Faith* I now make the following selections. I make them with
considerable difficulty. The whole *Confession* is so good that it is
hard to say what to quote and what to leave behind. I only ask my
readers to remember that the sack is as good as the sample.

In the twenty-sixth article of the *Confession*, Hooper says,

> I do believe and confess that Christ's condemnation is mine
> absolution; that His crucifying is my deliverance; His descending
> into hell is mine ascending into heaven; His death is my life; His
> blood is my cleansing, and purging, by which only I am washed,
> purified, and cleansed from all my sins: so that I neither receive,
> neither believe any other purgatory, either in this world, or in the
> other, whereby I may be purged, but only the blood of Jesus
> Christ, by which all are purged and made clean for ever.

In the twenty-eighth article of the *Confession*, Hooper says,

I believe that the Holy Supper of the Lord is not a sacrifice, but only a remembrance and commemoration of this holy sacrifice of Jesus Christ. Therefore it ought not to be worshipped as God, neither as Christ therein contained; who must be worshipped in faith only, without all corruptible elements. Likewise I believe and confess that the Popish Mass is the invention and ordinance of man, a sacrifice of Antichrist, and a forsaking of the sacrifice of Jesus Christ, that is to say, of His death and passion; and that it is a stinking and infected sepulchre, which hideth and covereth the merit of the blood of Jesus Christ—and, therefore, ought the Mass to be abolished, and the Holy Supper of the Lord to be restored, and set in his perfection again.

In the fifty-fourth article of the *Confession*, Hooper says,

I believe that the Word of God is of a far greater authority than the Church; the which Word only doth sufficiently show and teach us all those things that in any wise concern our salvation, both what we ought to do and what to leave undone. The same Word of God is the true pattern and perfect rule, after the which all faithful people ought to govern and order their lives, without turning either to the right hand or to the left hand, without changing anything thereof, without putting to it, or taking from it, knowing that all the works of God are perfect, but most chiefly His Word.

In the sixty-fourth article of the *Confession*, Hooper says,

I believe that in the holy sacrament the signs, or badges, are not changed in any point, but the same do remain wholly in their nature; that is to say, the bread is not changed and transubstantiated (as the fond Papists, and false doctors do teach, deceiving the poor people), into the body of Jesus Christ, neither is the wine transubstantiated into His blood; but the bread remaineth still bread, and the wine remaineth still wine, every one in his proper and first nature.

In the sixty-fifth article of the *Confession*, Hooper says,

I believe that all this sacrament consisteth in the use thereof; so that without the right use the bread and wine in nothing differ from other common bread and wine, that is commonly used:

and, therefore, I do not believe that the body of Christ can be contained, hid, or inclosed in the bread, under the bread, or with the bread; neither the blood in the wine, under the wine, or with the wine. But I believe and confess the very body of Christ to be in heaven, on the right hand of the Father (as before we have said), and that always and as often as we use this bread and wine according to the ordinance and institution of Christ, we do verily and indeed receive His body and blood.

In the sixty-sixth article of the *Confession*, Hooper says,
I believe that this receiving is not done carnally or bodily, but spiritually, through a true and lively faith; that is to say, the body and blood of Christ are not given to the mouth and belly, for the nourishing of the body, but unto our faith, for the nourishing of the spirit and inward man unto eternal life. And for that cause we have no need that Christ should come from heaven to us, but that we should ascend unto Him, lifting up our hearts through a lively faith on high, unto the right hand of the Father, where Christ sitteth, from whence we wait for our redemption; and we must not seek for Christ in these bodily elements.

I drop my quotations here. I have given enough to make it clear what kind of opinions Hooper held and what his theological views were. I know not what my readers may think of these quotations. But I will tell you what impression they leave on my mind.

They supply plain proof, for which I am deeply thankful, that Protestant and evangelical churchmen are not men of new-fangled and modern opinions, but churchmen of the stamp of the Reformation, churchmen whose views were held by an eminent churchman 300 years ago. Let them take courage. Let them not be moved by the sneers and taunts and hard words of those church- men who do not agree with them. They may boldly reply that theirs are the old paths, and that they are the true representatives of the Church of England. If evangelical churchmen are wrong, then Hooper was wrong too. If Hooper was right, then they are right. But as for a material difference between their views and those of the martyred Bishop of Gloucester, I defy any one to show that there is any at all.

My task is done. I have brought together as concisely as possible

the times, life, death, and opinions of one of our greatest English
Reformers. But I cannot leave off without offering two practical
suggestions to all into whose hands this paper may fall. I address
them to each reader personally and directly, and I entreat him to
ponder well what I say.

(1) For one thing, I charge all loyal churchmen to *resist manfully
the efforts now being made to un-Protestantize England*, and to bring her
once more into subjection to Popery. Let us not go back to
ignorance, superstition, priestcraft, and immorality. Our forefathers
tried Popery long ago, and threw it off with disgust and indignation. Let us not put the clock back and return to Egypt. Let us
have no peace with Rome, till Rome abjures her errors and is at
peace with Christ.

Let us read *our Bibles* and be armed with scriptural arguments. A
Bible-reading laity is a nation's surest defence against error. I have
no fear for English Protestantism, if the laity will only do their duty.

Let us read *history* and see what Rome did in days gone by. Read
how she trampled on your country's liberties, plundered your fore-
father's pockets, and kept the whole nation ignorant and immoral.
Read Fox and Strype and Burnet and Soames and Blunt. And do
not forget that Rome never changes. It is her boast and glory that
she is always the same. Only give her absolute power in England,
and she would soon put out the eyes of our country and make her
like Samson, a degraded slave.

Let us read *facts* standing out on the face of the globe. What has
made Italy what she is? Popery. What has made Mexico and the
South American States what they are? Popery. What has made
Spain and Portugal what they are? Popery. What has made Ireland
what she is? Popery. What makes Scotland, the United States, and
our own beloved England, the powerful, prosperous countries that
they are at present, and I pray God they may long continue? I
answer in one word, *Protestantism*—a free Bible and a Protestant
ministry, and the principles of the Reformation. Let us think twice
before we give ear to the specious arguments of liberalism falsely so
called. Let us think twice before we help to bring back the reign of
Popery.

(2) For another thing, I charge all loyal churchmen and all who
love pure evangelical religion *to stand together in these days of division,*

and not allow crotchets and scruples to keep them asunder. Let the friend of liturgical revision drop his favourite panacea for a little space and put his shoulder to the work of maintaining the Gospel in the Church of England. Let the friend of revivals not think it misspent time to give his aid in opposing Rome. If Popery once triumph, there will be no more liberty for revivals. We cannot afford to lose friends. Our ranks are already very thin. The Church of England demands of every Protestant and evangelical churchman that he will do his duty.

Things look black in every direction, I freely admit. But there is no cause to despair. The day is not lost. There is yet time to win a battle. Come what will, let us not desert our position or forsake the good old ship yet. Let us not please our enemies by spiking our guns and marching out of our fortress without a battle. Rather let us stand to our guns, like good Bishop Hooper, and in God's strength show a bold front to the foe. The Church of England has done some good in days gone by, and the Church is still worth preserving. If we do go down in the struggle, let us go down with colours flying. But let us stand firm, like the gallant sentinel of Pompeii; let no man leave his post. My own mind is fully made up. I say the Church of England had better perish and go to pieces than forsake John Hooper's principles and tolerate the sacrifice of the Mass and auricular confession.

Note

A letter which Master Hooper did write out of prison to certain of his friends, three weeks before his cruel burning at Gloucester.

The grace of God be with you. Amen.

I did write unto you of late, and told you what extremity the Parliament had concluded upon concerning religion, suppressing the truth, and setting forth the untruth, intending to cause all men by extremity to forswear themselves, and to take again for the head of the Church him that is neither head nor member of it, but a very enemy, as the Word of God and all ancient writers do record: and for lack of law and authority, they will use force and extremity, which have been the arguments to defend the Pope and Popery since this authority first began in the world. But now is the time of trial, to see whether we fear God or man. It was an easy thing to hold with Christ while the Prince and world held with Him; but now the world hateth Him, it is the true trial who be His. Wherefore, in the name and in the virtue, strength, and power of His Holy Spirit, prepare yourselves in any case to adversity and constancy. Let us not run away when it is most time to fight. Remember, none shall be crowned but such as fight manfully; and *he that endureth to the end shall be saved.* You must now turn all your cogitations from the peril you see, and mark the felicity that followeth the peril—either victory in this world of your enemies, or else a surrender of this life to inherit the everlasting kingdom. Beware of beholding too much the felicity or misery of this world; for the consideration and too earnest love or fear of either of them draweth from God. Wherefore think with yourselves, as touching the felicity of the world, it is good; but yet none otherwise than it standeth with the favour of God. It is to be kept; but yet so far forth, as by keeping of it we lose not God. It is good abiding and tarrying still among our friends here; but yet so, that we tarry not therewithal in God's displeasure, and hereafter dwell with the devils in fire everlasting. There is nothing under God but may be kept, so that God, being above all things we have, be not lost.

Of adversity judge the same. Imprisonment is painful; but yet liberty upon evil conditions is more painful. The prisons stink, but yet not so much as sweet houses where the fear and true honour of God lacketh. I must be alone and solitary; it is better so to be, and have God with me, than to be in company with the wicked. Loss of goods is great; but loss of God's grace and favour is greater. . . . It is better to make answer before the pomp and pride of wicked men than to stand naked in the sight of all heaven and earth before the just God at the latter day. I shall die by the hands of the cruel man: he is blessed that loseth this life, full of mortal miseries, and findeth the life full of eternal joys. It is pain and grief to depart from goods and friends; but yet not so much as to depart from grace and heaven itself. Wherefore there is neither felicity nor adversity of this world that can appear to be great, if it be weighed with the joys or pains of the world to come.

I can do no more but pray for you; do the same for me, for God's sake. For my part (I thank the heavenly Father), I have made mine accounts, and appointed myself unto the will of the heavenly Father; as He will, so I will, by His grace. For God's sake, as soon as ye can, send my poor wife and children some letter from you; and my letter also, which I sent of late to D. As it was told me, she never had letter from me, since the coming of M.S. unto her; the more to blame the messengers, for I have written divers times. The Lord comfort them, and provide for them; for I am able to do nothing in worldly things. She is a godly and wise woman. If my meaning had been accomplished, she should have had necessary things; but what I meant God can perform, to whom I commend both her and you all. I am a precious jewel now, and daintily kept, never so daintily; for neither mine own man, nor any of the servants of the house, may come to me, but my keeper alone—a simple, rude man, God knoweth; but I am nothing careful thereof. Fare you well. The 21st of January, 1555.

Your bounden,
JOHN HOOPER

5

ROWLAND TAYLOR: MARTYR

ROWLAND TAYLOR, Rector of Hadleigh, in Suffolk, one of the famous Protestant martyrs in Queen Mary's days, is a man about whom the Church possesses singularly little information. Excepting the facts related by John Fox in the *Book of Martyrs*, we know scarcely anything about him. Enough, however, is on record to show that among the noble champions of Christ's truth, who sealed their faith with their blood at the time of the English Reformation, Rowland Taylor was second to none.

The causes of this absence of information are easily explained. For one thing, the good man lived and laboured and died in a small country town, fifty miles from London. Such a position is fatal to a worldwide celebrity. It is the dwellers in large cities and the occupiers of metropolitan pulpits whose doings are chronicled by admirers and whose lives are carefully handed down to posterity. For another thing, he wrote no books, either expository or controversial or practical. Not even a single sermon of the martyred Rector of Hadleigh exists in print and enables him, though dead, to speak. When he died, he left nothing behind him to keep his memory alive in libraries. These two facts must not be forgotten.

The account of Taylor, which Fox has supplied, is so peculiarly graphic and vivid, that one might almost suppose that the martyrologist was a personal friend of the martyr, or an eyewitness of his sufferings. Of this, however, I can find no evidence. Yet it is worthy of notice that Fox, after Queen Elizabeth came to the throne, resided for a considerable time with Parkhurst, Bishop of Norwich, in whose diocese Hadleigh was then situated. He also seems to have had friends and acquaintances at Ipswich, which is only ten miles from Hadleigh. It is therefore highly probable that he had frequent opportunities of visiting Taylor's parish and very likely received much information from people who were actually present when the noble martyr was burned, and could supply full and accurate accounts both of his ministry and his sufferings. To condense and modernize Fox's narrative, and to present it to my readers in a convenient form, is the simple object of these pages.

Rowland Taylor, according to Strype, was born at Rothbury, in Northumberland, the same county, it may be remembered, from which Bishop Ridley came. The date of his birth, the rank or position of his family, his early history, and the place of his education are all things about which nothing whatever is known. We only gather from various sources that in due time he became a student at Cambridge and there imbibed the principles of the Protestant Reformation. Among other means by which he was influenced at this important crisis of his life, the sermons of Bishop Latimer are especially named.

The first distinct fact in his life that we know is his intimacy with Archbishop Cranmer. In that great man's household he seems to have occupied some office and to have worked with him in carrying forward the mighty building of the English Reformation. How long he lived with Cranmer, we have, unfortunately, no means of finding out. But there is strong internal evidence that he was so long and so intimately connected with him that he became a marked man among the English Reformers. Upon no other supposition can we explain the peculiar enmity with which he was sought out and persecuted to death in Queen Mary's reign. The old parson of Hadleigh must surely have obtained an honourable reputation in London, in the days of Edward VI.

Hadleigh, in Suffolk, was the first and only piece of preferment which we know of Rowland Taylor holding. To this he was appointed by his friend Archbishop Cranmer, but at what date we have no means of ascertaining. One thing only is quite certain: as soon as he was appointed to Hadleigh, he resigned all his offices in London, and devoted himself entirely to the work of his parish.

Hadleigh is a small town on the southwest border of Suffolk, containing at this time about four thousand people. The character of the place in the days of Edward VI and the nature of Rowland

Taylor's ministry are so well and graphically described by Fox in his *Acts and Monuments* that I cannot do better than quote his words:

> The town of Hadleigh was one of the first that received the Word of God in all England, at the preaching of Master Thomas Bilney, by whose industry the Gospel of Christ had such gracious success, and took such root there, that a great number in that parish became exceeding well learned in the Holy Scripture, as well women as men; so that a man might have found among them many that had often read the whole Bible through, and that could have said a great part of St. Paul's Epistles by heart, and very well and readily have given a godly learned sentence in any matter of controversy.
>
> Their children and servants were also brought up and trained diligently in the right knowledge of God's Word, so that the whole town seemed rather an university of the learned, than a town of cloth-making or labouring people; and what most is to be commended, they were for the most part followers of God's Word in their living.
>
> In this town of Hadleigh, Dr. Taylor was a good shepherd, abiding and dwelling among his sheep. He gave himself wholly to the study of Holy Scripture, most faithfully endeavouring himself to fulfil that charge which the Lord gave unto Peter, saying, "Peter, lovest thou Me? Feed my lambs;" "Feed my sheep;" "Feed my sheep." This love of Christ so wrought in him, that no Sunday nor holy day passed, nor other time, when he might get the people together, but he preached to them the Word of God, the doctrine of their salvation.
>
> Not only was his word a preaching unto them, but all his life and conversation was an example of unfeigned Christian life and true holiness. He was void of all pride, humble and meek as any child; so that none were so poor but they might boldly, as unto their father, resort unto him. Neither was his lowliness childish or fearful; but as occasion, time, and place required, he would be stout in rebuking the sinful and evil doers: so that none was so rich but he would tell him plainly his fault, with such earnest and grave rebukes as became a good curate and pastor. He was a man very mild, void of all rancour, grudge, or evil will, ready to do good to all men, readily forgiving his enemies, and never sought to do evil to any.

To the poor that were blind, sick, lame, bedridden, or that had many children, he was a very father, a careful patron, a diligent provider, insomuch that he caused the parishioners to make a general provision for them; and he himself (beside the continual relief that they always found at his house) gave an honest portion yearly to the common alms box. His wife, also, was an honest, discreet, and sober matron; and his children well nurtured, brought up in the fear of God and good learning.

To conclude, he was a right and lively image or pattern of all those virtuous qualities described by St. Paul in a true bishop—a good salt of the earth, savoury, biting the corrupt manners of evil men; a light in God's house set upon a candlestick, for all good men to imitate and follow.

How long Taylor's ministry lasted at Hadleigh we do not exactly know. Fox only says that he continued there "all the days of the most innocent and holy King, of blessed memory, King Edward VI." We may, however, safely conclude that he was there more than ten years. When he was put in prison in Queen Mary's days, he was the father of nine children; and as it is not probable that he would marry until he left Cranmer's household and had a home of his own, it seems likely that his children were all born at Hadleigh. All this, however, is only matter of conjecture. Enough for us to know that he was evidently Rector of Hadleigh long enough to be loved and honoured by the mass of his parishioners.

Rowland Taylor's quiet days at Hadleigh were soon brought to an end when Queen Mary came to the throne. A man of his eminence and high reputation as a Protestant was sure to be marked for destruction by the Popish party, and an excuse was soon found for putting him in prison.

In the best worked parishes, and under the most faithful preaching of the Gospel, there will always be found many who hate vital religion and remain hardened, impenitent, and unbelieving. It was so in the days of the Apostles. It is so at the present time, in our own parishes. It was so at Hadleigh, when Rowland Taylor was rector. There were men who hated him, because his doctrine condemned their own lives and opinions; and as soon as they had an opportunity of doing him an injury, they eagerly seized it. Two of these men, named Foster and Clerke, conspired to bring the worthy

Rector into collision with the higher powers by hiring one John Avreth, Rector of Aldham, to come to Hadleigh Church and celebrate the Popish Mass. The result answered their expectations. Rowland Taylor, with righteous indignation, rushed into the church as the Mass was about to begin and protested warmly against the whole proceeding as illegal and idolatrous. Then followed an unseemly altercation—the forcible expulsion of the Rector of Hadleigh from his own church—great excitement among the faithful parishioners—throwing of stones into the church, and a general ferment among the people. All this was duly reported to Stephen Gardiner, Bishop of Winchester and Lord Chancellor of England; and the upshot of the affair, as the malignants had foreseen, was a summons from Gardiner to Dr. Taylor to appear before him in London without delay. This summons the gallant Reformer promptly obeyed, and left Hadleigh, never to return till the day of his death.

When the summons arrived, Rowland Taylor's many friends tried in vain to persuade him to fly to the Continent to save his life, as many other faithful Protestants had done. But they had no more effect on the good old man than Paul's friends had on the Apostle, when they entreated him not to go up to Jerusalem. This was his reply:

> What will ye have me to do? I am now old, and have already lived too long to see these terrible and most wicked days. Fly you, and do as your conscience leadeth you. I am fully determined, with God's grace, to go to this Bishop, and to tell him to his beard that he doth naught. God shall well hereafter raise up teachers of His people, which shall with much more diligence and fruit teach them than I have done. For God will not forsake His Church, though now for a time He trieth and correcteth us, and not without just cause.
>
> As for me, I believe before God I shall never be able to do God so good a service as I may do now, nor shall I ever have so glorious a calling as I have now, nor so great mercy of God proffered me, as is now at this present. For what Christian man would not gladly die against the Pope and his adherents? I know that the Papacy is the kingdom of Antichrist, altogether full of falsehoods; so that all their doctrine is nothing but idolatry,

superstition, error, hypocrisy, and lies. Wherefore I beseech you and all other my friends to pray for me, and to doubt not but God will give me strength and His Holy Spirit, that all mine adversaries shall have shame of their doings.

Armed with this frame of mind, Rowland Taylor went voluntarily to London, and most manfully kept his word. The opening of his first interview with Gardiner is thus described by Fox:

Now when Gardiner saw Dr. Taylor, according to his common custom, he reviled him, calling him knave, traitor, heretic, with many other villainous reproaches. All this Dr. Taylor heard patiently, and at last said, "My lord, I am neither traitor nor heretic, but a true subject, and a faithful Christian man; and I am come according to your commandment, to know what is the cause why your lordship hath sent for me." Then said the Bishop, "Art thou come thus, villain? How darest thou look me in the face for shame? Knowest thou not who I am?" "Yea!" said Dr. Taylor, "I know who you are: you are Dr. Stephen Gardiner, Bishop of Winchester and Lord Chancellor, and yet but a mortal man. If I should be afraid of your lordly looks, why fear you not God, the Lord of us all? How dare you for shame look any Christian man in the face, seeing you have forsaken the truth, denied our Saviour Christ and His Word, and done contrary to your oath-taking? With what countenance will you appear before the judgment-seat of Christ, and answer to your oath made first to King Henry VIII, and afterward unto King Edward VI, his son?"

The interview, which began in this extraordinary manner, terminated as might have been expected. After several sharp arguments and wrangles, in which the Suffolk Rector showed himself more than a match for the Bishop of Winchester, Taylor was committed to the King's Bench prison. On hearing his committal, he kneeled down, and holding up both his hands, said, "Good Lord, I thank Thee. From the tyranny of the Bishop of Rome, and all his detestable errors, idolatries, and abominations, good Lord, deliver us. And God be praised for good King Edward."

Rowland Taylor lay in prison two years, and spent most of his time in prayer, reading the Scriptures, and writing. He had also opportunities of exhorting and addressing the prisoners. How much he saw of the other Reformers who were in prison at the same time, is not quite clear. It is certain, however, that he was very often in company of the famous John Bradford and told his friends that God had sent him to a prison where he "found an angel of God to comfort him." It is also highly probable that he had occasional interviews with the illustrious Reformers, Hooper, Rogers, Ferrar, and Saunders,[1] who all, like himself, were finally burned at the stake.

The end of Rowland Taylor's weary imprisonment came at last. On the 22nd of January, 1555, he was brought before the Lord Chancellor, Bishop Gardiner, and other commissioners, and subjected to a lengthy examination. To go into the details of all that was said on this occasion would be wearisome and unprofitable. The whole affair was conducted with the same gross unfairness and partiality which characterized all the proceedings against the English Reformers, and the result, as a matter of course, was the good man's condemnation. To use his own words, in a letter to a friend, he was pronounced a heretic because he defended the marriage of priests and denied the doctrine of transubstantiation. Never let it be forgotten in these days that the denial of any corporal presence of Christ's body and blood in the elements of bread and wine at the Lord's Supper was the turning point which decided the fate of our martyred Reformers. If they gave way on that point they might have lived. Because they would not admit any corporal presence they died. These things are recorded for our learning.

On the last day of January 1555, Taylor, together with Bradford and Saunders, was called to appear before the bishops of Winchester, Norwich, London, Salisbury, and Durham. They were all three charged with heresy and schism, and required to answer determinately whether they would submit themselves to the Bishop of Rome and abjure their errors. On their refusal they were condemned to death.

For this [says Fox] they gave God thanks, and stoutly said unto the

---

[1] Lawrence Saunders, sometime Vicar of Coventry, was martyred on February 8, 1555.

Bishops, "We doubt not but God, the righteous Judge, will require our blood at your hands, and the proudest of you all shall repent this receiving again of Antichrist, and your tyranny that ye now show against the flock of Christ."

On the evening of this day, Taylor was sent to the Compter prison and parted from his brethren.

On the 4th of February, Bonner, Bishop of London, came to the Compter prison and formally degraded Taylor from the office of priest, with many absurd ceremonies of which Fox supplies a ludicrous description. The night after his degradation, his wife and his son, Thomas, were permitted to visit and sup with him, and after supper they parted, with much affection and many tears. The next day, the 5th of February, he set out on his journey to Hadleigh, in order that he might be burned in the presence of his parishioners. The circumstances of his departure from London are so touchingly described by Fox, that I think it best to let the old historian speak for himself.

On the next morrow after that Dr. Taylor had supped with his wife in the Compter prison, which was the 5th day of February, the sheriff of London, with his officers came to the Compter by two o'clock in the morning, and so brought forth Dr. Taylor; and without any light led him to the Woolsack, an inn without Aldgate. Dr. Taylor's wife, suspecting that her husband should that night be carried away, watched all night in St. Botolph's Church porch, beside Aldgate, having with her two children, the one named Elizabeth, of thirteen years of age, whom, being left without father or mother, Dr. Taylor had brought up of alms from three years old; the other named Mary, Dr. Taylor's own daughter.

Now when the sheriff and his company came against St. Botolph's Church, Elizabeth cried, saying, "O my dear father! Mother, mother: here is my father led away!" Then cried his wife, "Rowland, Rowland: where art thou?" for it was a very dark morning, that the one could not see the other. Dr. Taylor answered, "Dear wife, I am here," and stayed. The sheriff's men would have led him forth, but the sheriff said, "Stay a little, masters, I pray you, and let him speak to his wife;" and so they stayed.

Then came she to him, and he took his daughter Mary in his arms, and he, his wife, and Elizabeth kneeled down and said the Lord's Prayer. At which sight the sheriff wept apace, and so did divers others of the company. After they had prayed, he rose up and kissed his wife, and shook her by the hand, and said, "Farewell, my dear wife: be of good comfort, for I am quiet in my conscience. God shall raise up a father for my children." And then he kissed his daughter Mary, and said, "God bless thee, and make thee His servant;" and, kissing Elizabeth, he said, "God bless thee. I pray you all stand strong and steadfast to Christ and His Word, and keep you from idolatry." Then said his wife, "God be with thee, dear Rowland: I will, with God's grace, meet thee at Hadleigh."

And so was he led forth to the Woolsack, and his wife followed him. As soon as they came to the Woolsack, he was put into a chamber, wherein he was kept, with four yeomen of the guard and the sheriff's men. Dr. Taylor, as soon as he was come into the chamber, fell down on his knees, and gave himself wholly to prayer. The sheriff then, seeing Dr. Taylor's wife there, would in no case grant her to speak any more with her husband; but gently desired her to go to his house, and take it as her own, and promised her she should lack nothing, and sent two officers to conduct her thither. Notwithstanding, she desired to go to her mother's, whither the officers led her, and charged her mother to keep her there till they came again.

Rowland Taylor's journey from London to Hadleigh is minutely described by Fox. He traveled on horseback, according to the custom of those days, and stopped at Brentwood, Chelmsford, and Lavenham. "All the way he was joyful and merry, as one that accounted himself going to a most pleasant banquet or bridal." But we must content ourselves with the account of the closing scene in the worthy martyr's history, which shall be given in Fox's own words:

On the 9th February, 1555 (the same day that Bishop Hooper was burnt at Gloucester), the sheriff and his company led Dr. Taylor towards Hadleigh; and coming within two miles of Hadleigh, he desired for somewhat to light off his horse; which done, he leaped, and set a frisk, or twain, as men commonly do in dancing.

"Why, master Doctor," quoth the sheriff, "how do you now?" He answered, "Well, God be praised, good master sheriff, never better; for now I know I am almost at home. I lack not past two stiles to go over, and I am at even at my Father's house. But, master sheriff," said he, "shall we not go through Hadleigh?" "Yes," said the sheriff, "you shall go through Hadleigh." Then said he, "O good Lord, I thank Thee! I shall yet once ere I die, see my flock whom Thou, Lord, knowest I have most heartily loved and most truly taught. Good Lord, bless them, and keep them steadfast in Thy Word and truth."

When they were now come to Hadleigh, and came riding over the bridge, at the bridge foot waited a poor man with five small children, who, when he saw Dr. Taylor, he and his children fell down upon their knees and held up their hands, and cried with a loud voice, and said, "O dear father and good shepherd, Dr. Taylor, God help and succour thee, as thou hast many a time succoured me and my poor children." Such witness had this servant of God of his virtuous and charitable alms-given in his lifetime; for God would now the poor should testify of his good deeds to his singular comfort, to the example of others, and confusion of his persecutors and tyrannous adversaries. For the sheriff and others that led him to death were wonderfully astonished at this, and the sheriff sore rebuked the poor man for so crying. The streets of Hadleigh were beset on both sides the way with men and women of the town and country who waited to see him; whom, when they beheld so led to death, with weeping eyes and lamentable voices they cried, saying one to another, "Ah, good Lord, there goeth our good shepherd from us, that so faithfully hath taught us, so fatherly hath cared for us, and so godly hath governed us. O merciful God! What shall we poor scattered lambs do? What shall come of this most wicked world? Good Lord, strengthen him and comfort him." With such other most lamentable and piteous voices. Wherefore the people were sore rebuked by the sheriff and the catchpoles, his men, that led him. And Dr. Taylor evermore said to the people, "I have preached to you God's Word and truth, and am come this day to seal it with my blood."

Coming against the almshouses, which he well knew, he cast to the good people money which remained of that which good people had given him in time of his imprisonment. As for his living, they took it from him at his first going to prison, so that he was sustained all the time of his imprisonment by the charitable alms of good people that visited him. Therefore the money that now remained he put in a glove ready for the same purpose, and, as is said, gave it to the poor almsmen standing at their door to see him. And coming to the last of the almshouses, and not seeing the poor that there dwelt ready at their doors as the others were, he asked, "Is the blind man and blind woman that dwelt here alive?" It was answered, "Yea, they are within." Then threw he glove and all in at the window, and so rode forth.

At the last, coming to Aldham Common, the place assigned where he should suffer, and seeing a great multitude of people gathered thither, he asked, "What place is this, and what meaneth it that so much people are gathered hither?" It was answered, "It is Aldham Common, the place where you must suffer, and the people are come to look upon you." Then said he, "Thanked be God, I am even at home"; and so alighted from his horse, and rent the hood from his head.

Now was his head knotted ill-favouredly, and clipped much as a man would clip a fool's head; which cost the good Bishop Bonner had bestowed upon him when he degraded him. But when the people saw his reverend and ancient face, with a long white beard, they burst out with weeping tears, and cried, saying, "God save thee, good Dr. Taylor! Jesus Christ strengthen thee; the Holy Ghost comfort thee," with such other like godly wishes. Then would he have spoken to the people, but the yeomen of the guard were so busy about him, that as soon as he opened his mouth, one or other thrust a tipstaff into his mouth, and would in no wise permit him to speak.

Dr. Taylor, perceiving that he could not be permitted to speak, sat down, and seeing one named Soyce, he called him, and said, "Soyce, I pray thee come and pull off my boots, and take them for thy labour. Thou hast long looked for them, now take them." Then rose he up, and put off his clothes unto his shirt, and gave them away; which done, he said with a loud voice, "Good people, I have taught you nothing but God's Holy Word, and those lessons that I have taken out of God's blessed Book—the Holy Bible; and I am come hither this day to seal it with my blood." With that word, a certain yeoman of the guard, who had used Dr. Taylor very cruelly all the way, gave him a great stroke upon the head with a waster, and said, "Is that the keeping of thy promise, thou heretic?" Then he, seeing they would not permit him to speak, kneeled down and prayed, and a poor woman that was among the people stepped in and prayed with him, but they thrust her away, and threatened to tread her down with horses; notwithstanding, she would not remove, but abode and prayed with him. When he had prayed, he went to the stake and kissed it, and set himself into a pitch-barrel, which they had set for him to stand in, and so stood with his back upright against the stake, with his hands folded together, and his eyes toward heaven, and so he continually prayed.

After some painful delay, and some miserable insults from the Popish helpers who were assisting, the fire was lighted. Then says Fox:

Dr. Taylor, holding up both his hands, called upon God, and said, "Merciful Father of heaven, for Jesus Christ my Saviour's sake, receive my soul into Thy hands." So stood he still, without either crying or moving, until one struck him on the head with a halbert, so that his brains fell out, and the dead corpse fell down into the fire.

Thus died one of the best and bravest of the English martyrs. An old rude stone still marks the spot where he was burned, in the midst of an enclosed field, which once formed part of Aldham Common. It bears the following quaint but pithy inscription:

1555.
Dr. Taylor, in defending that
which was good, at this
place left his blood.

In the year 1819 another and more pretentious monument was erected on the same spot, with a long poetical inscription written by the Rector of Hadleigh. But the martyr's history is still remembered in the parish, without the aid of stones and monuments. "Being dead, he yet speaketh."[1]

---

[1] Hebrews 11:4.

Taylor's last parting wishes to his wife and family and parishioners were written in a book which he gave his son as a parting
legacy, only five days before his martyrdom. They can hardly fail to
interest the reader:

I say to my wife and to my children, The Lord gave you unto me,
and the Lord hath taken me from you and you from me: blessed
be the name of the Lord! I believe that they are blessed which die
in the Lord. God careth for sparrows, and for the hairs of our
heads. I have ever found Him more faithful and favourable than is
any father or husband. Trust ye, therefore, in Him by the means
of our dear Saviour Christ's merits. Believe, love, fear, and obey
Him: pray to Him, for He hath promised to help. Count me not
dead, for I shall certainly live and never die. I go before, and you
shall follow after, to our long home. I go to the rest of my
children—Susan, George, Ellen, Robert, and Zachary. I have
bequeathed you to the only Omnipotent.

I say to my dear friends of Hadleigh, and to all others which
have heard me preach, that I depart hence with a quiet conscience
as touching my doctrine, for the which I pray you thank God
with me. For I have, after my little talent, declared to others those
lessons that I gathered out of God's Book, the blessed Bible.
'Therefore, if I, or an angel from heaven, should preach to you
any other Gospel than that ye have received,' God's great curse be
upon that preacher!

Beware, for God's sake, that ye deny not God, neither decline
from the word of faith, lest God decline from you, and so do ye
everlastingly perish. For God's sake beware of Popery, for though
it appear to have in it unity, yet the same is vanity and anti-
Christianity, and not in Christ's faith and verity.

Beware of the sin against the Holy Ghost, now after such a light
opened so plainly and simply, truly, thoroughly, and generally to all
England.

The Lord grant all men His good and Holy Spirit, increase of
His wisdom, contemning the wicked world, hearty desire to be
with God, and the heavenly company; through Jesus Christ, our
only Mediator, Advocate, Righteousness, Life, Sanctification, and
Hope. Amen. Amen. Pray. Pray.

Rowland Taylor, departing hence in sure hope, without all
doubting of eternal salvation. I thank God, my heavenly Father,

through Jesus Christ, my certain Saviour. Amen. 5th of February, anno 1555.

"The Lord is my Light and my Salvation, whom then shall I fear?" "God is He that justifieth: who is he that can condemn?" "In Thee, O Lord, have I trusted: let me never be confounded."

Does any one wish to know whether the Church of Rome is infallible? Let him carefully study the history of such martyrdoms as that of Rowland Taylor. Of all the stupid and suicidal mistakes that the Romish church ever made, none was greater than the mistake of burning the Reformers. It cemented the work of the Reformation, and made Englishmen Protestants by thousands. When plain Englishmen saw the Church of Rome so cruelly wicked and Protestants so brave, they ceased to doubt on which side was the truth. May the memory of our martyred Reformers never be forgotten in England until the Lord comes!

Hugh Latimer (*c.* 1485–1555)

6

HUGH LATIMER: BISHOP AND MARTYR

THE name of Bishop Latimer is well known to all readers of English church history. There are, probably, few who have not read that more than 300 years ago there was such a Queen of England as "Bloody Mary"—and that men were burnt alive in her reign because they would not give up Protestantism—and that one of these men was Bishop Latimer.

But English churchmen ought to know these things better in the present day. They ought to become thoroughly familiar with the lives, the acts, and the opinions of the leading English Reformers. Their *names* ought to be something better than hackneyed ornaments to point a platform speech, and rhetorical traps to elicit an Exeter Hall cheer. Their *principles* ought no longer to be vague, hazy shadows "looming in the distance," but something clear, distinct, and well-defined before our mind's eyes. My desire is that men may understand that the best interests of this country are bound up with Protestantism. My wish is that men may write on their hearts that the well-being of England depends not on commerce, or clever politicians, or steam, or armies, or navies, or gold, or iron, or coal, or corn—but on the maintenance of the principles of the English Reformation.

The times we live in call loudly for the diffusion of knowledge about English church history. Opinions are boldly broached nowadays of so startling a nature that they make a man rub his eyes and say, "Where am I?" A state of feeling is growing up among us about Romanism and Protestantism, which, to say the least, is most unhealthy. It has increased, is increasing, and ought to be diminished. Nothing is so likely to check this state of feeling as the production of a few plain facts. If you want to convince a Scotchman, they say you must give him a long argument. If you want to convince an Englishman, you must give him plain facts. Facts are the principal commodity I have brought together in this biographical paper. If anyone expects to find in these pages private speculations or oratorical display, I am afraid he will be disappointed; but if anyone likes plain facts, I think I shall be able to supply him with a few.

Does any reader doubt who is a true member of the Church of England? Are you perplexed by the rise and progress of what are foolishly called "church views"? Come with me today and pay a visit to one of the fathers of the English church. Let us put into the witness-box one of the most honest and outspoken bishops of the days of the English Reformation. Let us examine the life and opinions of good old Latimer.

Does any reader doubt what is the true character of the Church of Rome? Are you bewildered by some of those plausible gentlemen who tell you there is no fundamental difference between the Anglican and Romish churches? Are you puzzled by that intense yearning after so-called "*catholic* principles," which distinguishes some misguided churchmen, and which exhibits itself in "*catholic* teaching," "*catholic* ceremonies," "*catholic* books of devotion," and "*catholic* architecture"? Come with me today, and turn over a few old pages in English history. Let us see what England actually was when Romish teachers instructed the English people and had things all their own way. Let us see what the Church of Rome does when she has complete power. Let us see how she treats the friends of an open Bible, of private judgment, and of justification by faith. Let us see how the Church of Rome dealt with Bishop Latimer.

I. Latimer's Times

In examining the history of Bishop Latimer, *the times in which he lived* demand attentive consideration. It is impossible to form a just estimate of a man's conduct unless we know the circumstances in which he is placed, and the difficulties with which he has to contend. No one is aware of the whole extent of our obligations to the noble band of English Reformers, who is not acquainted with the actual state of England when they began their work, and the amazing disadvantages under which that work was carried on.

Latimer was born in the reign of Henry VII. He lived through the reigns of Henry the VIII and Edward VI, and was put to death in the reign of Queen Mary. He began life at a period when Popery bore undisputed sway in this country. He witnessed the beginning of the breach between Henry VIII and Rome, and the establishment of a transition state of religion in England. He lived to see the full development of Protestantism under Edward VI, and the compilation of a liturgy and articles very slightly differing from those we have at this day. About each of these three periods I must say a few words.

(a) The first period of Latimer's life, when Popery was supreme in England, was a period of *utter spiritual darkness.* The depth of superstition in which our worthy forefathers were sunk is enough to make one's hair stand on end. No doubt, there were many Lollards and followers of Wycliffe scattered over the land, who held the truth and were the salt of the nation. But the fierce persecution with which these good men were generally assailed prevented their making much progress. They barely maintained their own ground. And as for the mass of the population, gross darkness covered their minds.

Most of the priests and teachers of religion were themselves profoundly ignorant of everything they ought to have known. They were generally ordained without any adequate examination as to learning or character. Many of them, though they could read their breviaries, knew nothing whatever of the Bible. Some, according to Strype, the historian, were scarcely able to say the Lord's Prayer, and not a few were unable to repeat the Ten Commandments. The prayers of the Church were in the Latin language, which hardly anybody understood. Preaching—there was scarcely any, and what there was, was grossly unscriptural and unedifying.

Huge nests of ordained men were dotted over the face of England, in the shape of abbeys and monasteries. The inhabitants of these beautiful buildings were seldom very holy and self-denying and were often men of most profligate and disreputable lives. Their morals were just what might have been expected from "fulness of bread and abundance of idleness."[1] They did next to nothing for the advancement of learning. They did nothing for the spread of

---

[1] Ezekiel 16:49.

true religion. Two things only they cared for, and those two were to fill their own pockets and to keep up their own power. For the one purpose they persuaded weak and dying people to give money and lands to the Church under the specious pretence that they would in this way be delivered from purgatory, and their faith proved by their good works. For the other purpose they claimed to hold the keys of the kingdom of heaven. To *them* confession of sins must be made. Without *their* absolution and extreme unction, no man could be saved. Without *their* masses no soul could be redeemed from purgatory. In short, *they* were practically the mediators between Christ and man; and to injure them was the highest offence and sin. Old Fuller tells us, for example, that in 1489, a certain Italian got an immense sum of money in England, by "having power from the Pope to absolve people from usury, simony, theft, manslaughter, fornication, and adultery, and all crimes whatsoever, except smiting the clergy and conspiring against the Pope."* Such were Romish priests in Latimer's youth, when Popery was last rampant in England. To say that they were generally ignorant, covetous, sensual, and despotic tyrants over the souls and bodies of men is not saying one jot more than the truth.

When priests in Latimer's youth were men of this stamp, we shall not be surprised to hear that the *people* were utterly ignorant of true religion. It would have been miraculous indeed if it had been otherwise, when they had neither sound preaching to hear nor Bibles to read. A New Testament could not be bought for less than £12 16s. 3d., and the buyer was in danger of being considered a heretic for purchasing it. The Christianity of the vast majority was naturally enough a mere name and form. The Sabbath was a day of sport and pastime, and not a day of solemn worship. Not one in a hundred perhaps could have rightly answered the question, "What shall I do to be saved?"[1] or given the slightest account of justification, regeneration, sanctification, the office of Christ, or the work of the Spirit. A man's only idea of the way to heaven generally was to do as the priest told him and to belong to "the true Church"![2] Thus the blind led the blind, and all wallowed in the ditch together.

---

* 1, p. 532. Tegg's edition.
[1] Acts 16:30.
[2] Direct quote from the "infallible" *Papal Syllabus of Errors.*

All the practical religion that the mass of the laity possessed, consisted in prayers to the Virgin Mary and saints, paying the priests to say masses, pilgrimages to holy places, and adoration of images and relics. The list of their superstitious practices would make an appalling catalogue. They hastened to the church for holy water before a thunderstorm. They resorted to St. Rooke in times of pestilence. They prayed to St. Pernel in an ague. Young women, desiring to be married, sought the help of St. Nicholas. Wives, weary of their husbands, betook themselves to St. Uncumber. One hundred thousand pilgrims visited the tomb of St. Thomas à Becket, at Canterbury, in one year in order to help their souls towards heaven. In one year at Canterbury Cathedral, there was offered at Christ's altar £3 2s. 6d.; on the Virgin Mary's, £63 5s. 6d.; and on Thomas à Becket's, £832 12s. 3d. The *images* worshipped were often gross cheats as well as idols. The *relics* worshipped were as monstrous and absurd as the images. As to the bones of saints, there were whole heaps which had been venerated for years, which proved at length to be bones of deer and pigs. These are dreadful things to tell, but they ought to be known. All these things the Church of Rome knew, connived at, sanctioned, defended, taught, and enforced on her members. This was the state of religion in England in the early years of the sixteenth century, when the English Reformers were raised up. This was English Christianity in the childhood and youth of Hugh Latimer!

(*b*) The second period of Latimer's life, during which England was in a state of transition between Romanism and Protestantism, presents many curious features. We see, on the one hand, a reformation of religion begun by a king from motives which, to say the least, were not spiritual. It would be absurd to suppose that a sensual tyrant like Henry VIII came to a breach with the Pope for any other reason than that the Pope crossed his will. We see his pretended scruples about his marriage with Catherine of Aragon bringing him into communication with Cranmer and Latimer.

We see him, at *one time*, so far guided by the advice of these good men that, like Herod, he does many things that are right and likely to advance the cause of the Gospel. He makes Cranmer Archbishop of Canterbury and shows him favour to the end of his days. He allows the Bible to be printed in English and placed in churches. He

commands images to be broken and puts down many gross superstitions. He boldly denies the doctrine of the Pope's supremacy. He
dissolves the monasteries and puts to open shame the wickedness of
their inmates. All this we see and are thankful.

We see him, at *another time*, defending Popish dogmas and
burning men who, like the martyr Lambert, denied them. We see
him putting forth the famous Six Articles, which reasserted transubstantiation, private masses, clerical celibacy, vows of chastity,
auricular confession, and the denial of the cup to the laity.[1] Worst
of all, we see in him the marks of a proud, self-willed, sensual man
all his life long, and an utter want of evidence that his heart was
ever right in the sight of God. The employment of a man who was
guilty of such inconsistencies, to do God's work, is among the deep
things of God's providence. We cannot understand it. We must
wait.

Turning, on the other hand, from Henry VIII to the first English
Reformers, we see in them strong indications of what Fuller calls
"a twilight religion." We see them putting forth books in Henry
the Eighth's reign, which, though an immense improvement and
advance upon Romish teaching, still contain some things which
are not scriptural. Such were *The Necessary Erudition*,[2] and the
Institution of a Christian Man.[3] We see them, however, gradually
growing in spiritual knowledge, perhaps unawares to themselves,
and specially as to the error of transubstantiation. We see them
continually checked and kept back, partly by the arbitrary conduct
of the King, partly by the immense difficulty of working side by
side with a Popish party in the Church, and partly by the great
ignorance of the parochial clergy. Nevertheless, on comparing the
end of Henry Eighth's reign with the beginning, we see plain proof
that much ground was gained. We learn to admire the overruling

---

[1] Passed in 1539, the Six Articles were much closer to Rome than were
the Ten Articles. For good reason they have been called the "bloody
Articles" and a "whip with six strings"—subscription to them was
enforced upon pain of death.

[2] Published in 1543 and generally known as the *King's Book*, this work
was a fully revised version of the *Institution of a Christian Man*.

[3] Published in 1537 and popularly known as the *Bishop's Book*, this was
a manual on Christian doctrine for the laity.

power of God, who can use a Henry VIII just as He did a Nebuchadnezzar or Sennacherib, for the accomplishment of His own purposes. And last, but not least, we learn to admire the patient perseverance of the Reformers. Though they had but little strength, they used it. Though they had but a small door open, they entered in by it. Though they had but one talent, they laid it out heartily for God and did not bury it in the ground. Though they had but a little light, they lived fully up to it. If they could not do what they would, they did what they could, and were blessed in their deed. Such was the second period of Latimer's life. Never let it be forgotten that, at this time, the foundations of the Church of England were excavated, and vast heaps of rubbish removed out of the way of the builders who were to follow. Viewed in this light, it will always be an interesting period to the student of church history.

(c) The last period of Latimer's life, which comprises the reign of Edward VI, is, in many respects, very different from the two periods to which I have already adverted. The cause of English Protestantism made immense progress during Edward's short but remarkable tenure of power. It was truly said of him by Hooker, that "He died young, but lived long, if life be action."

Released from the bondage of a tyrannical king's interference, Cranmer and his friends went forward in the work of religious reformation with rapid strides. Bonner and Gardiner were no longer allowed to keep them back. Refusing to take part in the good work, these two Popish prelates were deposed and put to silence. Faithful men, like Ridley and Hooper, were placed on the episcopal bench. An immense clearance of Popish ceremonies was effected. A liturgy was compiled, which differed very slightly from our present Prayer Book. The Forty-two Articles of religion were drawn up, which form the basis of our own Thirty-nine. The first *Book of Homilies* was put forth, in order to supply the want of preachers. An accuracy and clearness of doctrinal statement was arrived at, which had hitherto been unknown. Learned foreigners, like Bucer and Peter Martyr, were invited to visit England and appointed regius professors of divinity at Oxford and Cambridge. How much further the Reformers might have carried the work of reformation, if they had had time, it is useless now to conjecture.

Judging by the changes they effected in a very few years, they would probably have made our church as nearly perfect as a visible church can be, if they had not been stopped by Edward's premature death.

There was, however, one thing which the Reformers of Edward the Sixth's reign could not accomplish. They could not change the hearts of the parochial clergy. Thousands of clergymen continued to hold office in the Church of England, who had no sympathy with the proceedings of Cranmer and his party. There was no getting rid of these worthies, for they were ready to promise anything, sign anything, and swear anything in order to keep their livings. But while they yielded compliance to Cranmer's injunctions and commands, they were graceless, ignorant, and semi-Papists at heart. The questions which Bishop Hooper found it necessary to put to the Dean, prebendaries, and clergy of the diocese of Gloucester on his first visitation, and the answers which he received, furnish us with a sad illustration of the state of English clergymen in Edward the Sixth's time.[*]

Facts such as these are painful and astounding; but it is most important that we should know them. They explain at once the ease with which Bloody Mary restored Popery when she came to the throne. Parochial clergymen like those just described were not likely to offer any resistance to her wishes. Facts such as these throw great light on the position of Cranmer and the Reformers of Edward the Sixth's days. We probably have little idea of the immense difficulties both within and without which beset them. Above all, facts such as these give us some idea of the condition of religion in England even in the brightest portion of Latimer's times. If things like these were to be seen when Latimer was an old man, what must have been seen when he was young! If ignorance like this prevailed under Edward VI, how thick must the darkness have been under Henry VIII!

I must dwell no longer on the subject of Latimer's times. The subject has been already exhausted in Hooper's biography, and I do not wish to weary my readers by a dry and tedious repetition of facts. But I firmly believe that a knowledge of these facts is

---

[*] See Hooper's life, in this volume, page 81.

absolutely essential to a right understanding of the English Reformation, and I therefore hope that the few which I have given will not prove useless.

On calm consideration, I trust my readers will agree with me that it is the height of absurdity to say, as some do nowadays, that this country has been a loser by getting rid of Popery. It is really astonishing to hear the nonsense talked "about merry England in the olden times," the "mediæval piety," the "ages of faith," and the "devout habits of our catholic forefathers." Walter Scott's fascinating writings and Pugin's beautiful architectural designs have lent a false glare to Romanism in England, and induced many to doubt whether our Reformation really was a gain. The state of English society, which Scott has sometimes made so interesting by his pen, and Pugin by his pencil, is a far more beautiful thing in poems and pictures than it ever was in honest reality. Depend upon it, "distance lends enchantment to the view."[1] We may rest satisfied that Netley, and Glastonbury, and Bury, and Fountains, and Melrose, and Bolton abbeys, are much more useful now in ruins than they ever were in Henry the Seventh's days. Few Englishmen probably have the least idea how much we have gained by the Reformation. We have gained light, knowledge, morality, and religious liberty. Few have any clear idea of the fruits which grew on the tree of Popery when last it flourished in England. Those fruits were ignorance, superstition, immorality, and priestly tyranny. God was angered. Souls were lost, and the devil was pleased.

I trust again my readers will feel with me that it is most unfair to suppose that the acts and writings of the English Reformers under Henry VIII are any real criterion of their matured opinions. It is as unfair as it would be to measure the character of a grownup man by his sayings and doings when he was a child. Cranmer and his helpers under Henry VIII were in a state of spiritual childhood. They saw many points in religion through a glass darkly. It was not till the reign of Edward VI that they put away childish things. We must beware, therefore, lest any man deceive us by artfully-chosen quotations drawn from works published in the beginning of the English Reformation. Judge the Reformers, if you will, by their

---

[1] Quoted from *Pleasures of Hope*, by Thomas Campbell.

writings in the reign of Edward VI, but not by their writings in the reign of Henry VIII.

I trust, lastly, my readers will agree with me that it is most unreasonable to decry the early English Reformers as men who did not go far enough. Such charges are easily made, but those who make them seldom consider the enormous obstacles the Reformers had to surmount and the enormous evils they had to remove. It is nonsense to suppose they had nothing more to do than to pare the moss off an old building and whitewash it afresh. They had to take down an old decayed house and rebuild it from the very ground. It is nonsense to criticise their proceedings, as if they voyaged over a smooth sea with a fair wind and a clear course. On the contrary, they had to pilot the ship of true religion through a narrow and difficult strait, against current, wind, and tide. Put all their difficulties together—the arbitrary, profligate character of Henry VIII, and the tender years of Edward VI—the general ignorance of the population—the bitter enmity of dispossessed monks and friars —the open opposition of many of the bishops, and the secret indifference of a vast proportion of the clergy—put all these things together and weigh them well; and then I think you will not lightly regard the work that the early Reformers did. For my own part, so far from wondering that they did so little, I wonder rather that they did so much. I marvel at their firmness. I am surprised at their success. I see immense results produced by comparatively weak instruments, and I can only account for it by saying that "God was with them of a truth."[1]

II. Bishop Latimer's Life

The next branch of my subject to which I shall invite the attention of my readers is *the story of Bishop Latimer's life*. Hugh Latimer was born about the year 1485 at Thurcaston, near Mount Sorrel, in the county of Leicester. He has left such a graphic account of his father and family, in one of his sermons preached before Edward VI, that I must in justice give it in his own words. He says:

> My father was a yeoman, and had no lands of his own. He had only a farm of three or four pounds a year at the uttermost, and

---

[1] Paraphrase of 1 Corinthians 14:25.

hereupon he tilled so much as kept half a dozen men. He had walk
for one hundred sheep, and my mother milked thirty kine. He was
able, and did bring the King a harness, with himself and his horse,
when he came to the place where he should receive the King's
wages. I can remember that I buckled his harness, when he went
to Blackheath Field.[1] He kept me to school, or else I had not been
able to have preached before the King's majesty now. He married
my sisters with five pounds apiece, and brought them up in
godliness and the fear of God. He kept hospitality for his poor
neighbours, and some alms he gave to the poor.[*]

Such is the good Bishop's homely account of his own family. It is
only fair to observe that Latimer is one among the thousand
examples on record that England, with all its faults, is a country
where a man may begin very low, and yet live to rise very high.

Latimer was sent to Cambridge at the age of fourteen and in
1509 was elected a Fellow of Clare Hall. We know very little of his
early history, except the remarkable fact, which he himself has told
us, that up to the age of thirty he was a most violent and bigoted
Papist. Just as St. Paul was not ashamed to tell men that at one time
he was a "blasphemer, and a persecutor, and injurious,"[2] so the old
Protestant Bishop used often to tell how he too had once been the
slave of Rome. He says in one of his sermons, "I was as obstinate a
Papist as any was in England, insomuch that when I should be
made bachelor of divinity, my whole oration went against Philip
Melancthon and his opinions."[†] He says in another sermon, "All
the Papists think themselves to be saved by the law, and I myself
was of that dangerous, perilous, and damnable opinion till I was
thirty years of age. So long had I walked in darkness and the
shadow of death."[‡] He says in a letter to Sir Edward Baynton,

I have thought in times past that if I had been a friar and in a cowl,
I could not have been damned nor afraid of death; and by reason
of the same I have been minded many times to have been a friar,

[1] In 1497 an army of Cornish rebels was defeated at Blackheath.
[*] *Works*, I, p. 101. Parker's Society edition.
[2] I Timothy 1:13.
[†] *Works*, I, p. 334.
[‡] I, p. 137.

namely, when I was sore sick or diseased. Now I abhor my superstitious foolishness.*

Latimer's testimony about himself is confirmed by others. It is recorded that he used to think so ill of the Reformers that he declared the last times, the day of judgment, and the end of the world must be approaching. "Impiety" he said, "was gaining ground apace, and what lengths might not men be expected to run, when they began to question even the infallibility of the Pope?" Becon mentions that when Stafford, the divinity lecturer, delivered lectures in Cambridge on the Bible, Latimer was sure to be present, in order to frighten and drive away the scholars. In fact his zeal for Popery was so notorious that he was elected to the office of cross-bearer in the religious processions of the University, and discharged the duty with becoming solemnity for seven years. Such was the clay of which God formed a precious vessel meet for His work! Such were the first beginnings of one of the best and most useful of the English Reformers!

The instrument which God used in order to bring this furious Papist to a knowledge of Christ's truth was a student named Bilney. Bilney was a contemporary of Latimer's at Cambridge, who had for some time embraced the doctrines of the Reformation and was finally burned as a martyr at Norwich. He perceived that Latimer was a sincere and honest man, and kindly thought it possible that his zeal for Popery might arise from lack of knowledge. He, therefore, went boldly to him after his public onslaught on Melancthon and humbly asked to be allowed to make a private confession of his own faith. The success of this courageous step was complete. Old Latimer tells us, "I learned more by his confession than before in many years. From that time forward I began to smell the Word of God, and forsook the school doctors and such fooleries."† Bilney's conduct on this occasion seems to have been most praiseworthy. It ought to encourage everyone to try to do good to his neighbour. It is a shining proof of the truth of the proverb, "A word spoken in season, how good is it!"[1]

---

* I, p. 332.
† I, p. 335.
[1] Proverbs 15:23.

Hugh Latimer was not a man to do anything by halves. As soon as he ceased to be a zealous Papist, he began at once to be a zealous Protestant, and gave himself up, body, soul, and mind, to the work of doing good. He visited, in Bilney's company, the sick and prisoners. He commenced preaching in the University pulpits, in a style hitherto unknown in Cambridge, and soon became famous as one of the most striking and powerful preachers of the day. He stirred up hundreds of his hearers to search the Scriptures and inquire after the way of salvation. Becon, afterwards Chaplain to Cranmer and Bradford, afterwards Chaplain to Ridley, both traced their conversion to his sermons. Becon has left us a remarkable description of the effects of his preaching. He says: "None, except the stiff-necked and uncircumcised in heart, went away from it without being affected with high detestation of sin, and moved unto all godliness and virtue."*

The consequences of this faithful discharge of ministerial duty were just what all experience might lead us to expect. There arose against Latimer a storm of persecution. Swarms of friars and doctors who had admired him when he carried the cross as a Papist, rose up against him in a body when he preached the cross like St. Paul. The Bishop of Ely forbade his preaching any more in the University pulpits at Cambridge; and had he not obtained permission from Dr. Barnes to preach in the Church of the Augustine Friars, which was exempt from episcopal jurisdiction, he might have been silenced altogether. But the malice of his enemies did not stop here. Complaints were laid against him before Cardinal Wolsey, and he had more than once to appear before him and Tonstall, Bishop of London, on charges of heresy. Indeed, when the circumstances of the times are considered, it is wonderful that Latimer did not at this period of his life share Bilney's fate and suffer death at the stake.

But the Lord, in whose hand our times are, had more work for Latimer to do and raised up for him unexpected friends in high quarters. His decided opinions in favour of Henry the Eighth's divorce from Catherine of Aragon brought him into communication with Dr. Butts, the King's physician, and ultimately secured

---

* *Becon's Works*, vol. 2, p. 224. Parker's Society edition.

to him the favour and patronage of the King himself. In the year 1530 he was made one of the royal chaplains and preached before the King several times. In the year 1531 the royal favour procured for him an appointment to the living of West Kington, near Chippenham, in Wiltshire; and in spite of his friend Dr. Butts' remonstrances, he at once left court and went to reside upon his cure.

At West Kington, Latimer was just the same man that he had been latterly at Cambridge and found the devil just as busy an adversary in Wiltshire as he had found him in the University. In pastoral labours he was abundant. In preaching he was instant in season and out of season, both within his parish and without. This he had full authority to do, by virtue of a general license from the University of Cambridge. But the more he did, the more angry the idle Popish clergy round West Kington became, and the more they laboured to stop his proceedings. So true is it that human nature is the same in all ages. There is generally a dog-in-the-manger spirit about a graceless minister. He neither does good himself nor likes anyone else to do it for him. This was the case with the Pharisees: they "took away the key of knowledge: they entered not in themselves, and them that were entering in they hindered" (Luke 11:52). And as it was in the days of the Pharisees, so it was in the days of Latimer.

On one occasion the mayor and magistrates of Bristol, who were very friendly to him, had appointed him to preach before them on Easter Day. Public notice had been given and everybody was looking forward to the sermon with pleasure, for Latimer was very popular in Bristol. Suddenly there came out an order from the Bishop forbidding anyone to preach in Bristol without his license. The clergy of the place waited on Latimer and informed him of the Bishop's order, and then, knowing well that he had no such license, told him "that they were extremely sorry they were deprived of the pleasure of hearing an excellent discourse from him." Their hypocritical compliments and regrets were unfortunately ill-timed. Latimer had heard the whole history of the affair. And he knew well that these smooth-tongued gentlemen were the very persons who had written to the Bishop in order to prevent his preaching.

For four years, while Vicar of West Kington, the good man was subjected to a constant succession of petty worrying attacks and attempts to stop him from doing good. He was cited to London, and brought before Archbishop Warham, and detained many months from home. He was convened before Convocation and excommunicated and imprisoned for a time. But the protecting care of God seems to have been always round him. His enemies appear to have been marvelously restrained from carrying their malice to extremities. At length, in 1535, the King put a sudden stop to their persecution by making him Bishop of Worcester. That such a man should make such an appointment is certainly very wonderful. Some have attributed it to the influence of Lord Cromwell; some to that of the Queen Anne Boleyn; some to that of Dr. Butts; some to that of Cranmer, who was always Latimer's fast friend. Such speculations are, to say the best, useless. "The King's heart is in the hand of the LORD, as the rivers of waters: He turneth it whithersoever He will." (Prov. 21:1). When God intends to give a good man a high office, He can always raise up a Darius to convey it to him.

The history of Latimer's episcopate is short and simple, for it only lasted four years. He was the same man in a bishop's palace that he had been in a country parsonage or a Cambridge pulpit. Promotion did not spoil him. The mitre did not prove an extinguisher to his zeal for the Gospel. He was always faithful—always simple-minded—always about his Father's business—always labouring to do good to souls. Fox, the historian, speaks highly of "his pains, study, readiness, and continual carefulness in teaching, preaching, exhorting, visiting, correcting, and reforming, either as his ability could serve, or the times would bear." But he adds,

the days then were so dangerous and variable that he could not in all things do what he would. Yet what he might do, that he performed to the uttermost of his strength, so that, although he could not utterly extinguish all the sparkling relics of old superstition, yet he so wrought that though they could not be taken away, yet they should be used with as little hurt and as much profit as might be.

In 1536 we find Bishop Latimer appointed by Archbishop Cranmer to preach before the Convocation of the Clergy. No

doubt this appointment was made advisedly. Cranmer knew well
that Latimer was just the man for the occasion. The sermons he
preached are still extant and fully justified the Archbishop's choice.
Two more faithful and conscience-stirring discourses were probably
never delivered to a body of ordained men. They will repay an
attentive perusal.

> Good brethren and fathers, [he said in one place] seeing we are
> here assembled, for the love of God let us do something whereby
> we may be known to be the children of light. Let us do somewhat,
> lest we, which hitherto have been judged children of the world,
> prove even still to be so. All men call us prelates; then seeing we be
> in council, let us so order ourselves that we be prelates in honour
> and dignity, that we may be prelates in holiness, benevolence,
> diligence and sincerity.
>
> Lift up your heads, brethren, and look about with your eyes,
> and spy what things are to be reformed in the Church of England.
> Is it so hard, so great a matter, for you to see many abuses in the
> clergy, and many in the laity?

He then mentions several glaring abuses by name: the state of the
Court of Arches and the bishop's consistories—the number of
superstitious ceremonies and holidays—the worship of images, and
visiting of relics and saints—the lying miracles and the sale of
masses—and calls upon them to consider and amend them. He
winds up all by a solemn warning of the consequence of bishops
neglecting notorious abuses:

> God will come, [he says] God will come: He will not tarry long
> away. He will come upon such a day as we nothing look for Him,
> and at such an hour as we know not. He will come and cut us in
> pieces. He will reward us as He doth the hypocrites. He will set us
> where wailing shall be, my brethren—where gnashing of teeth
> shall be, my brethren. These be the delicate dishes prepared for
> the world's well-beloved children. These be the wafers and junkets
> provided for worldly prelates: wailing and gnashing of teeth. . . .
> Ye see, brethren, what sorrow and punishment is provided for you
> if ye be worldlings. If you will not then be vexed, be not the
> children of the world. If ye will not be the children of the world,
> be not stricken with the love of worldly things; lean not upon

them. If ye will not die eternally, live not worldly. Come, go to; leave the love of your profit: study for the glory and profit of Christ; seek in your consultations such things as pertain to Christ, and bring forth at last somewhat that may please Christ. Feed ye tenderly, with all diligence, the flock of Christ. Preach truly the Word of God. Love the light, walk in the light, and so be ye the children of light while ye are in this world, that ye may shine in the world to come, bright as the stars, with the Father, Son, and Holy Ghost.*

Such was a sermon before Convocation by Latimer.

In 1537 we find Bishop Latimer placed on the Commission of Divines for the publication of a book to set forth the truth of religion; the result of which Commission was *The Institution of a Christian Man*. The same year we find him putting forth some injunctions to the Prior of Worcester Convent, a monastic house not yet dissolved, in which, among other things, he commands the Prior to have a whole Bible in English chained in the church. He orders every member of the convent to get himself an English New Testament; he directs a lecture of Scripture to be read in the convent every day, and Scripture to be read at dinner and supper. Shortly afterwards he published injunctions to the clergy of his diocese, in which he commands every one of them to provide himself with a whole Bible, or at any rate with a New Testament, and every day to read over and study one chapter, at the least. He also forbids them to set aside preaching for any manner of observance, ceremonies, or processions and enjoins them to instruct the children in their respective parishes. All these little facts are deeply instructive. They show us what an Augean stable an English diocese was in Henry the Eighth's day, and what enormous difficulties a reforming bishop had to overcome.

In 1538 we find Latimer pleading with Lord Cromwell that Great Malvern Abbey might not be entirely suppressed. He suggests that it should be kept up, "not for monkery," which he says, "God forbid," but "to maintain teaching, preaching, study, and prayer;" and he asks whether it would not be good policy to have two or three of the old monastic houses in every county set apart for such

---

* *Works*, vol. 1, p. 50.

purposes. This was a very wise design and shows great foresight of the country's wants. Had it been carried into effect, Durham, St. Bees, St. Aidan's, Lampeter, King's College London, and the London College of Divinity would have been unnecessary. The rapacity of Henry the Eighth's courtiers, who had an amazing appetite for the property of the suppressed abbeys, made the suggestion useless.

In 1539 Bishop Latimer's episcopate was brought to an end by the enactment of the Six Articles already referred to, in which some of the leading tenets of Romanism were authoritatively maintained. He strenuously withstood the passing of this act, in opposition to the King and the Parliament; and the result was that he was compelled to resign his bishopric. It is related that on the day when this happened, when he came back from the House of Lords to his lodgings, he threw off his robes, and leaping up, declared to those who stood about him that he found himself lighter than he had been for some time.

The next eight years of Latimer's life appear to have passed away in forced silence and in retirement. We read little of anything that he did. We do not exactly know where he spent his time and whether he returned to his old living at West Kington or not. The probability is that he was regarded as a dangerous and suspected man and had much difficulty in preserving his life. The only certain fact we know is that he was at length committed to prison as a heretic and spent the last year of Henry the Eighth's reign in confinement in the Tower.

When Edward VI came to the throne in 1547, Latimer was at once released from prison and treated with every mark of respect. His old bishopric of Worcester was offered to him, and the House of Commons presented an address to the Protector Somerset, earnestly requesting that he might be reappointed. Old age and increasing infirmities made Latimer decline the proffered dignity, and he spent the next six years of his life without any office, but certainly not as an idle man. His chief residence during these six years was with his old friend and ally, Archbishop Cranmer, under the hospitable roof of Lambeth Palace. While here, he took an active part in all the measures adopted for carrying forward the Protestant Reformation. He assisted Cranmer in composing the first *Book of Homilies* and was also one of the divines appointed to reform the Ecclesiastical Law, a work which was never completed. All this time he generally preached twice every Sunday. In the former part of Edward the Sixth's reign, he preached constantly before the King. In the latter part he went to and fro in the midland counties of England, preaching wherever his services seemed to be most wanted, and especially in Lincolnshire. This was perhaps the most useful period of his life. No one of the Reformers probably sowed the seeds of sound Protestant doctrine so widely and effectually among the middle and lower classes as Latimer. The late Mr. Southey bears testimony to this: he says, "Latimer, more than any other man, promoted the Reformation by his preaching."

The untimely death of Edward VI and the accession of Queen Mary to the English throne in 1553, put an end to Latimer's active exertions on behalf of the Gospel. Henceforward he was called to glorify Christ by suffering, and not by doing. The story of his sufferings, and the noble courage with which he endured them, is admirably told in *Fox's Martyrs*—a book which all churchmen in these days ought to study.

As soon as Queen Mary came to the throne, one of the first acts of her government was the apprehension of the leading English Reformers, and Latimer was among the first for whom a warrant was issued. The Queen's messenger found him doing his Master's work as a preacher in Warwickshire, but quite prepared for prison. He had received notice of what was coming six hours before the messenger arrived, from a good man named Careless, and might easily have escaped; but he refused to avail himself of the opportunity. He said, "I go as willingly to London at this present, being called by my Prince to render a reckoning of my doctrine, as ever I went to any place in the world. And I do not doubt but that God, as He hath made me worthy to preach His Word to two excellent princes, so He will enable me to witness the same unto the third." In this spirit he rode cheerfully up to London and said, as he passed through Smithfield where heretics were generally burned, "Smithfield has long groaned for me."

Latimer was at once committed to the Tower, in company with Cranmer, Ridley, and Bradford, and for want of room, all the four were confined in one chamber. There these four martyrs, to use old

Latimer's words, "did together read over the New Testament with great deliberation and painful study," and unanimously agreed that transubstantiation was not to be found in it. From the Tower the three bishops were removed to Oxford, in 1554; and there, in 1555, Latimer and Ridley were burnt alive at the stake as obstinate heretics.

The old Bishop's behaviour in prison was answerable to his previous life. For two long years he never lost his spirits, and his faith and patience never failed him. Much of his time was spent in reading the Bible. He says himself, "I read the New Testament over seven times while I was in prison." Much of his time was spent in prayer. Augustine Bernher, his faithful servant, tells us that he often continued kneeling so long that he was not able to get up from his knees without help. Three things he used especially to mention in his prayers at this time. One was that as God had appointed him to be a preacher and professor of His Word, so He would give him grace to stand to His doctrine till his death. Another was that God would of His mercy restore the Gospel of Christ to the realm once again; he often repeated these two words, "once again." The third was that God would preserve the Princess, Elizabeth, and make her a comfort to England. It is a striking fact that all these three prayers were fully granted.

Latimer's conduct at his various trials and examinations before his Popish persecutors was in some respects wiser and better than that of the other martyrs. He knew well enough that his death was determined on, and he was quite right. Gardiner, the Popish Bishop of Winchester, had said openly that "he would have the axe laid at the root of the tree: the bishops and most powerful preachers ought certainly to die." Bonner, the Popish Bishop of London, had said, "God do so to Bonner, and more also, if one of the heretics escape me." Acting on this impression, Latimer told Ridley before the trial that he should say little. "They talk of a free disputation," said he, "but their argument will be as it was with their forefathers: 'We have a law, and by our law he ought to die.'"[1] Acting on this impression, he did little at his various trials but make a simple profession of his faith. He refused to be led away into lengthy

---

[1] John 19:7.

discussions about the opinions of the Fathers, like Cranmer and Ridley. He told his judges plainly, that "the Fathers might be deceived in some points;" and that he only "believed them when they said true, and had Scripture with them!" A wiser and truer remark about the Fathers was probably never made.

The death of old Latimer is so beautifully described by Fox, that I cannot do better than give the account as nearly as possible in his words. I certainly shall not try to spoil it by any additions of my own, though I must abridge it considerably.

> The place appointed for the execution [says Fox] was on the north side of Oxford, in the ditch over against Balliol College. For fear of any tumult that might arise to prevent the burning, Lord Williams and the householders of the city were commanded by the Queen's letter to be assistant, sufficiently armed; and when all things were in readiness, the prisoners were brought forth together, on the 16th of October, 1555.
>
> Ridley came first, in a furred black gown, such as he was wont to wear as a bishop. After him came Latimer, in a poor Bristol frieze frock, all worn, with his buttoned cap and handkerchief over his head, and a long new shroud hanging over his hose, down to his feet.
>
> Ridley, looking back, saw Latimer coming after, to whom he said, "Oh, are ye there?" "Yea!" said Master Latimer, "as fast as I can follow." At length they came to the stake one after the other. Ridley first entered the place, and earnestly holding up both his hands, looked towards heaven. Shortly after, seeing Latimer, he ran to him, embraced and kissed him, saying, "Be of good cheer, brother, for God will either assuage the fury of the flames, or else strengthen us to abide it."
>
> With that he went to the stake, kneeled down by it, kissed it, and prayed; and behind him Latimer kneeled, earnestly calling upon God. After they arose, one talked with another a little while, but what they said Fox could not learn of any man.
>
> Then they were compelled to listen to a sermon preached by a renegade priest, named Smith, upon the text, "Though I give my body to be burned, and have not charity, I am nothing."[1] They attempted to answer the false statements of this miserable

---

[1] 1 Corinthians 13:3

discourse, but were not allowed. Ridley said, "Well, then, I commit our cause to Almighty God, who shall impartially judge all." Latimer added his own verse: "Well, there is nothing hid but it shall be made manifest";[1] and said, "He could answer Smith well enough, if he might be suffered."

They were commanded after this to make ready immediately, and obeyed with all meekness. Ridley gave his clothes and such things as he had about him to those that stood by, and happy was he that could get any rag of him. Latimer gave nothing, but quietly suffered his keeper to pull off his hose and his other apparel, which was very simple. And now being stripped to his shroud he seemed as comely a person to them that stood by as one could desire to see. And though in his clothes he appeared a withered, crooked old man, he now stood quite upright.

Then the smith took a chain of iron and fastened it about both Ridley's and Latimer's middles to one stake. As he was knocking in a staple, Ridley took the chain in his hands, and said to the smith, "Good fellow, knock it in hard, for flesh will have its course." A bag of gunpowder was tied about the neck of each. Faggots were piled around them, and the horrible preparations were completed.

Then they brought a faggot kindled with fire, and laid it down at Ridley's feet, to whom Latimer then spake in this manner: "BE OF GOOD COMFORT, BROTHER RIDLEY, AND PLAY THE MAN; WE SHALL THIS DAY LIGHT SUCH A CANDLE, BY GOD'S GRACE, IN ENGLAND, AS I TRUST NEVER SHALL BE PUT OUT."

And so the fire being kindled, when Ridley saw the fire flaming up towards him, he cried with a loud voice, "Lord, into Thy hands I commend my spirit: Lord, receive my spirit!" and repeated the latter part often. Latimer, crying as vehemently on the other side of the stake, "Father of heaven, receive my soul!" received the flame as if embracing it. After he had stroked his face with his hands, and as it were bathed them a little in the fire, he soon died, as it appeared, with very little pain.

And thus much, [says Fox] concerning the end of this old blessed servant of God, Bishop Latimer, for whose laborious services, fruitful life, and constant death, the whole realm has cause to give great thanks to Almighty God.

---

[1] Mark 4:22

Latimer lived and died unmarried, and I am not aware that any English family at this day lays claim to any connection with him. But he left behind him a name far better than that of sons and daughters, a name which will be held in honour by all true English Protestants, so long as the world stands.

Of all the Marian martyrs, [says Fuller] Mr. Philpot was the best-born gentleman, Bishop Ridley the profoundest scholar, Mr. Bradford the holiest and devoutest man, Archbishop Cranmer of the mildest and meekest temper, Bishop Hooper of the sternest and austerest nature, Dr. Taylor had the merriest and pleasantest wit, but Mr. Latimer had the plainest and simplest heart.

III. Latimer's Opinions

I turn from the subject of Latimer's life to *his opinions*. I have given a brief sketch of his history, from his birth to his death. My readers will easily believe that I have left many things untold.

I might dwell on the good man's *preaching*. Few, probably have ever addressed an English congregation with more effect than he did. No doubt his sermons now extant would not suit modern taste. They contain many quaint, odd, and coarse things. They are very familiar, rambling, and discursive, and often full of gossiping stories. But, after all, we are poor judges in these days of what a sermon ought to be. A modern sermon is too often a dull, tame, pointless, religious essay, full of measured, round sentences, Johnsonian English, bald platitudes, timid statements, and elaborately concocted milk and water. It is a leaden sword, without either point or edge: a heavy weapon, and little likely to do much execution. But if a combination of sound gospel doctrine, plain Saxon language, boldness, liveliness, directness, and simplicity, can make a preacher, few, I suspect, have ever equalled old Latimer.

I might supply many proofs of his *courage and faithfulness as a minister*. He did not shrink from attacking anybody's sins, even if they were the sins of a king. When Henry VIII checked the diffusion of the Bible, Latimer wrote him a plain-spoken letter, long before he was a bishop, remonstrating with him on his conduct. He feared God, and nothing else did he fear. "Latimer, Latimer," he exclaimed at the beginning of one of his sermons, "thou art going to speak before the high and mighty King Henry

VIII, who is able, if he think fit, to take thy life away. Be careful what thou sayest. But Latimer, Latimer, remember also thou art about to speak before the King of kings, and Lord of lords. Take heed that thou dost not displease Him."

I might speak of his *unworldliness.* He gave up a rich bishopric, and retired into private life, for conscience' sake, without a murmur. He refused that same bishopric again, because he felt too old to fulfil his duties, when he might have had it by saying, "Yes." I might speak of his *genuine kindliness* of heart. He was always the friend of the poor and distressed. Much of his time, while he stayed at Lambeth, was occupied in examining into the cases of people who applied to him for help. I might speak of his *diligence.* To the very end of his life he used to rise at two o'clock in the morning and begin reading and study. All this, and much more, I might tell, if I entered into more particulars in this biography.

I trust, however, I have given facts enough to supply some faint idea of what the man was. I trust my readers will agree with me that he was one of the best bishops this country has ever had, and that it would have been well for the Church of England if more of her bishops had been like Bishop Latimer.

Let us never forget, as we think over the history of his life, that he is a glorious instance of the miracles which the grace of God can work. The Holy Spirit can take a bigoted, fierce Papist and make him a faithful Protestant. Where the hand of the Lord is, nothing is impossible. Let us never think that any friend, relative, or companion is too much opposed to the Gospel to become a true Christian. Away with the idea! There are no hopeless cases under the Gospel. Let us remember Latimer and never despair.

From all these topics, however interesting, I turn to one which is even more important in the present day. That topic is the nature of Latimer's theological opinions. For dwelling on this topic at some length I shall make no apology. The circumstances of the times we live in invest the subject with more than ordinary importance.

We live in days when very strange statements are made in some quarters, as to the true doctrines of the Church of England. Semi-Popish views about the rule of faith—about justification—about regeneration—about the sacraments—about preaching are continually urged upon the attention of congregations, while the advocates and teachers of these views are coolly arrogating to themselves the credit of being the only sound churchmen.

It is to no purpose that those who repudiate these semi-Popish views challenge their advocates to prove them by Scripture. The ready answer is at once given—that whether these views are scriptural or not, there can be no doubt they are "church views." It is to no purpose that we deny these views are to be found in the Articles, Liturgy, and Homilies of the Church of England, when honestly and consistently interpreted. We are quietly told that we know nothing about the matter. We are stupid! We are dense! We are blind! We are ignorant! We do not understand plain English! They are the true men! Their views are the *true* "church views"; and if we disagree with them, we must be quite wrong! In short, we are left to infer that, if we are honest and consistent, we ought to leave our dear old church and give it up to the extreme ritualists. I appeal to the experience of everyone who lives with his eyes open and marks the signs of the times. My readers know well I am describing things which are going on in every part of the land.

Now, as matters have come to this pass, let us see whether we cannot throw a little light on the subject by looking back 300 years. Let us inquire what were the views of the men who laid the foundations of the Church of England and are notoriously the fathers of the Articles, Homilies, and Liturgy. Let us put old Latimer into the witness-box today and see what his opinions were upon the points in dispute. An honoured member of the Church of England, at the period when doctrines of the Church were first brought into shape and form—a near and dear friend and adviser of Archbishop Cranmer—an assistant in the composition of the first *Book of Homilies*—a bishop whose orthodoxy and soundness were never called in question for a moment by his contemporaries—if any man knows what a true churchman ought to hold, Bishop Latimer must surely be that man. If his views are not *true* "church views," I know not whose are.

I ask my readers, then, to bear with me for a few minutes, while I give some extracts from Latimer's works. Quotations from old writers, I am well aware, are very wearisome and seldom read. But I want to inform the minds of Englishmen on the important question of the present day: Who is, and who is not a true churchman?

(1) Scripture

First of all, what did Bishop Latimer think about SCRIPTURE? This is a point with which the very existence of true religion is bound up. Some churchmen tell us nowadays, notwithstanding the Sixth Article, that the Bible alone is not the rule of faith and is not able to make a man wise unto salvation. No! it must be the Bible and the Fathers, or the Bible and catholic tradition, or the Bible and the Church, or the Bible explained by the Prayer Book, or the Bible explained by an episcopally-ordained man, but not the Bible alone. Now let us hear Bishop Latimer.

He says, in a sermon before Edward VI:

> I will tell you what a bishop of this realm once said to me. He sent for me and marvelled that I would not consent to such traditions as were set out. And I answered him, that I would be ruled by God's Book, and rather than depart one jot from it I would be torn by wild horses. I chanced in our communication to name *the Lord's Supper*. "Tush!" saith the Bishop. "What do you call the *Lord's Supper*? What new term is this?" There stood by him one Dr. Dubber. He dubbed him by-and-by, and said that this term was seldom read in the doctors. And I made answer, that I would rather follow Paul in using his terms than them, though they had all the doctors on their side.*

He says again, in his conference with Ridley:

> A layman, fearing God, is much more fit to understand holy Scripture than any arrogant or proud priest; yea, than the Bishop himself, be he ever so great and glistering in his pontificals. But what is to be said of the Fathers? How are they to be esteemed? St. Augustine answereth, giving this rule: that we should not therefore think it true because they say so, do they never so much exceed in holiness and learning; but if they be able to prove their saying by canonical Scripture, or by good probable reasons; meaning that to be a probable reason, I think, which doth orderly follow upon a right collection and gathering out of the holy Scriptures.
>
> Let the Papists go with their long faith. Be you contented with the short faith of the saints, which is revealed to us in the Word of God written. Adieu to all Popish fantasies. Amen! For one man having the Scripture, and good reason for him, is more to be

---

* *Works*, I, p. 121.

esteemed himself alone, than a thousand such as they, either gathered together, or succeeding one another. The Fathers have both herbs and weeds, and Papists commonly gather the weeds, and leave the herbs.*

I make no comment on these passages, they speak for themselves.

(2) Justification by Faith

In the next place what did Bishop Latimer think about *justification by faith?* This is the doctrine which Luther truly called the criterion of a standing or falling church. This is the doctrine which, in spite of the Eleventh Article of our church, many are now trying to obscure, by mingling up with it baptism, the Lord's Supper, our own works, and I know not what besides. Now let us hear Bishop Latimer.

He says, in a sermon preached at Grimsthorpe, Lincolnshire:

Christ reputeth all those for just, holy and acceptable before God, which believe in Him, which put their trust, hope, and confidence in Him. By His passion which He suffered, He merited that as many as believe in Him shall be as well justified by Him as though they had never done any sin, and as though they had fulfilled the law to the uttermost. For we without Him are under the curse of the law. The law condemneth us. The law is not able to help us. And yet the imperfection is not in the law, but in us. The law itself is holy and good, but we are not able to keep it, and so the law condemneth us. But Christ with His death hath delivered us from the curse of the law. He hath set us at liberty, and promised that when we believe in Him we shall not perish, the law shall not condemn us. Therefore let us study to believe in Christ. Let us put all our hope, trust, and confidence only in Him. Let us patch Him with nothing, for, as I told you before, our merits are not able to deserve everlasting life. It is too precious a thing to be merited by man. It is His doing only. God hath given Him to us to be our Deliverer, and to give us everlasting life.†

He says again, in another sermon:

Learn to abhor the most detestable and dangerous poison of the

---

* *Ridley's Works*, p. 114. Parker's edition.
† 2, p. 125.

Papists, which go about to thrust Christ out of His office. Learn, I say, to leave all Papistry, and to stick only to the Word of God, which teacheth that Christ is not only a judge but a justifier, a giver of salvation, and a taker away of sin. He purchased our salvation through His painful death, and we receive the same through believing in Him, as St. Paul teacheth us, saying, Freely ye are justified through faith. In these words of St. Paul, all merits and estimation of works are excluded and clean taken away. For if it were for our works' sake, then it were not freely, but St. Paul saith *freely.* Whether will you now believe St. Paul or the Papists?*

He says again, in another sermon: "Christ only, and no man else, merited remission, justification, and eternal felicity, for as many as will believe the same. They that will not believe it, shall not have it; for it is no more, but believe and have."†

Once more I say, these passages require no comment of mine. They speak for themselves.

(3) Regeneration

In the next place, what did Bishop Latimer think about *regeneration*? This, as you are all aware, is the subject of one of the great controversies of the day. Multitudes of churchmen, in spite of the Seventeenth Article, and the Homily for Whit Sunday, maintain that all baptized persons are necessarily regenerate, and receive grace and the Holy Ghost at the moment they are baptized. In a word, they tell us that every man, woman, and child who has received baptism has also received regeneration, and that every congregation in the Church of England should be addressed as an assembly of regenerated persons. Now let us hear Bishop Latimer.

He says in a sermon preached in Lincolnshire: "There be two manner of men. Some there be that be not justified, not regenerate, not yet in the state of salvation, that is to say, not God's servants. They lack the renovation, or regeneration. They be not yet come to Christ."‡

He says, in a sermon preached before Edward VI:

Christ saith, Except a man be born from above, he cannot see the

---

* 2, p. 147.
† 1, p. 421.
‡ 2, p. 7.

kingdom of God. He must have a regeneration. And what is this regeneration? *It is not to be christened in water,* as those firebrands expound it, and nothing else. How is it to be expounded, then? St. Peter showeth that one place of Scripture declareth another. It is the circumstance and collection of places that maketh Scripture plain. We be born again, says Peter, and how? Not by a mortal seed, but an immortal. What is the immortal seed? By the Word of the living God: by the Word of God preached and opened. Thus cometh in our new birth.*

He says, in another Lincolnshire sermon: "Preaching is God's instrument, whereby He worketh faith in our hearts. Our Saviour saith to Nicodemus, Except a man be born anew, he cannot see the kingdom of God. But how cometh this regeneration? By hearing and believing the Word of God: for so saith St. Peter."†

Once more I say, these passages require no comment of mine. They speak for themselves.

(4) The Lord's Supper

In the next place, what did Bishop Latimer think about the *Lord's Supper?* This, I need hardly say, is a subject about which very un-Protestant doctrine is often taught in the present day. Some around us, in the face of the Twenty-eighth Article, speak of this sacrament in such a manner that it is hard to see the difference between their doctrine and Popish transubstantiation or the sacrifice of the Mass. Now let us hear Bishop Latimer.

He says, in his disputation at Oxford:

In the sacrament there is none other presence of Christ required than a spiritual presence. And this presence is sufficient for a Christian man, as the presence by which we abide in Christ and Christ in us, to the obtaining of eternal life, if we persevere in the true Gospel. And this same presence may be called a real presence, because to the faithful believer there is the real and spiritual body of Christ.‡

He says, in the same disputation:

Christ spake never a word of sacrificing or saying of mass; nor

---

* I, p. 202.
† I, p. 471.
‡ 2, p. 252.

promised the hearers any reward but among the idolaters with the devil and his angels, except they repent speedily. Therefore, sacrificing priests should now cease forever: for now all men ought to offer their own bodies a quick sacrifice, holy and acceptable before God. The Supper of the Lord was instituted to provoke us to thanksgiving, and to stir us up by preaching of the Gospel to remember His death till He cometh again.[*]

He says, in his last examination:

There is a change in the bread and wine, and such a change as no power but the omnipotency of God can make, in that that which before was bread, should now have the dignity to exhibit Christ's body. And yet the bread is still bread, and the wine is still wine. For the change is *not in the nature but the dignity*.[†]

He says, in one of his Lincolnshire sermons:

Whosoever eateth the mystical bread, and drinketh the mystical wine worthily, according to the ordinance of Christ, he receiveth surely the very body and blood of Christ spiritually, as it shall be most comfortable to his soul. He eateth with the mouth of his soul, and digesteth with the stomach of his soul, the body of Christ. And, to be short, whosoever believeth in Christ, putteth his hope, trust, and confidence in Him, he eateth and drinketh Him. For the spiritual eating is the right eating to eternal life, not the corporal eating.[‡]

Once more I say, I make no comment on these passages. They speak for themselves. It would be easy to multiply quotations of this kind to an endless length, if it were necessary or desirable. There is hardly a controverted subject in the present day on which I could not give some plain, scriptural, sensible, sound opinion of Bishop Latimer.

(5) Preaching

Would my readers like to know what he thought about the ordinance of *preaching*? Did he think little of it, as some do in this day, and regard it as a means of grace very subordinate to sacraments and services? No, indeed he did not! He calls it "the office of

---

[*] 2, p. 256.
[†] 2, p. 286.
[‡] 1, p. 459.

salvation, and the office of regeneration." He says, "Take away preaching, and take away salvation." He says, "This office of preaching is the only ordinary way that God hath appointed to save us all. Let us maintain this, for I know no other." He declares that, "preaching is the thing the devil wrestled most against. It has been all his study to decry this office. He worketh against it as much as he can. He hath made unpreaching prelates, and stirred them up by heaps to persecute this office in the title of heresy."*

(6) Gorgeous Ceremonial and Candles in Churches
Would my readers like to hear what he thought about a *gorgeous ceremonial and candles in churches*? He says plainly that these things come from the devil.

> Where the devil is resident, and hath his plough going, there away with book and up with candles; away with Bible and up with beads; away with the light of the Gospel and up with the light of candles, yea, even at noonday. Where the devil is resident, that he may prevail, up with all superstition and idolatry, censing, painting of images, candles, palms, ashes, holy water, and now services of man's inventing.†

(7) The Foreign Reformers
Would my readers like to know what he thought about the *foreign reformers*? Did he lightly esteem them, as some do nowadays, because they did not retain episcopacy? No, indeed he did not! He says:

> I heard say, Melancthon, that great clerk, should come hither. I would wish him, and such as he is, to have £200 a-year. The King would never want it. There is yet among us two great learned men, Peter Martyr and Bernard Ochin, which have a hundred marks a-piece. I would the King would bestow a thousand pounds on that sort.‡

(8) Unity
Would my readers like to know what he thought about *unity*? Did he think, as some do now, that it is the one thing needful, and

---

* I, pp. 203, 155, 306, 349, 302.
† I, p. 71.
‡ I, p. 141.

that we should give up everything in order to attain it? No, indeed! He says, "Unity must be according to God's Holy Word, or else it were better war than peace. We ought never to regard unity so much that we forsake God's Word for her sake."*

(9) Councils and Convocations

Would my readers like to know what he thought about *councils and convocations*? Did he regard them as the grand panacea for all ecclesiastical evils, like those around us, whose cry is, "Give us synodical action, or we die"? He says to Ridley,

> Touching councils and convocations, I refer you to your own experience to think of our own country's parliaments and con-vocations. The more part in my time did bring forth the Six Articles. Afterward the more part did repeal the same. The same Articles are now again restored. Oh, what uncertainty is this!†

And he says, in another place, "More credence is to be given to one man having the Holy Word of God for him, than to ten thousand without the Word. If it agrees with God's Word, it is to be received. If it agrees not, it is not to be received, though a council had determined it."‡

(10) Thorough Going Protestant Preaching

Would my readers like to know what he thought of *thorough going Protestant preaching*? Did he think, as some do now, that if a sermon contains a good deal of truth, a little false doctrine may be excused and allowed? No, indeed he did not! He says:

> Many preach God's Word, and shall preach a very good and godly sermon, but at the last they will have a blanched almond, one little piece of Popery patched in to powder their matter with, for their own lucre and glory. They make a mingling of the way of God and man's way, a mingle-mangle, as men serve pigs in my country.§

I will not multiply these extracts, though it would be easy to do so. Those who have never studied the works of Latimer, published

---

* I, p. 487.
† Ridley, p. 130.
‡ Latim. I, p. 288.
§ I, p. 290.

by the Parker Society, have little idea of the loss they have sustained. They are rich to overflowing with pithy, pointed Protestant truths. I will only ask my readers to remember well those words I have been quoting, and when they were spoken.

These words were not spoken last year. They did not fall from the lips of modern evangelical or low church clergymen. They were not spoken by the ministers of Park Chapel, Chelsea; or of Portman Chapel; or the Lock; or Belgrave Chapel; or by some platform orator at Exeter Hall. No: the words I have quoted are more than 300 years old. They are the words of one of the best bishops the Church of England ever had. They are the words of the man who helped to compose our first *Book of Homilies*. They are the words of the friend and adviser of Archbishop Cranmer. They are the words of one whom king and Parliament delighted to honour.

Why was the speaker of these words not cast out of the Church of England? Why was he not reprimanded? Why was he not reviled as a man of low, unchurchman-like opinions? Why was he not proceeded against and persecuted for his views? How is it that he was persecuted only by Papists, but always honoured by Protestants? persecuted by Bonner, Gardiner, and Bloody Mary, but honoured by Cranmer, Ridley, and Edward VI?

I will give a plain answer to these questions. I answer them by saying that at the time of which I write, no man in his senses doubted that Latimer's opinions were the real opinions of the Church of England. I go on further to affirm that the truest and best members of the Church of England, at the present day, are those whose views are most in harmony with those of good Bishop Latimer. And I say that to tell men who love the Church of England with deep affection that they are not sound churchmen, merely because they agree with Latimer, and not with Laud, is to bring against them a most unfair and unwarrantable charge.

IV. Conclusion

And now let me conclude this biography of Latimer with two practical remarks.

(*a*) For one thing, let me earnestly exhort my readers, as individuals, *never to be ashamed of holding what are called "evangelical" views within the Church of England.* Listen not to those supercilious gentlemen, on the one side, who would have you believe that if you are not high churchmen, like themselves, you are no church-men at all. Listen not to those exceedingly kind friends, on the other side, who try to persuade you that the Established Church maintains Popish doctrines and ought to be left at once. Both these are ancient tricks. Against both these tricks be on your guard.

Do not be bullied out of the Church of England by the high churchman's assertion that you are only a tolerated party and have no business by his side. No doubt you live in a communion where great freedom of opinion is allowed. But to tell men of evangelical views that they are merely *tolerated* is a downright insult to the memory of the Reformers. Let us make answer to people who tell us so, that if they have forgotten Latimer and three hundred years ago, we have not. Let us say that we are not going to desert the church of Latimer, in order to please men who wish to lord it over God's heritage and have things all their own way. Sure I am that if might should ever prevail over right, and the friends of Latimer should be thrust out of the Church by force, and the House of Commons should be mad enough to sanction it—sure am I that the men thrust out would be better churchmen than the men left behind.

And do not be wheedled out of the Church by the arguments of men outside, who would probably be glad to be in it if they only saw the way. When the fox, in an old fable, could not reach the grapes, he said they were sour. When the fox, in another fable, lost his tail in a trap, he tried to persuade his friends that foxes did much better without tails and advised them to get rid of their own. Do not forget the moral of that fable; do not be enticed into biting off your own tails. Rest assured that with all its faults and defects the Church of England has very high privileges to offer to its members. Think well about these privileges. Do not be always poring over the defects. Resolve that you will not lightly cast these privileges away.

Above all, never, never forget that evangelical views are not only theoretically sound and agreeable to the mind of the Reformers, but that they are also of vital importance to the very existence of the Church of England. Never has our beloved church stood so low in this country as when evangelical views have been at zero, and almost forgotten. Never has she stood so high as when the views of Latimer and the Reformers have been honestly preached and carried out. So far from being ashamed of evangelical opinions, you may be satisfied that the maintenance of them is rapidly becoming a matter of life or death to your own communion. Take away Latimer's views, and I firmly believe the whole Establishment would collapse before the pressure from without, and come to the ground.

(*b*) For another thing, let me entreat all English readers of this biography to *beware of countenancing any retrograde movement in this country towards the Church of Rome, and to resist such movement by every possible means, from whatever quarter it may come.*

I am sure that this warning is one which the times loudly call for. The Church of Rome has risen up amongst us with renewed strength in the last few years. She does not disguise her hope that England, the lost planet, will soon resume her orbit in the so-called *catholic* system and once more revolve in blind obedience round the centre of the Vatican. She has succeeded in blinding the eyes of ignorant persons to her real character. She has succeeded in securing the unexpected aid of misguided men within our own Establishment. A hundred little symptom's around us tell us how real the danger is. Laud and the nonjurors are cried up, while Latimer and the Reformers are cried down. Historical works are industriously circulated in which Bloody Mary is praised and Protestant Elizabeth blamed. A morbid tenderness towards Romanists, and a virulent bitterness towards Dissenters have sprung up side by side. An unhealthy attention is paid to what is called mediæval taste. Thousands of tracts are sown broadcast over the land in which the three leading phrases to be seen are generally these three ominous words, *priest, catholic,* and *church.* The use of the rosary, auricular confession, prayers for the dead, and the Hail, Mary, are deliberately recommended to the members of the English church. Little by little, I fear, the edge of English feeling about Popery is becoming blunt and dull. Surely I have good reason to tell my readers to beware of the Church of Rome.

Remember the darkness in which Rome kept England when she last had the supreme power. Remember the gross ignorance and degrading superstitions which prevailed in Bishop Latimer's youth. Think not for a moment that these are ancient things, and that Rome is changed. The holy coat of Trèves, the winking picture at Rimini, the mental thraldom in which the Papal states have been kept, the notorious practices which go on in the Holy City to this day, are all witnesses that Rome, when she has the power, is not changed at all. Remember this and beware.

Remember the horrible persecutions which Rome carried on against true religion, when she last had uncontrolled sway in this country. Remember the atrocities which disgraced the days of Bloody Mary and the burning of Bishop Latimer. Think not for a moment that Rome is altered. The persecution of Bible readers in Madeira, and the imprisonment of the Madiai, are unmistakable proofs that, after three hundred years, the old persecuting spirit of Rome still remains as strong as ever. Remember this also and beware.

Shall we, in the face of such facts as these, return to the bondage in which our forefathers were kept? Shall we give up our Bibles or be content to sue for sacerdotal license to read them? Shall we submit ourselves humbly to Italian priests? Shall we go back to confessional-boxes and the idolatrous sacrifice of the Mass. God forbid! I say for one—God forbid! Let the dog return to his vomit. Let the sow that was washed return to her wallowing in the mire. Let the idiotic prisoner go back to his chains. But God forbid that Israel should return to Egypt! God forbid that England should go back into the arms of Rome! God forbid that old Latimer's candle should ever be put out!

Let us work, every one of us, if we would prevent such a miserable consummation. Let us work hard for the extension of pure, scriptural, and evangelical religion at home and abroad. Let us labour to spread it among the Jews, among the Roman Catholics, among the heathen. Let us labour not least to preserve and maintain it by every constitutional means in our own church.

Let us cherish, every one of us, if we would prevent the increase of Romanism, a brotherly feeling towards all orthodox Protestants, by whatever name they may be called. Away with the old rubbishy opinion that the Church of England occupies a middle position, a *via media*, between Dissent and Rome. Cast it away, for it is false.

We might as well talk of the Isle of Wight being midway between England and France. Between us and Rome there is a gulf, and a broad and deep gulf too. Between us and orthodox Protestant Dissent there is but a thin partition wall. Between us and Rome the differences are about essential doctrines and things absolutely necessary to salvation. Between us and Dissent the division is about things indifferent, things in which a man may err, and yet be saved. Rome is a downright open enemy, attacking the very foundation of our religion. Dissent ought to be an ally and friendly power; not wearing our uniform, nor yet, as we think, so well equipped as we are—but still an ally, and fighting on the same side. Let not this hint be thrown away! Let us keep up a kind, brotherly feeling towards all who love the same Saviour, believe the same doctrines, and honour the same Bible as ourselves.

Finally, let us pray, every one of us, if we would prevent the increase of Romanism; let us pray night and day that God may preserve this country from Popery and not deal with it according to its sins. It is a striking fact that almost the last prayer of good King Edward VI, on his deathbed, was a prayer to this effect: "O my Lord God, defend this realm from Papistry, and maintain Thy true religion." There was a prayer in the Litany of our Prayer Book, in 1549, which many think never ought to have been cast out of it. "From all sedition, and privy conspiracy—FROM THE TYRANNY OF THE BISHOP OF ROME, AND ALL HIS DETESTABLE ENORMITIES—from all false doctrine and heresy—from hardness of heart, and contempt of Thy Word and commandments, good Lord, deliver us!" To that prayer may we ever be able to say heartily, Amen, and Amen!

John Bradford (*c.* 1520–1555)

7

JOHN BRADFORD: MARTYR

JOHN BRADFORD, the famous English Reformer, who was burned at Smithfield for Christ's truth in Queen Mary's days, is far better known as a martyr than as a writer. The splendour of his death has eclipsed the work of his pen. Few perhaps have the least idea what a rich treasure of English theology is laid up in his literary remains.

This ought not so to be. Among the many goodly volumes published by the Parker Society, not a few, I suspect, sleep quietly on library shelves, unopened and uncut. Like ancient weapons of war, they are too ponderous for the taste of our day. Like guns and shells in Woolwich Arsenal, they are regarded as stores to be only used in special times of need. Yet some of these volumes will richly repay an attentive perusal, even in the nineteenth century. Latimer, Hooper, and Jewell should never be neglected. Side-by-side with these three men I am disposed to rank the two volumes of *Bradford's Works and Remains*, from which I propose to make some selections at the conclusion of this paper.

Some account of Bradford's life and death will prove a suitable preface to the extracts I shall give from his writings. It is to many an old story and well known, yet in days like these it is well to stir up men's minds by putting them in remembrance of the champions of the English Reformation. For a large portion of the information I give, I am indebted to a biography of Bradford, written by the Rev. Aubrey Townsend, and prefixed to the Parker Society's edition of *Bradford's Works*.

John Bradford, Prebendary of St. Paul's and Chaplain to Bishop Ridley, was born at Blackley, near Manchester, about the year 1520, and educated first at Manchester Grammar School. Fox records that he was—

"brought up in virtue and good learning even from his very childhood and, among other fruits of his good education, he obtained as a chief gift the cunning and readiness of writing, which knowledge was not only an ornament unto him, but also an help to the necessary sustentation of his living."

Baines, the historian of the county of Lancaster, also observes that Bradford, having received a liberal education at the free grammar school in Manchester, founded by Bishop Oldham, who died in 1519, attained there a considerable proficiency in Latin and arithmetic. To this early period of his life Bradford, writing from prison in the days of Mary, feelingly adverts:

"I cannot but say that I have most cause to thank thee for my parents, schoolmasters, and others, under whose tuition thou hast put me. No pen is able to write the particular benefits, which I have already received in my infancy, childhood, youth, middle age, and always hitherto. . . . I could reckon innumerable behind me, and but few before me, so much made of and cared for as I have been hitherto."

Fox records that Bradford, at a later period, "became servant to Sir John Harrington, Knight, [of Exton, in Rutlandshire,] who, in the great affairs of Henry VIII, and King Edward VI, which he had in hand when he was treasurer of the King's camps and buildings, at divers times, in Boulogne, had such experience of Bradford's activity in writing, of his expertness in the art of auditors, and also of his faithful trustiness, that, not only in those affairs, but in many other of his private business, he trusted Bradford in such sort, that above all others he used his faithful service." At the siege of Montreuil in particular, conducted by the English army under the Duke of Norfolk in the year 1544, Bradford discharged, under Sir John Harrington, the office of paymaster.

Three years later, not long after the accession of Edward VI, on the 8th April, 1547, Bradford entered the Inner Temple as a student of common law. His character then underwent a complete change. Twenty-seven years later, Sampson, his friend and fellow-student at the Temple, and who, it has been said, was the human means, under a higher power of that great transformation, writes, in his preface to *Bradford's Works*:

"I did know when, and partly how, it pleased God, by effectual calling, to turn his heart unto the true knowledge and obedience of the most holy Gospel of Christ our Saviour; of which God did give him such an heavenly hold and lively feeling, that, as he did then know that many sins were forgiven him, so surely he declared by deeds that he 'loved much.' For, where he had both gifts and calling to have employed himself in civil and worldly affairs profitably, such was his love of Christ and zeal to the promoting of His glorious Gospel, that he changed not only the course of his former life, as the woman did (Luke 7), but even his former study, as Paul did change his former profession and study.

"Touching the first, after that God touched his heart with that holy and effectual calling, he sold his chains, rings, brooches and jewels of gold, which before he used to wear, and did bestow the price of this his former vanity in the necessary relief of Christ's poor members, which he could hear of or find lying sick or pining in poverty. Touching the second, he so declared his great zeal and love to promote the glory of the Lord Jesus, whose goodness and saving health he had tasted, that,"* "with marvellous favour to further the kingdom of God by the ministry of His Holy Word, he gave himself wholly to the study of the Holy Scriptures. The which his purpose to accomplish the better, he departed from the Temple at London, where the temporal law is studied, and went to the University of Cambridge, to learn, by God's law, how to further the building of the Lord's temple."†

An incident occurred, while he was in London, which occasioned him deep anxiety. He "heard a sermon which that notable preacher, Master Latimer, made before King Edward VI, in which he did earnestly speak of restitution to be made of things falsely gotten." This "did so strike him to the heart" on account of a fraud, committed by his master, Sir John Harrington, which "was to the deceiving of the King," and which it would seem Bradford had concealed, "that he could never be quiet till by the advice of the same Master Latimer a restitution was made." That he had not been an interested party to this fraud would appear from his words to Bishop Gardiner, January 30th, 1555:

"My lord, I set my foot to his foot, whosoever he be, that can come

---

* Vol. 1. Preface by Sampson, A.D. 1574, pp. 31, 2.
† Foxe, *Acts*, &c., ed. 1583, p. 1603, or ed. 1843–9, Vol. 7. p. 143.

forth, and justly vouch to my face that ever I deceived my master: and, as you are chief justice by office in England, I desire justice upon them that so slander me, because they cannot prove it."

This was a challenge, which he could scarcely have ventured to make, if he had himself defrauded the government. It was through his firmness, in fact, that Sir John Harrington was compelled to make restitution to the King of the sums falsely obtained, in the two successive years, 1549 and 1550.

In the year 1548, Bradford became a student at Cambridge, first at Catharine Hall, and afterwards at Pembroke Hall, where he became a fellow. His letter describing his fellowship is curious and interesting.

"I am now a fellow of Pembroke Hall, of the which I nor any other for me did ever make any suit; yea, there was a contention betwixt the Master of Catharine's Hall [Sandys] and the Bishop of Rochester, who is Master of Pembroke Hall, whether should have me. . . . My fellowship here is worth seven pounds a year; for I have allowed me eighteen-pence a week, and as good as thirty-three shillings four pence a year in money, besides my chamber, launder, barber, &c.; and I am bound to nothing but once or twice a year to keep a problem. Thus you see what a good Lord God is unto me."

His friend Sampson graphically depicts Bradford's holy walk with God at this period:
"His manner was, to make to himself a catalogue of all the grossest and most enorme sins, which in his life of ignorance he had committed; and to lay the same before his eyes when he went to private prayer, that by the sight and remembrance of them he might be stirred up to offer to God the sacrifice of a contrite heart, seek assurance of salvation in Christ by faith, thank God for his calling from the ways of wickedness, and pray for increase of grace to be conducted in holy life acceptable and pleasing to God. Such a continual exercise of conscience he had in private prayer, that he did not count himself to have prayed to his contentation, unless in it he had felt inwardly some smiting of heart for sin, and some healing of that wound by faith, feeling the saving health of Christ, with some change of mind into the detestation of sin, and love of obeying the good will of God. . . . Without such an

inward exercise of prayer our Bradford did not pray to his full contentation, as appeared by this: he used in the morning to go to the common prayer in the college where he was, and after that he used to make some prayer with his pupils in his chamber: but not content with this, he then repaired to his own secret prayer and exercise in prayer by himself, as one that had not yet prayed to his own mind; for he was wont to say to his familiars, 'I have prayed with my pupils, but I have not yet prayed with myself.'

"Another of his exercises was this: he used to make unto himself an ephemeris or a journal, in which he used to write all such notable things as either he did see or hear each day that passed. But, whatsoever he did hear or see, he did so pen it that a man might see in that book the signs of his smitten heart. For, if he did see or hear any good in any man, by that sight he found and noted the want thereof in himself, and added a short prayer, craving mercy and grace to amend. If he did hear or see any plague or misery, he noted it as a thing procured by his own sins, and still added, *Domine miserere mei*, 'Lord, have mercy upon me.' He used in the same book to note such evil thoughts as did rise in him; as of envying the good of other men, thoughts of un-thankfulness, of not considering God in his works, of hardness and unsensibleness of heart when he did see other moved and affected. And thus he made to himself and of himself a book of daily practices of repentance."

At Cambridge, Bradford became intimate with Bucer, Sandys, and Ridley, and was tutor to Whitgift, afterwards Archbishop of Canterbury. He was ordained by Ridley in 1550 and strongly recommended to King Edward VI, on account of his high talents and piety. Shortly afterwards, by Ridley's advice, the King appointed him to be one of the six royal chaplains who were sent about England, with a kind of roving commission, to preach up the doctrines of the Reformation. Bradford's commission was to preach in Lancashire and Cheshire, being connected with those counties; and he seems to have performed his duty with singular ability and success. He preached constantly in Manchester, Liverpool, Bolton, Bury, Wigan, Ashton, Stockport, Middleton, and Chester, with great benefit to the cause of Protestantism, and with great effect on men's souls.

At the close of 1552, when Bradford was at Manchester, he "treated of Noe's flood," and often forewarned the people of "those plagues" which would be "brought to pass." And on the twenty-sixth of December, St. Stephen's Day, "the last time that he was with them," he preached a remarkable sermon from the twenty-third chapter of St. Matthew. The last six verses, the gospel for the day, was the text, no doubt, he selected on that occasion—a passage eminently suggestive of that solemn and prophetic warning which he then delivered. Local tradition even yet points to the spot in Blackley, where the country people say that Bradford, during that last visit to Manchester, knelt down and made solemn supplication to Almighty God. His request at the throne of grace was, that the everlasting Gospel might be preached in Blackley, to the end of time, by ministers divinely taught to feed the flock with wisdom and knowledge. The martyr's prayer, it is alleged, has been answered in the continuance, with scarcely an exception, of faithful men in that place.

Sampson informs us, that "besides often preaching in London and at Paul's Cross, and sundry places in the country, and especially in Lancashire, Bradford preached before King Edward VI, in the Lent, the last year of his reign, upon the second Psalm; and there in one sermon, showing the tokens of God's judgment at hand for the contempt of the Gospel, as that certain gentlemen upon the Sabbath day going in a wherry to Paris Garden, to the bear-baiting, were drowned, and that a dog was met at Ludgate carrying a piece of a dead child in his mouth, he with a mighty and prophetical spirit said, 'I summon you all, even every mother's child of you, to the judgment of God, for it is at hand:' as it followed shortly after in the death of King Edward."

This was, perhaps, the occasion which John Knox so well describes in his "Godly Letter," 1554:
"Master Bradford . . . spared not the proudest, but boldly declared that God's vengeance shortly should strike those that then were in authority, because they loathed and abhorred the true Word of the everlasting God; and amongst many other willed them to take ensample by the late Duke of Somerset, who became so cold in hearing God's Word, that, the year before his last apprehension, he would go to visit his masons, and would

not dingy himself from his gallery to go to his hall for hearing of a sermon. 'God punished him,' said that godly preacher, 'and that suddenly: and shall He spare you that be double more wicked? No, He shall not. Will ye, or will ye not, ye shall drink the cup of the Lord's wrath. *Judicium Domini, judicium Domini!* The judgment of the Lord, the judgment of the Lord!' lamentably cried he with a lamentable voice and weeping tears."

Bishop Ridley, writing from prison in the reign of Mary, speaking of Bradford, Latimer, Lever, and Knox, bears the strongest testimony to the boldness and faithfulness with which they addressed the courtiers of Edward:

"Their tongues were so sharp, they ripped in so deep in their galled backs, to have purged them, no doubt, of that filthy matter that was festered in their hearts of insatiable covetousness, of filthy carnality and voluptuousness, of intolerable ambition and pride, of ungodly loathsomeness to hear poor men's causes and to hear God's Word, that these men of all other these magistrates then could never abide."

Sampson represents forcibly Bradford's habits in private life:

"They which were familiar with him might see how he, being in their company, used to fall often into a sudden and deep meditation, in which he would sit with fixed countenance and spirit moved, yet speaking nothing a good space. And sometimes in this silent sitting plenty of tears should trickle down his checks: sometime he would sit in it and come out of it with a smiling countenance. Oftentimes have I sitten at dinner and supper with him, in the house of that godly harbourer of many preachers and servants of the Lord Jesus, I mean Master Elsyng, when, either by occasion of talk had, or some view of God's benefits present, or some inward cogitation and thought of his own, he hath fallen into these deep cogitations: and he would tell me in the end such discourses of them, that I did perceive that sometimes his tears trickled out of his eyes, as well for joy as for sorrow. Neither was he only such a practiser of repentance in himself, but a continual provoker of others thereunto, not only in public preaching, but also in private conference and company. For in all companies where he did come he would freely reprove any sin, and misbehaviour which appeared in any person, especially swearers, filthy talkers, and Popish praters. Such never departed out of his company unreproved. And this he did with such a Divine grace and Christian majesty, that ever he stopped the mouths of the gainsayers. For he spoke with power and yet so sweetly, that they might see their evil to be evil and hurtful unto them, and understand that it was good indeed to the which he laboured to draw them in God."

The consequences of Bradford's zeal for the principle of the Reformation, as soon as Edward VI died, were precisely what might have been expected. Within a month of Queen Mary's accession he was put into prison, like Cranmer, Ridley, Latimer, and Hooper and never left it until he was burned. His youth, his singular holiness, and his great reputation as a preacher, made him an object of great interest during his imprisonment, and immense efforts were made to reason him out of his Protestantism, and pervert him to the Romish church. All these efforts, however, were in vain. As he lived, so he died.

Sentence of condemnation was passed January 31, 1555. It was at first intended to deliver him forthwith to the Earl of Derby, to be conveyed into Lancashire, and there to be burned in the town of Manchester, where he was born. The original purpose was subsequently abandoned. The Romish bishops, whether from secret fear of Bradford's friends (for Bradford was in favour among his own people), or from some more secret confidence of overcoming his opinion, retained him at London for some months, assailing him during that time with frequent conferences and embassies. And it appears from some pages, first reprinted in the former volume of his works from his examinations, that the Earl of Derby took great interest in his case, and (it was alleged) obtained from the Queen the concession that he should "have his books, and time enough to peruse them."

On the day of Bradford's execution he was led out from Newgate to Smithfield about nine o'clock in the morning of July 1, 1555, amidst such a crowd of people as was never seen either before or after. A certain Mrs. Honeywood, who lived to the age of ninety-six and died about 1620, often told her friends that she remembered going to see him burned, and her shoes being trodden off by the crowd, so that she had to walk barefoot to Ludgate Hill.

The account of his martyrdom, as described by Fox, is so

touching that I shall give it in the martyrologist's own words. In the afternoon of June 30th,

"Suddenly the keeper's wife came up, as one half amazed, and seeming much troubled, being almost windless, said, 'O Master Bradford, I come to bring you heavy news.' 'What is that?' said he. 'Marry,' quoth she, 'tomorrow you must be burned, and your chain is now a-buying, and soon you must go to Newgate.' With that Master Bradford put off his cap, and lifting up his eyes to heaven said, 'I thank God for it; I have looked for the same a long time, and therefore it cometh not now to me suddenly, but as a thing waited for every day and hour; the Lord make me worthy thereof': and so, thanking her for her gentleness, departed up into his chamber, and called his friend with him, who when he came thither, he went secretly himself alone a long time, and prayed. Which done, he came again to him that was in his chamber, and took him divers writings and papers, and showed him his mind in those things, what he would have done; and, after they had spent the afternoon till night in many and sundry such things, at last came to him half a dozen of his friends more, with whom all the evening he spent the time in prayer and other good exercises, so wonderfully that it was marvellous to hear and see his doings.

"A little before he went out of the Compter, he made a notable prayer of his farewell, with such plenty of tears, and abundant spirit of prayer, that it ravished the minds of the hearers. Also when he shifted himself with a clean shirt, that was made for his burning (by one Master Walter Marlar's wife, who was a good nurse unto him, and his very good friend), he made such a prayer of the wedding garment, that some of those that were present were in such great admiration, that their eyes were as thoroughly occupied in looking on him, as their ears gave place to hear his prayer. At his departing out of the chamber, he made likewise a prayer, and gave money to every servant and officer of the house, with exhortation to them to fear and serve God continually labouring to eschew all manner of evil. That done, he turned him to the wall, and prayed vehemently, that his words might not be spoken in vain, but that the Lord would work the same in them effectually, for his Christ's sake. Then being beneath in the court all the prisoners cried out to him, and bid him farewell, as the rest of the house had done before with weeping tears.

"The time they carried him to Newgate was about eleven or twelve o'clock in the night, when it was thought none would be stirring abroad; and yet, contrary to their expectation in that behalf, was there in Cheapside, and other places between the Compter and Newgate, a great multitude of people that came to see him, which most gently bade him farewell, praying for him with most lamentable and pitiful tears; and he again as gently bade them farewell, praying most heartily for them and their welfare. Now whether it were a commandment from the Queen and her council, or from Bonner and his adherents, or whether it were merely devised of the Lord Mayor, Alderman, and sheriffs of London, or no, I cannot tell; but a great noise there was overnight about the city by divers, that Bradford should be burnt the next day in Smithfield, by four of the clock in the morning, before it should be greatly known to any . . . But . . . the people prevented the device suspected: for the next day," Monday, July 1, "at the said hour of four o'clock in the morning, there was in Smithfield such a multitude of men and women, that many being in admiration thereof thought it was not possible that they could have warning of his death, being so great a number in so short a time, unless it were by the singular providence of Almighty God.

"Well, this took not effect as the people thought; for that morning it was nine o'clock of the day before Master Bradford was brought into Smithfield; which, in going through Newgate thitherward, spied a friend of his whom he loved, standing on the one side [of] the way to the keeper's houseward, unto whom he reached his hand over the people, and plucked him to him, and delivered to him from his head his velvet night-cap, and also his handkerchief, with other things besides. . . . After a little secret talk with him, and each of them parting from other, immediately came to him a brother-in-law of his, called Roger Beswick, which, as soon as he had taken the said Bradford by the hand, one of the sheriffs of London, called Woodrofe, came with his staff, and brake the said Roger's head, that the blood ran about his shoulders; which sight Bradford beholding with grief bade his brother farewell, willing [him] to commend him to his mother and the rest of his friends, and to get him to some surgeon betimes: and so they, departing, had little or no talk at all together. Then was he led forth to Smithfield with a great company of weaponed men, to conduct him thither, as the like was not seen at no man's burning: for in every corner of Smithfield there were some, besides those which stood about the stake. Bradford then, being come to the place, fell flat to the ground, secretly making his prayers to Almighty God." And he "lying prostrate on the one side of the stake, and a young man, an apprentice, John Leaf, who suffered with him on the other side, they lay flat on their faces, praying to themselves the space of a minute of an hour. Then one of the sheriffs said to Master Bradford, 'Arise, and make an end; for the press of the people is great.'

"At that word they both stood up upon their feet; and then Master Bradford took a faggot in his hand, and kissed it, and so likewise the stake. And, when he had so done, he desired of the sheriffs that his servant might have his raiment; 'for,' said he, 'I have nothing else to give him, and besides that he is a poor man.' And the sheriff said he should have it. And so forthwith Master Bradford did put off his raiment, and went to the stake; and, holding up his hands, and casting his countenance up to heaven, he said thus, 'O England, England, repent thee of thy sins, repent thee of thy sins. Beware of idolatry, beware of false antichrists: take heed they do not deceive you.' And, as he was speaking these words, the sheriff bade tie his hands, if he would not be quiet, 'O Master Sheriff,' said Master Bradford, 'I am quiet: God forgive you this, Master Sheriff.' And one of the officers which made the fire, hearing Master Bradford so speaking to the sheriff, said, 'If you have no better learning than that, you are but a fool, and were best to hold your peace.' To the which words Master Bradford gave no answer, but asked all the world forgiveness, and forgave all the world, and prayed the people to pray for him, and turned his head unto the young man that suffered with him, and said, 'Be of good comfort, brother; for we shall have a merry supper with the Lord this night;' and so spake no more words that any man did hear, but embracing the reeds said thus, 'Strait is the way, and narrow is the gate, that leadeth to eternal salvation, and few there be that find it.'"

The Burning of Master John Bradford and John Leaf

There seems to have been something peculiarly beautiful and attractive in Bradford's character, exceeding that of any of the Reformers.

Fuller remarks: "It is a demonstration to me that he was of a sweet temper because Parsons, who will hardly afford a good word to a Protestant, saith 'that he seemed to be of a more soft and mild nature than many of his fellows.' Indeed he was a most holy and mortified man, who secretly in his closet would so weep for his sins, one would have thought he would never have smiled again; and then, appearing in public, he would be so harmlessly pleasant, one would think he had never wept before."

The familiar story, that, on seeing evil-doers taken to the place of execution, he was wont to exclaim, "But for the grace of God there goes John Bradford," is a universal tradition, which has overcome the lapse of time. And Venning, writing in 1653, desirous to show that, "by the sight of others' sins, men may learn to bewail their own sinfulness and heart of corruption," instances the case of Bradford, who, "when he saw any drunk or heard any swear, &c., would railingly complain, 'Lord, I have a drunken head; Lord, I have a swearing heart.'"

His personal appearance and daily habits are graphically described by Fox:

"He was, of person, a tall man, slender, spare of body, somewhat a faint sanguine colour, with an auburn beard. He slept not commonly above four hours a night; and in his bed, till sleep came, his book went not out of his hand. . . . His painful diligence, reading, and prayer, I might almost account it his whole life. He did not eat above one meal a day, which was but very little when he took it; and his continual study was upon his knees. In the midst of dinner he used oftentimes to muse with himself, having his hat over his eyes, from whence came commonly plenty of tears, dropping on his trencher. Very gentle he was to man and child. . . . His chief recreation was, in no gaming or other pastime, but only in honest company and comely talk, wherein he would spend a little leisure after dinner at the board, and so to prayer and his book again. He counted that hour not well-spent, wherein he did not some good, either with his pen, study, or exhortation to others."

Mr. Townsend concludes his excellent biography with the following passage, which is so true and good that I give it in its entirety:

> He may be said to have lived a long life in a short space of time.
> From his ordination as deacon to the hour of martyrdom he was
> only permitted to exercise the ministerial office for five years, of
> which no fewer than two were passed in prison. Until the great
> day, when the secrets of all hearts shall be revealed, it cannot be
> fully known to what extent England has been indebted to the
> labours and the prayers of this devouted man. "Certainly he was
> neither the least able nor the least learned" of the fathers of the
> English church. He happily combined judgment with "learning
> elocution, sweetness of temper, and profound devotion toward
> God: . . . and of his worth the Papists themselves were so
> sensible, that they took more pains to bring him off from the
> profession of religion than any other." Had Edward longer
> occupied the English throne Bradford would have been raised to
> the episcopal bench. He obtained from the great Bishop of souls a
> higher promotion. By the holiness of his life and the testimony of
> his writings "he yet speaketh." By the flames of martyrdom
> "Bradford and Latimer, Cranmer and Ridley, four prime pillars of
> the Reformed Church of England," have, through the grace of
> God, lighted such a candle in this country as shall never be
> extinguished.

Bradford's literary remains occupy about 1,100 pages, and fill two
8vo volumes of the Parker Society's series. They consist chiefly of
sermons, short treatises, meditations, prayers, declarations, exhor-
tations, and letters. All are good, and all deserve reading. If I must
pick out any of his writings as specially good, I would name his
controversial treatises, entitled, *A Confutation of a few Romish
Doctrines*, and *The Hurt of Hearing Mass*; his sermons on repentance
and the Lord's Supper; his *Treatise Against the Fear of Death*; and his
Farewells to London, Cambridge, Lancashire, Cheshire, etc. Above
all, I commend his 100 letters to friends. He that can read any of
the above-mentioned writings without feeling his soul stirred
within him must be in an unsatisfactory condition. To my mind,
there is not only scriptural soundness in all that Bradford writes,
but a peculiar fire, unction, warmth, and directness, which entitle
him to a very high rank among Christian authors. Had he lived

longer and written more, one fancies it would have been an immense blessing to the Church.

(1) My first extract shall be taken from Bradford's *Treatise against the Fear of Death*:

Some man will say, O Sir, if I were certain that I should depart from this miserable life into that so great felicity, then could I be right glad, and rejoice as you will me, and bid death welcome. But I am a sinner; I have grievously transgressed and broken God's will; and therefore I am afraid I shall be sent into eternal woe, perdition, and misery.

Here, my brother, thou dost well that thou dost acknowledge thyself a sinner, and to have deserved eternal death; for, doubtless, "if we say we have no sin, we are liars, and the truth is not in us." A child of a night's birth is not pure in God's sight. In sin were we born, and "by birth (or nature) we are the children of wrath" and firebrands of hell: therefore, confess ourselves to be sinners we needs must; for "if the Lord will observe any man's iniquities, none shall be able to abide it:" yea, we must needs all cry, "Enter not into judgment, O Lord; for in Thy sight no flesh or man living can be saved." In this point, therefore, thou hast done well to confess thyself a sinner.

But now when thou standest in doubt of pardon of thy sins, and thereby art afraid of damnation, my dear brother, I would have thee answer me one question—that is, "Whether thou desirest pardon or no; whether thou dost repent or no; whether thou dost unfeignedly purpose, if thou shouldest live, to amend thy life or no?" If thou dost, even before God, so purpose, so desirest His mercy, then hearken, my good brother, what the Lord saith unto thee:

"I am He, that for Mine own sake will do away thine offences." "If thy sins be as red as scarlet, they shall be made as white as snow;" for "I have no pleasure in the death of a sinner." "As surely as I live, I will not thy death; but rather that thou shouldest live and be converted." I "have so loved the world," that I would not spare My dearly beloved Son, the image of My substance and brightness of My glory, "by whom all things are made," by whom all things were given; but gave Him for thee, not only to be man, but also to take thy nature, and to purge it from mortality, sin, and all corruption, and to adorn and endue it with immortality and eternal glory, not only in His own person, but also in thee and for thee: whereof now by faith I would have thee certain, as in very deed thou shalt at length feel and fully enjoy for ever. This My Son I have given to the death, and that a most shameful death, "even of the cross," for thee "to destroy death," to satisfy My justice for thy sins; therefore "believe," and "according to thy faith, so be it unto thee."

Hearken what my Son Himself saith to thee: "Come unto Me all ye that labour, and are heavy laden, and I will refresh you"; "I came not into the world to damn the world, but to save it. I came not to call the righteous, but sinners to repentance." "I pray not," saith He, "for these Mine apostles only, but also for all them that by their preaching shall believe in Me." Now what prayed He for such? "Father," saith He, "I will that where I am they may also be, that they may see and enjoy the glory I have, and always had with Thee. Father, save them and keep them in Thy truth." "Father," saith He, "I sanctify Myself, and offer up Myself for them." Lo, thus thou hearest how My Son prayeth for thee.

Mark now what My apostle Paul saith: "We know," saith he, "that our Saviour Christ's prayers were heard;" also, "This is a true saying, that Jesus Christ came into the world to save sinners." Hearken what he saith to the jailer, "Believe in the Lord Jesus Christ, and thou shalt be saved;" for He, by His own self, hath "made purgation for our sins." "To Him," saith Peter, "bear all the prophets witness, that whosoever believeth in His name shall receive remission of their sins." "Believe," man. Pray, "Lord, help mine unbelief;" "Lord, increase my faith." "Ask, and thou shalt have." Hearken what St. John saith: "If we confess our sins, God is righteous to forgive us all our iniquities; and the blood of our Lord Jesus Christ shall cleanse us from all our sins;" for, "if we sin, we have an Advocate," saith he, "with the Father, Jesus Christ the righteous, and He is the propitiation for our sins." Hearken what Christ is called: "Call His name Jesus," saith the angel; "for He shall save His people from their sins:" so that "where abundance of sin is, there is abundance of grace."

Say, therefore, "Who shall lay anything to my charge? It is God that absolveth me, Who then shall condemn me? It is Christ which is dead for my sins, yea, which is risen for my righteousness, and sitteth on the right hand of the Father, and prayeth for me." Be certain, therefore, and sure of pardon of thy sins; be certain and sure of everlasting life. Do not say in thy heart, "Who shall descend into the deep?" that is, doubt not of pardon of thy sins, for that is to fetch up Christ. Neither say thou, "Who shall ascend up into heaven?" that is, doubt not of eternal bliss, for that is to put Christ out of heaven. But mark what the Lord saith unto thee, "The Word is nigh thee, even in thy mouth and in thy heart; and this is the word of faith which we preach: If thou confess with thy mouth that Jesus Christ is the Lord, and believe with thy heart that God raised Him up from the dead, thou shalt be safe." If thou believe that Jesus Christ died and rose again," even so shalt thou be assured, saith the Lord God, that "dying with Christ, I will bring thee again with Him."

Thus, dear brother, I thought good to write to thee, in the name of the Lord, that thou, fearing death for nothing else but because of thy sins, mightest be assured of pardon of them; and so embrace death as a dear friend, and insult against his terror, sting, and power; saying, "Death, where is thy sting? Hell, where is thy victory?" Nothing in all the world so displeaseth the Lord as to doubt His mercy. In the mouth of two or three witnesses we should be content; therefore, in that thou hast heard so many witnesses, how that indeed desiring mercy with the Lord, thou art not sent empty away, give credit thereto, and say with the good Virgin Mary, "Behold Thy servant, O Lord; be it unto me according to Thy word."*

(2) My second extract shall be taken from Bradford's *Farewell to Lancashire and Cheshire*:

When I consider the cause of my condemnation, I cannot but lament that I do no more rejoice than I do, for it is God's verity and truth. The condemnation is not a condemnation of Bradford simply, but rather a condemnation of Christ and His truth. Bradford is nothing else but an instrument, in whom Christ and His doctrine are condemned; and, therefore, my dearly beloved, rejoice, rejoice, and give thanks, with me, and for me, that ever God did vouchsafe so great a benefit to our country, as to choose the most unworthy (I mean myself) to be one in whom it would

---

* Vol. 1, page 342, Parker Society's edition.

please Him to suffer any kind of affliction, much more this violent kind of death, which I perceive is prepared for me with you for His sake. All glory and praise be given unto God our Father for this His exceeding great mercy towards me, through Jesus Christ our Lord. Amen.

But perchance you will say unto me, "What is the cause for the which you are condemned? We hear say that ye deny all presence of Christ in His holy Supper, and so make it a bare sign and common bread, and nothing else." My dearly beloved, what is said of me, and will be, I cannot tell. It is told me that Master Pendleton is gone down to preach to you, not as he once recanted (for you all know how he hath preached contrary to that he was wont to preach afore I came amongst you), but to recant that which he hath recanted. How he will speak of me, and report before I come, when I come, and when I am burned, I much pass not; for he that is so uncertain, and will speak so often against himself, I cannot think he will speak well of me, except it make for his purpose and profit: but of this enough.

Indeed, the chief thing I am condemned for as an heretic is, because I deny the sacrament of the altar, which is not Christ's Supper, but a plain perverting of it (being used, as the Papists now use it, to be a real, natural, and corporal presence of Christ's body and blood, under the forms and accidents of bread and wine): that is, because I deny transubstantiation, which is the darling of the devil, and daughter and heir to Antichrist's religion, whereby the Mass is maintained, Christ's Supper perverted, the ministry taken away, repentance repelled, and all true godliness abandoned.

In the Supper of our Lord, or sacrament of Christ's body and blood, I confess and believe that there is a true and very presence of whole Christ, God and Man, to the faith of the receiver (but not of the stander by or looker on), as there is a very true presence of bread and wine to the senses of him that is partaker thereof. This faith, this doctrine, which consenteth with the Word of God, and with the true testimony of Christ's Church, which the Popish church doth persecute, will I not forsake; and therefore am I condemned as an heretic, and shall be burned.

But, my dearly beloved, this truth (which I have taught and you have received, I believed and do believe, and therein give my life), I hope in God, shall never be burned, bound, nor overcome, but shall triumph, victory, and be at liberty, maugre the head of all God's adversaries. For there is no counsel against the Lord, nor no device of man can be able to defeat the verity in any other than in such as be "children of unbelief," which have no 'love to the truth,' and, therefore, are given up to believe lies. From which plague the Lord of mercies deliver you and all this realm, my dear hearts in the Lord, I humbly beseech His mercy. Amen.*

(3) My third and last extract shall be taken from a letter written by Bradford to Francis Russell, Earl of Bedford, in the year 1551:

You have cause, my good lord, to be thankful. For look upon your vocation, I pray you, and tell me how many noblemen, earls' sons, lords, knights, and men of estimation hath God in this realm of England dealt thus withal. I daresay you think not you have deserved this. Only God's mercy in Christ hath wrought this on you, as He did in Jeremy's time on Ebedmelech, in Ahab's time on Obadias, in Christ's time on Joseph of Arimathea, in the Apostles' time on Sergius Paulus and the Queen Candace's chamberlain. Only now be thankful, and continue, continue, continue, my good lord, continue to confess Christ. Be not ashamed of Him before men, for then will not He be ashamed of you. Now will He try you: stick fast unto Him, and He will stick fast by you; He will be with you in trouble and deliver you. But then you must cry unto Him, for so it proceedeth: "He cried unto Me, and I heard: I was with him in trouble."

Remember Lot's wife, which looked back; remember Francis Spira; remember that "none is crowned, except he strive lawfully." Remember that all you have is at Christ's commandment. Remember He lost more for you than you can lose for Him. Remember you lose not that which is lost for His sake, for you shall find much more here and elsewhere. Remember you shall die; and when and where and how you cannot tell. Remember the death of sinners is most terrible. Remember the death of God's saints is precious in His sight. Remember the multitude goeth the wide way which windeth to woe. Remember the strait gate which leadeth to glory hath but few travellers. Remember

---

* Vol. I, p. 449.

Christ biddeth you strive to enter in thereat. Remember he that trusteth in the Lord shall receive strength to stand against all the assaults of his enemies.

Be certain all the hairs of your head are numbered. Be certain your good Father hath appointed bounds, on the which the devil dares not look. Commit yourself to Him; He is, hath been, and will be your keeper; cast your care on Him, and He will care for you. Let Christ be your scope and mark to prick at; let Him be your pattern to work by; let Him be your example to follow: give Him as your heart so your hand, as your mind so your tongue, as your faith so your feet; and let His Word be your candle to go before you in all matters of religion.

Blessed is he that walketh not to these Popish prayers, nor standeth at them, nor sitteth at them. Glorify God both in soul and body. He that gathereth not with Christ scattereth abroad. Use prayer; look for God's help, which is at hand to them that ask and hope thereafter assuredly. In which prayer I heartily desire your lordship to remember us, who as we are going with you right gladly, God be praised, so we look to go before you, hoping that you will follow us if God so will.*

Comment upon these extracts, I think my readers will agree, is needless. They speak for themselves. Scores of similar passages might easily be selected, if space permitted. But enough is as good as a feast. Enough, perhaps, has been quoted to prove that Bradford's literary remains are well worth reading.

Let us thank God that the foundations of the Reformed Church of England were laid by such men as John Bradford. Let us clearly understand what kind of men our martyred Reformers were, what kind of doctrines they held, and what kind of lives they lived. Let us pray that the work they did for the Church of England may never be despised or underrated. Above all, let us pray that there never may be wanting among us a continual succession of English clergy, who shall keep the martyrs' candle burning brightly, and shall hand down true Reformation principles to our children's children.

---

* *Bradford's Works*, vol. 2, p. 79.

Nicholas Ridley (*c.* 1500–1555)

8

NICHOLAS RIDLEY: BISHOP AND MARTYR
His Life, Times, and Writings

NICHOLAS RIDLEY, bishop and martyr, is a man whose name ought to be a household word among all true-hearted English churchmen. In the noble army of English Reformers, no one deserves a higher place than Ridley. Together with Cranmer, Latimer, and Hooper, he occupies the first rank among the worthies of our blessed Reformation, and in point of real merit is second to none. Ridley was born about the year 1500, at Willymontswick, in Northumberland, not far from the Scottish border. His early education was received at a school at Newcastle-on-Tyne, and in the year 1518 he was removed to Pembroke College, Cambridge. Here he soon became distinguished as a student of uncommon diligence and ability, and rapidly rose to a prominent position in the University. He became Fellow of Pembroke in 1524, Senior Proctor in 1533, Chaplain to the University and Public Orator in 1534, and Master of Pembroke in 1540.

The beginnings of Ridley's decided Protestantism are wrapped in some obscurity. Like Cranmer, he seems to have worked his way gradually into the full light of scriptural truth, and not to have attained full maturity of soundness in faith at once. He signed the decree against the Pope's supremacy in 1534.[1] In 1537 he became Chaplain to Archbishop Cranmer, and was appointed by him to

---

[1] Passed by Parliament in 1534, the Act of Supremacy decreed that the King "shall be taken, accepted, and reputed the only Supreme Head on earth of the Church of England," thus divorcing England from Rome.

the vicarage of Herne, in East Kent, in 1538. Here, in the retirement of a quiet country parsonage, he first read the famous treatise of Ratramnus, or Bertram,[1] about the Lord's Supper, and was led by it to search the Scriptures, and examine more carefully than before the writings of the Fathers. The result was that he began to entertain grave doubts of the truth of the Romish doctrine about the Lord's Supper. These doubts he communicated to his friend and patron, the Archbishop. The final event was the conviction of both Cranmer and Ridley that the received tenet of transubstantiation was unscriptural, novel, and erroneous. It was not, however, till the year 1545 that Ridley completely renounced the doctrine of the corporal presence of Christ's body and blood in the sacrament. About that time, the arguments and sufferings of Frith,[2] Lambert,[3] and others confirmed the impressions received at Herne, and he unhesitatingly embraced the doctrine of the Lord's Supper as now held in the Church of England and never swerved from it till his death.

In 1540 Ridley became Chaplain to Henry VIII and then rose from office to office of dignity and influence with rapid steps. In 1541 he was made Prebendary of Canterbury, and in 1545,

---

[1] Ratramnus (d. *c.* 868, known as "Bertram" to the Reformers) was an Augustinian monk made famous for his work *De Corpore et Sanguine Domini* (*On the Body and Blood of the Lord*), in which he firmly denied that the sacramental body of Christ is identical with the body born of Mary. The work was ordered to be burnt by the Council of Vercelli (1050).

[2] John Frith was martyred in 1531. Fox tells us that he "endured much torment, for the wind blew the flames away" from him so that he was "above two hours in agony" before he died.

[3] John Lambert, martyred by Henry VIII for denying *transubstantiation*, suffered an especially cruel death. Says Fox: "As touching the terrible manner and fashion of the burning of this blessed martyr, here it is to be noted, of all others that have been burned and offered up at Smithfield, there were yet none so cruelly and piteously handled as he." The fire was lit, then put out, and then lit again, so as to consume him piecemeal. His scorched and half-burned body was raised on the pikes of the halberdiers, and tossed from one to the other as far as his chain would allow. Then Lambert, says Fox, "lifting up such hands as he had, and his finger-ends flaming with fire, cried unto the people in these words, 'None but Christ, none but Christ!' and so being let down again from their halberds, fell into the fire, and gave up his life."

Prebendary of Westminster. In 1547 he was appointed Vicar of Soham, and in the same year was nominated Bishop of Rochester by Henry VIII. In 1550 he was made Bishop of London by Edward VI and in 1553 was nominated Bishop of Durham. This last change of position, however, never took place. The lamented death of the young King Edward put a complete stop to Ridley's earthly honours. In 1553 he was excepted by name from the amnesty by Bloody Queen Mary, who had a special dislike to him, and was committed to the Tower.

The circumstances under which Ridley came into direct collision with Queen Mary before the death of Edward VI are so graphically described by Fox that I think it best to give them in the martyrologist's own words:

About the eighth of September, 1552, Dr. Ridley, then Bishop of London, lying at his house at Hadham in Herts, went to visit the Lady Mary, then lying at Hunsden, two miles off, and was gently entertained of Sir Thomas Wharton and other her officers, till it was almost eleven of the clock, about which time the said Lady Mary came forth into her chamber of presence, and then the said Bishop there saluted her Grace, and said that he was come to do this duty to her Grace. Then she thanked him for his pains, and for a quarter of an hour talked with him very pleasantly, and said that she knew him in the court when he was chaplain to her father, and could well remember a sermon that he made before King Henry her father at the marriage of my Lady Clinton that now is to Sir Anthony Browne, &c., and so dismissed him to dine with her officers. After the dinner was done, the Bishop being called for by the said Lady Mary, resorted again to her Grace, between whom this communication was. First the Bishop beginneth in manner as followeth. "Madam, I came not only to do my duty to see your Grace, but also to offer myself to preach before you on Sunday next, if it will please you to hear me."

At this her countenance changed, and after silence for a space, she answered thus: "My Lord, as for this last matter, I pray you make the answer to it yourself."

Ridley—"Madam, considering mine office and calling, I am bound to make your Grace this offer to preach before you."

Mary—"Well, I pray you, make the answer, as I have said, to this matter yourself, for you know the answer well enough; but if there be no remedy, but I must make you answer, this shall be your answer, the door of the parish church adjoining shall be open for you, if you come, and ye may preach if you list, but neither I nor any of mine shall hear you."

Ridley—"Madam, I trust you will not refuse God's Word."

Mary—"I cannot tell what ye call God's Word—that is not God's Word now, that was God's Word in my father's days."

Ridley—"God's Word is one at all times, but hath been better understood and practised in some ages than in other."

Mary—"You durst not for your ears have avouched that for God's Word in my father's days that now you do; and as for your new books, I thank God, I never read any of them, I never did nor ever will do."

And after many bitter words against the form of religion then established, and against the government of the realm, and the laws made in the young years of her brother, which she said she was not bound to obey till her brother came to perfect age, and then she said she would obey them; she asked the Bishop whether he were one of the council? He answered, "No." "You might well enough," said she, "as the council goeth nowadays." And so she concluded with these words: "My Lord, for your gentleness to come and see me I thank you, but for your offering to preach before me I thank you never a whit."

Then the said Bishop was brought by Sir Thomas Wharton to the place where they had dined, and was desired to drink, and after he had drunk, he paused awhile, looking very sadly, and suddenly brake out into these words: "Surely I have done amiss." "Why so?" quoth Sir Thomas Wharton. "For I have drunk," said he, "in that place where God's Word offered hath been refused, whereas if I had remembered my duty, I ought to have departed immediately, and to have shaken off the dust of my shoes for a testimony against this house." These words were by the said Bishop spoken with such a vehemency, that some of the hearers afterward confessed their hair to stand upright on their heads. This done, the said Bishop departed, and so returned to his house.

From the Tower, Ridley was sent to Oxford in 1554, to be baited and insulted in a mock disputation; and finally, after two years' imprisonment, was burned at Oxford with old Latimer, on October 16th, 1555. Singularly enough, he seems to have had forebodings of the kind of death he would die. Humphrey, in his *Life of Jewel*, records the following anecdote:

> Ridley, on one occasion, being tossed about in a great storm, exhorted his terrified companions with these words, "Be of good cheer, and bend to your oars; this boat carries a bishop who is not to be drowned, but burned."

From the day that Ridley became a bishop, he appears to have been wholly absorbed in assisting Archbishop Cranmer to establish and consolidate the Reformation of the Church of England. For this huge and formidable work he was peculiarly well fitted by his acknowledged learning. To no one, perhaps, of the Reformers are we more indebted for our admirable articles and liturgy, than to Ridley. Altered and somewhat improved, as they undoubtedly were in Queen Elizabeth's time, we must never forget that in their rudimentary form they first received shape and consistency from the Edwardian Reformers; and that of the Edwardian Reformers, no one probably did a greater portion of the work than Bishop Ridley. In fact, the importance of his work in the English Reformation may be gathered from the saying of one of his most distinguished adversaries: "Latimer leaneth to Cranmer, Cranmer leaneth to Ridley, and Ridley leaneth to his own singular wit." No one, certainly, seems to have had more influence over the mind of Edward VI than Ridley. It was owing to his suggestion that the noble-minded young King founded no less than sixteen grammar schools, including Christ's Hospital; and designed, if his life had been spared, to erect twelve colleges for the education of youths. Besides this, the noble institution of St. Bartholomew's Hospital, in Smithfield, was first endowed and called into existence by Ridley's advice to the King.

The account given by Mr. Christmas, in his biography prefixed to Ridley's works, of the circumstances under which Edward VI founded St. Bartholomew's Hospital is so interesting that I shall give it in its entirety:

> A remarkable instance of the beneficial effect of Ridley's counsels is to be seen in the foundation of three institutions in

the reign of Edward VI, and which in point of date may be called the first fruits of the Reformation. Both in the council chamber and the pulpit did this eminent prelate resist the sacrilegious spirit of his day; and though the young King was but partially able to resist the tide of corruption, he yet founded, at the suggestion of Ridley, no less than sixteen grammar schools, and designed, had his life been spared, to erect twelve colleges for the education of youth. Shortly before his death he sent for the Bishop, and thanking him for a sermon in which he strongly pressed the duty of providing for the poverty and ignorance of our fellow-men, added:

"I took myself to be especially touched by your speech, as well in regard of the abilities God hath given me, as in regard of the example which from me He will require; for as in the kingdom I am next under God, so must I most nearly approach Him in goodness and mercy; for as our miseries stand most in need of aid from Him, so are we the greatest debtors—debtors to all that are miserable, and shall be the greatest accountants of our dispensation therein; and therefore, my Lord, as you have given me, I thank you, this general exhortation, so direct me (I pray you) by what particular actions I may this way best discharge my duty."

The Bishop, who was not prepared for such a request, begged time to consider, and to consult with those who were more conversant with the condition of the poor. Having taken the advice of the Lord Mayor and aldermen of London, he shortly returned to the King, representing that there appeared to be three different classes of poor. Some were poor by impotency of nature, as young fatherless children, old decrepit persons, idiots, cripples, and such like, these required to be educated and maintained; for them accordingly the King gave up the Grey Friars' Church, near Newgate Market, now called Christ's Hospital. Other he observed were poor by faculty, as wounded soldiers, diseased and sick persons who required to be cured and relieved, for their use the King gave St. Bartholomew's, near Smithfield; the third sort were poor by idleness or unthriftiness, as vagabonds, loiterers, &c., who should be chastised and reduced to good order; for these the King appointed his house at Bridewell, the ancient mansion of many English kings.

The inner life and habits of Ridley, during the brief period of his episcopate, are so beautifully described by Fox in his *Acts and Monuments* that I make no excuse for giving the passage in its entirety:

In his calling and office he so travelled and occupied himself by preaching and teaching the true and wholesome doctrine of Christ, that never good child was more singularly loved of his dear parents than he of his flock and diocese. Every holiday and Sunday he preached in some one place or other, except he were otherwise letted by weighty affairs and business. To whose sermons the people resorted, swarming about him like bees, and coveting the sweet flowers and wholesome juice of the fruitful doctrine, which he did not only preach, but showed the same by his life, as a glittering lantern to the eyes and senses of the blind, in such pure order and chastity of life (declining from evil desires and concupiscences), that even his very enemies could not reprove him in any one iota thereof.

Besides this, he was passingly well learned. His memory was great, and he of such reading withal, that of right he deserved to be comparable to the best of this our age, as can testify as well divers his notable works, pithy sermons, and sundry disputations in both the Universities, as also his very adversaries, all which will say no less themselves.

Besides all this, he was wise of counsel, deep of wit, and very politic in all his doings. How merciful and careful he was to reduce the obstinate Papists from their erroneous opinions, and by gentleness to win them to the truth, his gentle ordering and courteous handling of Doctor Heath, late Archbishop of York, being prisoner with him in King Edward's time in his house one year, sufficiently declareth. In fine, he was such a prelate, and in all points so good, godly, and ghostly a man, that England may justly rue the loss of so worthy a treasure. And thus hitherto concerning these public matters.

Now will I speak something further particularly of his person and conditions. He was a man right comely and well proportioned in all points, both in complexion and lineaments of the body. He took all things in good part, bearing no malice nor rancour from his heart, but straightways forgetting all injuries and offences done against him. He was very kind and natural to his kinsfolk, and yet not bearing with them anything otherwise than right would require, giving them always for a general rule (yea, to his own brother and sister) that they doing evil, should seek or look for nothing at his hand, but should be as strangers and aliens unto him, and they to be his brother or sister which used honesty and a godly trade of life.

He, using all kinds of ways to mortify himself, was given to much prayer and contemplation; for duly every morning, so soon as his apparel was done upon him, he went forthwith to his bed-chamber, and there upon his knees prayed the space of half-an-hour, which being done, immediately he went to his study (if there came no other business to interrupt him), where he continued till ten of the clock, and then came to common prayer, daily used in his house. The prayers being done he went to dinner, where he used little talk, except otherwise occasion by some had been ministered, and then it was sober, discreet, and wise, and sometimes merry, as cause required.

The dinner done, which was not very long, he used to sit an hour or thereabouts talking or playing at chess. That done, he returned to his study, and there would continue, except suitors or business abroad were occasion of the contrary, until five of the clock at night, and then would come to common prayer, as in the forenoon, which being finished he went to supper, behaving himself there as at his dinner before. After supper recreating himself in playing at chess the space of an hour, he would then return again to his study; continuing there till eleven of the clock at night, which was his common hour to go to bed, then saying his prayers upon his knees, as in the morning when he rose. Being at his manor of Fulham, as divers times he used to be, he read daily a lecture to his family at the common prayer, beginning at the Acts of the Apostles, and so going throughout all the Epistles of St. Paul, giving to every man that could read a New Testament, hiring them besides with money to learn by heart certain principal chapters, but especially the thirteenth chapter of the Acts; reading also unto his household oftentimes the 101st Psalm, being marvellous careful over his family, that they might be a spectacle of all virtue and honesty to other. To be short, he was as godly and virtuous himself, so nothing but virtue and godliness reigned in his house, feeding them with the food of our Saviour Jesus Christ.

Now remaineth a word or two to be declared of his gentle
nature and kindly pity in the usage of an old woman called
Mistress Bonner, mother to Doctor Bonner, sometime Bishop of
London: which I thought good to touch, as well for the rare
clemency of Doctor Ridley, as the unworthy immanity[1] and
ungrateful disposition again of Doctor Bonner. Bishop Ridley,
being at his manor of Fulham, always sent for the said Mistress
Bonner, dwelling in an house adjoining to his house, to dinner
and supper, with one Mistress Mungey, Bonner's sister, saying,
"Go for my mother Bonner"; who coming, was ever placed in
the chair at the table's end, being so gently entreated, welcomed,
and taken, as though he had been born of her own body, being
never displaced of her seat, although the King's council had been
present, saying, when any of them were there (as divers times they
were), "By your lordships' favour, this place of right and custom is
for my mother Bonner." But how well he was recompensed for
this his singular gentleness and pitiful pity after at the hands of the
said Doctor Bonner, almost the least child that goeth by the
ground can declare. For who afterward was more enemy to
Ridley than Bonner and his? Who more went about to seek his
destruction than he, recompensing his gentleness with extreme
cruelty? As well appeared by the strait handling of Ridley's own
natural sister, and George Shipside, her husband, from time to
time. The gentleness of Ridley did suffer Bonner's mother, sister,
and other his kindred, not only quietly to enjoy all that which
they had of Bonner, but also entertained them in his house,
showing much courtesy and friendship daily unto them. On the
other side Bishop Bonner, being restored again, would not suffer
the brother and natural sister of Bishop Ridley, and other his
friends, not only not to enjoy that which they had by the said
their brother Bishop Ridley, but also currishly, without all order
of law or honesty, by extort power wrested from them all the
livings they had.

And yet being not therewith satisfied, he sought all the means
he could to work the death of the aforesaid Shipside, saying that
he would make twelve godfathers to go upon him; which had
been brought to pass indeed, at what time he was prisoner at

---

[1] "Inhuman cruelty."

Oxford, had not God otherwise wrought his deliverance by means of Doctor Heath, Bishop then of Worcester.

Whereby all good indifferent readers notoriously have to understand, what great diversity was in the disposition of these two natures. Whereof as the one excelled in mercy and pity, so the other again as much or more excelled in churlish ingratitude and despiteful disdain. But of this matter enough.

The closing scene of Ridley's life, his famous martyrdom on October 16th, 1555, is described with such touching and masterly simplicity by Fox, that I think it best to let my readers have it in the martyrologist's own words:

Upon the north side of the town of Oxford, in the ditch over against Balliol College, the place of execution was appointed; and for fear of any tumult that might arise, to let the burning of them, the lord Williams was commanded, by the Queen's letters, and the householders of the city to be there assistant, sufficiently appointed. And when everything was in a readiness, the prisoners were brought forth by the mayor and the bailiffs.

Master Ridley had a fair black gown furred, and faced with foins, such as he was wont to wear, being bishop, and tippet of velvet furred likewise about his neck, a velvet nightcap upon his head, and a corner cap upon the same, going in a pair of slippers to the stake, and going between the mayor and an alderman.

After him came Master Latimer, in a poor Bristol frieze frock, all worn, with his buttoned cap, and a kerchief on his head, all ready to the fire, a new long shroud hanging over his hose down to the feet. All this at the first sight stirred men's hearts to rue upon them, beholding on the one side the honour they sometime had, and on the other the calamity whereunto they were fallen.

Then Master Ridley, looking back, espied Master Latimer coming after, unto whom he said, "Oh, be ye there?" "Yea," said Master Latimer, "I have after you as fast as I can follow." So he following a pretty way off, at length they came both to the stake, the one after the other; where first Dr. Ridley entering the place, marvellous earnestly holding up both his hands, looked towards heaven. Then shortly after espying Master Latimer, with a wondrous cheerful look he ran to him, embraced and kissed him;

and, as they that stood near reported, comforted him, saying, "Be of good heart, brother, for God will either assuage the fury of the flame, or else strengthen us to abide it."

With that went he to the stake, kneeled down by it, kissed it, and effectually prayed; and behind him Master Latimer kneeled, as earnestly calling upon God as he. After they arose the one talked with the other a little, while they which were appointed to see the execution removed themselves out of the sun. What they said I can learn of no man.

After a sermon by a renegade preacher named Smith, which they were not allowed to answer, they were commanded to make them ready, which they with all meekness obeyed. Master Ridley took his gown and his tippet, and gave it to his brother-in-law Master Shipside, who all his time of imprisonment, although he might not be suffered to come to him, lay there at his own charges to provide him necessaries, which, from time to time, he sent by the sergeant that kept him. Some other of his apparel that was little worth he gave away; other the bailiffs took.

He gave away besides divers other small things to gentlemen standing by, and divers of them pitifully weeping. As to Sir Henry Lea he gave a new groat; and to divers of my lord Williams' gentlemen some napkins, some nutmegs, and rases of ginger; his dial, and such other things as he had about him, to every one that stood next him. Some plucked the points off his hose. Happy was he that might get any rag of him.

Master Latimer gave nothing, but quietly suffered his keeper to pull off his hose and his other array, which to look unto was very simple; and being stripped unto his shroud, he seemed as comely a person to them that were there present, as one should lightly see; and whereas in his clothes he appeared a withered and crooked silly old man, he now stood bolt upright, as comely a father as one might lightly behold.

Then Master Ridley, standing as yet in his truss, said to his brother, "It were best for me to go in my truss still." "No," quoth his brother, "it will put you to more pain; and the truss will do a poor man good." Whereunto Master Ridley said, "Be it so, in the name of God;" and so unlaced himself. Then, being in his shirt, he stood upon the aforesaid stone, and held up his hand and said, "O heavenly Father, I give unto Thee most hearty thanks, for that Thou hast called me to be a professor of Thee, even unto death. I beseech Thee, Lord God, take mercy upon this realm of England, and deliver the same from all her enemies."

Then the smith took a chain of iron, and brought the same about both Dr. Ridley's and Master Latimer's middle: and as he was knocking in a staple, Dr. Ridley took the chain in his hand, and shaked the same, for it did gird in his belly, and looking aside to the smith said, "Good fellow, knock it in hard, for the flesh will have his course." Then his brother did bring him gunpowder in a bag, and would have tied the same about his neck. Master Ridley asked what it was. His brother said, "Gunpowder." "Then," said he, "I will take it to be sent of God; therefore I will receive it as sent of Him. And have you any," said he, "for my brother?" meaning Master Latimer. "Yea, sir, that I have," quoth his brother. "Then give it unto him," said he, "betime; lest ye come too late." So his brother went, and carried of the same gunpowder unto Master Latimer.

Then they brought a faggot, kindled with fire, and laid the same down at Dr. Ridley's feet. To whom Master Latimer spake in this manner: "BE OF GOOD COMFORT, MASTER RIDLEY, AND PLAY THE MAN. WE SHALL THIS DAY LIGHT SUCH A CANDLE, BY GOD'S GRACE, IN ENGLAND, AS I TRUST SHALL NEVER BE PUT OUT."

And so the fire being given unto them, when Dr. Ridley saw the fire flaming up towards him, he cried with a wonderful loud voice, *"In manus tuas, Domine, commendo spiritum meum: Domine, recipe spiritum meum."* And after repeated this latter part often in English, "Lord, Lord, receive my spirit"; Master Latimer crying as vehemently on the other side, "O Father of heaven, receive my soul!" who received the flame, as it were embracing of it.

After that he had stroked his face with his hand, and as it were bathed them a little in the fire, he soon died (as it appeared), with very little pain or none. And thus much concerning the end of this old and blessed servant of God, Master Latimer, for whose laborious travails, fruitful life, and constant death, the whole realm hath cause to give great thanks to Almighty God.

But Master Ridley, by reason of the evil making of the fire unto him, because the wooden faggots were laid about the gorse, and overhigh built, the fire burned first beneath, being kept down by the wood; which when he felt, he desired them for Christ's sake to let the fire come unto him. Which when his brother-in-law heard, but not well understood, intending to rid him out of his pain (for the which cause he gave attendance), as one in such sorrow not well advised what he did, he heaped faggots upon him, so that he clean covered him, which made the fire more vehement beneath, that it burned clean all his nether parts before it touched the upper; and that made him leap up and down under the faggots, and often desire them to let the fire come unto him, saying, "I cannot burn." Which indeed appeared well; for after his legs were consumed, by reason of his struggling through the pain (whereof he had no release but only his contentation in God) he shewed that side towards us clean, shirt and all untouched with flame. Yet in all this torment he forgot not to call unto God still, having in his mouth, "Lord, have mercy upon me," intermingling his cry. "Let the fire come unto me, I cannot burn." In which pangs he laboured till one of the standers by with his bill pulled off the faggots above, and where he saw the fire flame up, he wrested himself unto that side. And when the flame touched the gunpowder, he was seen to stir no more, but burned on the other side, falling down at Master Latimer's feet; which, some said, happened by reason that the chain loosed; others said, that he fell over the chain by reason of the poise of his body, and the weakness of the nether limbs.

Some said, that before he was like to fall from the stake, he desired them to hold him to it with their bills. However it was, surely it moved hundreds to tears, in beholding the horrible sight; for I think there was none, that had not clean exiled all humanity and mercy, which would not have lamented to behold the fury of the fire so to rage upon their bodies. Signs there were of sorrow on every side. Some took it grievously to see their deaths, whose lives they held full dear; some pitied their persons, that thought their souls had no need thereof. His brother moved many men, seeing his miserable case, seeing (I say) him compelled to such infelicity, that he thought then to do him best service when he hastened his end. Some cried out of the fortune, to see his endeavour (who most dearly loved him, and sought his release) turn to his greater vexation and increase of pain. But whoso considered their preferments in time past, the places of honour that they some time occupied in this Common-wealth, the favour they were in with their princes, and the opinion of learning they had in the University where they studied, could not choose, but sorrow with tears, to see so great dignity, honour, and estimation, so necessary members some time accounted, so many godly virtues, the study of so many years, such excellent learning, to be put into the fire, and consumed in one moment. Well: dead they are and the reward of this world they have already. What reward remaineth for them in heaven, the day of the Lord's glory, when He cometh with His saints, shall shortly, I trust, declare.

*   *   *

It only remains now to give some account of Ridley's writings. They are few in number, and occupy only one volume of the Parker Society's series. They consist chiefly of short treatises against transubstantiation and image-worship; conferences with Latimer and Bourne; a disputation held in 1549 about the sacra-ment; disputations and examination at Oxford, held shortly before his martyrdom; injunctions to the diocese of London; and thirty-five letters, chiefly written during his imprisonments. Scanty as these literary remains are from so great a divine, they are worthy of his pen, and make us wish he had written more. But, doubtless, the worthy Bishop had little time for writing. To work, and preach, and advise, and witness, and suffer, and die for God's truth, was his appointed lot. And who shall dare to say that his short life and glorious death have not done more for Christ's truth in England than fifty folio volumes of writings? I venture to think that the following extracts from Ridley's writings will be found interesting.

1. My first extract shall be taken from Ridley's Conference with Latimer:

In Tynedale, where I was born, not far from the Scottish borders, I have known my countrymen watch night and day in their har-ness, such as they had, that is, in their jacks, and their spears in their hands (you call them northern gads), especially when they

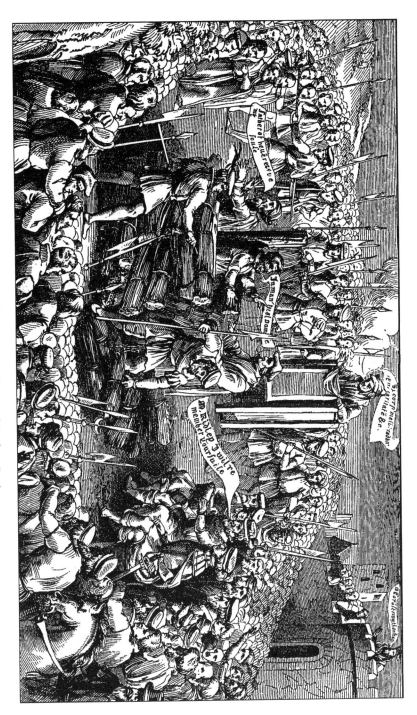

The Burning of Bishop Ridley and Father Latimer

had any privy warning of the coming of the Scots. And so doing, although at every such bickering some of them spent their lives, yet by such means, like pretty men, they defended their country. And those that so died, I think, that before God, they died in a good quarrel, and their offspring and progeny all the country loved them the better for their fathers' sake.

And in the quarrel of Christ our Saviour, in the defence of His own Divine ordinances, by the which He giveth unto us life and immortality, yea, in the quarrel of faith and Christian religion, wherein resteth our everlasting salvation, shall we not watch? Shall we not go always armed, ever looking when our adversary (which like a roaring lion, seeketh whom he may devour) shall come upon us by reason of our slothfulness? Yea, and woe be unto us, if he can oppress us at unawares, which undoubtedly he will do, if he find us sleeping. Let us awake therefore; for if the good man of the house knew what hour the thief would come, he would surely watch and not suffer his house to be broken up. Let us awake therefore, I say, and let us not suffer our house to be broken up. "Resist the devil," says St. James, "and he will fly from you." Let us therefore resist him manfully, and, taking the cross upon our shoulders, let us follow our Captain Christ, who by His own blood hath dedicated and hallowed the way, which leadeth unto the Father, that is, to the light which no man can attain—the fountain of everlasting joys. Let us follow, I say, whither He calleth and allureth us, that after these afflictions, which last but for a moment whereby He trieth our faith, as gold by the fire, we may everlastingly reign and triumph with Him in the glory of the Father, and that through the same our Lord and Saviour Jesus Christ, to whom with the Father and the Holy Ghost, be all honour and glory, now and for ever. Amen. Amen.*

2. My second extract shall be taken from Ridley's Injunctions to the Diocese of London, given in the year 1550:

It is injoined, that no minister do counterfeit the Popish Mass in kissing the Lord's board; washing his hands or fingers after the Gospel, or on the receipt of the Holy Communion; shifting the book from one place to another; laying down and licking the

---

* Parker Society's edition, p. 145.

chalice after the Communion; blessing his eyes with the sudarie thereof, or paten, or crossing his head with the same, holding his forefingers and thumbs joined together toward the temples of his head, after the receiving of the sacrament; breathing on the bread, or chalice; saying the Agnus before the Communion; shewing the sacrament openly before the distribution, or making any elevation thereof; ringing of the sacrying bell, or setting any light upon the Lord's board. And finally, that the minister, in the time of the Holy Communion, do use only the ceremonies and gestures appointed by the *Book of Common Prayer*, and none other, so that there do not appear in them any counterfeiting of the Popish Mass.

And whereas in divers places some use the Lord's board after the form of a table, and some of an altar, whereby dissention is perceived to arise among the unlearned; therefore, wishing a godly unity to be observed in all our diocese, and for that the form of a table may more move and turn the simple from the old superstitious opinions of the Popish Mass and to the right use of the Lord's Supper, we exhort the curates, churchwardens, and questmen, here present, to erect and set up the Lord's board after the form of an honest table decently covered, in such place of the quire or chancel as shall be thought most meet by their discretion and agreement, so that the ministers, with the communicants, may have their place separated from the rest of the people; and to take down and abolish all other by-altars or tables.*

3. My third extract shall be taken from Ridley's letter to Bishop Hooper when they were both in prison, expecting death. It is a remarkable letter when we remember that the two famous Reformers had once differed much about vestments:

My dearly beloved brother and fellow-elder, whom I reverence in the Lord, pardon me, I beseech you, that hitherto, since your captivity and mine, I have not saluted you by my letters: whereas, I do indeed confess, I have received from you (such was your gentleness) two letters at sundry times, but yet at such times as I could not be suffered to write unto you again; or if I might have written, yet was I greatly in doubt, lest my letters should not

* Parker's Society's edition, p. 319.

safely come unto your hands. But now, my dear brother, forasmuch as I understand by your works, which I have yet but super-
ficially seen, that we thoroughly agree and wholly consent
together in those things which are the grounds and substantial
points of our religion, against the which the world so furiously
rageth in these our days, howsoever in time past in smaller
matters and circumstances of religion, your wisdom and my
simplicity (I confess) have in some points varied: now, I say, be
you assured, that even with my whole heart (God is my witness)
in the bowels of Christ, I love you, and in truth, for the truth's
sake which abideth in us, and (as I am persuaded) shall by the
grace of God abide with us for evermore. And because the
world, as I perceive, brother, ceaseth not to play his pageant, and
busily conspireth against Christ our Saviour with all possible
force and power, exalting high things against the knowledge of
God, let us join hands together in Christ; and if we cannot
overthrow, yet to our power, and as much as in us lieth, let us
shake those things, not with carnal, but with spiritual weapons;
and withal, brother, let us prepare ourselves to the day of our
dissolution; whereby, after the short time of this bodily affliction,
by the grace of our Lord Jesus Christ, we shall triumph together
with Him in eternal glory.*

4. My last extract shall be taken from Ridley's farewell letter to
the prisoners for Christ's cause:

Why should we Christians fear death? Can death deprive us of
Christ, which is all our comfort, our joy, and our life? Nay,
forsooth. But contrary, death shall deliver us from this mortal
body, which loadeth and beareth down the spirit, that it cannot
so well perceive heavenly things, in the which so long as we
dwell, we are absent from God.

Wherefore, understanding our state in that we be Christians,
that if our mortal body, which is our earthly house, were
destroyed, we have a building, a house not made with hands, but
everlasting in heaven, etc.; therefore we are of good cheer, and
know that when we are in the body, we are absent from God; for
we walk by faith, and not by clear sight. Nevertheless we are
bold, and had rather be absent from the body and present with

* Parker Society's edition, p. 355.

God. Wherefore we strive, whether we be present at home or absent abroad, that we may always please Him.

And who that hath true faith in our Saviour Christ, whereby he knoweth somewhat truly what Christ our Saviour is, that He is the eternal Son of God, life, light, the wisdom of the Father, all goodness, all righteousness, and whatsoever is good that heart can desire, yea, infinite plenty of all these, above that man's heart can either conceive or think (for in Him dwelleth the fulness of the Godhead corporally), and also that He is given us of the Father, "and made of God to be our wisdom, our righteousness, our holiness, and our redemption;" who (I say) is he that believeth this indeed, that would not gladly be with his Master Christ? Paul for this knowledge coveted to have been loosed from the body, and to have been with Christ, for that he counted it much better for himself, and had rather to be loosed than to live. Therefore these words of Christ to the thief on the cross, that asked of Him mercy, were full of comfort and solace: "This day thou shalt be with Me in paradise." To die in the defence of Christ's Gospel, it is our bounden duty to Christ, and also to our neighbour. To Christ, "for He died for us, and rose again, that He might be Lord over all." And seeing He died for us, "we also (saith St. John) should jeopard, yea give, our life for our brethren." And this kind of giving and losing is getting and winning indeed; for he that giveth or loseth his life thus, getteth and winneth it for evermore. "Blessed are they, therefore, that die in the Lord;" and if they die in the Lord's cause, they are most happy of all.

Let us not then fear death, which can do us no harm, other-wise than for a moment to make the flesh to smart; for that our faith, which is surely fastened and fixed unto the Word of God, telleth us that we shall be anon after death in peace, in the hands of God, in joy, in solace, and that from death we shall go straight unto life. For St. John saith, "He that liveth and believeth in Me shall never die." And in another place, "He shall depart from death unto life." And therefore this death of the Christian is not to be called death, but rather a gate or entrance into everlasting life. Therefore Paul calleth it but a dissolution and resolution; and both Peter and Paul, a putting off of this tabernacle or dwell-house, meaning thereby the mortal body, as wherein the soul or spirit doth dwell here in this world for a small time. Yea, this death may be called, to the Christian, an end of all miseries. For so long as we live here, "we must pass through many tribulations, before we can enter into the kingdom of heaven." And now, after that death has shot his bolt, all the Christian man's enemies have done what they can, and after that they have no more to do. What could hurt or harm poor "Lazarus, that lay at the rich man's gate"? his former penury and poverty, his miserable beggary, and horrible sores and sickness? For so soon as death had stricken him with his dart, so soon came the angels and carried him straight up into Abraham's bosom. What lost he by death, who from misery and pain is set by the ministry of angels in a place both of joy and solace?

Farewell, dear brethren, farewell! and let us comfort our hearts in all troubles, and in death, with the Word of God: for heaven and earth shall perish, but the Word of the Lord endureth for ever.*

---

* Parker Society's edition, p. 425.

9

SAMUEL WARD

SAMUEL WARD, an eminent Suffolk divine, and one of the most famous Puritans of the seventeenth century, is a man whose name is comparatively unknown to most readers of English theology. This is easily accounted for. He wrote but little, and what he wrote has never been reprinted till very lately. The works of Owen, Baxter, Gurnall, Charnock, Goodwin, Adams, Brooks, Watson, Greenhill, Sibbes, Jenkyn, Manton, Burroughs, Bolton, and others have been reprinted, either wholly or partially. Of Samuel Ward, so far as I can ascertain, not a word had been reprinted till recently for more than two hundred years.

How far Samuel Ward's sermons have deserved this neglect, I am content to leave to the judgment of all students of theology into whose hands his sermons may fall. But I venture the opinion that it reflects little credit on the discretion of republishers of old divinity that such a writer as Samuel Ward has been so long passed over. His case, however, does not stand alone. When such works as those of Swinnock, Arrowsmith on John One, Gouge on Hebrews, Airay on Philippians, John Rogers on First Peter, Hardy on First John, Daniel Rogers on Naaman the Syrian (to say nothing of some of the best works of Manton and Brooks), have been only recently thought worthy of republication, we must not be surprised at the treatment which Ward has received.

As one who was for thirty-seven years a Suffolk minister and a thorough lover of Puritan theology, I desire to supply some information about Ward in this biographical paper. I should have been especially pleased if it had been in my power to write a complete memoir of the man and his ministry. I regret, however, to be obliged to say that the materials from which any account of him

can be compiled are exceedingly scanty and the facts known about
him are comparatively few. Nor yet, unhappily, is this difficulty the
only one with which I have had to contend. It is a very curious
circumstance that no less than three divines named "S. Ward" lived
in the first half of the seventeenth century, and were all members
of Sydney College, Cambridge. These three were Dr. Samuel
Ward, Master of Sydney College, who was one of the English
commissioners at the Synod of Dort and a correspondent of Archbishop Usher; Seth Ward, who was successively Bishop of Exeter
and Salisbury; and Samuel Ward of Ipswich, whose sermons have
been lately reprinted. Of these three, the two "Samuels" were
undoubtedly the most remarkable men, but the similarity of their
names has hitherto involved their biographies in much confusion. I
can only say that I have done my best, in the face of these accu-
mulated difficulties, to unravel a tangled skein and to supply the
reader with accurate information.

The story of Samuel Ward's life is soon told. He was born at
Haverhill, in Suffolk, in the year 1577, and was eldest son of the
Rev. John Ward, minister of the Gospel in that town. John Ward,
the father of Samuel Ward, appears to have been a man of considerable eminence as a minister and preacher. Fuller (in his *Worthies
of Suffolk*) says that the three sons together would not make up the
abilities of their father. The following inscription on his tomb in
Haverhill Church is well worth reading:

JOHANNES WARDE.

Quo si quis scivit scitius,
Aut si quis docuit doctius,
At rarus vixit sanctius,
Et nullus tonuit fortius.

Son of thunder, son of ye dove,
Full of hot zeal, full of true love;
In preaching truth, in living right,—
A burning lampe, a shining light.

LIGHT HERE.   STARS HEREAFTER.
John Ward, after he with great evidence
and power of ye Spirite, and with much fruit,
preached ye Gospel at Haverill and Bury in
Suff. 25 years, was heere gathered to his fathers.

Watch.   Susan, his widdowe, married Rogers, that   Warde.
                worthy Pastor of Wethersfielde. He left 3 sonnes,
                Samuel, Nathaniel, John, Preachers, who for
                them and theirs, wish no greater blessing
                than that they may continue in beleeving
                and preaching the same Gospel till ye coming
                of Christ. Come, Lord Jesus, come quicklye.
Watch.   Death is our entrance into life.   Warde.

Samuel Ward, the subject of this memoir, was admitted a scholar of St. John's College, Cambridge, on Lady Margaret's foundation, on Lord Burghley's nomination, November 6th, 1594, and went out B.A. of that house in 1596. He was appointed one of the first fellows of Sydney Sussex College in 1599, commenced M.A. 1600, vacated his fellowship on his marriage in 1604, and proceeded B.D. in 1607.

Nothing is known of Ward's boyhood and youth. His entrance on the work of the ministry, the name of the bishop by whom he was ordained, the date of his ordination, the place where he first began to do Christ's work as a preacher, are all things of which apparently there is no record. His first appearance as a public character was in the capacity of lecturer at his native town of Haverhill. Of his success at Haverhill, Samuel Clark[*] gives the following interesting example, in his life of Samuel Fairclough, a famous minister of Kedington, in Suffolk:

God was pleased to begin a work of grace in the heart of Samuel Fairclough very early and betimes, by awakening his conscience by the terror of the law, and by bestowing a sincere repentance upon him thereby, and by working an effectual faith in him; and all this was done by the ministry of the Word preached by Mr. Samuel Ward, then Lecturer of Haverhill. Mr. Ward had answered for him in baptism, and had always a hearty love to him. Preaching one day on the conversion of Zaccheus, and discoursing upon his fourfold restitution in cases of rapine and extortion, Mr. Ward used that frequent expression, that no man can expect pardon from God of the wrong done to another's estate, except he make

---

[*] In his *Lives of Eminent Persons*, p. 154, edit. 1683.

full restitution to the wronged person, if it may possibly be done. This was as a dart directed by the hand of God to the heart of young Fairclough, who, together with one John Trigg, afterwards a famous physician in London, had the very week before robbed the orchard of one Goodman Jude of that town, and had filled their pockets as well as their bellies with the fruit of a mellow pear tree.

At and after sermon, young Fairclough mourned much and had not any sleep all the night following; and, rising on the Monday morning, he went to his companion Trigg and told him that he was going to Goodman Jude's, to carry him twelve pence by way of restitution for three pennyworth of pears of which he had wronged him. Trigg, fearing that if the thing were confessed to Jude, he would acquaint Robotham their master therewith, and that corporal correction would follow, did earnestly strive to divert the poor child from his purpose of restitution. But Fairclough replied that God would not pardon the sin except restitution were made. To which Trigg answered thus: "Thou talkest like a fool, Sam; God will forgive us ten times sooner than old Jude will forgive us once." But our Samuel was of another mind, and therefore he goes on to Jude's house, and there told him his errand, and offered him a shilling, which Jude refusing (though he declared his forgiveness of the wrong), the youth's wound smarted so, that he could get no rest till he went to his spiritual father, Mr. Ward, and opened to him the whole state of his soul, both on account of this particular sin and many others, and most especially the sin of sins, the original sin and depravation of his nature. Mr. Ward received him with great affection and tenderness, and proved the good Samaritan to him, pouring wine and oil into his wounds, answering all his questions, satisfying his fears, and preaching Jesus to him so fully and effectually that he became a true and sincere convert, and dedicated and devoted himself to his Saviour and Redeemer all the days of his life after.[*]

---

[*] I think it right to remark that Clark, in all probability, has erred in his *dates* in telling this story. He says that Fairclough was born in 1594, and that the event he has recorded took place when he was thirteen years old. Now, in 1607 Ward had ceased to be Lecturer of Haverhill. Whether the explanation of this discrepancy is that Fairclough was born before 1594, or

From Haverhill, Samuel Ward was removed, in 1603, at the early age of twenty-six, to a position of great importance in those days. He was appointed by the Corporation of Ipswich to the office of Town Preacher at Ipswich, and filled the pulpit of St. Mary-le-Tower in that town, with little intermission, for about thirty years. Ipswich and Norwich, it must be remembered, were places of far more importance two hundred and fifty years ago than they are at the present day. They were the capital towns of two of the wealthiest and most thickly peopled counties in England. Suffolk, in particular, was a county in which the Protestant and evangelical principles of the Reformation had taken particularly deep root. Some of the most eminent Puritans were Suffolk ministers. To be chosen Town Preacher of a place like Ipswich two hundred and fifty years ago was a very great honour, and shows the high estimate which was set on Samuel Ward's ministerial character, even when he was so young as twenty-six. It deserves to be remarked that Matthew Lawrence and Stephen Marshall, who were among his successors, were both leading men among the divines of the seventeenth century.

The influence which Ward possessed in Ipswich appears to have been very considerable. Fuller says:

He was preferred Minister *in*, or rather *of*, Ipswich, having a care over, and a love from, all the parishes in that populous place. Indeed, he had a magnetic virtue (as if he had learned it from the loadstone, in whose qualities he was so knowing) to attract people's affections.*

The history of his thirty years' ministry in the town of Ipswich would doubtless prove full of interesting particulars, if we could

---

that he was only nine years old when he stole the pears, or that Ward was visiting at Haverhill in 1607 and preached during his visit, or that Fairclough was at school at Ipswich and not Haverhill, is a point that we have no means of deciding.

* I suspect that Fuller's remarks about the loadstone refer to a book called *Magnetis Reductorium Theologium*, which is sometimes attributed to Samuel Ward of Ipswich. But it is more than doubtful whether the authorship of this book does not belong to Dr. Samuel Ward, the Principal of Sydney College, of whom mention has already been made.

only discover them. Unhappily, I can only supply the reader with the following dry facts, which I have found in an antiquarian publication of considerable value, entitled *Wodderspoon's Memorials of Ipswich*. They are evidently compiled from ancient records, and throw some useful light on certain points of Ward's history.

Wodderspoon says:

> In the year 1603, on All Saints' Day, a man of considerable eminence was elected as Preacher, Mr. Samuel Ward. The Corporation appear to have treated him with great liberality, appointing an hundred marks as his stipend, and also allowing him £6 13s. 4d. quarterly in addition, for house rent.
>
> The Municipal Authorities (possibly because of obtaining so able a divine) declare very minutely the terms of Mr. Ward's engagement. In his sickness or absence he is to provide for the supply of a minister at the usual place three times a week, "as usual hath been." "He shall not be absent out of town above forty days in one year, without leave; and if he shall take a pastoral charge, his retainer by the Corporation is to be void. The pension granted to him is not to be charged on the Foundation or Hospital Lands."
>
> In the seventh year of James I, the Corporation purchased a house for the Preacher, or rather for Mr. Ward. This house was bought by the town contributing £120, and the rest of the money was made up by free contributions, on the understanding that, when Mr. Ward ceased to be Preacher, the building was to be resold, and the various sums collected returned to those who contributed, as well as the money advanced by the Corporation.
>
> In the eighth year of James I, the Corporation increased the salary of Mr. Ward to £90 per annum, "on account of the charges he is at by abiding here."
>
> In the fourteenth year of James I, Mr. Samuel Ward's pension increased from £90 to £100 yearly.
>
> The preaching of this divine, being of so free and puritanic a character, did not long escape the notice of the tale bearers of the Court; and after a short period, spent in negociation, Mr. Ward was restrained from officiating in his office. In 1623, August 6th, a record appears in the town books, to the effect that "a letter from the King, to inhibit Mr. Ward from preaching, is referred to the Council of the town."

About the remaining portion of Ward's life, Wodderspoon supplies no information. The little that we know about it is gleaned from other sources.

It is clear from Hackett's *Life of the Lord Keeper Bishop Williams** that, though prosecuted by Bishop Harsnet for Nonconformity in 1623, Ward was only suspended temporarily, if at all, from his office as preacher. Brook,† following Hackett, says that "upon his prosecution in the Consistory of Norwich, he appealed from the Bishop to the King, who committed the articles exhibited against him to the examination of the Lord Keeper Williams." The Lord Keeper reported that Mr. Ward "was not altogether blameless, but a man easily to be won by fair dealing; and persuaded Bishop Harsnet to take his submission, and not remove him from Ipswich. The truth is the Lord Keeper found that Mr. Ward possessed so much candour, and was so ready to promote the interests of the Church, that he could do no less than compound the troubles of so learned and industrious a divine. He was therefore released from the prosecution, and most probably continued for some time without molestation in the peaceable exercise of his ministry." Brook might here have added a fact, recorded by Hackett, that Ward was so good a friend to the Church of England that he was the means of retaining several persons who were wavering about conformity, within the pale of the Episcopal Communion.

After eleven years of comparative quiet, Ward was prosecuted again for alleged Nonconformity, at the instigation of Archbishop Laud. Prynne, in his account of Laud's trial, tells us that in the year 1635, he was impeached in the High Commission Court for preaching against bowing at the name of Jesus, and against the "Book of Sports," and for having said "that the Church of England was ready to ring changes in religion," and "that the Gospel stood on tiptoe ready to be gone."‡ He was found guilty, was enjoined to make a public recantation in such form as the Court should appoint, and condemned in costs of the suit. Upon his refusal to recant, he was committed to prison, where he remained a long time.

---

* p. 95, ed. 1603.

† In his *Lives of the Puritans*, vol. 2, p. 452.

‡ p. 361.

In a note to Brook's account of this disgraceful transaction, which he appears to have gathered out of *Rushworth's Collections* and Wharton's *Troubles of Laud*, he mentions a remarkable fact about Ward at this juncture of his life, which shows the high esteem in which he was held at Ipswich. It appears that after his suspension the Bishop of Norwich would have allowed his people another minister in his place; but "they would have Mr. Ward or none!"

The last four years of Ward's life are a subject on which I find it very difficult to discover the truth. Brook says that after his release from prison, he retired to Holland and became a colleague of William Bridge, the famous Independent minister of Yarmouth, who had settled at Rotterdam. He also mentions a report that he and Mr. Bridge renounced their episcopal ordination and were re-ordained: "Mr. Bridge ordaining Mr. Ward, and Mr. Ward returning the compliment." He adds another report that Ward was unjustly deposed from his pastoral office at Rotterdam, and after a short interval restored.

I venture to think that this account must be regarded with some suspicion. At any rate, I doubt whether we are in possession of all the facts in the transaction which Brook records. That Ward retired to Holland after his release from prison is highly probable. It was a step which many were constrained to take for the sake of peace and liberty of conscience in the days of the Stuarts. That he was pastor of a church at Rotterdam, in conjunction with Bridge—that differences arose between him and his colleague—that he was temporarily deposed from his office and afterward restored—are things which I think very likely. His *re-ordination* is a point which I think questionable. For one thing, it seems to me exceedingly improbable that a man of Ward's age and standing would first be re-ordained by Bridge, who was twenty-three years younger than himself, and afterward re-ordain Bridge. For another thing, it appears very strange that a man who had renounced his episcopal orders should have afterwards received an honourable burial in the aisle of an Ipswich church in the year 1639. One thing only is clear. Ward's stay at Rotterdam could not have been very lengthy. He was not committed to prison till 1635 and was buried in 1639. He "lay in prison long," according to Prynne. At any rate, he lay there long

enough to write a Latin work called *A Rapture*, of which it is
expressly stated that it was composed during his imprisonment "in
the Gate House." In 1638 we find him buying a house in Ipswich.
It is plain at this rate that he could not have been very long in
Holland. However, the whole of the transactions at Rotterdam, so
far as Ward is concerned, are involved in some obscurity. Stories
against eminent Puritans were easily fabricated and greedily swallowed in the seventeenth century. Brook's assertion that Ward died
in Holland, about 1640, is so entirely destitute of foundation that it
rather damages the value of his account of Ward's latter days.

Granting, however, that after his release from prison Ward retired
to Holland, there seems every reason to believe that he returned to
Ipswich early in 1638. It appears from the town books of Ipswich
(according to Wodderspoon) that in April 1638 he purchased the
house provided for him by the town for £140, repaying the
contributors the sum contributed by them. He died and was buried
in the month of March 1639, aged 62, in St. Mary-le-Tower,
Ipswich, on the 8th of that month. A certified copy of the entry of
his burial in the parish register is in my possession. On a stone
which was laid in his lifetime in the middle aisle of the church, the
following words (according to Clarke's *History of Ipswich*) are still
extant:

> Watch, Ward! yet a little while,
> And He that shall come, will come.

Under this stone it is supposed the bones of the good old Puritan
preacher were laid; and to this day he is spoken of by those who
know his name in Ipswich as "Watch Ward."

It only remains to add that Ward married, in 1604, a widow
named Deborah Bolton, of Isleham, in Cambridge, and had by her
a family.* It is an interesting fact, recorded in the town books of
Ipswich, that after his death, as a mark of respect, his widow and
his eldest son Samuel were allowed for their lives the stipend
enjoyed by their father: *viz.*, £100 annually. It is also worthy of
remark that he had two brothers who were ministers, John and
Nathaniel. John Ward lived and died Rector of St. Clement's,

* For this fact, and the facts about Ward's degrees at Cambridge, I am
indebted to a well informed writer in *Notes and Queries* for October 1861.

Ipswich; and there is a tablet and short inscription about him in that church. Nathaniel Ward was Minister of Standon, Herts., went to America in 1634, returned to England in 1646, and died at Shenfield, in Essex, 1653.

There is an excellent portrait of Ward still extant in Ipswich. He is represented with an open book in his right hand, a ruff round his neck, a peaked beard and moustaches. On one side is a coast beacon lighted, and there is an inscription:

Watche Ward. Ætatis suæ, 43. 1620.

The following extract, from a rare volume called *The Tombstone; or, a notice and imperfect monument of that worthy man, Mr. John Carter, Pastor of Bramford and Belstead, in Suffolk* (1653), will probably be thought to deserve insertion, as an incidental evidence of the high esteem in which Ward was held in the neighbourhood of Ipswich. The work was written by Mr. Carter's son; and the extract describes what occurred at his father's funeral. He says,

> In the afternoon, February 4th, 1634, at my father's interring, there was a great confluence of people from all parts thereabout, ministers, and others taking up the word of Joash, King of Israel, "O my father! my father! the chariots of Israel and the horsemen thereof!" Old Mr. Samuel Ward, *that famous divine, and the glory of Ipswich*, came to the funeral, brought a mourning gown with him, and offered very respectfully to preach the funeral sermon, seeing that such a congregation was gathered together, and upon such an occasion. But my sister and I durst not give way to it; for our father had often charged us in his lifetime, and upon his blessing, that no service should be at his burial. "For," said he, "it will give occasion to speak some good things of me that I deserve not, and so false things will be uttered in this pulpit." Mr. Ward rested satisfied, and did forbear. But the next Friday, at Ipswich, he turned his whole lecture into a funeral sermon for my father, in which he did lament and honour him, to the great satisfaction of the whole auditory.*

I have now brought together all that I can discover about Samuel Ward's history. I heartily regret that the whole amount is so small,

---

* pp. 26, 27.

and that the facts recorded about him are so few. But we must not forget that the best part of Ward's life was spent in Suffolk, and that he seldom left his own beloved pulpit in St. Mary-le-Tower, Ipswich.* That he was well known by reputation beyond the borders of his own county there can be no doubt. His selection to be a preacher at St. Paul's Cross, in 1616, is a proof of this. But it is vain to suppose that the reputation of a preacher, however eminent, who lives and dies in a provincial town, will long survive him. In order to become the subject of biographies, and have the facts of his life continually noted down, a man must live in a metropolis. This was not Ward's lot; and, consequently, after the lapse of so many years, we seem to know little about him.

It only remains to say something about Ward's sermons and treatises, which have been lately, for the first time, reprinted, and made accessible to the modern reader of theology.† It must be distinctly understood that these reprints do not comprise the whole of Ward's writings. Beside these sermons and treatises, he wrote, in conjunction with Yates, a reply to Montague's famous book, *Appello Cæsarem*.[1] There is also reason to think that he published one or two other detached sermons beside those which are now reprinted. I think, however, there can be little doubt that the nine sermons and treatises which have been lately republished by Mr. Nichol are the only works of Samuel Ward which it would have been worth while to reprint, and in all probability, the only works which he would have wished himself to be reproduced.

Of the merits of these sermons, the reading public will now be able to form an opinion. They were thought highly of in time past and have received the commendation of very competent judges. Fuller testifies that Ward "had a sanctified fancy, dexterous in designing expressive pictures, representing much matter in a little

---

* It seems that he expounded half the Bible during his ministry in Ipswich. See his preface to *The Happiness of Practice*.

† Ward's sermons are to be found in Nichol's valuable series of reprints of Puritan divines, at the end of the third volume of Adams' *Works*.

[Ward's sermons have recently been reprinted by the Banner of Truth Trust. The *Works of Thomas Adams*, out of print for more than 130 years, were reprinted by Tanski Publications in 1998.—*Ed.*]

[1] Latin, *I Appeal to Cæsar* (1625), Montague's self-defense against charges of Popery and Arminianism.

model." Doddridge says that Ward's "writings are worthy to be read through. His language is generally proper, elegant, and nervous. His thoughts are well digested, and happily illustrated. He has many remarkable veins of wit. Many of the boldest figures of speech are to be found in him, beyond any English writer, especially apostrophes, prosopopœias, dialogisms, and allegories."* This praise may at first sight seem extravagant. I shall, however, be disappointed if those who take the trouble to read Ward's writings do not think it well deserved.

It is only fair to Samuel Ward to remind the readers of his works that at least three of the nine sermons and treatises now reprinted were not originally composed with a view to publication. The sermons entitled *A Coal from the Altar, Balm from Gilead to Recover Conscience,* and *Jethro's Justice of the Peace* would appear to have been carried through the press by friends and relatives. They have all the characteristics of compositions intended for ears rather than for eyes, for hearers rather than for readers. Yet I venture to say that they are three of the most striking examples of Ward's gifts and powers out of the whole nine. The peroration of the sermon on conscience, in particular, appears to me one of the most powerful and effective conclusions to a sermon which I have ever read in the English language.†

The *doctrine* of Ward's sermons is always thoroughly evangelical. He never falls into the extravagant language about repentance, which disfigures the writings of some of the Puritans. He never wearies us with the long, supra-scriptural, systematic statements of theology, which darken the pages of others. He is always to the point, always about the main things in divinity, and generally sticks to his text. To exalt the Lord Jesus Christ as high as possible, to cast down man's pride, to expose the sinfulness of sin, to spread out broadly and fully the remedy of the Gospel, to awaken the

---

* How Doddridge could possibly have made the mistake of supposing that Ward died at the age of 28 is perfectly inexplicable!

† The engraved title pages of two of the nine sermons, in the edition of 1636, are great curiosities in their way. The one which is prefixed to the *Woe to Drunkards* is intended to be a hit at the degeneracy of the times in which Ward lived. If it was really designed by Ward himself, it supplies some foundation for the rumour that he had a genius for caricaturing.

unconverted sinner and alarm him, to build up the true Christian and comfort him—these seem to have been objects which Ward proposed to himself in every sermon. And was he not right? Well would it be for the churches if we had more preachers like him!

The *style* of Ward's sermons is always eminently simple. Singularly rich in illustration—bringing everyday life to bear continually on his subject—pressing into his Master's service the whole circle of human learning—borrowing figures and similes from everything in creation—not afraid to use familiar language such as all could understand—framing his sentences in such a way that an ignorant man could easily follow him—bold, direct, fiery dramatic, and speaking as if he feared none but God—he was just the man to arrest attention, and to keep it when arrested, to set men thinking, and to make them anxious to hear him again. Quaint he is, undoubtedly, in many of his sayings. But he preached in an age when all were quaint, and his quaintness probably struck no one as remarkable. Faulty in taste he is, no doubt. But there never was the popular preacher against whom the same charge was not laid. His faults, however, were as nothing compared to his excellencies. Once more I say, well would it be for the churches if we had more preachers like him!

The *language* of Ward's sermons ought not to be passed over without remark. I venture to say that in few writings of the seventeenth century will there be found so many curious, old-fashioned, and forcible words as in Ward's sermons. Some of these words are unhappily obsolete and unintelligible to the multitude, to the grievous loss of English literature.

*   *   *

It only remains to give a few extracts from Ward's sermons which may give some idea of what this famous divine was as a preacher.

1. The first extract is from a sermon entitled *Christ is All in All*:

All let Him be in all our thoughts and speeches. How happy were it if He were never out of our sight and minds, but that our souls were directed towards Him, and fixed on Him, as the sunflower towards the sun, the iron to the loadstone, the loadstone to the polestar. Hath He not for that purpose resembled Himself to all familiar and obvious objects:* to the light, that so often as we open our eyes we might behold Him; to bread, water, and wine, that in all our repasts we might feed on Him;† to the door, that in all our out and ingoing we might have Him in remembrance? How happy if our tongues would ever run upon that name, which is honey in the mouth, melody in the ear, jubilee in the heart. Let the mariner prate of the winds, the merchant of his gain, the husbandman of his oxen.‡ Be thou a Pythagorean to all the world, and a Peripatetian to Christ; mute to all vanities, and eloquent only to Christ, that gave man his tongue and his speech. How doth Paul delight to record, which Chrysostom§ first took notice of (1 Cor. 1:10). And how doth worthy Fox grieve to foresee and foretell that which we hear and see come to pass, that men's discourses would be taken up about trifles and nifles, as if all religion lay in the flight and pursuit of one circumstance or opinion; how heartily doth he pray, and vehemently wish that men would leave jangling about ceremonies, and spend their talk upon Him that is the substance; that learned men would write of Christ, unlearned men study of Him, preachers make Him the scope and subject of all their preaching.¶ And what else, indeed, is our office but to elevate, not a piece of bread, as the Romish priests, but Christ in our doctrine; to travail in birth till He be formed in a people, to crucify Him in their eyes by lively preaching His death and passion. The old emblem of St. Christopher is good, representing a preacher as one wading through the sea of this world, staying on the staff of faith, and lifting up Christ aloft to be seen of men. What else gained John the name of the Divine, and Paul of a wise master builder, but that he regarded not, as the fashion is nowadays, to have his reading, memory, and elocution, but Christ known, and Him crucified, and to build the Church skilfully, laying the foundation upon this Rock,‖ of which, if we hold our peace, the rocks themselves will cry. This being the sum of our art and task, by

---

* Musculus et Brentius in Johannem.
† Bernard.
‡ Nolanus.
§ In Præfat. ad Concionem de Christo crucifixo.
¶ Philip Melancthon in Rhetor.
‖ Lutherus.

the help of Christ, to preach the Gospel of Christ, to the praise of Christ, without whom a sermon is no sermon, preaching no preaching.*

The sum of the sum of all is, that the whole duty of all men is to give themselves wholly to Christ, to sacrifice not a leg, or an arm, or any other piece, but soul, spirit, and body, and all that is within us;† the fat, the inwards, the head and hoof, and all as a holocaust to Him, dedicating, devoting ourselves to His service all the days and hours of our lives, that all our days may be Lord's days. To whom, when we have so done, yet must we know we have given Him so much less than His due, as we worms and wretched sinners are less than the Son of God, who knew no sin. To Him therefore let us live, to Him therefore let us die. So let us live to Him that we may die in Him, and breathe out our souls most willingly, into His hands, with the like affection that John of Alexandria, surnamed the Almoner, for his bounty, is reported to have done, who, when he had distributed all he had to the poor, and made even with his revenues, as his fashion was yearly to do in his best health, thanked God he had now nothing left but his Lord and Master Christ, whom he longed to be with, and would now with unlimed and unentangled wings fly unto; or as, in fewer words, Peter of old and Lambert of later times, "Nothing but Christ, nothing but Christ."‡

2. The second extract is from a sermon on *conscience* entitled *Balm from Gilead*:

Hearken, O consciences! hear the word of the Lord. I call you to record this day, that it is your office to preach over our sermons again, or else all our sermons and labours are lost. You are the cuds of the soul, to chew over again. Against your reproofs, and against your and faithful admonitions, what exception can any take? Your balm is precious; your smitings break not the head, nor bring any disgrace. God hath given you a faculty to work wonders in private and solitude. Follow them home, therefore, cry aloud in their ears and bosoms, and apply what hath now and at other times been delivered.

---

* Perkins in Prophetica.
† Nazianzenus de Spiritu.
‡ *Ward's Sermons*, p. 10. Nichol's edition.

Conscience, if the house and owner where thou dwellest be a son of peace, let thy peace and thy Master's peace abide and rest on him; that peace which the world never knows, nor can give, nor take away. Be thou propitious and benign, speak good things, cherish the least sparks and smoke of grace; if thou findest desire in truth, and in all things, bid them not fear and doubt of their election and calling. With those that desire to walk honestly, walk thou comfortably. Handle the tender and fearful gently and sweetly; be not rough and rigorous to them. Bind up the broken hearted. Say unto them, Why art thou so disquieted and sad? When thou seest them melancholy for losses and crosses, say unto them in cheer, as Elkanah to Hannah, "What dost thou want? Am not I a thousand friends, wives, and children unto thee?"

Clap them on the back, hearten them in well-doing, spur them on to walk forward; yea, wind them up to the highest pitch of excellency, and then applaud them. Delight in the excellent of the earth.

Be a light to the blind and scrupulous.

Be a goad in the sides of the dull ones.

Be an alarm and trumpet of judgment to the sleepers and dreamers.

But as for the hypocrite, gall him and prick him at the heart. Let him well know that thou art God's spy in his bosom, a secret intelligencer, and wilt be faithful to God.

Bid the hypocrite walk "in all things."

Bid the civil add piety to charity.

Bid the wavering, inconstant, and licentious "walk constantly."

Bid the lukewarm and common Protestant for shame amend, be zealous, and "walk honestly."

But with the sons of Belial, the profane scorners, walk frowardly with them, haunt and molest them, give them no rest till they repent, be the gall of bitterness unto them. When they are swilling and drinking, serve them as Absalom's servants did Amnon, stab him at the heart. Yet remember, so long as there is any hope, that thine office is to be a pedagogue to Christ, to wound and kill, only to the end they may live in Christ, not so much to gaster and affright as to lead to Him; and, to that purpose, to be instant in season and out of season, that they may believe and repent.

But if they refuse to hear, and sin against thee, and the Holy Ghost also, then shake off the dust of thy feet, and either fall to torment them before their time, and drive them to despair; or if thou give them ease here, tell them thou wilt fly in their throat at the day of hearing when thou shalt and must speak, and they shall and must hear.

Conscience, thou hast commission to go into princes, chambers and council tables; be a faithful man of their counsel. Oh, that they would in all courts of Christendom, set policy beneath thee, and make thee president of their councils, and hear thy voice, and not croaking Jesuits, sycophants, and liars. Thou mayest speak to them, subjects must pray for them, and be subject, for thy sake, to honour and obey them in the Lord.

Charge the courtiers not to trust in uncertain favours of princes, but to be trusty and faithful, as Nehemiah, Daniel, Joseph; whose histories pray them to read, imitate and believe above Machiavelli's oracles.

Tell the foxes and politicians, that make the *main* the *by*, and the *by* the *main*, that an ill conscience hanged Ahithophel, overthrew Haman, Shebna, etc. Tell them it is the best policy, and Solomon's, who knew the best, to get and keep thy favour; to exalt thee, and thou shalt exalt them, be a shield to them, and make them as bold as the lion in the day of trouble, not fearing the envy of all the beasts of the forest, no, nor the roaring of the lion, in righteous causes.

Conscience, thou art the judge of judges, and shalt one day judge them; in the meanwhile, if they fear neither God nor man, be as the importunate widow, and urge them to do justice. Oh, that thou sattest highest in all courts, especially in such courts as are of thy jurisdiction, and receive their denomination from thee. Suffer not thyself to be exiled, make Felix tremble, discourse of judgment to them.

To the just judges, bid them please God and thee, and fear no other fear; assure them, for whatever they do, of partiality or popularity, thou wilt leave them in the lurch; but what upon thy suit and command, thou will bear them out in it, and be their exceeding great reward.

If thou meetest in those courts and findest any such pleaders as are of thine acquaintance and followers, be their fee and their promoter. Tell them, if they durst trust thee, and leave Sunday works, bribing on both sides, selling of silence, pleading in ill causes, and making the law a nose of wax, if they durst plead all and only rightful causes, thou hast riches in one hand, and honour in the other, to bestow on them.

As for the tribe of Levi, there mayest thou be a little bolder, as being men of God, and men of conscience by profession. Be earnest with them to add *con* to their *science*, as a number to cyphers, that will make it something worth. Desire them to preach, not for filthy lucre or vain glory, but for thy sake: wish them to keep thee pure, and in thee to keep the mystery of faith; assure them thou art the only ship and cabinet of orthodoxal faith, of which, if they make shipwreck by laziness and covetousness, they shall be given over to Popery and Arminianism, and lose the faith, and then write books of the apostacy, and intercession of faith, and a good conscience, which they never were acquainted withal, nor some drunkards of them, ever so much as seemed to have.*

I make no comment on the extracts I have given. I think they speak for themselves. No doubt tastes and opinions about sermons differ widely. But it is my own deliberate judgment that a man who preaches in the style of Ward will never lack hearers.

---

* *Ward's Sermons*, p. 109. Nichol's edition.

William Laud (1573–1645)

10

ARCHBISHOP LAUD AND HIS TIMES

WILLIAM LAUD, Archbishop of Canterbury, was beheaded on Tower Hill, London, in the year 1645. He was one of five archbishops in historical times who died violent deaths. Alphege was killed by the Danes in 1009 in Ethelred's reign. Thomas à Becket was suddenly murdered in Canterbury Cathedral, in the reign of Henry II.[1] Simon Sudbury was beheaded by Wat Tyler in the reign of Richard II.[2] Cranmer was burned by Papists at Oxford, in the days of Queen Mary. Laud alone died by Protestant hands, in Charles the First's time, at the beginning of the Long Parliament.

Now what have we got to do with Archbishop Laud in this present century? Many, I venture to suspect, are ready to ask that question. Two centuries have passed away since Laud died. Steam, electricity, railways, free trade, reform, education, science, have changed everything in England. Why rake up the melancholy story of a barbarous deed done in semi-barbarous times? What is Laud to us, or we to Laud, that we need trouble ourselves with him and his history?

Questions like these, I make bold to say, are rather short-sighted and inconsiderate. "History," it has been wisely said, "is philosophy teaching by examples,"[3] and of no history is that saying so true as of the history of the Church. "History," it has again been said, "has a strange tendency to repeat itself,"[4] and a close study of the history of the past will help us greatly to conjecture what will happen in the future. It is my firm belief that we have a great deal to do with

---

[1] 1170.
[2] 1381.
[3] Thucydides (c. 460–c. 400 B.C.), Athenian historian.
[4] English proverb traced back to Thucydides.

Laud, and that a knowledge of Laud's times is of great importance in the present day. I will go further. I believe that the history of Laud throws broad and clear light on the present position of the Church of England.

I must begin by throwing myself on the kind indulgence of my readers and soliciting a large measure of patience and consideration. My subject is an historical one. Few men, except Froude and Macaulay, can make history anything but dry and dull. When King Ahasuerus could not sleep, the chronicles, or history of his own times, were read to him. My subject, moreover, is peculiarly surrounded with difficulties. Never was there a character so differently estimated as that of Laud. According to some, he was a Papist and a monster of iniquity; according to others, he was a blessed martyr and an angel of light. Between the violent abuse of Prynne on the one hand, and the preposterous admiration of Heylin, Wharton, Lawson, and even Le Bas on the other, it is extremely hard to find out the truth. In short, the subject is a tangled skein, and at this distance of time it is difficult to unravel it. Nevertheless, I shall boldly try to set before my readers "the thing as it is."[1] After careful investigation my own mind is thoroughly made up. I hold that, wittingly or unwittingly, meaningly or unmeaningly, intentionally or unintentionally, Laud did more harm to the Church of England than any churchman that ever lived. He inflicted a wound that will never be healed; he worked mischief that will never be repaired.

Laud was born in the year 1573, about thirty-five years after the beginning of the Reformation, in the middle of Queen Elizabeth's reign, and came forward as a public man about the time of James the First's accession, in 1603. I ask particular attention to these dates. A moment's reflection will show that he appeared on the stage of English church history at a most critical period: that is to say, within the first seventy-five years after the commencement of the glorious English Reformation.

Seventy-five years only! How short a time that seems! Yet how many events of deepest interest to us all were crowded into that period. Within those seventy-five years the seed of Protestantism was first sown by Henry VIII, though I fully admit from low, carnal,

---

[1] Job 26:3.

and worldly motives. Then came the short but glorious reign of Edward VI, when the tender plant grew with hotbed rapidity under the fostering care of Cranmer, Ridley, Latimer, and Hooper. Then came the bloody reign of Mary, when it was cut down to the very ground by the ferocious proceedings of Bonner and Gardiner. Then came the happy reaction, on Elizabeth's accession to the throne, and the final reestablishment of the Church of England on the basis which it now occupies.

But even Elizabethan times, I am sorry to say, were not times of unmixed good to the Church of England. The truth must be spoken on this point. In our thankfulness for the good Elizabeth did, we are rather apt to overlook the harm which was done in her reign. Things were left undone that ought to have been done, and done that ought not to have been done. Partly from the Queen's characteristic Tudor love of power and jealousy of the bishops, and partly from her anxious desire to conciliate and win over the Papists, the work of the Reformation was not carried forward so energetically as it might have been. The *Zürich Letters*, published by the Parker Society, contain many hints about this. If Jewel and his companions had not been incessantly thwarted and hampered by royal interference, our church's worship and organization would probably have been made far better than it is. If Grindal had not been snubbed and stopped in the matter of the "prophesyings,"[1] the English clergy would have been a far better body than they were. His letter to the Queen on that painful occasion deserves unmixed admiration. Partly again, from the universal ignorance of toleration which prevailed among all parties, conscientious men were often persecuted for trifling offences, and the ground was prepared for an abundant crop of dissent in after times. Fuller, the historian, records some curious correspondence between Cecil and other privy councillors and Archbishop Whitgift on this subject. I am sorry to appear to depreciate Elizabeth. But truth is truth, and

---

[1] During the reign of Elizabeth, Archbishop Grindal regularly met with other Puritans for study of the Scriptures and mutual edification: *Church reform* was the primary item on their agenda. The Queen, however, interpreted those "prophesyings" (as they were called) as a political threat and ordered Grindal to cease; he refused and was then suspended by the Queen from the office of archbishop.

ought to be known; and we cannot properly understand Laud unless we understand the times which immediately preceded him.*

One bright point, however, should never be forgotten in estimating the reign of Elizabeth. The standard of doctrine in the Church of England was sound, clear, scriptural, and unmistakable. Rightly or wrongly, nothing was tolerated in pulpits which was not thoroughly Protestant, and thoroughly agreeable to all the Thirty-nine Articles. A clergyman who preached up the real presence of Christ's body and blood, under the forms of bread and wine in the sacrament—or recommended the practice of private confession to a priest—or advocated prayer to the Virgin Mary—or elevated the consecrated elements over his head in the Lord's Supper and adored them—or taught a gross, *opus operatum*[1] view of baptismal regeneration—or publicly denied the doctrine of predestination, or imputed righteousness, or justification by faith—or reviled the memory of Cranmer, Ridley, and Latimer—or called Edward VI "a young tiger-cub"[2]—or sneered at the Articles as "forty stripes save one"[3]—or recommended reunion with the Church of Rome—or hesitated to call the Pope *Antichrist*—such a man, I say boldly, unless he had been a very insignificant person, would have had a very hard time of it in the days of Good Queen Bess! The "powers that be"[4] would have come down upon him like a thunderbolt. These were subjects which were hardly even allowed to be controverted; you must either hold strong Protestant views about them, or hold your tongue.

In short, however faulty and deficient in many things, the Church of England in Queen Elizabeth's time was, in theory, downright Protestant and evangelical. Weak, by reason of her infancy, the Church may have been; defective in many points, judged by our light, no doubt she was; marred and damaged by

---

* The reader who cares to look into this subject will find a remarkable letter to Whitgift in favour of the persecuted Nonconformists, dated 1583, and signed by Burleigh, Warwick, Howard, Hatton, Shrewsbury, Leicester, Croft, Walsingham—eight leading privy councillors. See Fuller's *Church History*, vol. 3, p. 37. Tegg's Edition.

[1] "by the work working."
[2] Dr. Littledale the Tractarian. See page 3.
[3] A sarcastic use of 2 Corinthians 11:24.
[4] Romans 13:1.

stupid intolerance she certainly was; but at no period was her general standard of doctrine so scriptural and so Protestant as in the days of Elizabeth. Men and women were yet alive who had seen Rogers and Bradford burned in Smithfield—who had heard old Latimer say to Ridley at the stake, "Courage, we shall light a candle which shall never be extinguished"—who had watched gallant Hooper patiently agonizing in the fire for three quarters of an hour under the shadow of Gloucester Cathedral. Men and women in England had not yet forgotten these things. There was a widespread feeling that Popery was a false religion, and Protestantism was God's truth; that Popish doctrine in every shape was to be held in abhorrence, and that Reformation doctrines ought never to be given up. All classes held this, with very few exceptions, from the statesman in the Council Chamber down to the apprentice-boy in the shop. In short, the days of Elizabeth, with all their faults, were Protestant days. The nation was professedly a Protestant nation, and gloried in the name. This is a point which ought never to be forgotten. Well would it have been for our country if Elizabethan Protestantism had been as real and deep as it seemed.

Such were the critical times in which William Laud was allowed by God to come forward and become a power in England. Such was the state of things which he found in our church. How he deliberately set himself to oppose the current theology of his day—how he "practised and prospered"[1] for forty years—how he worked night and day to compass his ends, as "thorough" as Lord Strafford in driving on toward his mark[2]—how he rallied round him in an Arminian cave of Adullam every churchman who was discontented with the doctrines of the Reformation—how he gradually leavened our church with a distaste for true Protestantism, and a dislike for what he was pleased to call *Calvinism*—how, even after ruining Church and State by his policy, he left behind him a school of churchmen which has done immense harm to our church—all these are historical facts, which would fill a volume if fully described. In a paper like the present they can only be briefly pointed out. The utmost that I shall attempt to do is to supply a

[1] Daniel 8:12.
[2] Lord Strafford, known for his maxim, "Thorough," served with Laud as Charles the First's chief council. The Earl was executed in 1641.

bare outline of Laud's life and a brief estimate of his character, and to show the policy he had in view, the manner in which he carried it out, and the consequences to which it led. A few practical lessons for ourselves will then form a fitting conclusion to the whole.

*   *   *

William Laud was born at Reading in the year 1573, and was the son of respectable parents of the middle class. He received his early education at the grammar school of his native town and in the year 1589 entered St. John's College, Oxford. Little is known of his boyhood and youth, except that he was physically weak and puny, but intellectually vigorous, and a young man of untiring industry and application. His master at Reading School was so convinced from observation that he was one of those boys who are sure to rise in the world that he used to say, "When you are a great little man, remember Reading School." At Oxford he gradually, though slowly, made himself known and felt. In 1593 he was elected fellow of his college, and after losing two years from illness was made Master of Arts in 1598, and ordained deacon by Young, Bishop of Rochester, in 1600, and priest in 1601.

Of his ways and pursuits during the first ten years of his Oxford life very little is known, except the suspicious fact that Buckeridge, a notoriously unsound divine, was his tutor. It is evident that he was a careful observer of the times and one who thought for himself. Even at the period of his ordination he had already taken up a theological line of his own. Bishop Young is said to have observed that his studies had not been confined to the ordinary system of Geneva, but that his divinity was built "on the noble foundation of the fathers, the councils, and the ecclesiastical historians." Praise like this is suspicious. When a man makes an idol of Fathers and councils, and disparages the theology of the Reformation, we may be sure there is a screw loose in his theology. Wood, the author of *Athenæ Oxonienses*[1] says that even in his first ten years at Oxford, he was esteemed "a very forward, confident, and zealous man." Put together Bishop Young's and Wood's remarks, and you have the first

---

[1] A vast biographical dictionary of the writers and ecclesiastics who had been educated at Oxford, published in 1691.

ingredients of a very dangerous churchman. I venture the conjecture that these eleven quiet years at St. John's, Oxford, were the seed-time of all the mischief that Laud ever did and fixed the unhappy bias which characterized his whole career.

His appointment to read a divinity lecture at St. John's in 1602 was the first occasion when Laud came forward as the opponent of popular Protestantism and the avowed advocate of a new style of theology. The precise nature of the opinions he propounded is not recorded, but according to Heylin it was something like "the perpetual visibility of the Church of Christ, derived from the Apostles to the Church of Rome, and continued in that Church until the Reformation." What it was that he said exactly we do not know; but it is pretty clear that he took up ground about the Church of Rome which was quite opposed to the views of the Homilies, Jewel, and the Reformers, and most distasteful to the thorough Protestants of the University. The immediate result was that the lecturer came into collision with no less a person than Dr. George Abbot, then Vice-Chancellor of Oxford, Head of University College, and afterwards Archbishop of Canterbury—a man of great ability and deservedly high character. The afterconsequences were that from that day forward Abbot regarded Laud as a dangerous man, and Laud became marked and known as a very lukewarm Protestant, if not a friend of Popery, and an open enemy to the pure Gospel of Christ.

After serving the office of proctor in 1603, Laud took his degree as Bachelor of Divinity in 1604. The propositions he undertook to defend in his exercises for that degree supplied additional proof of his theological tendencies and increased the suspicion with which he was regarded. According to his biographers, he maintained, first, the "necessity of baptism"; and secondly that "there could be no true church without diocesan bishops." The precise nature of his statements, again, is not known but it is evident, from the stir which the exercises made, that they were thought unscriptural and unsound hitherto by Protestant churchmen. It seems most probable that, like the promoters of the Tracts for the Times, he maintained *apostolical succession* and *baptismal regeneration*. Whatever it was that he said, it is a fact that he was severely attacked by Dr. Holland, Rector of Exeter, who was at that time Regius Professor of

Divinity. As usual, nothing came of the attack, and Laud held his ground. Moral evidence of a man's theological unsoundness, and legal proof of it, are totally different things.

After damaging himself seriously in 1605 by countenancing and solemnizing a most discreditable marriage between the Earl of Essex and Lady Rich,[1] Laud got into another theological difficulty at Oxford in 1606. He delivered a sermon in St. Mary's of such a Romish tendency, that he was called in question for it by Dr. Airay, provost of Queen's, at that time Vice-Chancellor. Again we are left in ignorance of the nature of the sermon, and again we only know that, as usual, Laud contrived to escape public censure. But, like many others in a similar position, though not legally condemned, he established a strong impression in many minds that he was a thoroughly unsound divine, and deeply tainted with Romanizing opinions. Such, in short, was the scandal raised by this discourse that the famous Joseph Hall, afterwards Bishop of Norwich, took occasion to address a remarkable letter of expostulation to the preacher, which, as an indication of the estimate then made of Laud's character, deserves quoting at length. He says:

> I would I knew where to find you; then I could tell how to take direct aim. Whereas now I must pore and conjecture. Today you are in the tents of the Romanists, tomorrow in ours, the next day between both and against both. Our adversaries think you ours. We think you theirs. Your conscience finds you with both and neither. I flatter you not. This, of course, is the worst of all tempers. Heat and cold have their uses. Lukewarmness is good for nothing, but to trouble the stomach. Those that are spiritually hot find acceptation. Those that are stark cold have lesser reckoning. The mean between both is much worse, as it comes nearer to good and yet attains it not. How long will you be in this indifferency? Resolve one way, and know at last what you do hold, what you should. Cast off either your wings or your teeth; and, casting off this bat-like nature, be either a bird or a beast. To

---

[1] English noblewoman who, though married fourteen years and the mother of 7 children, bore 5 illegitimate children during the term of her marriage. After her husband left her, she lived openly with the father of her adulterines, obtained a divorce, and subsequently married him four years later.

die wavering or uncertain, yourself will grant fearful. If you must settle, when begin you? If you must begin, why not now? It is dangerous deferring that whose want is deadly, and whose opportunity is doubtful. God crieth with Jehu, "Who is on my side? who?" Look at last out of your window to Him, and in a resolute courage cast down the Jezebel that hath bewitched you. Is there any impediment which delay will abate? Is there any which a just answer cannot remove? If you would rather waver, who can settle you? But if you love not inconstancy, tell us why you stagger? Be plain, or else you will never be firm.*

In 1607, in the thirty-fourth year of his age, Laud began at last to climb the ladder of ecclesiastical preferment. A man of his stamp, who had come forward as an opponent of Protestant and evangelical theology, was sure not to lack patrons. Such men "speak of the world, and the world heareth them" (1 John 4:5). In fact, from this date, until he became a bishop, I can hardly find three years in which Laud did not obtain some piece of preferment. In 1607 he was made Vicar of Stamford, in Northamptonshire; in 1608, Rector of North Kibworth, in Leicestershire, and Chaplain to Neile, Bishop of Rochester; in 1609, Rector of West Tilbury, Essex; in 1610, Rector of Cuckstone, Kent, and then of Norton in the same county; in 1611, President of St. John's College, Oxford, and Chaplain to the King; in 1614, Prebendary of Buckden, in the diocese of Lincoln; in 1615, Archdeacon of Huntingdon; in 1616, Dean of Gloucester; in 1613, Rector of Ibstock in Leicestershire; in 1620, Canon of Westminster; and in 1622, Rector of Crick, in Northamptonshire.†

Such a number of successive preferments probably were never heaped on one man in an equal space of time! How many of them he held at once I am unable to ascertain. What he did at his various livings, whether he resided much, whether he preached much, whether he left any spiritual marks for good, are all points about which no information remains. Except the fact that in each parish he always assigned an annual pension to twelve poor persons, laid aside one-fifth of his income for charitable purposes, put the glebe

---

* Hall's *Letters*: Decade III Epist. 5.

† Laud appears to have taken the living of Crick after he became Bishop of St. David's. See his *Diary.*

house in repair, and saw that the church was supplied with becoming furniture, I can find nothing recorded. As to any evangelistic work bearing fruit in men's souls, in Stamford, North Kibworth, West Tilbury, Cuckstone, Norton, Ibstock, or Crick, we are left entirely in the dark. In truth, there is no evidence that work of this kind was at any time much in Laud's line.

Two public incidents in Laud's life during the thirteen years between 1607 and 1620 deserve special notice. One throws strong light on the estimate which was formed of him in the place where he was best known, the University of Oxford; the other supplies a striking example of the thorough, unbending style in which he drove on his own schemes for un-Protestantizing the Church of England, and thrust them down men's throats in the face of opposition.

The *first* of these incidents is the public rebuke which he received at Oxford, in consequence of a sermon which he preached before the University on Shrove Tuesday, 1614. This sermon contained matter so offensive to Protestant churchmen that the Vice-Chancellor, Robert Abbot, brother of the Archbishop of Canterbury, and afterwards Bishop of Salisbury, a man of great piety and learning, thought fit to give it a public answer the following Easter Sunday, in a sermon at St. Mary's. The following passage from Abbot's sermon is highly important, as showing what Laud's theological opinions really were:

> Some men, [said Abbot in his sermon] are partly Romish and partly English, as occasion serves them; so that a man may say unto them, "Art thou for us or for our adversaries?" They are men who under pretence of truth, and preaching against the Puritans, strike at the heart and root of the faith and religion now established among us. This preaching against the Puritans was the practice of Parsons and Campian the Jesuits, when they came into England to seduce young students. When many of them were afraid to lose their places, if they should professedly be thus, the counsel they then gave them was, that they should speak freely against the Puritans, and that would suffice. These men cannot plead that they are only accounted Papists because they speak against the Puritans, but because they speak nothing against the Papists. If they do at any time speak anything against the Papists, they do but

beat about the bush; and that but softly, for fear of awakening, and disquieting the birds that are in it. They speak nothing but that wherein one Papist will speak against another, or against equivo-cations and the Pope's temporal authority, and the like; and perhaps against some of their blasphemous opinions. But on the points of free-will, justification, concupiscence being sin after baptism, inherent righteousness, and certainty of salvation, the Papists beyond the sea can say they are wholly theirs, and the recusants at home make their brags of them. And in all things they keep so near the brink, that upon any occasion they may step over to them.

I make no comment on this passage: it speaks for itself. My readers will probably agree with me that it would have been well if vice-chancellors of Oxford had always spoken as plainly and faithfully as Robert Abbot, and that Laud is not the only person who has required such public rebuke to be given. I only ask then to mark carefully the charges against Laud which the passage contains. It shows clearly and unmistakably what was the Oxford estimate and the real nature of Laud's theology.

The *other* incident to which I ask attention in this period of Laud's life is the collision which took place between him and the Bishop of Gloucester, immediately after his appointment to the deanery of Gloucester, in the year 1616. His very first act on taking office in the cathedral was to remove the communion table from the place where it had long stood, in the midst of the choir, to the wall at the east end, where he ordered it to stand altar-wise. The change may seem a trifling one to many now, accustomed, as we have been for 200 years, to see the table in this position; but a right understanding of the old position of the table throws broad light on the famous expression, "On the north side." The change appeared a very serious matter to all good Protestants in 1616, as tending to bring back the Papal notion of an altar and to encourage the idea of a sacrifice, and a priest, and the Mass in the Lord's Supper. The people of Gloucester were of all English citizens the least likely to approve the slightest appearance of a leaning towards Popery. They had not forgotten good Bishop Hooper and the doctrine he had so often preached about the Lord's Supper before his martyrdom. Miles Smith, the Bishop of Gloucester, a holy and learned man, and one of the leading translators of the Authorised Version of the Bible, was more offended by the change than anyone and declared, if it was carried into effect, he would never enter the cathedral again. But none of these things moved Laud; in spite of bishop and people the table was moved. The Dean had his own way. The Bishop was publicly set at nought and never entered his own cathedral again, though living within fifty yards of it, until the day of his death in 1624. The feelings of the Protestant people of Gloucester were deeply wounded. It is a striking and significant fact that afterwards, when the Commonwealth Wars began, no place resisted the Cavaliers and fought for Parliament so stubbornly as this very city of Gloucester!

This unhappy transaction requires little comment from me. Like the affair of Abbot's sermon, however, it gives another insight into Laud's character. It shows him determined to carry out his own views without regard to the offence they might give to the feelings of Protestant churchmen. It shows him, like many in modern times, perfectly indifferent to his bishop's wishes and opinions the very moment they ran counter to his own. Here is the very man who preached up "Apostolical Succession" at Oxford, flying in the face of a venerable bishop, and trampling contemptuously on his conscientious scruples! It shows him, above all, beginning his official duties in a public position by making a great and suspicious stir about the sacrament of the Lord's Supper, and attaching an ominous importance to the precise position of the Lord's Table.* Need I remind many of my readers that the first step of the whole Tractarian Movement was exactly in the same direction? To exalt the Lord's Supper into a position neither warranted by the Bible, the Articles, nor the Prayer Book, and to invest the Lord's Table

---

* What Laud really thought about the Lord's Table may be seen in a very painful extract from a speech afterwards delivered by him in the Star Chamber, on the occasion of the prosecution of Prynne in 1637. He there says, "The altar" (a word, we must remember, never used in the Prayer Book), "the altar is the greatest place of God's residence upon earth. I say the greatest, yea, greater than the pulpit; for there it is, 'This is my body,' but in the pulpit it is, 'This is my word.' And a greater reverence, no doubt, is due to the body than to the word of our Lord; and so to the throne where His body is actually present than to the seat where His word useth to be proclaimed."

and all around it with a superstitious sanctity, these were among the first lessons taught by that school of which so many scholars have passed over to the Church of Rome. "I speak as to wise men; judge ye what I say?"[1]

In 1621, after five years at Gloucester deanery, Laud's ambition was once more gratified, and his power of mischief greatly increased, by his elevation to the bench as Bishop of St. David's. To thrust upon the bench, once filled by Latimer and Jewel, a man who had been publicly opposed by three vice-chancellors and a regius professor of divinity, required of course no small influence and exertion. Laud's friends were found equal to the occasion. For the appointment, he was mainly indebted to the Marquis of Buckingham, and to Williams, the well-known Bishop of Lincoln. King James, at any rate, seems to have given a very unwilling consent to his nomination. Partly, no doubt, from the character which Laud had notoriously obtained as a very lukewarm Protestant; partly from the open distrust with which Abbot, Archbishop of Canterbury, regarded him; and partly from a certain shrewdness in discerning unsound doctrine, the King raised serious objections to Laud being made a bishop. The conversation on the subject between His Majesty and Bishop Williams, preserved by Hackett in his life of Williams, is a very curious one, and shows plainly that "the British Solomon" (as people called James) was not quite such a fool as he was often thought to be:

"I keep Laud back," said the King, "from all place of rule and authority, because I find that he hath a restless spirit, and cannot see when matters are well; but loves to toss and change, and bring matters to a pitch of reformation floating in his own brain, which may endanger the steadfastness of that which is at a good pass, God be praised. I speak not at random: he hath made himself known to me to be such an one." To this Williams could only reply that Laud was "of a great and tractable wit, and would presently see the way to come out of his error." At last, wearied out by Williams' importunity, the King said, "Is there no way but you must carry it? Then take him to you: but on my soul, you will repent it;" and went away in a rage, using other words of fierce and ominous import.

[1] 1 Corinthians 10:15.

How true a prophet the King was, and how bitterly Williams afterwards smarted under Laud's base ingratitude, are notorious historical facts. But this was the way, and this the ladder, by which Laud climbed to the episcopal bench in 1621, in the forty-eighth year of his age.*

       *   *   *

We have now reached the period of Laud's life when his unhappy influence began to be felt most powerfully in every department of Church and State. For the next twenty years after 1621, his history is so intermixed with the history of every great movement in our country that to go fully into it would be to overload my subject and make a plain biographical paper a volume of history. I cannot pretend to do anything of the kind. The utmost I shall attempt to do is to supply the leading incidents of his story and the dates at which they occurred.

In 1622 I find he was appointed "Confessor"[1] to the Duke of Buckingham. In 1626 he was made Bishop of Bath and Wells, and Dean of the Chapel Royal. In 1628 he became Bishop of London. In 1630 he became Chancellor of Oxford. In 1633 he rose to be Archbishop of Canterbury and Chancellor of Dublin University. In 1640 he began at last to fall from his high estate, and in 1641 he was committed to the Tower.

How he conducted himself throughout these last twenty years of his life—how he plunged into politics with as much energy as any layman—how he became the intimate friend of such men as Buckingham, Strafford, Windebank, and others of doubtful character—how he contrived to get the reputation of having a hand in everything that went on both in Church and State—how he

---

* Hackett's story is corroborated by one told by Bishop Burnet. "I have heard," says Bishop Burnet, "my own father relate it from the mouth of old Sir William Armourer, who was of King James the First's court, being bred up from a page, that his Majesty, as Laud (then only Bishop of St. David's) walked by, but at some distance, took Prince Charles by the arm, and in his Scottish dialect said to him, 'Son, ken you yon knave Laud? He has a restless head: he'll ne'er ha' done till he has lost his own head and endangered yours.'" (*Memorials of Princess Sophia,* pp. 54, 55).

[1] Of the Romish church, a priest who hears the confessions of others and has power to grant them absolution.

managed to make himself the most unpopular man in England, from the Isle of Wight to Berwick-on-Tweed, and from the Land's End to the North Foreland—how at last not a mistake could be made, either political or ecclesiastical, without the cry being raised, "Is not the hand of Laud in all this?"—all these things are duly recorded in the historians of the times. They are far too many, and would occupy too much time to be detailed here. One general remark applies to all his career throughout these twenty years: He was always consistent, always the same, always in mischief, always playing the same game, always driving at the same end, always advocating the same theological principles, for which he had made himself notorious at Oxford.

—In 1622, before he had been a bishop a year, I find him assisting in the issue of six royal injunctions to the Clergy, in which, among other things, it is ordered "that no one, under the degree of a bishop or dean, shall preach on such deep points as predestination, or election, or the universality, efficacy, resistibility, or irresistibility of God's grace."

—In 1621 I find him procuring the suppression of an admirable association for buying up presentations and appointing good clergymen, mainly got up by the famous Dr. Gouge. The association was broken up, and the money subscribed was confiscated.

—In 1631 I find him consecrating the Church of St. Catherine Cree, London, with such superstitious ceremonies and idolatrous veneration of the Lord's Table and the elements of bread and wine, that he made every one suppose he longed to reintroduce downright Popery.

—In 1632 I find him prosecuting Sherfield, Recorder of Salisbury, for breaking a painted window in St. Edmund's Church, Salisbury, which the vestry had ordered to be removed, and this with such savage severity that the unfortunate man was fined £1,000 by the Star Chamber.

—In 1633 I find him first offending the feelings of the nation about the Sabbath by reviving and republishing "the Book of Sports," and then ungratefully trampling on the feelings of Williams, Bishop of Lincoln, by visiting his diocese as metropolitan, and opposing his known opinion about the Lord's Table.

—In 1634 I find him persecuting the French and Walloon

congregations in London, and pressing the Irish church only too successfully to give up its admirable articles.

—In 1636 I find him preparing and sending down to Scotland the notorious Scotch Liturgy, in which the *real presence* is as plainly taught as any Papist could wish, and setting all Scotland in a flame by attempting to introduce it in public worship.

—In 1637 I find him forbidding the migration to America of a large body of Puritans, among whom was the famous Oliver Cromwell, and compelling some of the very men, who afterwards upset Church and State, to remain in England against their will.

—In the same year I find him prosecuting Prynne, Burton, and Bastwick, for publishing violent writings, and actually punishing them with a fine of £5,000 each, imprisonment for life, and the hideous penalty of having their ears cut off.

—In 1640 I find him transgressing one of the first principles of our constitution by getting canons passed in Convocation without the consent of Parliament.

This list of monstrous follies might easily be increased. To enter into the particulars of them is, of course, impossible. For twenty years a petty warfare was kept up by him and his allies on the episcopal bench against some of the holiest and best ministers of the land. The catalogue of famous men who, at one time or another during Laud's day of power, were prosecuted, silenced, fined, imprisoned, or driven to retire to the Continent, is a melancholy roll, and of itself speaks volumes. John Rogers, Daniel Rogers, Thomas Hooker, Dod, Hildersham, Ward, Cotton, Bridge, Ames, Sheppard, Burroughs, Greenhill, Calamy, Whateley, Wilkinson, Goodwin, were all men who had more divinity in their little fingers than Laud had in his whole body. Yet every one of them was visited with Laud's displeasure, and in one way or another, disgracefully treated. In short, the public came to the conclusion that Laud and his companions thought Puritanism a greater sin than open immorality, and trifling acts of nonconformity worse than breaking the Ten Commandments! It really came to this that men said you might lie, or swear, or get drunk, and little notice would be taken; but to be a Puritan, or a Nonconformist, was to commit the unpardonable sin!

Never, I think, did mortal man labour so unceasingly to advance his own particular theological views as Laud, and never did any one seem so blind to the mischievous effects of his proceedings. Had half the zeal he displayed in snubbing Calvinists, persecuting Puritans, promoting Arminians, and making advances towards Rome, been shown by Grindal, Whitgift, and Abbot in propagating evangelical religion, it would have been a great blessing to the Church of England. Unhappily, we see in his case, as in many others, how much "wiser in their generation"[1] the children of this world are than the children of light. Besides, untiring activity is far more often the characteristic of the friends of error than of the friends of truth. Pharisees, Jesuits, heresiarchs, in every age, will compass sea and land and leave no stone unturned to accomplish their ends, while the so-called Protestant soldier slumbers and sleeps. It was so in the days of Laud; I fear it is too much the case in the present day.

*　　　　*　　　　*

The end came at last. The patience of the English people was at length fairly exhausted. After a long and unseemly endeavour to govern without a parliament, that unhappy monarch, Charles I, was obliged to summon the famous Long Parliament in 1640. From the very first meeting of the House of Commons the Archbishop of Canterbury's doom was sealed. Hollis, Pym, Dering, and their companions attacked Strafford and Laud without delay, and gave them no respite till they had brought them to the scaffold. The virulence of the attack made upon both these great officials, the singular unanimity with which the proceedings were carried on, the strong language which men of all parties, even quiet people like Lord Falkland, used in speaking of the Church of England are all most curious facts, and should be studied in *Rushworth's Collections*, May's *History of the Long Parliament*, or Stoughton's *Church of the Civil Wars*. They all help to show the deep dissatisfaction which Laud's policy had long created in the mind of the public, and the intensity of the dislike with which he was personally regarded. Englishmen are notoriously slow to move and curiously backward to resist constituted authority. When, therefore, Englishmen moved with such tremendous violence as the

---

[1] Luke 16:8.

House of Commons moved against Laud, it is impossible not to feel that a very strong sense of long-standing grievances must have existed.

Laud was kept a prisoner from the 18th December 1640, to the 10th of January 1645, and the greater part of that time he was confined to the Tower. The articles laid to his charge were fourteen in number. In substance they were as follows:*

1. That he had traitorously endeavoured to subvert the fundamental laws of the realm, and to persuade the King that he might levy money without the consent of Parliament.

2. That he had encouraged sermons and publications tending to the establishment of arbitrary power.

3. That he had interrupted and prevented the course of justice at Westminster Hall.

4. That he had traitorously and corruptly sold justice, and advised the King to sell judicial and other offices.

5. That he had surreptitiously caused a book of canons to be published without lawful authority, and had unlawfully enforced subscription to it.

6. That he had assumed a Papal and tyrannical power, both in ecclesiastical and temporal matters.

7. That he had laboured to subvert God's true religion, and to introduce Papal superstition and idolatry.

8. That he had usurped the nomination to many ecclesiastical benefices, and promoted persons who were Popishly affected, or otherwise unsound in doctrine or corrupt in manners.

9. That he had committed the licensing of books to chaplains notoriously disaffected to the reformed religion.

10. That he had endeavoured to reconcile the Church of England to the Church of Rome, and held intelligence with priests and the Pope, and had permitted a Popish hierarchy to be established in this kingdom.

11. That he had silenced many godly ministers, hindered the preaching of God's Word, cherished profaneness and ignorance, and caused many of the King's subjects to forsake the country.

---

* I copy Le Bas.

12. That he had endeavoured to raise discord between the Church of England and other Reformed churches, and had oppressed the Dutch and French congregations in England.

13. That he had laboured to introduce innovations in religion and government into the kingdom of Scotland, and to stir up war between the two countries.

14. That to preserve himself from being questioned for these traitorous practices, he had laboured to divert the ancient course of parliamentary proceeding, and to incense the King against all Parliaments.

Such were the charges brought against the unfortunate Archbishop, and upon these, with the addition of ten minor articles, he was finally brought to trial in March 1641. It will be seen by comparison of dates that he lingered in prison for four years. It must have been a bitter time for the fallen prelate! The execution of his friend Strafford, the battles of the Civil War, the King's ill-success, and the imposition of a fine of £20,000 on himself, no doubt were not the least part of his sorrows. At one time, in 1643, a motion was actually made in the House of Commons that Laud should be transported, untried and unheard, to New England, in America; and it is by no means quite clear that some of his enemies would not have been glad to get rid of him in this fashion.[1] But the motion fell to the ground, and at length, in the autumn of 1644, he was finally placed on his trial.

Of the trial itself I shall say but little. It was perhaps as unfair and discreditable to English history as any State trial that figures in our chronicles. The prosecution was committed to Prynne, who was the virulent and bigoted personal enemy of the prisoner.[2] Laud's

---

[1] From 1628 to 1640, in twelve years of Laud's administration, 4,000 Puritans fled to America, 77 of them ordained ministers of the Church of England.

[2] William Prynne, Puritan pamphleteer and trained lawyer, was arrested in 1633 for his tracts, sentenced to life, and (as punishment) had his ears partially cut off. Unrepentant, from his cell he issued yet more pamphlets attacking Laud and other Anglicans resulting in still further punishment: the stumps of his ears were shorn, and his cheeks were branded with the letters "S.L.", meaning "Seditious Libeler," though he preferred "Stigmata Laudis" (*the marks of Laud*). After being freed in 1640

own private papers and diary were seized and relentlessly used, and he had to defend himself under immense disadvantages. As the case went on, the evidence on many points was manifestly insufficient and would never have satisfied a really fair and impartial court. Those who wish to read up the subject should study Prynne's own narrative of this trial, in a folio called *Canterbury's Doom.* But it is as clear as daylight that Laud's condemnation was a foregone conclusion with his judges. In spite of a defence which even Prynne admits was "full, gallant, and pithy," in spite of a conspicuous absence of legal proof that he had committed anything worthy of death, at length, after great delays, the Archbishop of Canterbury was found guilty and sentenced to die.

Of his execution at Tower Hill, on the 9th of January 1645, I shall also say little. The only favour shown him on this occasion was that he was beheaded and not hanged. His demeanour on the scaffold was courageous, dignified, calm, and in every way honourable to him. His address before death was worthy of a better cause. In fact, you may say of him, as it was said of another, "Nothing in all his life became him so much as the leaving of it."[1] That his execution was as much a judicial murder as that of Sir Thomas More[2] or Cranmer, I feel no doubt at all: but I cannot for a moment admit that he deserves to be called a *martyr.* It is the cause, not the amount of suffering, which makes the martyr. That Laud met his death bravely and gallantly, I fully admit: but I never can admit that he had done nothing to exasperate men's minds against him, or that he was wholly innocent of everything laid to his charge, or that he died in support of a good cause.

*   *   *

We have now traced the life of Laud from his cradle to his grave. It only remains for me to point out the great and instructive lessons which his life appears to teach us, and the broad and clear light

---

by the Long Parliament, Prynne devoted himself to seeking revenge against Laud.

   [1] Quoted from Shakespeare's *Macbeth.*

   [2] More, a staunch Roman Catholic, refused to acknowledge Henry VIII as "head of the Church of England." In 1535 he was found guilty of treason and beheaded.

which it throws on the position of the Church of England at the present day. But before I do this, I wish to say a few words on three disputed points. These points are Laud's real character, his real policy and aims, and the real consequences of his policy. I am well aware that this is debatable ground. In walking over it I cannot expect that all will agree with me. But I give my opinion freely, and men must take it for what it is worth.

(*a*) His real *character*, then: What was it? What is the estimate that we ought to put on him? The answer, as is often the case, lies, in my judgment, between two extremes. Laud was neither so good nor so bad a man as he is often represented. To call him a saint, a martyr, an English Cyprian,[1] on one side, is simply ridiculous. I can discover no warrant for such extravagant praise. To paint him as a monster of iniquity and a child of the devil, on the other side, is equally absurd. The charge falls to the ground as *not proven*. Let us give him his due. He was not an immoral or a covetous man. Few archbishops seem to have spent so little on themselves, and to have given so largely and liberally of their substance to promote learning and to strengthen the material part of the Church of England. He was a zealous and earnest churchman. No one can deny that he spent himself and was spent in the promotion of what he thought sound "church views" and conscientiously believed he was doing right. But earnestness alone, if not rightly directed, is a very mischievous thing. Experience abundantly proves that in every age of the Church, well-meaning and conscientious men, when they are narrow-minded, short-sighted, ignorant of human nature, and obstinate, are the greatest causes of trouble. Never did man prove it so thoroughly as Laud.

He was not, I believe, a Jesuit or a Papist. His conference with Fisher and his successful dealings with Chillingworth completely negative that supposition. But to call him a sound Protestant churchman is simply absurd. He never disguised his dislike to thorough Protestant theology and laboured all his life to discourage it. The mere fact that he was twice offered a cardinal's hat by the Pope, after he became Archbishop of Canterbury, of itself speaks

---

[1] Thascius Cæcilius Cyprianus (*c.* A.D. 200–58), theologian, Bishop of Carthage, and first bishop-martyr of Africa, was executed under Valerian as an enemy of the Roman gods and law.

volumes. It shows the general impression that he made on the minds of foreigners.

That he was a spiritually-minded man, and really received the Gospel of God's grace into his heart, is a point of which we have very scanty proofs. This is a delicate matter. God forbid that we should judge him! Yet it is vain to deny that there is an absence of anything like thoroughly evangelical, experimental religion in his literary remains. There is a painful lack of anything really calculated to do good to hearts and souls. His seven sermons are poor things, and not worthy to be compared even with the discourses of men of his own school, like Andrews. His private *Diary* contains much superstition and weakness. His letters are not spiritual or striking. It is not too much to say that you will find more good divinity in ten pages of such men as his contemporaries, Usher, Davenant, Hall, and Sibbes, than in all the works of Laud. The plain truth must be spoken. Laud was much more a political churchman, an ecclesiastical Ahithophel, a zealous champion of his party, his cause, and his order, than a minister of Christ, a preacher of the Gospel, a shepherd of souls. For the work of the former character he laid himself out entirely and laboured in it night and day. For the work of the latter character he had no vocation and gave himself no time. It was not work in his line. What he really was, and what he really felt personally in his heart of hearts, is a question which I cannot pretend to solve. The last day alone will declare it. In hope and charity I leave it alone.

(*b*) Laud's real *policy* next demands our attention. What was it? What was he driving at all his life? What did he want to do? What was his object and aim? I do not believe, with some, that he really desired to Romanize the Church of England, or meant and intended, if possible, to reunite it with the Church of Rome. I think those who say this go too far and have no sufficient ground for their assertions. But I decidedly think that what he did labour to effect was just as dangerous, and would sooner or later have brought back downright Popery, no matter what Laud meant or intended. I believe that Laud's grand idea was to make the Church of England less Protestant, less Calvinistic, less evangelical, than it was when he found it. I believe he thought that our excellent Reformers had gone too far—that the clock ought to be put back a good deal. I believe his favourite theory was that we ought to occupy a medium position between the Reformation on the one side, and Rome on the other, and that we might combine the ceremonialism and sacramentalism of St. Peter's on the Tiber with the freedom from corruption and ecclesiastical independence of St. Paul's on the Thames. He did not, in short, want to go back to the Vatican, but he wanted to borrow some of its principles and plant them in Lambeth Palace. I see in those ideas and theories a key to all his policy. His one aim from St. John's, Oxford, till he was sent to the Tower, was not to Romanize, but to un-Protestantize the Church of England. Some may think this a nice and too refined a distinction. I do not. A *Romanizer* is one thing, an *un-Protestantizer* is another.

This was the explanation of his always opposing what he called *Calvinism*. He would fain have made popular Protestant theology odious by painting the doctrines of grace as inseparable from anti-nomianism and extreme views of election and reprobation. He knew too well that nothing so damages a theological cause as a cleverly chosen nickname.

This was the explanation of his making so much ado about the position of the Lord's Table. It was not merely to preserve the Table from irreverent and profane uses, but to exalt the sacrament of the Lord's Supper, and make a slight approach to the sacrifice of the Mass.

This was the explanation of his advocating extravagant views of the episcopal office, as if it were essential to a church. It helped his favourite notion that the Church of England occupied a middle position between the Presbyterian Church of Geneva and the Church of Rome—an idea, by the way, often brought forward nowadays, and about as absurd as to say the Isle of Wight occupies a middle position between England and France!

This was the explanation of his incessantly persecuting and teasing lecturers, and discouraging doctrinal preaching all over the land. He wished to make people think that the sacraments, and not the preaching of God's Word, were the principal part of Christianity.

This was the explanation of his introducing, as far as possible, such histrionic ceremonials as those with which he astonished

London at the consecration of St. Catherine Cree. He desired to show the public that churchmen could have as much sensuous and showy religion as Papists; and that if we did not have the Mass itself, the Communion Service of the Prayer Book might be so managed and manipulated as to make an excellent imitation of it.

This was the explanation of his discouraging and checking all attacks on Popery whether in the pulpit or the press, and obliging whole passages in many good books of the time to be expurgated and suppressed. He wished to lower the tone of the country about the nature of Popery and to make people less alive to its enormous evils and less awake to his own movements.

This, in the last place, but not least, was the explanation of his constantly promoting and bringing forward in the Church Arminian and semi-Protestant divines of his own school of theology. Wren, Montague, and Mainwaring are specimens of the kind of men he delighted to honour. He never threw away an opportunity of this kind. He knew the importance of backing your friends and of securing all the good things of place, power and influence for your own party. One plan was always kept in view, and that was to fill up the bench, as far as possible, with high churchmen.

Such, I believe firmly, is the true account of Laud's Policy. He had always one aim before him. Of that aim he never lost sight for a day. And while we admire his consistency, his persistency, his dogged tenacity of purpose, we must never forget the real nature of his aim. It was to *un-Protestantize* the Church of England.

(*c*) One more question demands a few words. What were the *consequences* of Laud's policy? I shall say but little on this point. Some people, I believe, who regard him as a slandered person, and venerate him as the reviver of so-called "*catholic* principles," would tell you that he did a great deal of good. From such I take leave to differ entirely. I hold that he did more harm to the Reformed Church of England than any man that ever lived—more than Gardiner, Bonner, Cardinal Pole and Queen Mary all put together. I have already said that he probably meant well and acted conscientiously. I quite believe that he thought his policy was doing God and the Church of England good service. But the consequences of his policy, both direct and indirect, were disastrous, mischievous and evil in the extreme. Let me show you what they were.

(i) One direct consequence of Laud's policy was a widespread decline of sound Protestant feeling among the clergy from which our church has never recovered. The principles and opinions of a forward, pushing archbishop like him, who practically had the key of all patronage in his pocket, were only too greedily swallowed by many. A school of divines was rapidly gathered and consolidated within our pale which has weakened our church most seriously from that period. How deep and widespread this decline was may be gathered from the *Memoirs of Panzani*, the Romish emissary to England in Laud's days, where he gives an account of the state of things in this country. He particularly mentions that Laud's great friend, Bishop Montague, told him privately, in 1636,

> that he and many of his brethren were prepared to conform themselves to the method and discipline of the Gallican Church . . . that there were only three bishops on the bench that could be counted violently bent against the Church of Rome: *viz.*, Morton, Davenant, and Hall; [and] as for the aversion to Popery which we discover in our sermons and printed books, [said Montague] they are things of form, chiefly to humour the populace and not to be much regarded.

Pretty language this from an English bishop! But what an idea it gives us of the rapid spread of Laud's theology!

(ii) But another direct consequence of Laud's policy was of a very different kind. There arose throughout the land a spirit of thorough alienation of the middle classes from the Church of England. The mass of English people gradually began to dislike a religious body which they saw principally occupied in persecuting Puritanism, silencing preachers, checking zeal, exalting forms, deifying sacraments, and complimenting Popery. The multitude seldom draws nice distinctions. It measures institutions chiefly by their working and administration, and cares little for theories and great principles. Little by little men's minds throughout the country began to connect *episcopacy* with *tyranny*, the liturgy with formality, and the Church of England with fines, imprisonments and punishments. Baxter's autobiography gives a vivid picture of the universal feeling of the kind which prevailed. Hence, when the Long Parliament assembled, there was a most painful unanimity of ill-feeling towards the poor old Church of England. The members representing all the counties and boroughs in England, with few exceptions, were found thoroughly dissatisfied with the Establishment; and the assailants, both in number and influence, completely swamped and overwhelmed the defenders. And all this was the doing of Laud! He had disgusted the bulk of the laity, lost the middle classes, and turned the Church's friends into foes.

(iii) The last and worst direct consequence of Laud's policy was the temporary destruction of the Church of England. An ecclesiastical revolution took place, which swelled at length into a kind of reign of terror. The pent-up feelings of the middle classes, once let loose, broke out into a hurricane, before which everything in the framework of the Church of England was clean swept away. Bishops and deans and clergy and liturgy were all shovelled off the stage like so much rubbish. Good things as well as bad were involved in one common ruin. A bloody civil war broke out. Charles I followed Strafford and Laud to the scaffold. Everything in Church and State was turned upside down. Order at last was only kept by the iron hand of a military dictator, Oliver Cromwell. The crown and the mitre were both alike proscribed, excommunicated, and rolled in the dust. And all this was the doing of Laud! He sowed the wind and reaped the whirlwind.

Such were the direct consequences of Laud's policy. I wish they had been all the harm that he did. But, unhappily, there were other indirect consequences of which we feel the bad effects to this very day. The whole balance of English feeling about the Church of England was completely disarranged and disturbed by his proceedings. Equilibrium has never been recovered.

A pendulum was set swinging by his mischievous folly which has now oscillated violently for over 200 years. First came a strong reaction in favour of the Church when the Stuarts returned to the throne at the Restoration, having learned nothing and forgotten nothing. Moderation and tolerance, you will remember, were then thrown to the winds. The wretched Act of Uniformity was passed, by which two thousand of the best clergy of the age were turned out of our pale and lost to our ranks for ever. Then came a long and dreary time of exhaustion and stagnation, a time during which the Church of England, like a torpid sloth, existed indeed and hung on the state tree, but scarcely lived, moved, or breathed. Then came, after a century, the revival of true Protestant religion under the auspices of those glorious clergymen Wesley and Whitefield; but a revival which our bishops could neither understand, appreciate, direct, manage, utilise, encourage, or retain. Then came the permanent establishment of Methodism and a vast increase of Nonconformity. Finally, we see in our own days the spectacle of a pure Protestant church in England which has allowed half the population to stray out of its fold and slip out of its fingers, and is neither liked, nor trusted, nor valued by the great majority of dissentients! And what was the first cause of all this? I answer again, in one sentence, the fatal policy of Archbishop Laud! He sowed the seed of which we reap the consequences. He made a whole generation of Englishmen hate the Church of England and feel no confidence in her; and the feeling survives and lingers down to the present day.

*   *   *

It only remains for me now to point out the leading lessons which Laud's history ought to teach us. I have done my best to show you the man and his character, and his policy and the consequences of it. On each of these topics, you will readily believe, much more might be said. But I am obliged to skim the surface of things and leave much to be filled up by my readers. If I can only set men thinking and reading and send them to such books as Marsden's *History of the Puritans* and Stoughton's *Ecclesiastical History*, I shall, even in this short sketch, have not laboured in vain. Let me now try to make some practical use of the whole subject.

1. The first lesson that I draw from the subject is this: Laud's history shows us that *any attempt to un-Protestantize the Church of England is fraught with peril and mischief to the Establishment*. Any man—no matter how high his rank—archbishop, bishop, dean, or archdeacon; no matter how high his character—earnest, zealous, conscientious, learned, devout, charitable, and self-denying; any man who tries to reintroduce Romish doctrines and Romish

ceremonies into the Church of England is an enemy to the Establishment and is damaging its best interests.

I am no more infallible than the Pope. I have no access to peculiar information more than other men. But it is my firm and decided conviction that the bulk of churchmen in our days will not have Romanism brought back within our pale. Some, perhaps, of the aristocracy and the nobility may approve a sensuous, histrionic religion, and see no harm in a nearer approximation to the ways of Rome. But the majority of the middle classes, and the most intelligent of the lower orders, will not have Romanism in any shape, or at any price; and if you try to thrust it down their throats, they will just leave the Church to shift for itself and walk away. There will be no more reign of terror, or ecclesiastical earthquakes. There will be no repetition of State trials. The Lauds and Montagues on our bench, if any, will not be taken to Tower Hill and beheaded. But the middle classes will just leave bishops, deans and clergy alone in their glory and forsake the Establishment. The cry will be raised, "This is not our rest, for it is polluted with Romanism: we must depart hence. To your tents, O Israel!"[1]

And what will happen then? Why, the Church will perish for want of churchmen. Generals and colonels and band alone do not make up an army; and bishops and deans and choristers and clergy alone do not make up a church. Disestablishment will come as a matter of course. The Church of a minority will not be long spared on this side of St. George's Channel any more than on the other. The tender mercies of liberal statesmen may perhaps leave the poor old church, her cathedrals, parish churches, and possibly some part of her endowments. But if the "multitude of people"[2] is the glory of a church as well as of a prince, the glory of the Church of England will have passed away for ever. "Ichabod"[3] will be written over empty naves and choirs. The Establishment will split up, or become one of the sects, like the Scotch Episcopal Church, and the page of history will record that she made shipwreck of all her greatness by the suicidal attempt to recede from Protestantism and reintroduce Popery.

[1] 1 Kings 12:16.
[2] Proverbs 14:28.
[3] 1 Samuel 4:21.

No! If I know anything of the middle classes and intelligent lower orders, they wish to have a Protestant Establishment, or no Establishment at all. They may not be hard readers or deep thinkers. But they know what Romanism was 350 years ago, and they do not want it back. They know what priestly tyranny, and the sacrifice of the Mass, and the odious confessional did before the Reformation. They have an innate, instinctive, wholesome dislike of the slightest symptom of any return to these things. They cannot draw nice distinctions; they are apt to call a spade a spade and to give things their right names. And if they see any attempt to imitate Romanism in our churches and to counterfeit Romish ceremonies, their suspicions are roused at once. The clergyman who rouses these suspicions, I say boldly, however earnest, conscientious, well-meaning, and charitable, is no friend to the Church of England and is doing immense harm.

2. The second lesson of the subject is this: Laud's history shows us *what harm may be done to a church by a very small party.* Great is the power of a minority when it acts together and is united. Great is the influence of a few determined men when they combine for mischief, see their object clearly, and endeavour incessantly and unscrupulously to carry it out. Laud's beginnings at St. John's, Oxford, were very small, but his latter end greatly increased.

This is a point, I venture to say, which is far too much overlooked. Nothing has injured the Church of England so much in the last thirty years as the habit of underrating and despising the Tractarian Movement. How small it seemed when it first began under Newman, Pusey, Keble and Richard Froude. It was a cloud which looked no bigger than a man's hand! To what portentous proportions, comparatively, it has now grown. A black thunderstorm seems to overspread one half the heavens. Well do I remember a valued Oxford friend, now dead, calling the attention of Bishop Sumner (of Chester) and Chancellor Raikes to this subject fifty years ago in a private conversation. Well do I remember the quiet smile of incredulity with which those venerable men listened, evidently thinking us young, short-sighted alarmists. "It was but a temporary delusion; it would soon pass away." *Nubecula est; transibit.* I thought, then, that they did not rightly estimate the extent of the danger. I suspect they both lived to change their minds.

Let us, then, not underrate the power of Ritualism because its adherents seem a small party, and the churches where they play at Popery are comparatively few in number. The party is not so small as it appears. It has many sympathisers throughout the country who only wait for the time when they can show their colours, and at the first shift of wind will put to sea. It must not be despised because it is small. Minorities often prove winners in the long run.

No! We ought to remember the great Duke of Wellington's maxim, that it is a cardinal mistake in war, and a cause of great disasters, to undervalue your enemy. We must make up our mind that the Ritualistic movement of this day is a very serious affair, and that it requires the utmost exertions of sound churchmen to prevent it ruining the Church of England. When we can afford to despise a little spark in a powder magazine, a little crack in a sea-wall embankment, a little leak in a ship, a little flaw in a chain cable, a few traitors in the garrison of a citadel, then, and not till then, it will be time to pooh-pooh ritualism, because its avowed adherents, like Laud's party at first, seem at present comparatively few.

3. The last lesson I draw from our subject is this: *Laud's history shows us the immense importance of the laity taking timely interest in the condition of the Church of England.* Nothing, it is clear to me, preserved the Church of England from returning bodily to Popery 200 years ago, but the active interference of the laity. I do not say it would have happened in Laud's time. I do not think he ever meant the Pope at Lambeth to be subject to the Pope at the Vatican. But I do believe that another twenty years of unopposed, systematic, persistent un-Protestantizing would have *educated* a generation of semi-Papists, and paved the way for downright Popery. From this we were not preserved by the bishops and clergy, but by the laity taking up the matter in the House of Commons. I grant their remedies were violent, and their surgery coarse and savage. They let blood profusely and did great harm in some directions, if they did good in others. But one thing I always maintain was done by Hollis, Dering, Pym, Hampden and their companions. They prevented the nation going back to Babylon. They stamped out Popery for the time in the Church of England. Even the Civil War was better than the return of Popery.

I hope the laity of this day will never forget this. They are the real hope of the Church of England. Our future depends greatly on their conduct and line of action. If they sit still and let things take their own course, I see nothing but evil before us. If they arise in their might, like their forefathers, and demand that there shall be no Romish innovations, no un-Protestantizing practices allowed in our communion, there is yet ground for hope. It is not too late to win a battle. Once let the laity raise the old cry, "*Nolumus leges Angliæ mutari*; We will have a Protestant Establishment or none at all," and I shall not despair of the Church of England.

One thing, in conclusion, is very clear. Whatever we may think about Laud, the Church of England is in a very critical position. Every one who reflects must confess this. Her rowers have brought her into troubled waters. Rent and torn by conflicting parties, her very existence is in peril. Never was there a church which had within her pale such totally opposite schools of theology. This state of things cannot last. The question may well rise in many minds, "What shall be the end? We cannot go on as we are. Will the sick man live, or will he die?"

As usual in such cases, advice is plentiful, the doctors are many, and the prescriptions abound—some homœopathic and some allopathic. Every one has his *panacea* and his *Eirenicon*.[1] "Only use it," he cries, "and the Church will be cured." Wider terms of communion, relaxation of creeds and articles, liturgical revision, synodical action, increase of the episcopate, union of the Western churches—all these are remedies gravely propounded and earnestly thrust on our attention. Each has its advocates, and each is war-ranted to cure. I have not the slightest faith in any of these healing measures. Two or three of them are downright mischievous. The best of them is not the medicine for the time. I regard them all as utterly beside the mark and unable to touch the disease.

My own mind is thoroughly made up. I know of only one cure and remedy for the ailments of our beloved church. That remedy is a revival among us of thorough Protestant principles and Protestant theology—the principles of the glorious Reformation, the theology of Latimer and Hooper and Jewel. Whether God will

---

[1] Greek, "Peace," a reference to Tractarian, E.B. Pusey, and his controversial book *Eirenicon* (1865).

grant us such a revival I cannot tell: perhaps our days are numbered. Without such a revival I have little hope for the future. We shall only fall lower and lower, and at last our candlestick will be removed, like that of Ephesus. Give us such a revival, and I hope everything. The laity would rally round us once more—the Spirit of God would be poured on our congregations. God, even the Lord God of our fathers, would give us His blessing.

I said the laity would rally round us. I say it advisedly. At present a large number of the best of them ride at single anchor and hold by the Church of England with a very loose hand. They are tired, wearied and disgusted with the undisturbed growth and progress of semi-Popery. They see no use in Protestant bishops and articles if Romanism is allowed to sit in the house of God. They may not be deep theologians, or very conversant with catholic principles and primitive antiquity. But they are not hard to satisfy. They know and feel what does them good. They want plain Protestant worship and plain Protestant preaching, and if they cannot have these in the Establishment they will soon migrate and swarm off elsewhere. The bulk of our middle classes and educated lower orders in the Church do not want chasubles, copes, dalmatics, birettas, banners, processions, incense, pastoral staffs, crucifixes, incessant bowings, turnings, and genuflections, or any such pernicious trumpery. Such things are mere gaudy toys, which may please children, and satisfy idle young men and women, and the whole herd of the ignorant, the weak-minded, and the superstitious. But they do not meet the wants of the middle-aged, the hard-headed, the hard-working men and women of the middle and lower orders. They want food —food for heart, and food for conscience; and if they do not find it in the Established Church of England, they will walk off and seek it elsewhere. Give them plain, simple, hearty Bible worship— plain, simple, hearty Bible preaching—give them the old, old story of Christ upon the cross, the real work of the Holy Ghost felt and experienced in the inner man—give them the noble lessons of repentance, faith, holiness—give them these, and they will never forsake the Church of England.* I repeat it emphatically. A return

---

* The *Times* of March 29, 1869, says most truly, "Ritualistic services may attract curious or admiring crowds, but they neither bring the poor to church nor bring religion into the homes of the poor."

to downright Protestant principles and Protestant theology is the Church's want in the present day. It is the only medicine which will heal the Church's disease.

I now wind up my paper with a short passage from the pen of a great man, which deserves special attention, partly because of his name and character, and partly because he wrote it with death before his eyes. The man I speak of is Lord William Russell, who was beheaded in Lincoln's Inn Fields on a false charge of treason, in the reign of James II, 1683. The book I find it in is *The Life of Lord W. Russell*, written by the late Earl Russell in 1820. The paper in which the passage occurs was given by the noble sufferer to his friends only a few moments before his execution. He says:

> I did believe, and do still believe, that Popery is breaking in upon this nation, and that those who advance it will stop at nothing to carry on their designs . . . I am heartily sorry that so many Protestants give their helping hand to it. But I hope God will preserve the Protestant religion and this nation, though I am afraid it will pass under very great trials and very great sufferings.

Solemn words these, and painfully prophetic! Well would it be for this country in the nineteenth century, if English peers and English prelates, English members of Parliament and English clergymen, saw the danger of Popery "breaking in upon this nation" as clearly as did in the seventeenth century the dying patriot, Lord W. Russell.

Note

The following extracts from Mr. Hallam's *Constitutional History of England* appear to me to deserve particular attention. I think so because they contain the deliberate opinion of a well-read layman, of no extreme theological views, and of one who has justly obtained a worldwide reputation on account of his learning, his correct judgment, and his impartiality:

> Laud's talents, though enabling him to acquire a large portion of theological learning, seem to have been by no means considerable. There cannot be a more contemptible work than this Diary; and his letters to Strafford display some smartness, but no great capacity. He managed, indeed, his own defence when impeached with some ability; but on such occasions ordinary men are apt to put forth a remarkable readiness and ability. . . . Though not literally destitute of religion, it was so subordinate to worldly interest, and so blended in his mind with the impure alloy of temporal pride, that he became an intolerant persecutor of the Puritan clergy, not from bigotry, which in its usual sense he never displayed, but systematic policy. And being subject, as his friends call it, to some infirmities of temper—that is, choleric, vindictive, harsh, and even cruel to a great degree—he not only took a prominent share in the severities of the Star Chamber, but perpetually lamented that he was restrained from going further lengths.[*]
>
> All the innovations of the school of Laud were so many approaches in the exterior worship of the Church to the Roman model. Pictures were set up or repaired; the Communion Table took the name of an altar; it was sometimes made of stone; obeisances were made to it; the crucifix was sometimes placed upon it; the dress of the officiating priests became more gaudy; churches were consecrated with strange and mystical pageantry. These petty superstitions, which would of themselves have disgusted a nation accustomed to despise as well as abhor the pompous rites of the Catholics, became more alarming from the

---

[*] Hallam's *Constit. Hist. of England*, vol. 2, p. 54.

evident bias of some leading churchmen to parts of the Romish theology. The doctrine of a real presence, distinguishable only by vagueness of definition from that of the Church of Rome, was generally held. Montague, Bishop of Chichester, already conspicuous and justly reckoned the chief of the Romanizing faction, went a considerable length towards admitting the invocation of saints. Prayers for the dead, which lead at once to the tenet of purgatory, were vindicated by many. In fact, there was hardly any distinctive opinion of the Church of Rome which had not its abettors among the bishops, or those who wrote under their patronage.[*]

---

[*] *Ibid.* p. 86, edit. 1832.

Richard Baxter (1615–1691)

II

RICHARD BAXTER

THERE are subjects about which it is well to look behind us. There are matters in which a knowledge of the past may teach us wisdom for the present and the future. The history of religion is pre-eminently such a subject and matter. Steam, electricity, railways, and gas have made a wonderful difference in the temporal condition of mankind in the last two hundred years. But all this time the Bible and the hearts of men have remained unaltered. That which men did and thought in religious matters two hundred years ago, they are capable of doing and thinking again. What they thought and did in England in the seventeenth century it is well to know.

And just as there are subjects about which it is wise to look behind us, so also there are times long gone by which deserve our special attention. There are times when the character of a nation receives an indelible impression from events which take place in a single generation. There have been times when the dearest privileges of a people have been brought to the birth and called into vigorous existence through the desperate agony of civil war and religious strife. Such, I take leave to say, were the times of which I am about to speak in this biography. To no times are Englishmen so deeply indebted for their civil and religious liberty as the times in which Baxter lived. To no body of men do they owe such an unpaid debt of gratitude as they do to that noble host of which Baxter was a standard bearer—I mean the Puritans. To no man among the Puritans are the lovers of religious freedom under such large obligations as they are to Richard Baxter.

I am fully sensible of the difficulties which surround the subject. It is a subject which few historians handle fairly, simply because they do not understand spiritual religion. To an unconverted man the religious differences of the day of the Puritans must necessarily appear foolishness. He is no more qualified to give an opinion about them than a blind man is to talk of pictures. It is a subject which no clergyman of the Church of England can approach without laying himself open to misrepresentation. He will be suspected of disaffection to his own church if he speaks favourably of men who opposed bishops. But it is a subject on which it is most important for Englishmen to have distinct opinions, and I must ask for it a patient hearing. If I can correct some false impressions, if I can supply a few great principles to guide men in these perilous times, I feel I shall have done my readers an essential service. And if I fail to interest them in "Baxter and his Times," I am sure the fault is not in the subject, but in me.

I. Baxter's Times

The *times* in which Baxter lived comprehend such a vast amount of interesting matter that I must of necessity leave many points in their history entirely untouched. My meaning will be plain when I say that he was born in 1615 and died in 1691. Nearly all his life was passed under the dynasty of a house which reigned over England, with no benefit to the country and no credit to itself—I mean the Stuarts.

He lived through the reign of James I, Charles I, Charles II, and James II, and was buried in the reign of William III. He was in the prime of life and intellectual vigour all through the days of the Commonwealth and the Civil Wars. He witnessed the overthrow of the Monarchy and the Church of England, and their subsequent reestablishment. He was a contemporary of Cromwell, of Laud, of Strafford, of Hampden, of Pym, of Monk, of Clarendon, of Milton, of Hale, of Jeffreys, of Blake. In his days took place the public execution of an English monarch, Charles I; of an Archbishop of Canterbury, Laud; and of a Lord Lieutenant of Ireland, Strafford. Within the single period of his life are to be found the Plague, the Fire of London,[1] the Westminster Assembly, the Long

---

[1] In a remarkable stroke of providence, the Fire of London (1666) followed directly after the Plague (1665–66), which immediately succeeded the Five Mile Act (1665), the Conventicle Act (1664), and the Act of

Parliament, the Savoy Conference, and the rejection of two thousand of the best ministers of the Church of England by the Act of Uniformity.

Such were the eventful times in which Baxter lived. I cannot, of course, pretend to enter fully into them. Their history forms a huge picture, like the moving panorama of the Mississippi, which it is utterly impossible to take in at a glance. I shall simply try to fix attention on a few of the leading features of the picture, and I shall choose those points which appear to me most likely to be useful in the present day.

(a) One remarkable feature in the history of Baxter's times is *the move backward from the principles of the Protestant Reformation*, which commenced in his youth. Doctrines and practices began to be maintained, both by preachers and writers in the Church of England, which Latimer and Jewell would never have sanctioned. Sound evangelical teaching was decried and run down under the specious name of *Calvinism*. Good bishops, like Davenant, were snubbed and reprimanded. Bad bishops, like Montague and Wren, were patted on the back and encouraged. Preaching and lecturing were depreciated, and forms and ceremonies were exalted. The benefits of episcopacy were extravagantly magnified. Candlesticks and crosses and all manner of Popish ornaments were introduced into some of the churches. The sanctity of the Lord's Day was invaded by the abominable "Book of Sports," and common people were encouraged to spend Sunday in England as it is now spent in France. The communion tables, which up to this time had stood in the middle of the chancel, were removed to the east end of the churches, put behind rails, and profanely called *altars*. Against all these sapping and mining operations some, no doubt, protested loudly; but still the sappers and miners went on.

The prime agent in the whole movement was Archbishop Laud.

Uniformity (1662). When the Great Plague struck, 68,000 died the first year alone, inspiring many of the conforming ministers to flee the City. Nonconformists then gathered up congregations from the abandoned flocks and preached to the people. After more than 78,000 deaths, the Plague was finally stopped by the Great Fire, the worst fire in London's history. Raging for four days, it destroyed a large part of the City, including 13,000 houses and 89 churches.

Whether that unhappy man really intended to reunite the Church of England with the Church of Rome is a question which will probably never be settled till the last day. One thing is very certain: no one could have played the game of Rome more thoroughly than he did. Like many a mischief-maker before and since, Laud pulled the house in which he lived upon his own head. He raised a storm at length, before which the Church, the throne, and the bishops all went down together, and in the midst of which he himself was put on his trial and lost his life. But the Church of England received an injury in Laud's days from which it has never entirely recovered. Since his time there never has been wanting a succession of men amongst its ministers who have held most of Laud's principles, and occasionally have boldly walked in his steps. So true are the words of Shakespeare: "The evil that men do lives after them."[1] The harm that Queen Mary did to the Church of England was nothing compared to the harm done by Laud.

We must never underrate the mischief that one bold, bad man can do, and especially in matters of religion. The seeds of error are like thistledown. One head of a thistle scattered by the wind will sow a whole field. One Tom Paine can rear up infidels all over the world.[2] One Laud can leaven generations with untold mischief. Never let us suppose that extreme ritualism is a legitimate child of the Church of England. It is not so. It was scarcely heard of till the time of the Stuarts. Never let us suppose that Tractarianism, or *ritualism*, so called, is a new invention of these latter days. It is not so. It is more than two hundred years old. The father of extreme ritualists is Archbishop Laud. Let us remember these things, and we shall have learned something from Baxter's times.

(*b*) Another remarkable feature in the history of Baxter's times is *the famous Civil War between Charles I and his Parliament*. All war is an evil—a necessary evil sometimes—but still an evil; and of all wars, the most distressing is a civil war. It is a kind of huge family quarrel. It is a struggle in which victory brings no glory, because the strife has been the strife of brethren. Edge Hill and Newbury and

---

[1]   Quoted from *Julius Cæsar*.

[2]   Thomas Paine (1737–1809) was an English-American writer remembered by his generation as the "worlds greatest infidel," for his work *Age of Reason* (1794).

Marston Moor and Naseby and Worcester are names which call up none but painful reflections. The victors in each battle had spilt the blood of their own countrymen and lessened the general strength of the nation.

But there is a point of view in which the Civil War between Charles I and his Parliament was peculiarly distressing. I allude to the striking fact that the general irreligion and immorality of the King's party did more to ruin his cause than all the armies which the Parliament raised. There were hundreds and thousands of steady, quiet men, who, at the beginning of the war, were desirous to be still and help neither side. But when they found that a man could not read his Bible to his dependents and have prayer in his family without being persecuted as a Roundhead, they felt obliged, in self-defence, to join the Parliamentary forces. In plain words, the wickedness and profligacy of many of the Cavaliers drove godly men into the ranks of their enemies. That there was plenty of hypocrisy, fanaticism, and enthusiasm on the Parliamentary side, I make no question. That there were some good men among the Cavaliers, such as Lord Falkland, I do not deny. But, after every allowance, I have no doubt there was far more true religion among those who fought for the Parliament than among those who fought for the King.

The result of the Civil War, under these peculiar circumstances, never need surprise anyone who knows human nature. The drinking, swearing, roystering troopers, who were led by Prince Rupert and Wilmot and Goring proved no match for the praying, psalm-singing, Bible-reading men whom Cromwell and Fairfax and Ireton and Harrison and Fleetwood and Desborough brought into the field. The steadiest men will, in the long run, make the best soldiers. A side which has a strong religious principle among its supporters will seldom be a losing one. "Those who honour God, God will honour; and they that despise Him shall be lightly esteemed."[1]

I shall dismiss the subject of the Civil War with one *general remark* and one *caution*.

My *general remark* is that deeply as we must regret the Civil War,

---

[1] 1 Samuel 2:30.

we must in fairness remember that we probably owe to it the free and excellent Constitution which we possess in this country. God can bring good out of evil. The oscillations of England between despotism and anarchy, and anarchy and despotism, for many years after the breach between Charles I and the House of Commons, were certainly tremendously violent. Still we must confess that great political lessons were probably imprinted on the English mind at that period, of which we are reaping the benefit at this very day. (i) Monarchs were taught that, like planets in heaven, they must be content to move in a certain orbit, and that an enlightened people would not be governed and taxed without the consent of an unfettered House of Commons. (ii) Nations were taught that it is a far easier thing to pull to pieces than to build, and to upset an ancient monarchy than to find a government which shall be a satisfactory substitute. Many of the foundations of our choicest national privileges, I make no doubt, were laid in the Common-wealth times. We shall do well to remember this. We may rest satisfied that this country owes an immense debt of gratitude to Brooke and Hampden and Eliot and Whitelock and Pym.

The *caution* I wish to give respects the execution of Charles I. We shall do well to remember that the great bulk of the Puritans were entirely guiltless of any participation in the trial and death of the King. It is a vulgar error to suppose, as many do, that the whole Parliamentary party are accountable for that wicked and impolitic act. The immense majority of the Presbyterians protested loudly against it. Baxter tells us expressly in his autobiography[1] that, to-gether with many other ministers, he declared his abhorrence of it and used every exertion to prevent it. The deed was the doing of Cromwell and his immediate adherents in the army, and it is at their door that the whole guilt must lie. That the great body of the Puritans espoused the Parliamentary side there is no doubt. But as to any abstract dislike to royalty, or assent to King Charles's death, the Puritans are entirely innocent. Let us remember this, and we shall have learned something from the history of Baxter's times.

(*c*) The next feature in the history of Baxter's times to which I shall venture to call attention is *the rise and conduct of that remarkable*

---

[1] *Reliquiæ Baxterianæ* (1696)

man, Oliver Cromwell. There are few men on whose character more obloquy has been heaped than Oliver Cromwell. He has been painted by some as a monster of wickedness and hypocrisy. Nothing has been too bad to say of him. Such an estimate of him is simply ridiculous. It defeats the end of those who form it. They forget that it is no compliment to England to suppose that it would so long tolerate the rule of such a monster. The man who could raise himself from being the son of a brewer at Huntingdon to be the most successful general of his age, and absolute dictator of this country for many years, must, on the very face of facts, have been a most extraordinary man.

For my own part I say frankly that I think we ought to consider the estimate of Cromwell, which Carlyle and D'Aubigné have formed, to be a near approach to the truth. I own I cannot go the lengths of the latter writer. I dare not pronounce positively that Cromwell was a sincere Christian. I leave the question in suspense. I hazard no opinion about it, one way or the other, because I do not find sufficient materials for forming an opinion. If I were to look at his private letters only, I should not hesitate to call him a converted man. But when I look at some of his public acts, I see much that appears to me quite inexplicable. And when I observe how doubt-fully Baxter and other good men, who were his contemporaries, speak of him, my hesitancy as to his spirituality is much increased. In short, I turn from the question in a state of doubt.

That Oliver Cromwell was one of the greatest Englishmen that ever lived I feel no doubt at all. No man, perhaps, ever won supreme power by the sword, and then used that power with such moderation as he did. England was probably more feared and respected throughout Europe during the short time that he was Protector than she ever was before, or ever has been since. His very name carried terror with it. He declared that he would make the name of an Englishman as great as ever that of a Roman had been. And he certainly succeeded. He made it publicly known that he would not allow the Protestant faith to be insulted in any part of the world. And he kept his word. When the Duke of Savoy began to persecute the Vaudois in his days, Cromwell interfered at once on their behalf and never rested till the Duke's army was recalled from their villages, and the poor people's goods and houses restored.

When certain Protestants at Nismes, in France, were threatened with oppressive usage by the French Government, Cromwell instructed his ambassador at Paris to insist peremptorily that proceedings against them should be dropped, and in the event of a refusal, to leave Paris immediately. In fact, it was said that Cardinal Mazarin, the French Minister, would change countenance when Cromwell's name was mentioned; and that it was almost proverbial in France that the Cardinal was more afraid of Cromwell than of the devil. As for the Pope, he was so dreadfully frightened by a fleet which Cromwell sent into the Mediterranean under Blake to settle some matters with the Duke of Tuscany that he commanded processions to be made in Rome, and the Host to be exposed for forty hours, in order to avert the judgments of God and save the Church. In short, the influence of English Protestantism was never so powerfully felt throughout Europe as it was in the days of Oliver Cromwell.

I will only ask my readers to remember, in addition to these facts, that Cromwell's government was remarkable for its toleration, and this, too, in an age when toleration was very little understood—that his private life was irreproachable—and that he enforced a standard of morality throughout the kingdom which was, unhappily, unknown in the days of the Stuarts. Let us remember all these things, and then I think we shall not lightly give way to the common opinion that Cromwell was a wicked and hypocritical man. Let us rest assured that his character deserves far better treatment than it has generally received hitherto. Let us regard him as one who, with all his faults, did great things for our country. Let not those faults blind our eyes to the real greatness of his character. Let us give him a high place in the list of great men before our mind's eye. Let us do this, and we shall have learned something from Baxter's times.

(d) There is one more feature in the history of Baxter's times which I feel it impossible to pass over. I allude to *the suicidal blindness of the Church of England under the Stuarts.* I touch on this subject with some reluctance. I love the Church of which I am a minister, heartily and sincerely. But I have never found out that my church lays claim to infallibility, and I am bound to confess that in the times of the Stuarts she committed some tremendous mistakes. Far be it from me to say that these mistakes were chargeable upon all her members. Abbot and Carlton and Davenant and Hall and Prideaux and Usher and Reynolds and Wilkins were bright exceptions among the bishops, both as to doctrine and practice. But, unhappily, these good men were always in a minority in the Church; and the manner in which the majority administered the affairs of the Church is the subject to which I wish to call attention. We ought to know something about the subject, because it serves to throw immense light on the history of our unhappy religious divisions in this country. We ought to know something of it, because it is one which is intimately bound up with Baxter's life.

One part of the suicidal blindness of the Church to which I have referred was its long-continued attempt to compel conformity, and prohibit private religious exercises by pains and penalties. A regular crusade was kept up against everybody who infringed its canons or did anything contrary to its rubrics. Hundreds and thousands of men, for many years, were summoned before magistrates, fined, imprisoned, and often ruined; not because they had offended against the Gospel or the Ten Commandments, not because they had made an open attack on the churches; but merely because they had transgressed some petty ecclesiastical bylaw, more honoured in the breach than in the observance; or because they tried by quiet, private meetings to obtain some spiritual edification over and above that which the public services of the Church provided.

At one time we read of good men having their ears cut off and their noses slit for writing unfavourably of bishops! This was the fate of the father of Archbishop Leighton![1] At another time we read of an enactment by which anyone present at a meeting of five or more persons, where there was any exercise of religion in other

---

[1] Prosecuted in 1630 in the Star Chamber for writing *Zions's Plea Against Prelacy*, Alexander Leighton was deprived of his holy orders and imprisoned. Having escaped, he was then recaptured whereupon he was first severely whipped, put in the pillory, had one of his ears cut off, his nose was slit, and he was branded on the cheek with a red-hot iron. He was then taken back to the Fleet prison, kept there for a week, and "his sores upon his back, ears, nose and face being not cured, he was whipped again in the pillory in Cheapside, and there had the remainder of his sentence executed upon him, by cutting off the other ear, slitting the other side of the nose, and branding the other cheek."

manner than that allowed by the Liturgy of the Church of England, was to be fined, or imprisoned for three months for the first offence, six months for the second offence, and for the third, transported for seven years! Many were afraid to have family prayer if more than four acquaintances were present! Some families had scruples about saying grace if five strangers were at table![1] Such was the state of England in the seventeenth century under the Stuarts.

The result of this miserable policy was just exactly what might have been expected. There arose a spirit of deep discontent on the part of the persecuted. There sprung up among them a feeling of disaffection to the Church in which they had been baptized, and a rooted conviction that a system must necessarily be bad in principle which could bear such fruits. Men became sick of the very name of the Liturgy, when it was bound up in their memories with a fine or a gaol. Men became weary of episcopacy, when they found that bishops were more frequently a terror to good works than to evil ones. The words of Baxter, in a striking passage on this subject in his autobiography, are very remarkable: "The more the bishops thought to cure schism by punishment, the more they increased the opinion that they were persecuting enemies of godliness, and the captains of the profane."

And who that knows human nature can wonder at such a state of feeling? The mass of men will generally judge an institution by its administration, more than by its abstract excellencies. When plain Englishmen saw that a man might do almost anything so long as he did not break an ecclesiastical canon—when they saw that people might gamble, and swear, and get drunk, and no one made them afraid, but that people who met after service to sing psalms and join in prayer were heavily punished—when they saw that godless, ignorant, reprobate, profligate spendthrifts sat under their own vines and fig trees in peace, so long as they conformed and went to their parish churches, but that humble, holy, conscientious, Bible-reading persons, who sometimes went out of their parishes to church, were severely fined—when they found that Charles II and

---

[1] The Conventicle Act of 1664 banned meetings for worship of more than five persons unless they used the Prayer Book, thus barring Dissenters from holding separate church services.

his boon companions were free to waste a nation's substance in riotous living, while the saints of the nation, like Baxter and Jenkyn, were rotting in gaols—I say, when plain Englishmen saw these things, they found it hard to love the Church which did them. Yet all this might often have been seen in many counties of England under the Stuarts. If this was not suicidal blindness on the part of the Church of England, I know not what is. It was helping the devil by driving good men out of her communion. It was literally bleeding herself to death.

The crowning piece of folly which the majority in the Church of England committed under the Stuarts was procuring the Act of Uniformity to be enacted in the year 1662. This, you must remember, took place at the beginning of Charles the Second's reign, and shortly after the reestablishment of the Monarchy and the Church. This famous act imposed terms and conditions of holding office on all ministers of the Church of England which had never been imposed before, from the time of the Reformation. It was notoriously so framed as to be offensive to the consciences of the Puritans, and to drive them out of the Church. For this purpose it was entirely successful. Within a year no less than two thousand clergymen resigned their livings rather than accept its terms. Many of these two thousand were the best, the ablest, and the holiest ministers of the day. Many a man who had been regularly ordained by bishops, and spent twenty or thirty years in the service of the Church without molestation, was suddenly commanded to accept new conditions of holding preferment, and turned out to starve because he refused. Sixty of the leading parishes in London were at once deprived of their ministers, and their congregations left like sheep without a shepherd. Taking all things into consideration, a more impolitic and disgraceful deed never disfigured the annals of a Protestant church.

It was a disgraceful deed, because it was a flat contradiction to Charles the Second's own promise at Breda, before he came back from exile. He was brought back on the distinct understanding that the Church of England should be reestablished on such a broad and liberal basis as to satisfy the conscientious scruples of the Puritans. Had it not been for the assistance of the Puritans he would never have got back at all. And yet as soon as the reins of power were fairly in the King's hands, his promise was deliberately broken![1]

It was a disgraceful deed, because the great majority of the ejected ministers might easily have been retained in the Church by a few small concessions. They had no abstract objection to episcopacy, or to a liturgy. A few alterations in the prayers and a moderate liberty in the conduct of Divine worship, according to Baxter's calculation, would have satisfied 1,600 out of the 2,000. But the ruling party were determined not to make a single concession. They had no wish to keep the Puritans in the Church. When someone observed to Archbishop Sheldon, the chief mover in the business, that he thought many of the Puritans would conform and accept the Act of Uniformity, the Archbishop replied, "I am afraid they will."[2] To show the spirit of the ruling party in the Church, they actually added to the number of apocryphal lessons in the Prayer Book calendar at this time. They made it a matter of congratulation among themselves that they had thrust out the Puritans, and got in Bel and the Dragon!

It was a disgraceful deed, because the ejected ministers were, many of them, men of such ability and attainments that great concessions ought to have been made in order to retain them in the Church. Baxter, Poole, Manton, Bates, Calamy, Brooks, Watson, Charnock, Caryl, Howe, Flavel, Bridge, Jenkyn, Owen, Goodwin, are names whose praise is even now in all the churches. The men who turned them out were not to be compared to them. The names of the vast majority of them are hardly known. But they had power on their side, and they were resolved to use it.

It was a disgraceful deed, because it showed the world that the

---

[1] Charles' promise included "a liberty to tender consciences, and that no man shall be disquieted or called in question for differences of opinion in matters of religion which do not disturb the peace of the kingdom" (D.M. Lloyd-Jones, *From Puritanism to Nonconformity*, Evangelical Press of Wales, 1991, p. 27).

[2] Disappointed by the number of Puritans who complied with the Act, Sheldon said, "If we thought so many would have conformed, we would have made the Act stricter" (Ibid., 32). Sheldon also dictated the agenda at the Savoy Conference, called to make revisions to the Prayer Book. There he ignored the Reformed Liturgy presented by Baxter and refused to consider most Puritan objections to the Prayer Book.

leaders of the Church of England, like the Bourbons in modern times, had learned nothing and forgotten nothing during their exile. They had not forgotten the old bad ways of Laud, which had brought such misery on England. They had not learned that conciliation and concession are the most becoming graces in the rulers of a church, and that persecution in the long run is sure to be a losing game.

I dare not dwell longer on this point. I might easily bring forward more illustrations of this sad feature in Baxter's times. I might speak of the infamous Oxford Act in 1665, which forbade the unhappy ejected ministers to live within five miles of any corporate town, or of any place where they had formerly preached. But enough has been said to show that when I spoke of the suicidal blindness of the Church of England, I did not speak without cause. The consequences of this blindness is manifest to anyone who knows England. The divided state of Protestantism in this country is of itself a great fact, which speaks volumes.

Against the policy of the ruling party in the Church of England under the Stuarts, I always shall protest. I do not feel the scruples which Baxter and his ejected brethren felt about the Act of Uniformity. Much as I respect them, I think them wrong and misguided in their judgments. But I think that Archbishop Sheldon and the men who refused to go one step to meet them were far more wrong and far more misguided. I believe they did an injury to the cause of true religion in England, which will probably never be repaired, by sowing the seeds of endless divisions. They were the men who laid the foundation of English dissent. I believe they recklessly threw away a golden opportunity of doing good. They might easily have made my own beloved church far more effective and far more useful than she ever has been by wise and timely concessions. They refused to do this, and instead of a healing measure, brought forward their unhappy Act of Uniformity. I disavow any sympathy with their proceedings and can never think of them without the deepest regret.

I cannot leave the subject of Baxter's times without offering one piece of counsel to my readers. I advise you, then, not to believe everything you may happen to read on the subject of the times of the Stuarts. There are no times, perhaps, about which prejudice and party-spirit have so warped the judgment and jaundiced the eyesight of historians. If anyone wants a really fair and impartial history of the times, I strongly advise him to read Marsden's *History of the Puritans*. I regard these two volumes as the most valuable addition which has been made to our stock of religious history in modern times.

II. Baxter Himself

I now turn from Baxter's times to Baxter *himself*. Without some knowledge of the times, we can hardly understand the character and conduct of the man. A few plain facts about the man will be more likely than anything I can write to fasten in our minds the times. Richard Baxter was the son of a small landed proprietor of Eaton Constantine, in Shropshire, and was born, in 1615, at Rowton, in the same county where Mr. Adeney, his mother's father, resided.

He seems to have been under religious impressions from a very early period of his life, and for this, under God, he was indebted to the training of a pious father. Shropshire was a very dark, ungodly county in those days. The ministers were generally ignorant, graceless, and unable to preach; and the people, as might be expected, were profligate and despisers of them that were good. In Eaton Constantine, the parishioners spent the greater part of the Lord's Day in dancing round a Maypole near old Mr. Baxter's door, to his great distress and annoyance. Yet even here grace triumphed over the world in the case of his son, and he was added to the noble host of those who "serve the LORD from their youth."[1]

It is always interesting to observe the names of religious books which God is pleased to use in bringing souls to the knowledge of Himself. The books which had the most effect on Baxter were Bunny's *Resolution*; Perkins on *Repentance*, on *Living and Dying Well*, and on *The Government of the Tongue*; Culverwell on *Faith*; and Sibbes's *Bruised Reed*. Disease and the prospect of death did much to carry on the spiritual work within him. He says in his autobiography, "Weakness and pain helped me to study how to die. That set me on studying how to live, and that on studying the

---

[1] 1 Kings 18:12.

doctrines from which I must fetch my motives and my comforts."

At the age of twenty-two he was ordained a clergyman by Thornborough, Bishop of Worcester. He had never had the advantage of an university education. A free-school at Wroxeter and a private tutor at Ludlow had done something for him; and his own insatiable love of study had done a good deal more. He probably entered the ministry far better furnished with theological learning than most young men of his day. He certainly entered it with qualifications far better than a knowledge of Greek and Hebrew. He entered it truly moved by the Holy Ghost, and a converted man. He says himself:

> I knew that the want of academical honours and degrees were like to make me contemptible with the most. But yet, expecting to be so quickly in another world, the great concernment of miserable souls did prevail with me against all impediments. And being conscious of a thirsty desire of men's conscience and salvation, I resolved, that if one or two souls only might be won to God, it would easily recompense all the dishonour which, for want of titles, I might undergo from men.

From the time of his ordination to his death, Baxter's life was a constant series of strange vicissitudes, and intense physical and mental exertions. Sometimes in prosperity and sometimes in adversity—sometimes praised and sometimes persecuted—at one period catechising in the lanes of Kidderminster, at another disputing with bishops in the Savoy Conference—one year writing the *Saint's Rest*, at the point of death, in a quiet country house, another year a marching chaplain to a regiment in Cromwell's army —one day offered a bishopric by Charles II, another cast out of the Church by the Act of Uniformity—one year arguing for monarchy with Cromwell, and telling him it was a blessing, another tried before Jeffreys on a charge of seditious writing—one time living quietly at Acton in the society of Judge Hale, at another languishing in prison under some atrocious ecclesiastical persecution—one day having public discussions about infant baptism with Mr. Tombes in Bewdley Church, another holding the reading-desk of Amersham Church from morning to night against the theological arguments of antinomian dragoons in the gallery—sometimes preaching the plainest doctrines, sometimes handling the most abstruse meta-physical points—sometimes writing folios for the learned, some-times writing broadsheets for the poor—never perhaps, did any Christian minister fill so many various positions; and never, certainly, did anyone come out of them all with such an un-blemished reputation. Always suffering under incurable disease, and seldom long out of pain—always working his mind to the utter-most, and never idle for a day—seemingly overwhelmed with business, and yet never refusing new work—living in the midst of the most exciting scenes, and yet holding daily converse with God —not sufficiently a partisan to satisfy any side, and yet feared and courted by all—too much of a Royalist to please the Parliamentary party, and yet too much connected with the Parliament and too holy to be popular with the Cavaliers—too much of an Episco-palian to satisfy the violent portion of the Puritan body, and too much of a Puritan to be trusted by the bishops—never, probably, did Christian man enjoy so little rest, though serving God with a pure conscience, as did Richard Baxter.

In 1638 he began his ministry by preaching in the Upper Church at Dudley. There he continued a year. From Dudley he removed to Bridgnorth. There he continued a year and three-quarters. From Bridgnorth he removed to Kidderminster. From thence, after two years, he retired to Coventry, at the beginning of the Commonwealth troubles, and awaited the progress of the Civil War. From Coventry, after the Battle of Naseby, he joined the Parliamentary Army in the capacity of regimental chaplain. He took this office in the vain hope that he might do some good among the soldiers, and counteract the ambitious designs of Cromwell and his friends. He was obliged by illness to give up his chaplaincy in 1646, and lingered for some months between life and death at the hospitable houses of Sir John Coke of Melbourne, in Derbyshire, and Sir Thomas Rous of Rouslench, in Worcester-shire. At the end of 1646 he returned to Kidderminster and there continued labouring indefatigably as parish minister for fourteen years. In 1660 he left Kidderminster for London, and took an active part in promoting the restoration of Charles II, and was made one of the King's chaplains. In London, he preached successively at St. Dunstan's, Black Friars', and St. Bride's. Shortly after this he was offered the bishopric of Hereford, but thought fit to refuse it. In 1662 he was one of the two thousand ministers who were turned out of the Church by the Act of Uniformity. Immediately after his ejection he married a wife who seems to have been every way worthy of him, and who was spared to be his loving and faithful companion for nineteen years. Her name was Margaret Charlton, of Apley Castle, in Shropshire. After this he lived in various places in and about London—at Acton, Totteridge, Bloomsbury, and at last in Charterhouse Square. The disgraceful treatment of his enemies made it almost impossible for him to have any certain dwelling-place. Once, at this period of his life, he was offered a Scotch bishopric, or the mastership of a Scotch university, but declined both offices. With few exceptions, the last twenty-nine years of his life were embittered by repeated prosecutions, fines, imprisonment, and harassing controversies. When he could he preached, and when he could not preach he wrote books; but something he was always doing. The revolution and accession of William III brought him some little respite from persecution, and death at last removed the good old man to that place "where the wicked cease from troubling and the weary are at rest,"[1] in the year 1691, and the seventy-sixth year of his age.

Such is a brief outline of the life of one of the most distinguished Puritans who lived under the Stuarts, and one of the most devoted ministers of the Gospel this country has ever seen. It is an outline which, we may readily believe, might be filled up to an indefinite length. I cannot, of course, pretend to do more than direct attention to a few leading particulars. If I do not tell more, it is not from want of matter. But if anyone wishes to know why Baxter's name stands so high as it does in the list of English worthies, I ask him to give me his attention for a few minutes, and I will soon show him cause.

(a) For one thing, Baxter was a man of most *eminent personal holiness.* Few men have ever lived before the eyes of the world for fifty or sixty years, as he did, and left so fair and unblemished a reputation. Bitterly and cruelly as many hated him, they could find no fault in the man, except "concerning the law of his

---

[1] Job 3:17.

God."[1] He seems to have been holy in all the relations of life, and in all the circumstances in which man can be placed: holy as a son, a husband, a minister, and a friend—holy in prosperity and in adversity, in sickness and in health, in youth and in old age. It is a fine saying of Orme, in his admirable life of him, that he was, in the highest sense, a most "unearthly" man. He lived with God and Christ and heaven and death and judgment and eternity continually before his eyes. He cared nothing for the good things of this world: a bishopric, with all its emoluments and honours, had no charms for him. He cared nothing for the enmity of the world: no fear of man's displeasure ever turned him an inch out of his way. He was singularly independent of man's praise or blame. He could be bold as a lion in the presence of Cromwell or Charles II, and his bishops; and yet he could be gentle as a lamb with poor people seeking how to be saved. He could be zealous as a crusader for the rights of conscience, and yet he was of so catholic a spirit that he loved all who loved Jesus Christ in sincerity. "Be it by Conformists or by Nonconformists," he would say, "I rejoice that Christ is preached." He was a truly humble man. To one who wrote to him expressing admiration for his character, he replied, "You admire one you do not know: knowledge would cure your error." So fair an epistle of Christ, considering the amazing trials of patience he had to go through, this country has seldom seen as Richard Baxter. Let us remember this point in Baxter's character. No argument has such lasting power with the world as a holy and consistent life. Let us remember that this holiness was attained by a man of like passions with ourselves. Let Baxter be an encouragement and an example. Let us remember the Lord God of Baxter is not changed.

(b) For another thing, Baxter was *one of the most powerful preachers that ever addressed an English congregation.* He seems to have possessed all the gifts which are generally considered to make a perfect "master of assemblies."[2] He had an amazing fluency—an enormous store of matter—a most clear and lucid style—an unlimited command of forcible language—a pithy, pointed, emphatic way of

---

[1] Daniel 6:5.
[2] Ecclesiastes 12:11.

presenting truth—a singularly moving and pathetic voice—and an earnestness of manner which swept everything before it like a torrent. He used to say, "It must be serious preaching which will make men serious in hearing and obeying it." Two well-known lines of his show you the man: "I'll preach as though I ne'er should preach again, and as a dying man to dying men." Dr. Bates, a contemporary, says of him:

> He had a marvellous felicity and copiousness in speaking. There was a noble negligence in his style. His great mind could not stoop to the affected eloquence of words. He despised flashy oratory. But his expressions were so clear and powerful, so convincing to the understanding, so entering into the soul, so engaging the affections, that those were as deaf as an adder who were not charmed so wise a charmer.

The effects that his preaching produced were those which such preaching always has produced, and always will. As it was under the pulpit of Latimer and Whitefield, so it was under the pulpit of Baxter. At Dudley the poor nailers would not only crowd the church, but even bang upon the windows and the leads without. At Kidderminster it became necessary to build five new galleries in order to accommodate the congregation. In London the crowds who attended his ministry were so large that it was sometimes dangerous, and often impossible, to be one of his hearers.

Once, when he was about to preach at St. Lawrence, Jewry, he sent word to Mr. Vines, the minister, that the Earl of Suffolk and Lord Broghill were coming in a coach with him, and would be glad to have seats. But when he and his noble companions reached the door, the crowd had so little respect for persons that the two peers had to go home again because they could not get within hearing. Mr. Vines himself was obliged to get up into the pulpit and sit behind the preacher, from want of room; and Baxter actually preached standing between Mr. Vines' feet.

On another occasion, when he was preaching to an enormous crowd in St. Dunstan's, Fleet Street, he made a striking use of an incident which took place during the sermon. A piece of brick fell down in the steeple, and an alarm was raised that the church, an old and rotten building, was falling. Scarcely was the alarm allayed, when a bench, on which some people were standing, broke with their weight, and the confusion was worse than ever. Many crowded to the doors to get out, and all were in a state of panic. One old woman was heard loudly asking God forgiveness for having come to the church at all and promising, if she only got out safe, never to come there again. In the midst of all the confusion Baxter alone was calm and unmoved. As soon as order was restored, he rose and said, "We are in the service of God to prepare ourselves that we may be fearless at the great noise of the dissolving world, when the heavens shall pass away, and the elements melt with fervent heat."

This was Baxter all over. This was the kind of thing he had not only grace, but gifts and nerve, to do. He always spoke like one who saw God and felt death at his back. Such a man will seldom fail to preach well. Such a man will seldom be in want of hearers. Such a man deserves to be embalmed in the memory of all who want to know what God can do for a child of Adam by His Spirit. Such a man deserves to be praised.

(c) For another thing, Baxter was *one of the most successful pastors of a parish and congregation that ever lived*. When he came to Kidderminster he found it a dark, ignorant, immoral, irreligious place, containing perhaps 3,000 inhabitants. When he left it at the end of fourteen years, he had completely turned the parish upside down. "The place before his coming," says Dr. Bates, "was like a piece of dry and barren earth; but, by the blessing of heaven upon his labour, the face of Paradise appeared there. The bad were changed to good, and the good to better." The number of his regular communicants averaged 600. "Of these," Baxter tells us, "there were not twelve of whom I had not good hope as to their sincerity." The Lord's Day was thoroughly reverenced and observed. It was said, "You might have heard an hundred families singing psalms and repeating sermons as you passed through the streets." When he came there, there was about one family in a street which worshipped God at home. When he went away, there were some streets in which there was not more than one family on a side that did not do it; and this was the case even with inns and public houses. Even of the irreligious families, there were very few which had not some converted relations.

Some of the poor people became so well versed in theology that they understood the whole body of divinity, and were able to judge difficult controversies. Some were so able in prayer that few ministers could match them in order, fulness, apt expressions, holy oratory and fervour. Best of all, the temper of their minds and the innocency of their lives were much more laudable even than their gifts.

The grand instrument to which Baxter used to attribute this astounding success was his system of household visitation and regular private conference with his parishioners. No doubt, this did immense good, and the more so because it was a new thing in those days. Nevertheless, there is no denying the fact that the most elaborate parochial machinery of modern times has never produced such effects as those you have just heard of at Kidderminster. And the true account of this I believe to be, that no parish has ever had such a wonderful mainspring in the middle of it as Baxter was. While some divines were wrangling about the Divine right of episcopacy or presbytery, or splitting hairs about reprobation and freewill, Baxter was always visiting from house to house, and beseeching men, for Christ's sake, to be reconciled to God and flee from the wrath to come. While others were entangling themselves in politics and "burying their dead"[1] amidst the potsherds of the earth, Baxter was living a crucified life and daily preaching the Gospel. I suspect he was the best and wisest pastor that an English parish has ever had, and a model that many a modern rector or vicar would do well to follow. Once more I say, have I not a right to say such a polished instrument as this ought not to be allowed to rust in oblivion? Such a man as this deserves to be praised.

(d) For another thing, Baxter was *one of the most diligent theological writers the world has ever seen*. Few have the slightest idea of the immense number of works in divinity which he wrote in the fifty years of his active life. It is reckoned that they would fill sixty octavo volumes, comprising not less than 35,000 closely-printed pages. These works, no doubt, are not all of equal merit, and many of them probably will never repay perusal. Like the ships from Tarshish, they contain not only gold and silver and ivory, but also a

---

[1] Matthew 8:22.

large quantity of apes and peacocks. Still, after every deduction, the writings of Baxter generally contain a great mass of solid truths, and truths often handled in a most striking and masterly way. Dr. Barrow, no mean judge, says "That his practical writings were never mended, and his controversial ones seldom confuted." Bishop Wilkins declares "That he had cultivated every subject he had handled, that if he had lived in the primitive times he would have been one of the Fathers of the Church, and that it was enough for one age to produce such a man as Mr. Baxter." That great and good man, William Wilberforce, says "His practical writings are a treasury of Christian wisdom;" and he adds, "I must beg to class among the brightest ornaments of the Church of England this great man, who was so shamefully ejected from the Church in 1662."

No one man has certainly ever written three such books as Baxter's three masterpieces, *The Saint's Rest, The Reformed Pastor,* and *The Call to the Unconverted.* I believe they have been made blessings to thousands of souls and are alone sufficient to place the author in the foremost rank of theological writers. Of *The Call to the Unconverted,* 20,000 were printed in one year. Six brothers were converted at one time by reading it. Eliot, the missionary, thought so highly of it that he translated it into the Indian language, the first book after the Bible. And really, when we consider that all Baxter's writings were composed in the midst of intense labour and fierce persecution, and often under the pressure of heavy bodily disease, the wonder is not only that he wrote so much, but that so much of what he wrote should be so good. Such wonderful diligence and redemption of time the world has never seen. Once more I say, have I not a right to say such a man deserves to be praised?

(*e*) For another thing, Baxter was *one of the most patient martyrs for conscience' sake that England has ever seen.* Of course I do not mean that he was called upon to seal his faith with his blood, as our Protestant Reformers were. But there is such a thing as "wearing out the saints of the Most High"[1] by persecutions and prisons, as well as shedding the blood of the saints. There is a "dying daily,"[2]

---

[1] Daniel 7:25.
[2] 1 Corinthians 15:31.

which, to some natures, is worse even than dying at the stake. If anything tries faith and patience, I believe it to be the constant dropping of such wearing persecution as Baxter had to endure for nearly the last twenty-nine years of his life. He had robbed no one. He had murdered no one. He had injured no one. He held no heresy. He believed all the articles of the Christian faith. And yet no thief or felon in the present day was ever so shamefully treated as this good man. To tell you how often he was summoned, fined, silenced, imprisoned, driven from one place to another, would be an endless task. To describe all the hideous perversions of justice to which he was subjected would be both painful and unprofitable. I will only allow myself to give one instance, and that shall be his trial before Chief Justice Jeffreys.

Baxter was tried before Jeffreys in 1685, at Westminster Hall, on a charge of having published seditious matter, reflecting on the bishops in a *Paraphrase on the New Testament*, which he had recently brought out. A more unfounded charge could not have been made. The book is still extant, and anyone will see at a glance that the alleged seditious passages do not prove the case. Fox, in his history of James the Second's reign, tells us plainly "that the real motive for bringing him to trial was the desire of punishing an eminent dissenting teacher, whose reputation was high among his sect, and who was supposed to favour the political opinions of the Whigs."

A long and graphic account of the trial was drawn up by a bystander, and it gives so vivid a picture of the administration of justice in Baxter's days that it may be useful to give a few short extracts from it. From the very opening of the trial it was clear which way the verdict was intended to go. The Lord Chief Justice of England behaved as if he were counsel for the prosecution, and not judge. He condescended to use abusive language towards the defendant, such as was more suited to Billingsgate[1] than a court of law. One after another the counsel for the defence were brow-beaten, silenced, and put down, or else interrupted by violent invectives against Baxter. At one time the Lord Chief Justice exclaimed:

---

[1] A London fish market known for its coarse, abusive language.

This is an old rogue, who hath poisoned the world with his Kidderminster doctrine. He encouraged all the women and maids to bring their bodkins and thimbles to carry on war against the King of ever blessed memory. An old schismatical knave! A hypocritical villain!

By and by he called Baxter "an old blockhead, an unthankful villain, a conceited, stubborn, fanatical dog. Hang him!" he said, "this one old fellow hath cast more reproaches on the constitution and discipline of our church than will be wiped off for this hundred years. But I'll handle him for it, for he deserves to be whipped through the city." Shortly afterwards, when Baxter began to say a few words on his own behalf, Jeffreys stopped him, crying out,

Richard, Richard, dost thou think we'll hear thee poison the Court? Richard, thou art an old fellow, an old knave; thou hast written books enough to load a cart, every one as full of sedition, I might say treason, as an egg is full of meat. Hadst thou been whipped out of thy writing trade forty years ago, it had been happy. Thou pretendest to be a preacher of the Gospel of peace, and thou hast one foot in the grave: it is time for thee to think what kind of an account thou intendest to give. But leave thee to thyself and I see thou wilt go on as thou hast begun; but, by the grace of God, I will look after thee. I know thou hast a mighty party, and I see a great many of the brotherhood in corners, waiting to see what will become of this mighty dove; but, by the grace of God Almighty, I'll crush you all! Come, what do you say for yourself, you old knave? Come, speak up!

All this, and much more of the same kind, and even worse, went on at Baxter's trial. The extracts I have given form but a small portion of the whole account. It is needless to say that in such a court as this, Baxter was at once found guilty. He was fined five hundred marks, which it was known he could not pay, condemned to lie in prison till he paid it, and bound over to good behaviour for seven years. And the issue of the matter was that this poor, old, diseased, childless widower of threescore years and ten, lay for two years in Southwark gaol!

It is needless, I hope, to remark in this present century that such a trial as this was a disgrace to the judicial bench of England, and a still greater disgrace to those persons with whom the information originated, understood commonly to have been Sherlock and L'Estrange. Thank God! I trust England, at any rate, has bid a long farewell to such trials as these, whatever may be done in other lands! Wretched, indeed, is that country where low, sneaking informers are encouraged—where the terrors of the law are directed more against holiness, and scriptural religion, and freedom of thought, than against vice and immorality—and where the seat of justice is used for the advancement of political purposes, or the gratification of petty ecclesiastical spite!

But it is right that we should know that under all this foul injustice and persecution, Baxter's grace and patience never failed him. "These things," he said in Westminster Hall, "will surely be understood one day, what fools one sort of Protestants are made to prosecute the other." When he was reviled, he reviled not again. He returned blessing for cursing, and prayer for ill-usage. Few martyrs have ever glorified God so much in their one day's fire as Richard Baxter did for twenty years under the ill-usage of so-called Protestants! Once more, I say, have I not a right to tell you such a man as this deserves to be remembered? Such a man surely deserves to be praised.

And now I hope I have proved my case. I trust it will be allowed that there are men who lived in times long gone by whose character it is useful to review, and that Baxter is undeniably one of them: a real man—a true spiritual hero. I do not ask men to regard him as a perfect and faultless being, any more than Cranmer or Calvin or Knox or Wesley. I do not at all defend some of Baxter's doctrinal statements. He tried to systematise things which cannot be systematised, and he failed. You will not find such a clear, full gospel in his writings as in those of Owen and Bridge and Traill. I do not think he was always right in his judgment. I regard his refusal of a bishopric as a huge mistake. By that refusal he rejected a glorious opportunity of doing good. Had Baxter been on the episcopal bench and in the House of Lords, I do not believe the Act of Uniformity would ever have passed.

But in a world like this we must take true Christians as they are and be thankful for what they are. It is not given to mortal man to be faultless. Take Baxter for all together, and there are few English ministers of the Gospel whose names deserve to stand higher than his. Some have excelled him in some gifts, and some in others. But it is seldom that so many gifts are to be found united in one man as they are in Baxter. Eminent personal holiness—amazing power as a preacher—unrivalled pastoral skill—indefatigable diligence as a writer—meekness and patience under undeserved persecution—all meet together in the character of this one man. Let us place him high in our list of great and good men. Let us give him the honour he deserves. It is no small thing to be the fellow-countryman of Richard Baxter.

And here let me remark that few bodies of men are under greater obligation to Baxter and his friends than the members of voluntary religious societies in the present day. We are allowed to associate together upon evangelical principles and for religious ends, and no one hinders us. We are allowed to meet in large numbers, and take sweet counsel with one another, and strengthen one another's hands in the service of Christ, and no one interferes to prevent us. We are allowed to assemble for devotional purposes, to read the Word of God, and stir one another up to perseverance in the faith, and no one dares to prohibit us. How great are all these privileges! How incalculable the benefit of union, conference, sympathy, and encouragement to Christians who are voyaging over the stormy waters of this evil world, and trying to do good. Blessed is the labour of those by whose care and attention these societies are kept together! They are sowing precious seed. They may sow with much toil and discouragement, but they may be sure they are sowing seed which shall yet bear fruit after many days.

But never let us forget to whom we are indebted for all this liberty of conference and association which we enjoy. Never let us forget that there was a time when informers would have tracked all our steps—when constables and soldiers would have rudely broken up our gatherings at Exeter Hall, and when our proceedings would have entailed upon us pains, penalties, fines, and imprisonments. Never let us forget that the happy and profitable freedom which we enjoy was only won by long-continued and intense struggles, by the blood and sufferings of noble-minded men, of whom the world was not worthy; and never forget that the men who won this freedom for us were those much-abused men—the Puritans.

Yes! We all owe a debt to the Puritans which I trust we shall never refuse to acknowledge. We live in days when many are disposed to run them down. As we travel through life, we often hear them derided and abused as seditious, rebellious levelers in the things of Cæsar, and ignorant, fanatical, hypocritical enthusiasts in the things of God. We often hear some conceited stripling fresh from college, puffed up with new-fledged views of what he calls "apostolical succession," and proud of a little official authority, depreciating and sneering at the Puritans as men alike destitute of learning and true religion, while, in reality, he is scarcely worthy to sit at their feet and carry their books. To all such calumnies and false statements, I trust we shall never give heed.

Let us settle it down in our minds that for sound doctrine, spirituality, and learning combined, the Puritans stand at the head of English divines. With all their faults, weaknesses, and defects, they alone kept the lamp of pure, evangelical religion burning in this country in the times of the Stuarts—they alone prevented Laud's Popish inclinations carrying England back into the arms of Rome. It was they who fought the battle of religious freedom, of which we are reaping such fruits. It was they who crushed the wretched spirit of inquisitorial persecution which misguided high churchmen tried to introduce into this land. Let us give them the honour they deserve. Let us suffer no man to speak lightly of them in our presence. Let us remember our obligations to them, reverence their memory, stand up boldly for their reputation, and never be afraid to plead their cause. It is the cause of pure, evangelical religion. It is the cause of an open Bible and liberty to meet and read and pray together. It is the cause of liberty of conscience. All these are bound up with Baxter and the Puritans. Let us remember this and give them their due.

(f) *Baxter's last days* were almost as remarkable as any in his life. He went down to his grave as calmly and peacefully as the setting sun in summer. His deathbed was a glorious deathbed indeed. I like to know how great men die. I am not satisfied with knowing that men are great Christians in the plenitude of riches and honour. I want to know whether they were great in view of the tomb. I do not want merely to know how men meet kings and bishops and parliaments; I want to know how they meet the king of terrors, and how they feel in the prospect of standing before the King of kings. I suspect that greatness which forsakes a man at last. I like to know how great men die, and I must be allowed to dwell for a few moments upon Baxter's death.

Few deathbeds, perhaps, were ever more truly instructive than that of this good old Puritan. His friend, Dr. Bates, has given a full description of it, and I think a few facts drawn from it may prove a suitable conclusion to this biography. Baxter's last illness found him quietly living in Charterhouse Square, close to the meeting-house of his friend, Dr. Sylvester. Here for the four years preceding his death, he was allowed to enjoy great quietness. The liberty of preaching the things concerning the Lord Jesus Christ, no man forbidding him, was at length fully conceded. "Here," says Dr. Calamy, "he used to preach with great freedom about another world, like one that had been there, and was come as a sort of express to make a report of it." The storm of persecution was at length over. The winds and waves that had so long burst over him were at last lulled. The saintly old Puritan was mercifully allowed to go down to the banks of Jordan in a great calm.

He continued to preach so long, notwithstanding his wasted body, that the last time he almost died in the pulpit. When disease compelled him to give over his beloved work and take to his dying bed, it found him the same man that he had been for fifty years. His last hours were spent in preparing others and himself to meet God. He said to the friends who visited him,

> You come hither to learn to die. I am not the only person that must go this way. Have a care of this vain, deceitful world, and the lust of the flesh. Be sure you choose God for your portion, heaven for your home, God's glory for your end, God's Word for your rule, and then you need never fear but we shall meet again with comfort.

Never was penitent sinner more humble, and never was sincere believer more calm and comfortable. He said, "God may justly condemn me for the best duty I ever did; and all my hopes are from the free mercy of God in Christ." He had often said before, "I can more readily believe that God will forgive me, than I can forgive myself."

After a slumber, he waked, saying, "I shall rest from my labours." A minister present said, "And your works will follow you." He replied, "No works; I will leave out works, if God will grant me the other." When a friend comforted him with the remembrance of the good many had received from his writings, he replied, "I was but a pen in God's hand, and what praise is due to a pen?"

When extremity of pain made him long for death, he would check himself and say, "It is not fit for me to prescribe: when Thou wilt—what Thou wilt—how Thou wilt!" Being in great anguish, he said, "How unsearchable are His ways!" and then he said to his friends, "Do not think the worse of religion for what you see me suffer."

Being often asked by his friend how it was with his inward man, he replied, "I have a well-grounded assurance of my eternal happiness, and great peace and comfort within; but it is my trouble that I cannot triumphantly express it, by reason of extreme pain." He added, "Flesh must perish, and we must feel the perishing; and though my judgment submit, sense will make me groan."

Being asked by a nobleman whether he had great joy from his believing apprehension of the invisible state, he replied, "What else, think you, Christianity serves for?" And then he added, "that the consideration of the Deity, in His glory and greatness, was too high for our thoughts, but the consideration of the Son of God in our nature, and of the saints in heaven whom we knew and loved, did much sweeten and familiarise heaven to him." The description of heaven in the 12th chapter of Hebrews, beginning with the "innumerable company of angels," and ending with "Jesus the Mediator, and the blood of sprinkling,"[1] was very comfortable to him. "That scripture," he said, "deserves a thousand thousand thoughts!" And then he added, "Oh, how comfortable is that promise, 'Eye has not seen, nor ear heard, neither hath it entered into the heart of man to conceive, the things God hath laid up for them that love Him.'"[2]

At another time he said that "he found great comfort and sweetness in repeating the words of the Lord's Prayer, and was sorry that

[1] Hebrews 12:22–24.
[2] 1 Corinthians 2:9.

some good men were prejudiced against the use of it; for there were all necessary petitions for soul and body contained in it."

He gave excellent counsel to young ministers who visited him on his deathbed. He used to pray earnestly "that God would bless their labours, and make them very successful in converting many souls to Christ." He expressed great joy in the hope that God would do a great deal of good by them, and that they would be of moderate, peaceful spirits.

He did not forget the world he was leaving. He frequently prayed "that God would be merciful to this miserable, distracted world; and that he would preserve His Church and interest in it."

He advised his friends "to beware of self-conceitedness, as a sin likely to ruin this nation." Being asked at the same time whether he had altered his mind in controversial points, he replied, "Those that please may know my mind in my writings. What I have done was not for my own reputation, but the glory of God."

The day before he died, Dr. Bates visited him; and on his saying some words of comfort, he replied, "I have pain: there is no arguing against sense; but I have peace: I have peace!" Bates told him he was going to his long-desired home. He answered, "I believe: I believe." He expressed great willingness to die. During his sickness, when the question was asked how he did, his reply was, "Almost well!" or else, "Better than I deserve to be, but not so well as I hope to be." His last words were addressed to Dr. Sylvester, "The Lord teach you how to die!"

On Tuesday, the 8th of December 1691, Baxter's warfare was accomplished; and at length he entered what he had so beautifully described—*the saint's everlasting rest.* He was buried at Christ Church, amidst the tears of many who knew his worth, if the world and the Established Church of that day did not. The funeral was that kind of funeral which is above all in real honour: "devout men carried him to his grave, and made great lamentation over him."[1]

He left no family, but he left behind him hundreds of spiritual sons and daughters. He left works which are still owned by God in every part of the world to the awakening and edification of

---

[1] Acts 8:2.

immortal souls. Thousands, I doubt not, will stand up in the morning of the resurrection, and thank God for the grace and gifts bestowed on the old Puritan of Shropshire. He left a name which must always be dear to every lover of holiness, and every friend of religious liberty. No Englishman, perhaps, ever exemplified the one, or promoted the other, more truly and really than did Richard Baxter.

Let me conclude by quoting the last paragraph of Dr. Bates' funeral sermon on the occasion of Baxter's death:

> Blessed be the gracious God, that He was pleased to prolong the life of His servant, so useful and beneficial to the world, to a full age, and that He brought him slowly and safely to heaven. I shall conclude this account with my own deliberate wish: May I live the short remainder of my life as entirely to the glory of God as he lived; and when I shall come to the period of my life, may I die in the same blessed peace wherein he died; may I be with him in the kingdom of light and love for ever.

12

WILLIAM GURNALL

William Gurnall, Rector of Lavenham, in Suffolk, and author of
The Christian in Complete Armour, is a man about whom the world
possesses singularly little information. Perhaps there is no writer
who has left a name so familiar to all readers of Puritan theology,
but of whose personal history so little is known. Except the three
facts—that he was a Puritan divine of the seventeenth century—
that he was minister of Lavenham—and that he wrote a well-
known book of practical divinity, most persons know nothing of
William Gurnall.

This dearth of information about so good a man appears at first
sight extraordinary and unaccountable. Born, as he was, in a seaport
town of no mean importance—the son of parents who held a
prominent position in the town—educated at Cambridge, at one of
the best known colleges of the day—the contemporary of leading
divines of the Commonwealth times—minister of the largest
church in West Suffolk for the uninterrupted period of thirty-five
years—author of a work which, from its first appearance, was
eminently popular—Gurnall is a man, we naturally feel, of whom
more ought to be known. How is it then that more is not known?
How shall we account for the absence of any notice of him in the
biographical writings of his day?

I believe that these questions admit of a very simple answer. That
answer is to be found in the line of conduct which Gurnall followed
in the year 1662, on the passing of the unhappy Act of Uniformity.
He did not secede from the Church of England! He was not one of the
famous two thousand ministers who gave up their preferment on
St. Bartholomew's Day and became Nonconformists. He retained
his position and continued Rector of Lavenham. Puritan as he

undoubtedly was, both in doctrine and practice, he did not do what many of his brethren did. When Baxter, Manton, Owen, Goodwin, and a host of other giants in theology seceded from the Church of England, Gurnall stood fast and refused to move. He did not act with the party with which he had generally acted, and was left behind.

The result of this line of conduct can easily be imagined. Whatever opinions we may hold about Gurnall's conformity, we must all allow that the course he took was not likely to make him a favourite with either of the two great religious parties into which England at that time was divided. A neutral is never popular in a season of strife and controversy. Both sides suspect him. Each party is offended at him for not casting his weight into their scale. This, I suspect, was precisely Gurnall's position. He was a Puritan in doctrine, and yet he steadfastly adhered to the Church of England. He was a minister of the Church of England and yet a thorough Puritan, both in preaching and practice. In fact, he was just the man to be disliked and slighted by both sides. I throw out the conjecture I have made with considerable diffidence. It is undoubtedly nothing but a conjecture. But I look at the broad fact that the biographical writers who have handled Gurnall's age have chronicled scores of names of far less weight than his, and have refused to say a word about the author of *The Christian in Complete Armour*. Calamy, Clarke, Neal, and Brooke have written hundreds of pages about men for whom the world cares nothing now, but not a page about Gurnall! I leave it to others to offer a better explanation of this fact, if they can. I must be allowed to retain my own settled conviction, that we should know far more about Gurnall if he had not submitted to the Act of Uniformity in 1662 and retained the pulpit of Lavenham parish church.

To supply a correct history of this good man and his times is the object of the biography I am now writing. Ever since I read *The Christian in Complete Armour* I have felt that the author of such a book was a man whose life ought to be known. From the day that I was transplanted into the eastern counties and became a Suffolk incumbent, I have made it my business to study the lives of eminent Suffolk divines. None of them all appears to deserve excavation from undeserved oblivion so much as Gurnall.

Almost the only source of information about Gurnall which we now possess is a small volume, published in 1830, by a writer named M'Keon, entitled, *An Inquiry into the Birthplace, Parentage, Life, and Writings of the Rev. William Gurnall, formerly Rector of Lavenham, in Suffolk, and author of "The Christian in Complete Armour."* This book was printed and published for the author at Woodbridge, in Suffolk, and not in London. It is owing to this circumstance, perhaps, that it seems to have attracted little notice, and to have become comparatively unknown.

Mr. M'Keon was an inhabitant of Lavenham, and likely to procure information about Gurnall, if anyone could. He was undoubtedly a painstaking man, and an antiquarian of considerable research. His accuracy and correctness are worthy of all commendation. There is hardly a single date or fact in his book which I have not taken the trouble to verify by inquiry and investigation; and there is hardly one, I feel bound to say, in which I have found him wrong. But it cannot be said that his *Inquiry* is written in a popular and attractive style. In accumulating facts he was most successful; in arranging and exhibiting them to the reading public, I certainly think he failed.

However, whatever may be the faults of Mr. M'Keon's book, it is certainly the only attempt at any account of Gurnall which has hitherto existed. A funeral sermon, to be sure, was preached by Gurnall's friend and neighbour, the well-known commentator Burkitt; but the information it contains is comparatively very small. I must therefore frankly avow that I am indebted to Mr. M'Keon's work for the greater part of the facts about Gurnall which I have brought together in the following pages. I have tried to rearrange these facts. I have endeavoured to present them to the reader in an attractive form, by illustrating them with some cross lights from the history of Gurnall's times. I have added a few facts which Mr. M'Keon was probably unable to obtain. But I think it only fair to state that Mr. M'Keon's book is the principal mine from which the biographical account of Gurnall now presented to the reader has been drawn. If I have added anything of interest to his work, it is almost always by following up clues which his volume indicated or put into my hand.

William Gurnall was born at Lynn, in the county of Norfolk, in

the year 1616, and was baptized at St. Margaret's Church in that
town, on the 17th of November 1616. His father and mother were
married at St. Margaret's Church on the 31st of December 1615,
and the subject of this memoir was therefore their eldest child.* It
has often been observed that the mothers of great men, and
especially of great divines, have been remarkable for strong mind
and force of intellect. Mothers have been found, as a general rule,
to influence children's character far more than fathers. How far
this was true in the case of Gurnall we have, unfortunately, no
means of judging. We only know that his mother's maiden name
was Catherine Dressit, and that in all probability she was a native
of Lynn.

Gregory, the father of William Gurnall, appears to have been
one of the principal inhabitants of Lynn. At any rate he was an
alderman of his native town in the year when his son was born and
was mayor of the borough eight years afterwards, in 1624. Nothing
is known of his calling or occupation. The fact that his son died
possessed of certain landed property at Walpole, a country parish
not far from Lynn, makes it highly probable that Gregory Gurnall
was a landed proprietor. But on this point again nothing certain is
known.

Gurnall had the misfortune to lose his father when he was only
fifteen years old. His death is recorded in the register of St.
Margaret's, Lynn, as having taken place on the 14th of October
1631. He was buried in St. Margaret's Church, and a tomb was
erected to his memory, with a curious inscription. This tomb is no
longer extant, as the spire of St. Margaret's Church was blown
down in a violent hurricane in the year 1741, and falling on the
body of the church, destroyed a large portion of the building.
Mackerell's *History of Lynn*, published about four years before the
hurricane, records the inscription. If epitaphs were worth

---

* Mr. Hankinson, once Rector of St. Margaret's, Lynn, informed me
that the name *Gurnall*, to the best of his knowledge, is no longer known
in Lynn. But he says that the name *Gurling* is not uncommon, and that he
has little doubt it was originally *Gurnal*. He adds, "I find an entry of
baptism in 1799, where the name is *Gurnell* or *Gurling*." In Suffolk, the
names of *Girling* and *Grinling*, as I happen to know from the parish
register of Stradbroke, are very common.

anything, the language of Gregory Gurnall's epitaph might lead us to the conclusion that he was a godly man. But unhappily it is too well known that tombstones are not always to be trusted.

How long Gurnall's mother survived his father there is no evidence to show. M'Keon conjectures that she married again. It is certainly a curious fact that Burkitt, the commentator, in his funeral sermon on William Gurnall, uses the following language: "How great was that tribute of veneration and respect which he constantly paid to the hoary hairs of his aged parents!" Considering that his father died when he was only fifteen years old, these words can hardly be supposed to apply to Gregory Gurnall. Unless, therefore, the word *parents* in Burkitt's sermon is a printer's mistake for *parent*, it seems a very probable idea that Gurnall's mother married again, and that he had a kind and loving stepfather. But who he was, and how long his mother lived, we do not know.

The first fifteen years of Gurnall's life appear to have been spent in his native town of Lynn. There is, at any rate, no doubt that he was educated at the free grammar school of that town up to the time when he went to Cambridge. The fact is recorded in the books of the school. The first fifteen years of life have often so much weight in the formation of a man's character that it would be very interesting to find out the influences under which William Gurnall spent his early years. Unhappily we possess no materials for doing this. Ambrose Fish was appointed Master of Lynn Grammar School in 1626, in the place of Mr. Robinson, deceased, and Robert Woodmansea was appointed master in 1627. But we know nothing of these men. I can only point out two things which appear to me deserving of attention.

For one thing, we may probably trace up to Lynn, Gurnall's Puritan predilections and opinions. Lynn was one of the chief towns of the most thoroughly Protestant district in England in the seventeenth century. In the days of Queen Mary and Elizabeth the inhabitants of Norfolk and Suffolk were famous for their deep attachment to the doctrines of the Reformation. In the days of the Stuarts and the Commonwealth they were no less famous for their steadfast adherence to Puritan principles. In no part of England were High Church opinions so thoroughly disliked as in the diocese of Norwich, and in no diocese were the minds of people so continually exasperated by vexatious persecutions of Non-conformists.*

Brought up in a large market town like Lynn, we cannot doubt that the religious atmosphere in which young Gurnall moved was essentially Puritan. If, as it seems not unlikely, from a comparison of dates, the famous John Arrowsmith and Samuel Fairclough were ministers at Lynn during Gurnall's school days, we get an additional ray of light thrown on the source of his doctrinal opinions. To hear men like Arrowsmith and Fairclough preach every Sunday, and perhaps to be solemnly catechised or examined by Arrowsmith on stated public occasions, were just the things likely to produce an indelible impression on a mind like Gurnall's.†

---

* Harsnet, White, Corbet. Wren, and Montague were bishops of Norwich between 1619 and 1641. Three of them, at least, *viz.*, Harsnet, Wren, and Montague were notoriously very high churchmen and strongly opposed to the Puritans.

† John Arrowsmith was born at Gateshead, in 1602. He was educated at St. John's College, Cambridge, and was chosen Fellow of Katherine Hall. He was elected one of the University Preachers, was beneficed at Lynn, and was afterwards Preacher at St. Margaret's, Ironmonger's Lane, London. He was a leading member of the Westminster Assembly and had a principal share in drawing up the Assembly's Catechism. He was elected Master of St. John's College in 1644, and was chosen Vice-Chancellor of Cambridge in 1647. In 1651 he was appointed Regius Professor of Divinity, and Rector of Somersham. He was chosen Master of Trinity College in 1653, died in 1659, and was buried in Trinity College Chapel. His commentary on the first seventeen verses of the first chapter of St. John's Gospel, entitled *God-Man*, gives a very favourable impression of his ability.

Samuel Fairclough was born at Haverhill in 1594 and was educated at Queen's College, Cambridge. He was appointed Lecturer at Lynn by the mayor and aldermen in 1619, and continued there, according to Samuel Clarke, who gives a long and most interesting account of him, "for some time." The opposition and persecution of Harsnet, Bishop of Norwich, obliged him to resign this lecture. He was afterwards Lecturer at Clare, in Suffolk, and was then appointed Rector of Keddington, by Sir N. Barnardiston. He resigned this living in 1662, on account of the Act of Uniformity. He died in retirement in 1677, aged 84. Though a retiring man, and not known by any writings, he seems to have been a man of singular gifts and graces. There is an interesting tablet in Heveningham Church, erected by his daughter, wife of Mr. Jones, Rector of Heveningham. He lived at Heveningham for two years but died at Stowmarket.

For another thing, we probably owe to Gurnall's early residence at Lynn his remarkable familiarity with the sea, sailors, and shipping. I was once puzzled to make out the reason why nautical illustrations so frequently occur in his writings. It did not surprise me to find an author like Gurnall, who delighted in illustrations, pressing everything in town and country into his service. I could understand the man who was rector of a Suffolk town for thirty-five years drawing comparisons from shops, and farms, and streets, and fields, and horses, and cattle, and corn, and grass, and flowers. I could understand the minister who lived through the bloody wars of the Commonwealth times using abundant imagery from the habits of soldiers, and from the battlefield. But I never could understand Gurnall's familiarity with the sea and shipping, until I found out that he was born and bred in Lynn. He knew well what a sailor's life was. He had seen the quaint-looking craft which carried on the coasting trade of Lynn. He had doubtless talked with sailors who could tell the perils of "the Wash," the Lincoln-shire coast, the Norfolk Sands, and the Voyage to the Humber. Hence came his nautical illustrations in Lavenham pulpit. How true it is that all knowledge is useful to a minister of Christ! The man of God makes everything he has seen become serviceable to his Master's cause.

*   *   *

The next thing that we know about Gurnall is his connection with Cambridge as a pensioner of Emmanuel College. It appears that Lynn Corporation had two scholarships at Emmanuel in its gift, connected with the grammar school of the town. To one of these Gurnall was presented by the Corporation, in December 1631, not long after his father's death. A correspondent of M'Keon, at Lynn, says:

> I find, on reference to the Corporation books, that on the 2nd December, 1631, William Gurnall, son of Gregory Gurnall, Alderman there, lately deceased, and one of the scholars of Lynn School, was nominated to one of the Scholarships in Emmanuel College, Cambridge, called Lynn Scholarship, or Mr. Titley's Scholarship; and that on the 11th of June, 1632, the nomination, dated 29th March then last, passed the corporation seal.

Of Gurnall's history during his residence at Cambridge we know literally nothing, with the exception of the following bald facts. The college books record that William Gurnall, pensioner, of Norfolk, was admitted March 29, 1632, was B.A., 1635, and M.A., 1639. It is certain that he was never elected a fellow of his college, and as the Lynn Scholarship was only tenable for seven years, it is highly probable that he ceased to reside at Cambridge in the year 1639, when he took his degree as M.A., and received no further assistance from his scholarship.

It would, no doubt, be highly interesting if we knew something of Gurnall's history during the seven years of his university life. The character of a young man is generally moulded for life during the period between sixteen and twenty-three, and the author of *The Christian in Complete Armour* was probably no exception to this rule. Who were his friends and companions? Who were his tutors and lecturers? Was he a reading man? Whom did he walk with, and talk with? What great preachers did he hear in the University pulpit? What were his habits and ways of employing his time? What side did he espouse in the mighty controversies of the day? All these are questions which it would be very pleasant to have answered. The answers would throw great light on many a passage in his afterlife and writings. But the answers, unhappily, are not forthcoming. The only light that we can throw on Gurnall's university life consists of a few facts about his college and the general state of England between 1632 and 1639.

The college to which Gurnall belonged was always famous in the seventeenth century for its theological tendencies. It was eminently a Puritan college. Sir Walter Mildmay, of Chelmsford, in Essex, was the founder of Emmanuel College, and even from its very foundation in 1585, it seems to have been notorious for its attachment to Puritan principles. Fuller, in his *History of Cambridge*, relates that on,

> Sir Walter Mildmay coming to Court, soon after he had founded his College, Queen Elizabeth said to him, "Sir Walter, I hear you have erected a Puritan foundation." "No, madam," saith he, "far be it from me to countenance anything contrary to your established laws; but I have set an acorn, which, when it becomes an oak, God alone knows what will be the fruit thereof." Sure I am

[adds Fuller, writing about 1650] at this day it hath overshadowed all the University, more than a moiety of the present Masters of Colleges being bred therein.

*   *   *

The number of leading divines of the seventeenth century who were educated at Emmanuel College, Cambridge, is certainly extraordinary. Beside Bishop Hall and Bishop Bedell, we find in the list of its members the names of Stephen Marshall, Jeremiah Burroughs, Thomas Sheppard, Thomas Hooker, Ezekiel Culverwell, Ralph Cudworth, Samuel Crooke, John Cotton, John Stoughton, Anthony Burgess, Laurence Chaderton, John Preston, Anthony Tuckney, Lazarus Seaman, Matthew Poole, Samuel Clarke, Ralph Venning, Thomas Watson, Stephen Charnock, William Bridge, Peter Sterry, Samuel Cradock. Anyone familiar with Puritan divinity will see at a glance that this catalogue embraces the names of some of the most eminent Puritan writers. Some of them, no doubt, were contemporaries and fellow-students of Gurnall himself.

From inquiries which I have made, I have succeeded in obtaining some information about Emmanuel College between the years 1632 and 1639, which I think will not be devoid of interest to all admirers of Gurnall. At any rate it will show who were at Emmanuel when he was there, both as an undergraduate and a graduate, and with what kind of minds he was associated.

The masters at Emmanuel in Gurnall's time were (1) William Sancroft, uncle of the Archbishop, who held the office from 1628 to 1637; and (2) Holdsworth, who held the office from 1637 to 1645, when he was ejected by the Earl of Manchester. He was a zealous advocate of the King, and attended him during his confinement in the Isle of Wight, and soon after, according to Neal, died of grief. The reason why Gurnall was never elected fellow of his college was probably, if I may venture a conjecture, the high character and attainments of his competitors. According to the books of Emmanuel, Ralph Cudworth was elected fellow in 1639, Worthington (afterward Master of Jesus) in 1641, and Sancroft (afterward Archbishop of Canterbury) in 1642. The fellows of Emmanuel between 1632 and 1639 were the following:

Walter Foster, Richard Clarke, John Ward, Thomas Ball, Ezekiel Wright, Thomas Hill, Nicholas Hall, William Bridge, Samuel Bowles, Henry Salmon, David Ensigne, Anthony Burgess, Thomas Holbeck, Thomas Horton, Malachi Harris, R. Sorsby, Benjamin Whichcot, John Henderson, John Almond, R. Weller, Peter Sterry, Laurence Sarson, John Saddler, Ralph Cudworth.

> All the fellows, [says a member of Emmanuel] appear to have been tutors in their day, though some had more pupils than others. As far as our books lead us to infer, Hill, Hall, Burgess, Holbeck, Ensigne, Salmon, Whichcot, all seem to have been most popular tutors in their day. We have no tutors' books which tell us under whom Gurnall was admitted.

When I add to the above information the fact that Horrox, the astronomer, was admitted at Emmanuel in 1632, the same year as Gurnall, and that Archbishop Sancroft, the famous nonjuror, was admitted in 1633, I shall have exhausted all the stock of information that I have been able to scrape together about Gurnall's college life and his contemporaries.

Seven years spent at a college like Emmanuel could not fail to have an effect on Gurnall's mind. Brought up from his boyhood to honour and reverence the Puritans as the excellent of the earth, at Lynn—trained afterwards at a college where the whole atmosphere was peculiarly Puritan—it would have been strange indeed if Gurnall had grown up without decided Puritan opinions.

The state of England during the seven years of Gurnall's university life was very peculiar. It was the crisis of the troubled period between the Reformation and the Commonwealth times. The suicidal and blind misgovernment of Charles I was rapidly paving the way for the destruction of the throne. The undisguised Romish tendencies and bitter persecutions of Archbishop Laud and his fellow-workers were doing the same for the Church of England. From one end of the country to the other there were discontent, murmuring, controversy, bitterness, and party spirit. On every side there were symptoms of a coming breakup, or a violent conflict both in Church and State.

Cambridge, we need not doubt, had its full share of all the troubles and discomfort of this stormy period. The following passage from Fuller's *History of Cambridge* records things which happened there in 1632, the very year that Gurnall entered Emmanuel, things which, no doubt, he saw with his own eyes and heard with his own ears:

> This year, [says Fuller] a grave divine, preaching before the University at St. Mary's, had this passage in his sermon: "That as at the Olympian games he was counted the conqueror who could drive his chariot wheels nearest to the mark, yet so as not to hinder his running, or stick thereon, so he, who in his sermons could preach near Popery, and yet no Popery, there was your man." And, indeed, it now began to be the complaint of most moderate men, that many in the University, both in school and pulpit, approached the opinion of the Church of Rome more than ever before.
>
> Mr. Bernard, Lecturer of St. Sepulchre's in London, preached at St. Mary's in the afternoon of May 6th, his text, 1 Sam. 4:21, "The glory is departed from Israel," etc. In handling whereof he let fall some passages which gave distaste to a prevalent party in the University, as for saying: (1) That God's ordinances, when blended and adultered with innovations of men, cease to be God's ordinances, and He owneth them no longer. (2) That it is impossible any should be saved, living and dying without repentance, in the doctrine of Rome, as the Tridentine Council hath decreed it. (3) That treason is not limited to the blood royal; but that he is a traitor against a nation that depriveth it of God's ordinances. (4) That some shamefully symbolize in Pelagian error and superstitious ceremonies with the Church of Rome. Let us pray such to their conversion or to their destruction, etc.
>
> Dr. Cumber, Vice-Chancellor, gave speedy notice hereof to Dr. Laud, Bishop of London, though he (so quick his University intelligence) had information thereof before. Therefore he was brought into the High Commission, and a recantation tendered to him, which he refused to subscribe, though professing his sincere sorrow and penitency, in his petition and letter to the Bishop, for any oversight and unbecoming expression in his sermon. Hereupon he was sent back to the new prison, where he died. If he was miserably abused therein by his keepers, as some have reported, to the shortening of his life, He that maketh inquisition for blood, either hath, or will be, a revenger thereof.

This deplorable affair took place, let us remember, in the year 1632, the very year that Gurnall came up to reside at Emmanuel. How much stir it would excite among the undergraduates of a thoroughly Puritan college we can easily imagine. All who know anything of an English university, know how ready undergraduates are, as a body, to sympathize with the persecuted and oppressed, and to side with the minority.

It was during Gurnall's residence at Cambridge that Dr. Ward, one of the representatives of the Church of England at the Synod of Dort, gave the following unsatisfactory description of the state of the University, in a letter to Archbishop Usher, dated 1634. He says, "It may be you are willing to hear of our University affairs. I may truly say I never knew them in worse condition since I was a member thereof, which is almost forty-six years."*

It was during Gurnall's residence at Cambridge that the infamous sentence on Prynne, Bastwick, and Burton was passed in the Court of Star Chamber. For publishing certain alleged libels on the Church of England, these unfortunate men were condemned to stand in the pillory and have their ears publicly cut off. The sentence was actually carried into effect June 30, 1637, in Palace Yard. Bastwick was a physician, who had been educated at Emmanuel College. We can easily imagine the sensation which his punishment would create within the walls of his old college.

It was during Gurnall's residence at Cambridge that the famous disturbances in Scotland arose, out of Archbishop Laud's attempt to introduce the notorious Scotch Liturgy, with its Popish Communion Office, into the churches of Edinburgh. The well-known riot in St. Giles' Church, when a stool is said to have been thrown at the Bishop of Edinburgh's head, by a zealous woman called Jenny Geddes, took place on Sunday, July 23, 1637.

It was during Gurnall's residence at Cambridge that John Hampden began the unhappy struggle between the King and his subjects by refusing to pay ship-money. The decision of the Chief Justice was given against him on the 9th of June, 1637.

I mention these facts and dates in order to give the reader some idea of the times in which Gurnall passed through his university

---

* Usher's Correspondence, No. 179.

career. We cannot doubt that his character and opinions must have been strongly influenced by them. No one could be at Cambridge from 1632 to 1639 without seeing and hearing things which would leave a mark on his memory for life, and without coming across a stream of conflicting opinions which he would remember to his dying day. No doubt Gurnall became acquainted with some of the best specimens of the Puritan divines. No doubt also he saw in the heart of a Puritan college enough to make him feel that all Puritans were not perfect men. I venture the conjecture that his afterlife at every step was greatly influenced by the recollection of what he saw at Emmanuel, Cambridge.

*   *   *

The five years of Gurnall's life immediately after he left Cambridge, in 1639, are a period in his history of which nothing whatever seems to be known. I must honestly confess that I can throw little light upon it and can only offer surmises and conjectures. He disappears from our notice on leaving Emmanuel, in 1639. He does not appear again till he is made Rector of Lavenham, in 1644. But how, and where, and in what manner, and in what official capacity he spent the intervening interval of five years we have no certain record.

It would be difficult to name five years of English history in which so many important events occurred, as between 1639 and 1644. Within these five years the famous Long Parliament commenced its sittings, the no less famous Westminster Assembly of divines was convened, Lord Strafford was beheaded, Archbishop Laud committed to prison, and the courts of High Commission and Star Chamber abolished. Within these five years the Civil War between the King and the Parliament actually broke out, the standard was raised at Nottingham, the battles of Edgehill, Newbury, and Marston Moor were fought, and Hampden, Pym, and Lord Falkland were all laid in their graves. Last, but not least, the Solemn League and Covenant was subscribed by the adherents of the Parliament side, in which, among other things, they pledged themselves to "endeavour the extirpation of Popery and Prelacy: that is, church government by archbishops, bishops, their chancellors and commissaries, deans and chapters, archdeacons, and all other ecclesiastical officers depending on that hierarchy."

And what was Gurnall doing all these five years? We cannot tell. Perhaps he was staying quietly with his friends at Lynn. Perhaps he was hearing and learning what he could in London. Perhaps he was turning to account his university education by acting as tutor to some noble or wealthy family, as many young divines did in that day. These are idle conjectures after all. There are only two facts that we know about him. One is that he must have been ordained some time between 1639 and 1644. The other is that he must have preached at Sudbury within this period. This last point is made clear by his own words, in a letter addressed to Sir Symond D'Ewes, in which he speaks of the Sudbury people making difficulties about his removal to Lavenham.

The subject of Gurnall's entrance into the ministry is shrouded in complete obscurity. There is no one point in his personal history about which we know so little. When he was ordained, where he was ordained, to what cure of souls he was ordained, by whom he was ordained, whether he was first ordained by episcopal or by Presbyterian ordination, are things about which we are entirely in the dark. After a good deal of troublesome research and investigation into the subject, I must honestly confess that I can find out nothing about it. I have only discovered, by the kindness of the present Bishop of Norwich and the late Bishop of Ely, that his name does not appear in the ordination registers of Norwich and Ely between 1639 and 1644. It is, of course, possible that he was ordained by the bishop of some other diocese, though even then it is certain that he was only ordained deacon. But it is far more probable that he entered the ministry without receiving episcopal orders at all. Most likely he was set apart for the work as a Presbyterian minister, by "the laying on of the hands of the presbytery."[1]

I am not disposed to waste the reader's time by entering into any discussion of the comparative merits of episcopal and Presbyterian orders, though, of course, I have my own opinions as a conscientious Episcopalian. I only venture the remark that we have no right

---

[1] 1 Timothy 4:14.

to infer anything as to Gurnall's opinions about episcopacy from his want of episcopal orders. We must remember the peculiar times in which he entered the ministry. There was probably no alternative left to him. He must either have been ordained by Presbyterian ordination, or not have been ordained at all.

The plain truth is that the times when Gurnall entered the ministry were times of disorder and confusion. It was a period of transition. Everything that had been settled and established in Church and State was being pulled to pieces. They were strange times, and strange things happened in them. We may well expect to find that there were all sorts of irregularities and diversities of practice about ordination.

Bishop Hall, in his famous account of himself called *His Hard Measure*, makes the following statement, which deserves the more notice because he was Bishop of Norwich, and Lavenham was then in his diocese. He says:

After the Covenant was appointed to be taken (September 26, 1643), and was generally swallowed of both clergy and laity, my power of *ordination* was with some violence restrained. For when I was going on in my wonted course, which no law or ordinance had inhibited, certain forward volunteers in the city, banding together, stirred up the mayor, and aldermen, and sheriffs (of Norwich), to call me to an account for an open violation of their Covenant.

To this purpose, divers of them came to my gate at a very unseasonable time, and knocking very vehemently, required to speak with the Bishop. Messages were sent to them to know their business; nothing would satisfy them but the Bishop's presence. At last I came down to them, and demanded what the matter was; they would have the gate opened, and then they would tell me. I answered that I would know them better first; if they had anything to say to me I was ready to hear them. They told me they had a writing for me from the mayor and some other of their magistrates. The paper contained both a challenge of me for breaking the Covenant, in ordaining ministers, and withal required me to give in the names of those which were ordained by me both then and formerly since the Covenant. My answer was that the mayor was much abused by those who had misinformed him and drawn that paper from him; that I would the next day give a full answer to the writing. They moved that my answer might be my personal appearance at the guildhall. I asked them when they ever heard of a Bishop of Norwich appearing before a mayor. I knew mine own place, and would take that way of answer which I thought fit, and so dismissed them, who had given out that day, that had they known before of mine ordaining, they would have pulled me and those whom I ordained out of the chapel by the ears.*

Let us add to this curious testimony the following passage from Neal, the well-known historian of the Puritans. He says:

From the time of taking the Covenant (September 28, 1643), we may date the entire dissolution of the hierarchy, though it was not as yet abolished by an ordinance of Parliament. There were no ecclesiastical courts, no visitations, no wearing the habits, no regard paid to the canons or ceremonies, or even to the Common Prayer.

He says immediately afterwards:

Upon the sitting of the Assembly of Divines all church worship went through their hands. The parishes elected their ministers. The Assembly examined and approved of them, and the Parliament confirmed them in their benefices without any regard to the Archbishop or his vicar. Thus the Earl of Manchester filled the vacant pulpits in the associated counties.†

After reading these passages we may well understand why there is no record of Gurnall's ordination as deacon in the registers of Norwich or Ely. He began his ministry in the diocese of Norwich and was an inhabitant of one of the most thoroughly Puritan districts of the seven "associated counties." Whether he desired episcopal ordination or not we do not know, though his subsequent ordination by Bishop Reynolds, at a later period of his ministry, ought not to be forgotten. But it is highly probable that at the time when he entered the ministry he could not have received episcopal ordination even if he had wished it.

---

* *Hall's Works*, vol. 1, p. 54. P. Hall's Edition.
† Neal's *History*, vol. 3, pp. 79, 80. Toulmin's Edition.

The matter, after all, is not one of primary importance. The Divine right of episcopacy, to the exclusion of all other forms of church government, and the absolute necessity of episcopal ordination to make a right minister of Christ, are positions that cannot be established from Scripture. The Twenty-third Article of the Church of England has exhibited a wise moderation in handling the whole question. It says: "It is not lawful for any man to take upon him the office of public preaching, or ministering, the Sacrament in the congregation, before he be lawfully called and sent to execute the same." But the Article cautiously avoids defining too closely what are valid orders. It goes on: "Those we ought to judge lawfully called and sent, which be chosen and called to the work by men who have public authority given unto them in the congregation to call and send ministers into the Lord's vineyard." This, we need not doubt, was Gurnall's position. Episcopal ordination he probably did not receive on entering the ministry and most likely could not have obtained it. But that he was "lawfully called and sent into the Lord's vineyard" we need not doubt, though in all probability it was only "by laying on of the hands of the presbytery."[1]

*   *   *

We now come to the most important event in Gurnall's life, and the one which fixed him down in one spot for the remaining thirty-five years of his life. That event was his appointment to be minister of the parish of Lavenham, in Suffolk. This, it appears, happened about the month of December 1644, when he was twenty-eight years old.

The manner of Gurnall's appointment was somewhat singular, and curiously illustrative of the strange and troublesome times in which it took place. Sir Symond D'Ewes, the famous antiquary, was patron of the living of Lavenham, and chief proprietor in the parish. It appears that he gave the living to Gurnall at the request of the parishioners, and the appointment was ratified by order of the House of Commons. The order of the House of Commons is so peculiar a document, that I venture to transcribe it whole and

---

[1] 1 Timothy 4:14.

entire, as M'Keon gives it, from an extract from the *Journals of the House*, furnished to him by the Clerk of the *Journals*:

16°· *Decembris*, 1644, 20 *Car.* 1.

Lavenham Rectory. } WHEREAS the Church of Lavenham, in the county of Suffolk, lately became void by the decease of Ambrose Coppinger, Doctor of Divinity, and that Sir Symond D'Ewes, patron of the said Church, hath conferred the advowson of the same upon William Gurnall, Master of Arts, a learned, godly, and orthodox divine: It is ordered by the House of Commons that the said William Gurnall shall be, and continue, Rector and Incumbent of the same Church during the term of his natural life, and shall have, receive, and enjoy all such tithes, as other Rectors and Incumbents of same Church before him have had, received, and enjoyed. Provided always that the same William Gurnall do pay upon his avoidance all such first fruits and tithes unto his Majesty, as by the laws of this realm are, and shall be due from time to time.*

A careful reader can hardly fail to notice some amusing points in this document. The right of Sir Symond D'Ewes to present is stated and allowed, and yet the presentation must be ratified by the order of the House of Commons! Gurnall's qualifications are broadly stated. The House declares him to be "learned, godly, and orthodox!" The King's name is carefully brought in (though the Parliament was at open war with him), and provision is inserted for the payment of first fruits to his Majesty! The name, office, and authority of the Bishop of Norwich, in whose diocese Lavenham was, are as utterly ignored as if they had never existed! Truly we may say that Gurnall lived in strange times!

What chain of providential circumstances led Gurnall to a town in the southwest corner of Suffolk, after leaving Cambridge, we do not know. Why the good man should turn up at Sudbury and Lavenham, five years after leaving Emmanuel, is a point which must be left to conjecture. We know nothing certain about it. It is,

---

* Vol. 3, p. 725. The same record of Gurnall's presentation, word for word, is to be found in the *Norwich Register of Institutions*, No. 24, 1638–1648.

however, not unworthy of notice that there was a certain James Gurnall living at Lavenham in 1644, who had a daughter baptized there on the 4th of September in that year. It is by no means improbable, as M'Keon suggests, that this James Gurnall was a relative of the Gurnalls of Lynn, and that the relationship was the cause of William Gurnall visiting Lavenham and becoming known in the neighbourhood. It is also worthy of notice that Henry Coppinger, who died Rector of Lavenham in 1622, and was father of Gurnall's predecessor, Ambrose Coppinger, was connected by marriage with Gurnall's native place, Lynn. It is stated on a monument erected to his memory in Lavenham Church that he married Ann, daughter of Henry Fisher, of Lynn, in Norfolk. Lynn was not so large a place that the families of Gurnall and Mr. Coppinger would not be acquainted with one another, and this may have been another cause of his settling in Lavenham. These are, of course, only conjectures, but I think them worth mentioning, and they must be taken for what they are worth.

How Gurnall became acquainted with Sir Symond D'Ewes, and whether he was appointed by him to the rectory of Lavenham on public or private grounds, we have no means of ascertaining. A statement, quoted by M'Keon from a manuscript in Herald's College, by Mr. Appleton, about Suffolk, is manifestly a mistake. He says Sir Symond D'Ewes "freely and very willingly gave the Rectory of Lavenham unto Mr. William Gurnall, now Incumbent there, although to him then unknown, at the request of the parish, which hath been much for the benefit of the town in many ways." Appleton was clearly misinformed here. There is a correspondence extant in the Harleian MSS. between Gurnall and Sir Symond D'Ewes, of which the first letter is dated March 1644. Beside this, Sir Symond was elected M.P. for Sudbury in 1640, and resided in the parish of Lavenham, so that he could hardly fail to know something about Gurnall.

The correspondence between Gurnall and Sir Symond D'Ewes, to which reference has been made, is a curiosity in its way. It consists of eight Latin letters, composed in the most approved classical style, and affording evidence that Gurnall was a tolerably good Latin scholar. Judged by the standard of modern times the matter of these letters is not much to be admired. There is a tone of obsequiousness and flattery about them which to our eyes seems very unworthy of a Christian, and very unlike what we should have expected from a Puritan. But it is only fair to remember the fashion of Gurnall's age. Dedications and letters to public men in the seventeenth century are often stuffed with high-flown language and hyperbolic compliments. It was as common to write in such a strain as it is for us to sign ourselves "your obedient servant." The words meant nothing and were only used because it was the custom to use them. If Gurnall had not written his Latin letters to Sir Symond D'Ewes in a very verbose, extravagant, and complimentary style, he would probably have been set down as an illiterate and unpolished man.

Some account of the contents of these eight letters will perhaps be found interesting. They throw a little light, at any rate, on Gurnall's presentation to Lavenham; and if we knew the meaning of the allusions which they contain, we should understand a good deal better than we do now the history of his settlement in the place with which his name is inseparably connected.*

(1) The first letter is dated Lavenham, March 26, 1644. It is a petition on behalf of a man who had been wounded in the service of the State and appears to have been bearer of the letter. It contains some general remarks on the discredit thrown upon religion when wounded soldiers are neglected, and on the duty of providing them with comfortable maintenance. Beside this, there is nothing worth notice.

(2) The second letter is dated July 24, 1644. It is endorsed "to the Right Worthy Sir Symond D'Ewes, at his lodgings in Margaret's, Westminster." The place from which it is written is not stated. In this letter for the first time the subject of Gurnall's appointment to Lavenham is mentioned. There seems to have been some difficulty about the matter, which at this distance of time we cannot, of course, explain. The letter was evidently written while the difficulty was pending. It contains the following passage, which I give in M'Keon's translation in its entirety:

> I have received your letter breathing nothing but love, and should immediately have answered it, had I not been called into Norfolk

---

* As a general rule, I have given the letters as translated by M'Keon. In a few instances I have attempted to mend his translation.

on public business. On my return I promised myself some certain grounds for a reply. But alas! the knot which I left to be untied I found still more perplexed and involved, so that I appeared, like the ship of St. Paul, to have "fallen into a place where two seas met."[1] While my mind is fixed on Lavenham, there threatens a storm at Sudbury, which accuses me of being lured by a golden bait. But were I to refuse this Providence held out to me by your hands, I might, not unjustly, appear disobedient to God, and ungrateful to you, who offer it to me. In such a storm a skilful pilot (I mean Solomon) suggested to me, "in the multitude of counsellors there is safety."[2] Most willingly, therefore, did I submit the hearing and determining the whole cause to certain ministers in my neighbourhood. If I must die, I could wish it should be in the hands of the most skilful physicians; if I must err, I should wish it to be among men most famous for their learning and piety. In a short time I hope to finish this whole business, and then I will write again to your honour.

This is a curious letter. One would like to know what was the knotty point which Gurnall could not untie, and who were the "certain ministers" whom he consulted. One thing, at any rate, it helps to confirm. It seems to indicate that Gurnall was a minister at Sudbury before he was Rector of Lavenham. Yet it is a singular fact, that at the present time no inhabitant of Sudbury, to whom I have applied, seems to know anything about Gurnall's connection with the town.

(3) The third letter is dated Sudbury, September 1, 1641. At the time when it was written it was evidently a settled thing that Gurnall should have the living of Lavenham, though the appointment was not yet completed. Amidst a quantity of verbose and fulsome compliments, which can only be excused by the customs of Gurnall's day, the following paragraphs are worth quoting:

I firmly believe, most worshipful, that the only happiness which you hope or wish for in this filthy world, is that of doing good. In this humble and grateful disposition, therefore, you may triumph that the numerous population of Lavenham now enjoy under your shadow the Gospel.

---

1 Acts 27:41
2 Proverbs 24:6

If God should bless my slender labours, whatever they may be, as many as may be imbued with Divine light, or cherished with its dew, will be a solace, and even a crown to you, under whose shield I fight. Happy indeed, still more and more, might we have had the English nation, which we now see so universally torn by civil wars, if with the same care with which you have laboured, all our patrons had striven in the propagation of the Gospel. But, alas, many make market of the souls of others while they peril their own! This will redound to your great honour. Not less do you strive to give than others to sell the priesthood.

The postscript to this letter is curious. Gurnall says:

One thing at the end of your letter I had almost forgot. You therein just mention the Bishop. My doubts increase as to the propriety of going to him, particularly since the opinions both of the clergy and of the people have become known to me.

(4) The fourth letter is dated Lavenham, October 26, 1644. It is a complimentary letter written on the occasion of Sir Symond D'Ewes giving Gurnall a copy of some antiquarian work he had lately published. It contains no allusion to the subject of the living of Lavenham, and there is nothing in it worth quoting.

(5) The fifth letter is dated Lavenham, November 21, 1644, and is one of the most important of the whole series. I shall therefore give it entire.

Right worshipful Sir: At length my frail bark, after a difficult navigation, has safely reached the port of Lavenham. Nothing now remains for me but to return my thanks to you, under whose shadow I enjoy this happiness, and with sound principles to imbue, and with paternal care to instruct, the numerous people which you have committed to me, particularly in times like these, fermenting with many errors, when, like Rome of old, who borrowed gods from all parts of the world, we also borrow errors which have already been buried, and yet after burial again revive. My only solace in this world will now be to preserve, by earnest and continued prayer, this my congregation, pure and unspotted amongst so many corruptions.

By your letter to Henry Coppinger, I find that certain of the Sudbury people, in your hearing, have said that some new agreement had been entered into between us. I wonder from whence this fable has taken its origin. I do not admit one atom of it. It is nothing new for the sweetest wine of love sometimes to degenerate into vinegar. I hope, however, in a short time that my Sudbury friends will be restored to their former serenity, although like the troubled sea they are now in a state of considerable agitation. With respect to the Bishop, I hope he will find some other way of instituting me, or else your most honourable House will do it. And all the inhabitants of Lavenham most humbly congratulate you, right worshipful, for that in this affair you have left no stone unturned. We also earnestly desire that the matter may, if possible, be completed within these six months, which are now fast wearing away. I would willingly go to London in order that whatever remains to be done may receive the finishing stroke. May the great and good God pour His blessing on thee and thine, and may He continue to be thy sun and shield. So prays most earnestly your very humble servant in Christ, WILLIAM GURNALL.

The matter referred to in the letter can, of course, only be explained by conjecture. It certainly seems to indicate that Gurnall was once a popular minister at Sudbury, and that his removal to the rectory of Lavenham was not approved by the Sudbury people. The six months mentioned most probably mean the six months immediately following the last rector's death. The precise date of the death of Coppinger, Gurnall's predecessor, is not known.

(6) The sixth letter is dated Lavenham, January 6th, 1645. It is clear from its contents, that whatever may have been the difficulties which stood in the way of his appointment to Lavenham, they were now all overcome, and he was finally settled in possession of the living. He says:

Honoured Sir, most opportunely have I received the order of your honourable House. By your care and exertion alone has it been obtained; and all your favours toward me have, by this fresh proof of your kindness, been brought to a completion—this last having given perfection to the rest. What is a presentation without orders? What are orders without institution? Successfully, however, have you finished all these things, so that my thanks are due to you, not only as patron, but as ordainer and institutor, for under your auspices all these things have been performed. I well know how much of your time is occupied by public business, while the arduous affairs of the nation are under consideration, and also with what indefatigable labour you pursue more severe studies. The weight therefore of this your favour is so much the more increased, when we see that among matters of greater importance you still find leisure to attend to these our affairs, trifling indeed in comparison, but such as would, I believe, from our want of skill, have been a complete snare to us, had we not been speedily delivered from them by your prudence.

About the matters referred to in this letter, we know nothing more than what Gurnall tells us. His expressions certainly seem to imply that he owed his ordination, by whatever hands he was ordained, to the interest of Sir Symond D'Ewes.

(7) The seventh letter is dated Lavenham, March 20, 1647. It contains nothing worth quoting, and is entirely occupied with lamentations over the troublous times which the nation was passing through, and words of devout encouragement to Sir Symond D'Ewes, whose position in Parliament was probably not a very easy one at this period.

(8) The eighth and last letter is dated October 30, 1648, and was evidently written in reply to an order of the House of Commons, calling on Gurnall to preach before the House. He says, among other things:

> Your letter reached me yesterday as I was descending from the pulpit, thoroughly fatigued; and today, having finished one sermon, I am preparing another for tomorrow. You will therefore, I trust, readily pardon both the brevity and unpolished style of my answer. As to the affair mentioned in your letter to me, that I have been, by an order of the House, appointed to preach before you on the 29th of November next, it is a burden much too weighty for my shoulders, particularly at this time, when so many infirmities oppress me, that I can scarcely, without danger to my health, remain a short time in the open air. Much less, therefore, could I undertake so long a journey in so winterly a season. I am persuaded that the gentlemen who have proposed this know not the shattered state of my body, and have scarcely considered the distance of the place. Most humbly and earnestly, therefore, I entreat that, by your persuasion, which I know to be unparalleled, and in that honourable House most weighty, this burden may be

laid on other shoulders; for, under it, in my infirm state of health, I must of necessity sink.

This letter is interesting on more than one account. It shows the high esteem in which Gurnall was held as a preacher. None but the most eminent and gifted divines of the day were summoned to preach before the House of Commons. It also shows the weak state of health in which Gurnall was at a comparatively early period of his ministry at Lavenham. To this state of health we may perhaps attribute the retired life which he seems to have lived, and the comparatively small information which we possess about him.

*   *   *

Having now brought Gurnall to the place where he lived and exercised his ministry for no less than thirty-five years, some information about Lavenham will probably be interesting to most readers.

Lavenham is a small town in the southwest corner of Suffolk, lying in a rural parish of about 2,800 acres, and containing at this time about eighteen hundred people. In Gurnall's time it was in the diocese of Norwich. It is now in the diocese of Ely. It had once a market, and before the invention of the steam-engine, was famous for the manufacture of blue cloth and serge, for the better regulation of which three guilds, or companies, of St. Peter's, Holy Trinity, and Corpus Christi, were established. Its manufactures have now dwindled down into one silk-mill, and its market is no longer held. The marketplace, with an ancient cross in the centre, exists still. The De Veres, earls of Oxford, were once the principal proprietors of Lavenham, and had a large park here, comprising nearly half the parish. In the reign of Elizabeth, Edward, then Earl of Oxford, sold his property at Lavenham, together with the advowson of the living, to Paul D'Ewes, Esq., father of Sir Symond D'Ewes, the patron of William Gurnall, and to this sale, therefore, the good man's connection with Lavenham must be traced.

The living to which Gurnall was appointed was, no doubt, a very valuable one. At this day the tithes are commuted at £850 a year, and there are 140 acres of glebe attached to the rectory. Allowing for the difference in the value of money two hundred years ago, the Rector of Lavenham must have been comparatively very well off. It is, however, a curious fact, recorded by Fuller in his *Church History*, that in the year 1577 the living of Lavenham had a narrow escape of being reduced to half its value, and was only saved by the firmness of the Rector. The whole transaction is worth reading as illustrating the disorders and irregularities in ecclesiastical matters which great laymen too often attempted to perpetrate in the sixteenth century, and too often with success. Fuller says:

> In the year 1622, Henry Coppinger, formerly Fellow of St. John's College in Cambridge, Prebendary of York, once Chaplain to Ambrose, Earl of Warwick (whose funeral sermon he preached), made Master of Magdalen College, Cambridge, by his Majesty's mandates, though afterwards resigning his right at the Queen's request (shall I call it?), to prevent trouble, ended his religious life. He was the sixth son of Henry Coppinger, Esq., of Buxhall in Suffolk, by Agnes, daughter of Sir Thomas Jermyn. His father, on his deathbed, asking him what course of life he would embrace, he answered he intended to be a divine. "I like it well," said the old gentleman, "otherwise what shall I say to Martin Luther when I shall see him in heaven, and he knows that God gave me eleven sons, and I made not one of them a minister?" An expression proportionable enough to Luther's judgment, who maintained, some hours before his death, that the saints in heaven shall knowingly converse one with another.
>
> Lavenham living fell void, which both deserved a good minister, being a rich parsonage, and needed one, it being more than suspected that Dr. Reynolds, late Incumbent, who ran away to Rome, had left some superstitious leaven behind him. The Earl of Oxford being patron, presents Mr. Coppinger to it, but adding withal, that he would pay no tithes of his park, being almost half the land of the parish. Coppinger desired to resign it again to his lordship, rather than by such sinful gratitude to betray the rights of the Church. "Well!" said the Earl, "if you be of that mind, then take the tithes; I scorn that my estate should swell with church goods." However, it afterwards cost Mr. Coppinger sixteen hundred pounds in keeping his questioned, and recovering his detained right, in suit with the agent for the next minor Earl of

Oxford and others; all which he left to his church's quiet possession, being zealous in God's cause, but remiss in his own.

He lived forty and five years the painful parson at Lavenham, in which market-town there are about nine hundred communicants, among whom, all this time, no difference did arise which he did not compound. He had a bountiful hand and plentiful purse (his paternal inheritance by death of elder brothers, and other transactions descending upon him), bequeathing twenty pounds in money, and ten pounds per annum, to the poor of the parish; in the chancel whereof he lieth buried under a fine monument, dying on St. Thomas' day, in the threescore and twelfth year of his age.

The lawsuit referred to by Fuller seems, at any rate, not to have prevented Henry Coppinger being succeeded by his son Ambrose as Rector of Lavenham, at whose death Gurnall was appointed to the living. The Henry Coppinger referred to by Gurnall in one of his letters to Sir Symond D'Ewes, was, no doubt, a member of the family of Gurnall's predecessor, and a descendant of the Rector whose firmness preserved half the tithes of Lavenham from the Earl of Oxford's shameful attempt to deprive the living of them.

The parish church of Lavenham, in which Gurnall preached for thirty-five years, must naturally possess much interest in the eyes of all true admirers of his works. The pulpit in which the good man preached the substance of *The Christian in Complete Armour* no longer exists. But the fabric of the church is, in all probability, exactly what it was two hundred years ago. Lavenham Church is one of the finest and handsomest ecclesiastical buildings in the county of Suffolk.

It stands at the west end of the town, and was erected on the site of the ancient fabric, in the fifteenth and early part of the sixteenth centuries, chiefly at the cost of the Earl of Oxford, and the wealthy family of Spring, whose arms are to be seen in many parts of the building. It is in the later style of decorated English architecture, and is constructed of freestone, curiously ornamented with flint, a material commonly used in Suffolk churches, from the scarcity of stone. It is 156 feet long and 68 broad. The tower, which is of singular beauty, is 141 feet high and 42 in diameter, and contains an excellent peal of eight bells, of which the tenor weighs 23 cwt., and was cast in 1625. In the interior the roof is richly carved, and two pews, formerly belonging to the Earls of Oxford and the Springs, though now somewhat decayed, are highly finished specimens of Gothic work, in the elaborate style of Henry the Seventh's Chapel at Westminster. In the windows are considerable remains of ancient stained glass, and the porch is of highly ornamental architecture, adorned with armorial bearings.★

At the present day there can be no doubt that Lavenham is a far less important place than it was two hundred years ago. The county in which it is situated no longer occupies the position it once occupied among the counties of England. Without mines or manufactures, or large seaport towns, the eastern counties have stood still in material prosperity, while the rest of England has moved on. The village towns, with which Suffolk is rather thickly dotted, are almost all in a decaying or stationary condition. The old glory of such places as Eye, Framlingham, Bungay, Orford, Southwold, Dunwich, Aldeburgh, Hadleigh, Bildeston, Needham, Stradbroke, and Debenham, has clean passed away. Lavenham has shared the fate of these places. It is now nothing more than a quiet village in an agricultural district, remarkable only for its beautiful church and its numerous old charitable institutions.

The thirty-five years during which Gurnall lived at Lavenham, and filled the pulpit of the old parish church, were years full of stirring incidents in English history. The final overthrow of the King's party in the Commonwealth wars, the beheading of Charles I, the establishment of the Protectorate, the death of Oliver Cromwell, the restoration of the Stuarts to the throne, the passing of the Act of Uniformity, the ejection of two thousand ministers of the Church of England which followed that Act, and the intolerant persecution of all Nonconformists which disgraced this country for many years after the Act was passed, are events with which every student of English history is familiar. What Gurnall thought of most of these we have no means of knowing. What part he took, if any, and how he acted amidst the political and ecclesiastical

★ The above account is principally extracted from White's *History of Suffolk*, and I have no reason to doubt the accuracy of the details it contains.

convulsions which distracted the country we cannot say. His health, in all probability, prevented him from frequently leaving his own home, or doing much outside his own parish. Be the cause what it may, I am obliged to confess that the facts on record about the last thirty-five years of his life are exceedingly few.

It is certainly somewhat remarkable that during the period of Gurnall's ministry at Lavenham, that is between 1644 and 1679, some of the best and holiest Puritan divines were at one time or another living within twenty miles of Gurnall's home at Lavenham. I will give their names.

The famous John Owen, whose name is familiar to every reader of pure English theology, began his ministry at Fordham and Coggeshall in Essex, and only left the latter place when Cromwell made him Dean of Christ Church, and Vice-Chancellor of Oxford, in 1650, six years after Gurnall became Rector of Lavenham.

Stephen Marshall, one of the most celebrated divines in the Westminster Assembly, and a prominent character in the Commonwealth times, was Minister of Wethersfield and Finchingfield, in Essex, shortly before Gurnall came to Lavenham, and spent the last two years of his life at Ipswich, where he died in 1655.

Matthew Newcomen, another eminent member of the Westminster Assembly, and an assistant of Arrowsmith and Tuckney in drawing up the well-known Assembly's Catechism, was Vicar of Dedham in Essex, after the famous John Rogers was ejected in 1629, until the time of his own ejection by the Act of Uniformity, in 1662.

Thomas Young, another distinguished member of the Westminster Assembly, and Milton's tutor, was Vicar of Stowmarket, in Suffolk, for the thirty years before 1643, when he became pastor of a church in Duke's Place, London. Afterwards, being ejected in 1650, he retired to Stowmarket and died there in 1655. He was one of the five authors of the famous controversial work called *Smectymnuus*,[1] which made a great stir in the first half of the seventeenth century. It was so called from the initial letters of the names of its five writers: *viz.*, Stephen Marshall, Edmund Calamy, Thomas

---

[1] Published in 1641 as a Presbyterian response to Bishop Hall's *A Humble Remonstrance.*

Young, Matthew Newcomen, and William Spurstow. Of these five men, let us remember, no less than three died within a few hours' reach of Gurnall.

It would be easy to add other great names to this list such as those of *Daniel Rogers*, who died at Wethersfield in 1652; *Blackerby*, who died at Great Thurlow in 1648; *Fairclough*, who was ejected from Kedington in 1662, and was succeeded by Tillotson; and *Owen Stockton*, who was ejected from St. Andrews, Colchester, in 1662. Beside these good men, there were some who are less well known, such as William Sparrow of Halstead in Essex, John Fairfax of Barking in Suffolk, Matthias Candler of Coddenham in Suffolk, Samuel Spring of Creeting St. Mary in Suffolk, Stephen Scanderet of Haverhill in Suffolk, Tobias Leg of Hemingstone in Suffolk, Brunning and Stonham of Ipswich, Storer of Stowmarket—all of whom were eminent Puritan ministers, and were ejected in 1662. Their histories will be found in Calamy's *Nonconformists' Memorial*. All these men, I repeat, lived within twenty miles of Gurnall and must have come in contact with him occasionally.

It would be deeply interesting if we knew whether Gurnall had much communication with these good men. My own private impression is that he had not. Ill-health, in all probability, kept him much at home. But I suspect this was not all. I am inclined to think that Gurnall was a man of retiring and cautious temperament, and naturally disinclined to go much into society. Above all, I am strongly inclined to think that he liked the Episcopal Church and the Prayer Book better than many of his neighbours did, and naturally withdrew from close intimacy with them. All these, however, are only conjectures, and I shall therefore pass on to the only remaining facts that remain to be told about Gurnall's history.

In the year 1645, the year following his appointment to Lavenham, Gurnall was married to Sarah Mott, daughter of the Rev. Thomas Mott, Vicar of Stoke-by-Nayland. By this lady, who survived him some years, he had ten children, eight of whom were living at his death.

        *   *   *

In the year 1662, when no less than two thousand ministers were ejected from the Church of England by the Act of Uniformity,

Gurnall signed the declaration required by the Act, on August 20th, was ordained priest by the Bishop of Norwich, the well-known Bishop Reynolds, on August 21st, and went through the forms of episcopal institution to Lavenham on the presentation of Thomas Bowes, of Bromley Hall, in Essex, a connection of the D'Ewes family, on August 22nd. The close proximity of these three dates is very remarkable! The result was, that while many of his Puritan brethren resigned their preferments, he retained his position as Rector of Lavenham until his death.

This part of Gurnall's history undoubtedly demands some consideration. At first sight undeniably there is something curious about it. That a minister of at least eighteen years' standing should submit to receive priest's orders at a bishop's hands—that a preacher of notoriously Puritan sentiments should sit still and retain his connection with the Church of England, while nearly all his Puritan brethren around him seceded—in all this there is something strange. That it really was so is as certain as possible. A facsimile of his subscription, which I have obtained from the Registry of Norwich, places the matter beyond doubt. It is a doubly interesting document, as containing the only specimen I know of Gurnall's handwriting.[*]

That Gurnall's conformity brought on him great obloquy and reproach we may well suppose. A libellous attack[†] on him was published in the year 1665, quoted by Bishop Kennett, which contains the following passage:

Neither is Mr. Gurnall alone in these horrible defilements, hateful

---

[*] By the kindness of the Bishop of Norwich, I have been enabled to verify all the three remarkable dates above given from the Registry at Norwich.

[†] The title of this libellous attack is so curious that I give it entire. *Covenant Renouncers Desperate Apostates, opened in two letters, written by a Christian friend to Mr. W. Gurnall, of Lavenham, Suffolk, which may indefinitely serve as an admonition to all such Presbyterian ministers or others, who have forced their conscience, not only to leap over, but to renounce their solemn covenant obligation to endeavour a reformation according to God's Word, and the extirpation of all prelatical superstitions, and contrary thereunto conform to those superstitious vanities against which they had so solemnly sworn. Printed in Anti-turn-coat Street, and sold at the sign of Truth's Delight, right opposite to Backsliding Alley. 4to, 1665.*

to the Word of God and His saints, but is compassed about with a cloud of witnesses, even in the same county where himself liveth, men of the same order of anti-Christian priesthood and brethren in the same iniquity with himself.

That he brought on himself much private sorrow and discomfort by his conformity we may easily believe. His own wife's father, Mr. Mott, of Stoke-by-Nayland, was one of the two thousand who went out of the Church of England for conscience' sake. Above all, the value of his living at Lavenham, and the large size of the family dependent on him, would be sure to cause men to cast suspicion on what he did, and to question the sincerity of his motives.

But, after all, the point remains to be considered: Did Gurnall do anything inconsistent with his character as a minister of Christ? Was there anything abstractedly wrong in his conformity? Was there anything in the antecedents of his history to make it base or dishonourable to retain his post at Lavenham, to subscribe the declaration of the Act of Uniformity, to assent to the liturgy, and to submit to receive priest's orders at Bishop Reynolds' hands? On these points I have something to say.

I shall clear the way by saying that I thoroughly disapprove the Act of Uniformity, although personally I feel no difficulty about its requirements. To show my own feeling about it, I need only refer my readers to a long passage in my biography of Baxter in this volume, in which the Act of Uniformity is plainly condemned.

But while I protest against the Act of Uniformity as an unjust, unwise, impolitic, unstatesmanlike, and hard measure, I do not for a moment admit that no good man could possibly submit to its requirements. On the contrary, I can quite understand that many holy and faithful ministers would do as Gurnall did, and act as he acted. They would argue that we cannot have everything to our mind in this world below—that the way of patience is better than the way of secession—that there is nothing abstractedly wrong in forms of prayer—that it is better to put up with some things we do not like in a church than to throw away opportunities of usefulness —that it was better to accept the Prayer Book with all its blemishes, and have liberty to preach the Gospel, than to refuse the Prayer Book and be silenced altogether—that so long as the

Thirty-nine Articles were sound and uninjured, they could not be compelled to preach unsound doctrine—and that so long as they were allowed to preach sound doctrine, they ought not to refuse the opportunity, but to preach, and stand by their flocks. All this I can conceive a good man saying to himself. Whether Gurnall reasoned in this manner I cannot pretend to say. But I think he might have done so.

The plain truth is, that before anyone condemns Gurnall for submitting to the Act of Uniformity, he ought in common justice to remember the times and circumstances in which Gurnall first entered the ministry. He became a minister of the Gospel at a period in English history when it was impossible to obtain episcopal ordination, and the use of the Prayer Book was almost forbidden. I have no doubt he was quite right in accepting the position of things which he found around him. The imposition of episcopal hands is not absolutely necessary to make a valid ordination. The use of the Church of England liturgy is not essential to the being of a church. At the time when Gurnall entered the ministry he could neither have episcopacy nor the Prayer Book, and he entered the ministry without them. Let others say what they will, I do not think he was wrong. It is better to have the Gospel preached without bishops and Prayer Books, than not to have any preaching at all.

But, after all, there is not the slightest proof that Gurnall had any conscientious objection either to episcopacy or the Liturgy of the Church of England. For anything we can discover, he had never committed himself to any such condemnation of them as to make it inconsistent to approve and adopt them. What right, then, have we to find fault with him because he submitted to the requirements of the Act of 1662? He was ordained priest by Bishop Reynolds, because he could not be an Incumbent in the diocese without priest's orders. But who shall say that he would not gladly have received episcopal orders twenty years before, if it had been possible to obtain them? He declared his assent and consent to all things contained in the Prayer Book. But who shall say that he would not have done the same at any period in his life? He had never been a member of the Westminster Assembly, like many of the two thousand ejected divines. He had never been mixed up in their public proceedings, discussions, and controversies like Owen, Newcomen, Baxter, and many more. He had been a quiet, retired preacher in a country parish, and there is really no proof whatever that his retention of his position at Lavenham was inconsistent with anything in his previous life.

One more circumstance ought not to be forgotten in forming our estimate of Gurnall's conduct at this crisis of his life. The Bishop in whose diocese he was living, and at whose hands he accepted re-ordination, was Bishop Reynolds, himself a Puritan in doctrine, and notoriously the most mild and lenient man on the episcopal bench in dealing with scrupulous clergymen. We cannot doubt that such a man as Reynolds would use every effort to meet Gurnall's scruples, if he had any. We cannot doubt that he would strain every nerve to retain as many of the clergy as possible within the pale of the Church, and to prevent secessions. I confess to a strong suspicion that this circumstance weighed much in Gurnall's mind. Few men can do more by kindness, and less by harshness, in dealing with men, than bishops. If Gurnall ever had any doubts about remaining in the Church of England in 1662, I think it very likely that his good bishop's character turned the scale. In short, I venture the guess that he might have gone out of Lavenham rectory and followed his father-in-law, Mr. Mott, in secession, if the occupier of Norwich palace had been any other bishop than Reynolds.*

I leave the subject of Gurnall's conduct in 1662 with the reader. It is one on which different men will have different opinions,

---

* Reynolds was made Bishop of Norwich by Charles II in 1661. He was a thorough Puritan and a prominent member of the famous Westminster Assembly of divines. When the bishopric of Norwich was offered to him, the bishopric of Hereford at the same time was offered to Baxter, the bishopric of Lichfield to Calamy, the deanery of Rochester to Manton, and the deanery of Coventry to Bates. All these eminent Puritan divines refused preferment when Reynolds accepted it. Their refusal, I venture to think, was the greatest misfortune that ever befell the Church of England, and the most singular instance of mistaken judgment on record in Church history. If Reynolds, Baxter, and Calamy had all been bishops, and sat in the House of Lords, and Manton and Bates had been deans, I doubt if the Act of Uniformity, in its present shape, could ever have been passed.

according to the standpoint which they occupy. Some in the present day would have thought more highly of Gurnall if he had refused to submit to the Act of Uniformity, and had gone out with the famous two thousand. I, and many others perhaps, think more highly of him because he held his ground and did not secede. Which of us is right will never, probably, be settled in this world. I only desire to record my own opinion, that Gurnall was probably just as courageous, conscientious and high-principled in deciding to stay in, as hundreds of his two thousand ejected brethren were in deciding to go out. In movements like that of 1662, the seceding party has not always a monopoly of grace and courage. There were many cases, I have no doubt, in which it showed more courage to submit to the Act of Uniformity than to refuse submission, and in which it cost a man far more to hold his living than to throw it up. I should not wonder if Gurnall's was one.

*   *   *

About Gurnall's life after the year 1662 we know literally nothing at all. We may well suppose that his latter years were saddened by the events of the year 1662. Human nature would not be what it is, if his retention of his position, and subscription to the Act of Uniformity, did not create some estrangement of feeling between himself and his seceding brethren. But we really have no right to speak decidedly on the matter. There are floating traditions in the neighbourhood of Lavenham that he never was the same man as a minister after 1662 that he had been before; that there was no power or blessing attending his ministry from that time forward. But I must plainly say that I cannot discover any foundation for these traditions. I regard them as nothing better than lying stories. Such stories are often current about eminent servants of Christ. His refusal to give up his post at Lavenham, when many other ministers seceded, would, no doubt, give great annoyance to the bitterest and most extreme Nonconformists in that part of Suffolk, since it would weaken their hands and strengthen the Church of England. I should therefore expect, as a matter of course, that all manner of false reports would be current about him. Lies are Satan's chief weapons against God's saints.

Gurnall died October 12th, 1679, and was buried at Lavenham, in the sixty-third year of his age. There is internal evidence, we have already seen, in his letters and elsewhere, that he was always a man of weak health. But we know not whether he died suddenly or of a lingering illness. The fact, however, that he made his will the day before he died would rather point to the conclusion that he had been ill some time. M'Keon, to whose biography of Gurnall I have so frequently referred, has procured a copy of Gurnall's will, which I here subjoin, as it may interest many readers:

In the name of God, Amen. The Eleventh day of October, in the year of our Lord, One Thousand Six Hundred and Seventy-nine, I, William Gurnall of Lavenham, in the county of Suffolk, clerk, weak of body, but, thanks be to God, of sound mind and memory, resigning up my soul in the first place into the hands of God, my Lord, Redeemer, and Saviour, and yielding my body to the earth, to be buried at the discretion of my executrix, as concerning that worldly estate which it has pleased God to bestow upon me, do make and ordain, this, my last will and testament as followeth: That is to say, I give and decree all my free land and tenements, with all their appurtenances whatsoever, lying and being in Walpole or elsewhere, in Monkland, in the county of Norfolk, unto Sarah, my well-beloved wife and her heirs, to hold to her, the said Sarah, to her own proper use, for, and during the time of her natural life, and after her decease to some one of my children, as she shall declare in, and by her last will and testament. And I do give and decree also all my goods and chattels, debts, and personal estate whatsoever, unto the said Sarah, my well-beloved wife, as well for her own comfortable subsistence and maintenance, and the better to enable her for the bringing up of my younger children, as also in trust and confidence that she will preserve and dispose of the residue and surplusage thereof amongst my children, respecting the circumstances of those of them which are not yet provided for, in such manner, and in such proportion as in her discretion she shall think most meet and fit; only I decree, if my son John shall be a scholar, that she will give my books to him. And I do hereby nominate, constitute, and appoint the said Sarah, my well-beloved wife, to be sole executrix of this my will, which I have caused to be written and have thereunto set my hand and seal, the day of grace aforesaid. Subscribed, sealed, published, and declared by the said William Gurnall, to be his last will and testament, in the presence of us, Thomas Mott, Bezaleel Peachie, John Pinchbeck.

The first of these three witnesses was most probably the father or brother of Mrs. Gurnall. She was daughter of Thomas Mott. The second was evidently the husband of his third daughter, Catherine. The third was perhaps the lawyer who drew up the will. The books mentioned in the will are probably the very books which Gurnall's son, John, afterwards left by his will, in 1699, to his brother Joseph, and his nephew Leonard Shaftoe of Newcastle. The English books were left to Joseph Gurnall, and the "rest of the books and manuscripts" to Leonard Shaftoe. They are now probably scattered to the four winds, and dispersed, if not destroyed. The end to which good men's libraries finally come is a melancholy subject. Few things are so much loved by some, and despised and neglected by others as books, and specially theological books.

The precise spot in which Gurnall was buried is not known. We cannot tell whether his bones are lying in the church or in the churchyard. No tombstone or monumental slab marks the place of his interment. Nothing, from some cause or other, seems to have been erected to his memory.

> The only sepulchral notice to be found of him, [says M'Keon] is on a black marble slab in the chancel, which has this inscription: "Here lieth the body of Mary, late wife of Mr. Henry Boughton, of this parish, and daughter of the late Reverend Mr. Samuel Beachcroft, Rector of Semer, and grand-daughter of the late Reverend Mr. William Gurnall, who was Rector of this parish thirty-five years. She died the 14th of October, 1741, aged 78 years."

Under this slab in the chancel is a vault, which M'Keon conjectured is Gurnall's resting-place, from the fact of Mrs. Boughton having been buried here instead of being buried with the Boughton family in the family vault, near the great south door. However, it is only a conjecture.

A funeral sermon was preached in Lavenham Church, in commemoration of Gurnall, shortly after his funeral, by the well-known commentator on the New Testament, Burkitt, who was at that time Rector of Milden, near Lavenham. It is still extant, and bears the following title: *The people's zeal provoked to an holy emulation by the pious and instructive example of their dead Minister; as a seasonable memento to the parishioners of Lavenham in Suffolk.*

Burkitt's sermon was on Heb. 13:7, "Remember them that have the rule over you," etc. It was both preached and published "by request," and is prefaced by an epistle dedicatory "to my honoured friend, Mrs. Sarah Gurnall, the sorrowful relict of Mr. William Gurnall, late of Lavenham, deceased, and to the rest of the sorrowing inhabitants of that town." It is a respectable composition, though somewhat quaint, and rather flowery and high-flown in style. But it is but fair to Burkitt to remember that he was comparatively young when he preached it, being only twenty-nine years old. A few extracts from it will probably be found interesting. I shall select those parts only which refer to Gurnall. Burkitt's epistle dedicatory concludes with the following passage:

> To inform and convince you how highly accountable you are to Almighty God, both for the long enjoyment of his ministry, and also for the happy advantage of his example, is the honest design of the following sermon; and also to let this censorious age (in which some persons are so overgrown with the anti-episcopal jaundice, that their eye can see nothing in a Conformist but what is discoloured and of a different tincture), understand and know that you had a Conformist for your minister, who rendered solid religion amiable, by a conversation in all things worthy of it; who did by a regular piety, a strict sobriety, a catholic and diffusive charity, render religion venerable to the world; one whose whole time, strength, and parts, were piously devoted to God and His sacred service.
>
> Moses, I observe, was in one particular privileged by God above all other holy persons. Their souls (in common with his) at death have angels for their convoy towards the mansions of bliss and glory: but he had an angel for his sexton, who buried his body in an unknown place, lest the Israelites should superstitiously idolize and adore it. There would be no fear at all of any such offensive adoration on your part, were I able (as indeed I am not) to draw to the life the fair effigies of your absent minister,

who was, like Moses, faithful in all God's house whilst he lived, and not unlike him at his death: his meek soul gliding from him in a fine, imperceptible vehicle; and he dying as the modern Jews by tradition tell us Moses did, *ad nutum Dei, et osculo oris ejus*, at God's beck, and as it were with a kiss of God's mouth. It was no more betwixt God and them but this—Go up and die.

To conclude, then, may all your practices appear to the world in a faithful compliance with what was truly imitable and praise-worthy in him. May the living example of your dead minister be exemplified in the lives of you his people. May you daily dress by his glass, and walk in his pious and devout footsteps. May you all meet him with astonishing joy, and behold him also with unutter-able delight and comfort, in the day of your great audit: this is, and ever shall be, the hearty and affectionate supplication of your sympathising friend and servant,

WILLIAM BURKITT

Milden, Dec. 10, 1679

The sermon contains the following sentences which are worth transcribing:

How lovely was that copy of religion which he set before you in his daily conversation! So forcible was the majesty of that holiness that shined forth in him, that it did extort a veneration from its most violent opposers; and so convictive also that it pierced the very consciences of his enemies, and constrained them whom prejudice only had made his foes, tacitly to acknowledge that God was in him of a truth.[*]

Again:

He being dead, yet speaketh: yea, dead as well as living, he is still your preacher, his shroud and coffin are his pulpit—his grave and tombstone are his temple, and he still preaches to you though he lies in silence before you and utters never a word; I mean by his pious and most instructive example left among you, and by that fair character and good report which he hath so deservedly obtained with you.[†]

---

[*] p. 9, Baynes' reprint, 1829.
[†] pp. 10, 11.

Again:

> I am sure it did not a little conduce to the support of your dying minister's spirit, when he had death before him in immediate prospect, to hope upon good grounds that he (as a spiritual father) should leave many children behind him, to carry on the work of Christ in the world, when his head should be laid among the clods.*

The last five pages of the sermon are so entirely occupied with Gurnall's character, that I think it best to give them unabridged:

> I infer from hence, in the last place, how signal your obligations are to Almighty God for the long enjoyment of that exemplary pattern of all true piety and virtue (your deceased Minister, I mean), whom (for your sins, I fear) He hath lately taken from you. Show now your obedience to God, your respects to him, your kindness and charity to your own souls, by a zealous and faithful care to transcribe impartially in your own lives whatever was truly imitable in your Minister's. And not to carry you beyond the confines of the text, let me earnestly bespeak your Christian compliance with a double duty here enjoined.
>
> I. To follow his faith.
> II. To imitate his exemplary conversation.
>
> I. *Follow his faith*, and that in a double respect, in the soundness of his faith, and in the steadfastness of his faith.
>
> 1. Follow him in the soundness of his faith. The faith which he perseveringly professed, and taught, was that doctrine which is according to godliness; that faith which owns God for its immediate Author and the Scripture for its infallible rule, the faith that was once delivered to the saints, which is not the result of fancy and imagination, but the product of an eternal counsel, which was confirmed by the miracles and sealed with the blood of a Saviour. In a word, that faith which he so zealously taught had sure footing in the Holy Scriptures. Whenever he propounded any truth which required not only the assent of your understandings, but also the obedience and adoration of your faith, he constantly showed you the Canon of the Scriptures for its confirmation. *If any then (which God forbid) should appear after him in this place, and attempt the proselyting of you to another Gospel, or*

---

* p. 17.

to any new doctrine of faith foreign to the Scriptures, should he pretend to the authority of a commissioned angel from heaven, let him be held accursed.

2. Follow him in the steadfastness of his faith. The same rule of faith which he laid before you at his first coming amongst you, he lived and preached by till the day of his death. And this I take the greater liberty to assert, because some persons have not blushed to tell the world publicly that since his conformity to the discipline of the Church he had apostatized and revolted from that faith which he had formerly professed and taught. But be ye all assured, that, as to the great fundamentals of faith and religion, he was ever the same, and what he taught you to his last breath, I doubt not but he stood ready to confirm and seal with his blood, even in the fiercest flames of martyrdom, if God had called him to that fiery trial.

II. *Imitate his Christian conversation.* My meaning is, exemplify those evangelical graces and Christian virtues in your lives, which did so oriently shine forth in his. To propound a few:

1. His eminent humility. This was the garment which covered all his excellent accomplishments, although indeed their beauty was rendered more conspicuous and amiable by casting this veil over it. O what mean thoughts had he of himself! And was not only content, but desirous also, that others should have so too: no man ever expressed so low a value of his worth and merits as himself did. Everything in others that was good he admired as excellent, whilst the same or better in himself he thought not unworthily contemned: his eyes were full of his own deficiencies and others' perfections.

In a word, he was a lovely valley, sweetly planted, well watered, richly fruitful: imitate him then herein, and by a holy emulation study to excel him in this adorning grace; and for your help herein recollect what you heard from him in his elaborate discourses among you upon Phil. 2:5: "Let this mind be in you, which was also in Christ Jesus"—this humble mind.

2. His extensive love. This grace did variously exert itself.

(1) His love to God. He loved Him exceedingly whom he could not love excessively, having such high and raised apprehensions of his Maker's excellencies, as caused him to judge his prime and best affections unworthy to be placed on so Divine an object.

(2) His love to the holy Jesus. This was such a seraphic and Divine fire in his soul, as did marvellously consume his love to the world and all sublunary comforts. You are witnesses, and all that knew him, in how eminent a measure and degree the world was crucified unto him, and he unto the world by the cross of Christ.

(3) His love to souls. This was it, no doubt, that made him so indefatigable both in his study and in the pulpit; from hence it was, that the throne of grace, his study, the pulpit, and his sick neighbours, had the whole of his time divided amongst them, and devoted to them.

(4) HIS UNBOUNDED LOVE TO ALL CHRISTIANS; though they differed in their sentiments from him. He loved Christians for their Christianity, and did adore the image of his Saviour wherein he saw it in any of his members *unhappily persecuting one another with hard names* and characters of reproach. How often did he PUBLICLY DEPLORE AND BEWAIL, that the greatest measure of love that is found at this day amongst the professors of the cross, was not true Christian love, *but only love of a party!* Follow him, then, in the impartial exercise of this grace, and for your help therein remember what he taught you from Eph. 5:2, "And walk in love, as Christ also hath loved us"; and as you have any regard for the Author of your profession, take heed that a spirit of division (now) crowd not in among you. Your unity is your strength as well as your beauty; persist therefore, I beseech you, in that Christian order amongst yourselves in which it was his great ambition all his days to preserve and keep you. Timely oppose the crafty design of the subtle adversary of souls, who will take this occasion (if possible), now the spiritual parent is out of the way, to set the children together by the ears.

3. His diffusive charity. His alms were as exuberant as his love: misery and want, wherever he met them, did sufficiently endear their objects to him. He was none of those that hide their faces from the poor, nor of the number of them who satisfy their consciences with a single exercise of their charity once a year, but daily were the emanations of his bounty. Yet although he cast the seeds of his charity upon all sorts of ground, he sowed them thickest upon God's inclosure: my meaning is, he did good unto all, "but especially to those that were of the household of faith." Make him herein, and his example, the pattern of your daily

imitation; for the world, which is chained together by inter-mingled love, will soon shatter and fall in pieces if charity shall once fail and die; and for your better help herein, call over those potent arguments for the exercise of this evangelical duty, which he urged upon you, from that apostolical injunction, Heb. 13:16, "But to do good, and to communicate, forget not, for with such sacrifices God is well pleased."

4. His persevering diligence and faithfulness in his place and station. You could not but observe that his whole disposal of himself was to perpetual industry and service. He not only avoided idleness, but seemed to have a forcible antipathy against it, and was often recommending it to you with great concern and vigour in his public advices, to be always furnished with some-what to do; *ut te inveniat semper diabolus occupatum:* that the devil may never find thee at leisure to listen to his temptations, as St. Hierom adviseth. The idle man's brain being, in truth, not only the devil's shop, but his kingdom too, a model of and an appendage unto hell; a place (like that) given up to torture and mischief. As to himself, his chiefest recreation was variety of work; for beside those portions of time which the necessities of nature and of civil life extorted from him, there was not a minute of the day which he left vacant. Now to stimulate your zeal to a pious imitation of him herein also, let me admonish you to ruminate upon those accurate sermons you heard from him upon Matt. 20:6: "Why stand ye here all the day idle?"

5. His tender sympathy with the afflicted Church of Christ. Like a true son of Zion he could not rejoice when his mother mourned, he daily felt as much by sympathy as he did by sense; and no wonder, for he that hath a stock going in the Church's ship, cannot but lament and quake at every storm. O how frequent were his inquiries after her, how fervent were his prayers for her, how bowelly and compassionate were his mournings over her! The deplorable condition of the Church and nation lay exceeding near his heart both living and dying; he preferring their happiness and welfare above his chief joy. Now in order to your attaining the same Christ-like temper with him, frequently meditate on what you heard from him upon Neh. 1:4, where the sympathising prophet refuseth to drink wine, when the afflicted Church drank water.

6. And lastly, to sum up all, imitate him in his daily care and endeavour to live religion in all his capacities. As a minister, ye are witnesses, and God also, how faithfully, how conscientiously he discharged his duty towards you in the exercise of his ministerial function, if censure itself be able to tax him for any neglect, it must be in not more frequent visiting his flock, from which nothing but a weak body kept him, not a proud or unwilling mind. The obstruction he met with in this part of his duty, from his tender habit of body (which would not suffer him so frequently to perform it as he desired) was, his great sorrow both living and dying; yet having this to comfort him, that the frailty of his body was his affliction, but not his sin. Consider him in his next relative capacity, as a child, how dutiful and obsequious! O how great was that tribute of veneration and respect which he so constantly paid to the hoary hairs of his aged parents! As a husband, how tender and compassionate; as a parent, how indulgent and affectionate; as a minister, how kind and munificent! Thus was he universally good in all stations, and lived religion in every capacity. And if you desire to imitate him herein also, as becomes you, dress your souls by that glass daily, which his dying hand last held up before your eyes: I mean by heavenly meditation, make those useful truths your own, which you last heard from him upon Tit. 2:12, "That, denying ungodliness and worldly lusts, we should live soberly, righteously, and godly in this present world." Which Christian lesson, if it shall be as practically learned by you as it was faithfully taught by him, I will be bold to say thus much in the singular commendation of you his people, that you will thereby give the world a convictive instance that this age hath virtues as stupendous as its vices!

THE CONCLUSION: Thus I have given myself the satisfaction of doing my duty in propounding your Minister's example to your Christian view. Let none censoriously say I have been all this while painting the prophet's sepulchre. No, but describing the prophet himself, and with this single and sincere intention, that you may timely know you have had a prophet of the Lord among you; a person that had *omnia in se sempiterna præter corpusculum:* all things living and lasting to eternity except his body, which was the only thing he had, subject to mortality, and besides which nothing of him doth see corruption. It will be below the merit of his person, as well as the greatness of our loss, to celebrate his death in womanish complaints, or indeed by any verbal lamentations; nor can anything beseem his memory but what is sacred and Divine, as his writings are. May his just fame from them, and from his virtues, be precious to all succeeding ages. And when elegies committed to the trust of marble shall be as illegible as if they had been writ in water, when all stately pyramids shall be dissolved in dust, and all the venerable monuments of antiquity be devoured by the corroding teeth of time, then let this short character, describing him in his best and fullest portraiture, remain of him: *viz.*, that he was a CHRISTIAN IN COMPLETE ARMOUR.

Circumstances at Lavenham, we can easily see, are referred to in this funeral sermon, of which we know nothing certain now. It is evident that Gurnall's troubles during the latter part of his incumbency were neither few nor small. His conformity in 1662 was probably never forgotten; and the last years of his life were probably darkened by the implacable enmity of some of his parishioners. That Burkitt, who doubtless knew more of Gurnall's inner life than anyone, should have given the world no biography of him, is much to be regretted. He could have done it well, and it is a pity that he did not do it.

*　　　　*　　　　*

Gurnall's widow survived her husband nineteen years, and seems to have resided at Lavenham. At any rate, she was buried at Lavenham on September 7, 1698, and the grant of administration to her property called her "Sarah Gurnall, widow, of Lavenham, deceased." Gurnall left at least eight children, according to M'Keon, two having died young:

1. Sarah, baptized April 2, 1646, married to Mr. Mayor, of Newcastle-on-Tyne.
2. Susannah, baptized April 4, 1650, married the Rev. Samuel Beachcroft, of Emmanuel College, Cambridge, Rector of Semer, Suffolk.
3. Catherine, the date of whose baptism we do not know, married the Rev. Bezaleel Peachie, of Emmanuel College,

Cambridge, Vicar of Bures St. Mary, near Sudbury, who was one of the witnesses of Gurnall's will.

4. Elizabeth, baptized April 25, 1655, married the Rev. Philip Richardson, of Christ's College, Cambridge, a clergyman of Ipswich.

5. Ann, baptized February 11, 1655, continued to live with her mother at Lavenham until her decease in 1698, and married in June, 1700, Mr. William Manthorpe, of Lowestoft.

6. Another sister, whose name is not known, married a Mr. Shaftoe, of Newcastle-on-Tyne.

7. Thomas, baptized March 13, 1659, settled at Little Waldringfield, and was buried there in 1723.

8. Joseph, baptized July 23, 1662, was an attorney, and according to M'Keon's belief, resided at Lavenham.

9. John, baptized December 24, 1664, was sent to Christ's College, proceeded B.A. in 1685, and afterwards became Curate of Brockley, until 1698. He was buried at Lavenham on February 6, 1700.

10. Leonard, baptized May 11, 1669, is one of whom nothing is known.

I can find no trace of Gurnall's descendants in the present day. There is no one, so far as I can learn, of his name at Lavenham. The rectory house in which he lived is no longer standing. The living of Lavenham has passed into the hands of Caius College, Cambridge. Everything connected with the good man, except his book, seems to have passed away. By it alone, "he being dead yet speaketh."[1]

*   *   *

I have now completely exhausted all the information I can supply about the author of *The Christian in Complete Armour*, and can only express my deep regret that I can tell the reader nothing more. It certainly does seem rather tantalizing that a writer of the seventeenth century—who is better known by name than almost any of the Puritans—who lived within twenty miles of such men as Owen, Marshall, Newcomen, Young, and Stockton—who resided for thirty-five years in a town of some little importance two hundred years ago, in a county so well known at that time as

[1] Hebrews 11:4.

Suffolk—that such a man should have passed away and so very little be known about him! But so it is, Gurnall's case, perhaps, does not stand alone. Perhaps the last day will prove that some of the best and holiest men that ever lived are hardly known.

Nothing now remains for me to do except to say a few words about Gurnall's literary works, which have been lately, for the first time, brought together in a complete form.*

The first of Gurnall's works, and indeed the one by which he is commonly known, is his famous book, *The Christian in Complete Armour*. This well-known book consists, like many of the theological writings of the seventeenth century, of sermons or lectures delivered by the author in the course of his regular ministry, in a consecutive course, on Eph. 6:10–20. It was originally published in three small quarto volumes, and in three portions, at three different times. The first volume, containing Eph. 6:10–13, was published in 1655. This volume is dedicated to "the Inhabitants of Lavenham, my dearly beloved friends and neighbours"; and the dedication contains a distinct statement that the book consists of sermons preached at Lavenham. "What I present you," says Gurnall, "within this treatise, is a dish from your own table, and so (I hope) will go down the better. You cannot despise it, though the fare be mean, except you will blame yourselves who chose the cook." There is a date at the end of the dedication which happily serves to show when the work was published. It is dated January 1, 1655. My copy is the second edition.

The second volume of the course, containing Eph. 6:14–16, was published in 1658. It contains a dedication to "Thomas Darcy, Esq., and Mrs. Sisilia Darcy, his religious consort," at Kentwell Hall in Suffolk; from which it appears that Mrs. Darcy was daughter of Sir Symond D'Ewes, Gurnall's patron. The dedication is dated Lavenham, October, 1657. My copy is the first edition.

The third volume of the work, containing Eph. 6:17–20, was published in 1662. It is dedicated to Lady Mary Vere, Baroness of Tilbury, a lady well known in the seventeenth century, and daughter of William Tracey, Esq., of Toddington, in Gloucestershire.

---

* I refer to Blackie's complete edition of Gurnall's works, which I take the opportunity of strongly recommending to all buyers of theology.

The dedication is dated August 28, 1661. My copy is the first edition.

Comment, or recommendation, is perhaps needless in speaking of Gurnall's great work. The fact that a sixth edition was published in the year the author died, 1679, is enough to show that its merits were early recognised. The high reputation it has always borne among lovers of sound English divinity down to the present day is another fact which ought not to be forgotten. Other theological works of the seventeenth century were famous in their day, but are now seldom read. *The Christian in Complete Armour* is a work that is read and enjoyed by thousands up to this time.

One grand peculiarity of *The Christian in Complete Armour* is the soundness and scriptural proportion of its doctrinal statements. There is nothing extravagant and overstretched in Gurnall's exhibition of any point either in faith or practice. Nothing is glaringly over-coloured, nothing is completely thrown into the shade. In this respect it is eminently like Bunyan's *Pilgrim's Progress*, a work so beautifully proportioned in doctrine that Calvinists and Arminians, churchmen and Dissenters, are all alike agreed in admiring it.

Another striking peculiarity of Gurnall's book is its profusion of illustrations and comparisons. You can hardly open a page of the work without meeting with some vivid image or picture of Divine things, which lights up the whole subject under consideration like a sunbeam. I am not prepared to say that in this respect Gurnall surpasses Brooks, Watson, or Swinnock, but I am quite sure that he deserves to be classed with them. Happy would it be for the Church if this gift of illustration was more common and more cultivated by preachers! The man whose sermons are best remembered is the man who, like his Divine Master, *uses similitudes*. "He is the eloquent man," says an Oriental proverb, "who turns his hearers' ears into eyes, and makes them see what he speaks of."

One more beautiful feature in Gurnall's book is its richness in pithy, pointed, and epigrammatical sayings. Page after page might be filled, if a collection were made of all the short, golden sentences which are to be found in *The Christian in Complete Armour*. You will often find in a line and a half some great truth, put so concisely, and yet so fully, that you really marvel how so much thought could be got into so few words.

It would be easy to heap up testimonies to the value of Gurnall's *Christian in Complete Armour*. Baxter and Flavel both thought most highly of the book. Toplady used to make copious extracts from it in his common-place book. John Newton said that if he was confined to one book beside the Bible, he dared say Gurnall's *Christian Armour* would be his choice. Cecil spent many of the last days of his life in reading it, and repeatedly expressed his admiration of it. But I have said enough already to weary the reader, and the best advice I can give him is to read the book for himself in the beautiful edition in which it has lately been brought out by Messrs. Blackie, and to judge for himself.

Two other books, and two only, are known to have been published by Gurnall, in addition to his great work, *The Christian in Complete Armour*. Both of these are single sermons preached on special occasions.

One of these sermons is called *The Magistrate's Portraiture drawn from the Word*. It was preached at Stowmarket, in Suffolk, upon August 20, 1656, "before the election of Parliament recurs for the same county," and published the same year. The subject of the sermon is Isaiah 1:26. It is an excellent sermon, and worthy of the author in every way.

The other sermon is called *The Christian's Labour and Reward*. It was preached at Castle Hedingham in Essex, on January 10, 1671, and published in 1672. It consists chiefly of a discourse preached at the funeral of Lady Mary Vere, widow of Sir Horace Vere of Tilbury, the lady to whom the third volume of *The Christian in Complete Armour* is dedicated. It contains a dedication to Elizabeth, Countess Dowager of Clare, who was Lady Mary Vere's daughter. It is a good sermon, undoubtedly, but would have been better if it had been more compressed. However, the preachers of funeral sermons are seldom allowed much time for their preparation, and perhaps Gurnall had no time to make his sermon shorter.

I have seen it asserted that Gurnall, in addition to the works already mentioned, published a volume of sermons in 1660. M'Keon says that this volume is mentioned in Cooke's *Preacher's Assistant*, published in 1783, and that a bookseller in London told him that he had himself seen a copy.

In reply to this I can only say that no such volume of sermons is to be found in the British Museum, nor in the Bodleian Library at Oxford, nor in the Redcross Street Library in London. Neither can I hear of any living man, whether bookseller or collector of old divinity, who ever saw the volume. I must therefore be allowed to think that M'Keon made a mistake, and that no such volume was ever published.

I now conclude this lengthy biography by expressing my earnest hope that Gurnall's works may yet find many readers as well as purchasers. It is indeed to be desired that solid, scriptural theology, like that contained in *The Christian in Complete Armour*, should be valued and studied in the Church. Books in which Scripture is reverently regarded as the only rule of faith and practice—books in which Christ and the Holy Ghost have their rightful office—books in which justification, and sanctification, and regeneration, and faith, and grace, and holiness are clearly, distinctly, and accurately delineated, and exhibited, these are the only books which do real good. Few things need reviving more than a taste for such books as these among readers.

For my own part, I can only say that I read everything I can get hold of which professes to throw light on my Master's business, and the work of Christ among men. But the more I read, the less I admire modern theology. The more I study the productions of the new schools, of theological teachers, the more I marvel that men and women can be satisfied with such writing. There is a vagueness, a mistiness, a shallowness, an indistinctness, a superficiality, an aim-lessness, a hollowness about the literature of the catholic or broader systems, as they are called, which, to my mind, stamps their origin on their face. They are of the earth, earthy. I find more of definite soul-satisfying thought in one page of Gurnall than in five pages of such books as the leaders of the so-called *catholic* and *broad church schools* put forth. In matters of theology "the old is better."[1]

---

[1] Luke 5:39.

James II (1633–1701)
King of Great Britain (1685–1688)

13

JAMES II AND THE SEVEN BISHOPS

THE reign of James II is a period of English history which has left a greater mark on this country than any period since the Reformation. It is a period to which we owe our civil and religious liberties, and the maintenance of our Protestantism, and as such it deserves the attention of every true-hearted Englishman. I propose in this paper to give a general sketch of the leading events in the reign of James II, and a more particular account of the famous trial of the Seven Bishops. If the whole subject does not throw broad, clear light on our position and duties in the present day, I am greatly mistaken.

The reign of James II was a singularly short one. It began in February 1685, and ended in December 1688. Short as his reign was, it is no exaggeration to say that it contains a more disgraceful list of cruel, stupid, unjust, and tyrannical actions, for which the Sovereign alone can be held responsible, than the reign of any constitutional monarch of this land, with the single exception of Bloody Mary. It is a reign, in fact, in our English annals, without one redeeming feature. Not one grand victory stirs our patriotic feelings; not one first-class statesman or general, and hardly a bishop beside Ken and Pearson, rouses our admiration; and the majestic name of Sir Isaac Newton among men of science stands almost alone. There were few giants in the land. It was an era of mediocrity; it was an age not of gold or silver or brass or iron—but of lead. We turn away from the picture with shame and disgust, and it abides in our memories as a picture in which there is no light and all shade.

The *chief* explanation of this singularly disgraceful reign is to be found in the fact that James II was a narrow-minded, obstinate, zealous, thorough-going member of the Church of Rome. As soon as he ascended the throne, he surrounded himself with priests and Popish advisers and placed confidence in none but Papists. Within a month of his accession, says Evelyn in his diary, "the Romanists were swarming at Court with greater confidence than had ever been seen in England since the Reformation."[*] At his coronation he refused to receive the sacrament according to the rites of the Church of England. He set up a Popish chapel at his Court and attended mass. He strained every nerve throughout his reign to encourage the spread of Popery and discourage Protestantism. He procured the visit of a Popish nuncio, and demeaned himself before him as no English sovereign ever did since the days of King John.[1] He told Barillon, the French Ambassador, that his first object was to obtain for the Romanists the free exercise of their religion, and then at last to give them absolute supremacy.[†] All this was done in a country which, little more than a century before, had been freed from Popery by the martyred Reformers, and blessed with organized Protestantism by the reign of Elizabeth. Can anyone wonder that the God of Providence was displeased and refused to show the light of His countenance on the land? James the Second's reign was an unhappy and discreditable time in the annals of England, because the King was a thorough-going Papist.

The *second* explanation of the disgraceful character of James the Second's times is to be found in the low moral condition of the whole nation when he came to the throne. The misgovernment of James I and Charles I, the semi-Popish proceedings of Archbishop Laud, the fierce Civil War of the Commonwealth, the iron rule of Oliver Cromwell, the rebound into unbridled licentiousness which attended the Restoration and reign of Charles II, the miserably unwise and unjust Act of Uniformity, the unceasing persecution of true religion, under the pretence of doing God service and making men of one mind—all these things had borne their natural fruit. The England of James the Second's time was morally vile and rotten to the core. The Court seems to have thrown aside common

---

[*] Knight, *History of England*, 4, p. 383.
[1] 1199–1216.
[†] If anyone doubts this, I refer him to the *Histories of England*, Hallam, 3, p. 73; Ranke, 4, pp. 216, 218, 219; Stoughton, 2, p. 108.

decency, and to have regarded adultery and fornication as no sin at all. Evelyn's description of what he saw at Whitehall the very week that Charles II died is sad and disgusting. On Sunday evening, the 1st of February 1685, Evelyn, it seems, was at Whitehall. A week after he recorded his impressions of the scene which he then witnessed:

> I can never forget the inexpressible luxury and profaneness, and, as it were, total forgetfulness of God, it being Sunday evening. The King sitting and toying with his concubines, Portsmouth, Cleveland, Mazarin, etc.; a French boy singing love songs in that glorious gallery; whilst above twenty of the great courtiers and other dissolute persons were at Basset around a large table, a bank of at least two thousand in gold before them.

On Monday morning, the 2nd of February, the King was struck with apoplexy. Charles Knight truly says:

> The high public spirit, the true sense of honour, which had characterized the nobles and gentry of England during the Civil War, was lost in the selfishness, the meanness, the profligacy, of the twenty-eight years that succeeded the Restoration. Traitors were hatched in the sunshine of corruption. The basest expediency had been the governing principle of statesmen and lawyers; the most abject servility had been the leading creed of divines. Loyalty always wore the livery of the menial. Patriotism was ever flaunting the badges of faction. The bulk of the people were unmoved by any proud resentments or eager hopes. They went on in their course of industrious occupation, without much caring whether they were under an absolute or a constitutional government, as long as they could eat, drink, and be merry. They had got rid of the Puritan severity; and if decency was outraged in the Court and laughed at on the stage, there was greater license for popular indulgences.*

The leading statesmen were too often utterly untruthful, and ready to take bribes. The judges were, as a rule, mean, corrupt, ignorant creatures of the Court. The Church of England, which ought to have been a bulwark against wickedness, had never recovered the suicidal loss of its life-blood caused by the Act of

---

* *History of England.*

Uniformity in 1662, and was a weak, timid, servile body. The bishops and clergy, with a few brilliant exceptions, were very unlike the Reformers, and always unwilling to find fault with any great man, or to dispute the Divine right of kings to do as they pleased. The Dissenters were crushed to the earth by petty intolerant restrictions; and, between fines, imprisonments, and persecutions, were little able to do anything to mend the times and could barely keep their heads above water.

Last, but not least, we must not forget that for at least a hundred years England had been incessantly exposed to the untiring machinations of the Jesuits. Ever since the accession of Elizabeth, those mischievous agents of Popery had been compassing sea and land to undo the work of the Reformation, and to bring back our country to the thraldom of the Church of Rome. Disguised in every possible way and professing anything by the Pope's permission and dispensation in order to accomplish their end, these Jesuits throughout the days of the Stuarts were incessantly at work. To set churchmen against Dissenters, Calvinists against Arminians, sect against sect, party against party, and so to weaken the Protestant cause, was their one constant employment. How much of the bitter divisions between churchmen and Nonconformists, how much of the religious strife which defiled the early part of the seventeenth century is owing to the Jesuits, I believe the last day alone will declare. Those only who read *Panzani's Memoirs* or Dean Goode's *Rome's Tactics* can have any idea of the mischief they did.

In short, if there ever was an era in modern history when a Popish King of England could promote Popery and do deeds of astounding cruelty and injustice without let or hindrance, that era was the reign of James II. What might have been the final result with such a king and such a field of action if he had not gone too fast and overshot his mark, is impossible to say. God in His infinite goodness had mercy on England and delivered us from his wicked designs. But the things that he did while he reigned,* and the singular manner in which he at last overreached himself by the trial of the Seven Bishops, and lost his throne, ought never to be

---

* Those who wish to make themselves acquainted with the reign of James II would do well to study Burnet, Hallam, Macaulay, Charles Knight, Ranke, and Stoughton's *History of the Church of the Restoration*.

forgotten by any Englishman who is a true Protestant and loves his country.

I. Five Disgraceful Pages from the Reign of James II

There are five leading events, or salient points, in this reign which are specially worth remembering. They follow each other in regular order, from the accession of James to his abdication. One common aim and object underlaid them all; that aim was to pull down Protestantism and to plant Popery on its ruins.

(a) The first disgraceful page in the history of James the Second's reign is *his savage and brutal treatment of the Nonconformists and Dissenters.* Our great historian, Macaulay, says: "He hated the Puritan sect with a manifold hatred, theological and political, hereditary and personal. He regarded them as the foes of heaven as well as the foes of all legitimate authority in Church and State."* The plain truth is that James, with all his natural dullness of character, had sense enough to know that for many years the most decided and zealous advocates of Protestantism had been the Nonconformists, and that when churchmen under Archbishop Laud's mischievous influence had become lukewarm, Nonconformists had been the most inveterate enemies of Popery. Knowing this, he began his reign by attempting to crush the Nonconformists entirely. If his predecessors had chastised them with rods, he tried to chastise them with scorpions. If he could not convert them, he would silence them by prosecutions, fines, and imprisonments, and, like Pharaoh, "make their lives grievous" by hard measures. He argued, no doubt, that if he could only stop the mouths of the Nonconformists, he would soon make short work of the Church of England, and he cunningly began with the weaker party. In both cases, happily, he reckoned without his host.

To describe how the unhappy Nonconformists at that period were summoned, fined, silenced, driven from their homes, and allowed no rest for the sole of their foot, would be an endless task. Two pictures will suffice to give an idea of the treatment to which they were subjected. One picture shall be taken from England, and the other from Scotland. Each picture shows things

---

* Macaulay, I, p. 494.

which happened with the King's sanction within three months after he came to the throne.

(i) The English picture is the so-called trial of Baxter, the famous author of *The Saint's Rest*, a book which is deservedly held in honour down to this day. Baxter was tried at Westminster Hall before James' detestable tool, Chief Justice Jeffreys, in May 1685. He was charged with having published seditious matter reflecting on the bishops, in his *Paraphrase on the New Testament*. A more absurd and unfounded accusation could not have been made. The book is still extant, and anyone will see at a glance that there was no ground for the charge. From the very opening of the trial it was clear which way the verdict was intended to go. The Lord Chief Justice of England behaved as if he were counsel for the prosecution and not judge. He used abusive language towards the defendant, such as was more suited to Billingsgate[1] than a court of law, while the counsel for the defence were browbeaten, silenced, and put down, or else interrupted by violent invectives against their client. At one stage the Lord Chief Justice exclaimed:

> This is an old rogue who hath poisoned the world with his Kidderminster doctrines. He encouraged all the women and maids to bring their bodkins and thimbles to carry on war against the King of ever blessed memory. An old schismatical knave! A hypocritical villain!

By and by he called Baxter "an old blockhead, an unthankful villain, a conceited, stubborn, fanatical dog." "Hang him!" he said, "this one old fellow hath cast more reproaches on the constitution and discipline of our church than will be wiped off for a hundred years. But I'll handle him for it; for he deserves to be whipped through the city." Shortly afterwards, when Baxter began to say a few words on his own behalf, Jeffreys stopped him, crying out:

> Richard, Richard, dost thou think we'll hear thee poison the court? Richard, thou art an old fellow, and an old knave; thou hast written books enough to load a cart, every one as full of sedition, I might say of treason, as an egg is full of meat. Hadst thou been whipped out of thy writing trade forty years ago, it had been happy.

---

[1] A London fish market known for its coarse, abusive language.

It is needless to say in such a court as this Baxter was at once found guilty. He was fined five hundred marks, which it was known he could not pay, condemned to lie in prison till he paid it, and bound over to good behaviour for seven years. And the issue of the matter was that the holy author of *The Saint's Rest*, a poor, old, diseased, childless widower, lay for two years in Southwark gaol.

(ii) The Scotch picture of the Nonconformists' sufferings under James II is even blacker than the English one. I shall take it substantially from Wodrow's and Macaulay's history. In the very same month that Baxter was tried, two women named Margaret Maclachlan and Margaret Wilson, the former an aged widow, the latter a girl of eighteen, suffered death for their religion in Wigton-shire, at the hands of James the Second's myrmidons. They were both godly women, innocent of any crime but Nonconformity. They were offered their lives if they would abjure the cause of the insurgent covenanters and attend the episcopal worship. They both refused; and they were sentenced to be drowned. They were carried to a spot on the shore of the Solway Firth, which the tide over-flowed twice a day, and were fastened to stakes fixed in the sand between high and low watermark. The elder woman was placed nearest to the advancing water, in the hopes that her last agonies might terrify the younger one into submission. The sight was dreadful. But the courage of the young survivor did not fail. She saw her fellow-sufferer drowned, and saw the sea draw nearer and nearer to herself, but gave no signs of alarm. She prayed and sang verses of psalms, till the waves choked her voice. When she had tasted the bitterness of death, she was, by cruel mercy, unbound and restored to life. When she came to herself, pitying friends and neighbours implored her to yield. "Dear Margaret," they cried, "only say, God save the King." The poor girl, true to her theology, gasped out, "May God save him if it be God's will." Her friends crowded round the presiding officer, crying, "She has said it, indeed, sir, she has said it." "Will she take the abjuration?" he sternly demanded. "Never," she exclaimed. "I am Christ's; let me go." And once more bound to the stake, the waters of the Solway closed over her for the last time. Her epitaph may be seen to this day in Wigton churchyard.

Such were the dealings of James with Protestant Nonconformists

at the beginning of his reign. I make no comment on them. These
two examples speak for themselves; and they do not stand alone.
The story of the murder of John Brown,[1] of Priesthill, by
Claverhouse, is as sad as that of Margaret Wilson. No wonder that a
deep dislike to episcopacy is rooted down in the hearts of Scotch
people to this very day! They never forget such stories as Margaret
Wilson's. Even in England I wish I could add that vile prosecutions
like that of Baxter had called forth any expression of disapproval
from English churchmen. But, alas! for a season, James persecuted
and prospered, and no man opposed him.

(b) The second black page in the history of James the Second's
reign is *the detestable cruelty with which he punished those English
counties which had taken any part in Monmouth's rebellion*, in the
autumn of 1685.[2] Concerning that miserable rebellion there can, of
course, be but one opinion among sensible men. It is vain to deny
that the brief insurrection, which ended with the Battle of Sedgemoor, was an enormous folly as well as a crime. We all know how
Monmouth, its unhappy leader, paid for it by dying on the scaffold.
But it is equally vain to deny that the bloodthirsty ferocity with
which James avenged self on all who had favoured Monmouth's
cause, or taken arms in his support, is unparalleled in the annals of
English history.

---

[1] John Brown founded Bible classes and Sunday schools. In 1685 he
was questioned by Claverhouse about *treasonable papers*, and informed that
he "shall immediately die." "Take goodbye of your wife and children,"
Brown was told. Having said his prayers, he kissed his family farewell
wishing "Blood-bought and Gospel-promised blessings" be multiplied to
them. Claverhouse then ordered six dragoons to shoot Brown on the spot,
but they refused—their hearts were all melted. Then, unbelting his pistol,
Claverhouse walked up to Brown, "placed it to his head, and blew his
brains out, scattering them all over the ground." With a smile, he turned to
Mrs. Brown and asked, "What do you think of your fine husband now?"
"I ever thought much good of him," she said, "and more than ever now."
[2] After the death of Charles II, his brother, James II, was crowned. At
the Battle of Sedgemoor, J.S. Monmouth, the illegitimate son of Charles,
and an army of 7,000 challenged James. "They were slaughtered where
they stood, and a merciless pursuit, with wholesale executions, ended their
forlorn endeavour" (Winston Churchill, *A History of the English Speaking
Peoples*, vol. 2, Barnes and Noble, 1993, pp. 388, 389). On the scaffold
Monmouth declared, "I die a Protestant of the Church of England."

(i) The proceedings of that military monster, Colonel Kirke, immediately after the defeat and dispersion of the rebel army, surpassed anything that we heard of in the Indian Mutiny.[1] At Taunton he is said to have hanged at least one hundred so-called *rebels* within a week after the Battle of Sedgemoor, and many without even the form of a trial. Not a few of his wretched victims were quartered, and their heads and limbs sent to be hanged in chains in the neighbouring villages. "So many dead bodies were quartered," says Macaulay, "that the executioner under the gallows stood ankle deep in blood."[*]

(ii) But even the diabolical cruelties of Colonel Kirke were surpassed by the execrable sentences of Judge Jeffreys, when he went on circuit to the Assizes in Hampshire, Dorsetshire, and Somersetshire, two months after the Battle of Sedgemoor. In Dorsetshire he hanged about 70, in Somersetshire no less than 233. The number of those transported for life was 841. The greater part of these were poor ignorant rustics, many of them men of blameless private character, who had taken arms under the idea that Protestantism was at stake; and they died for no other offence than that of simply following Monmouth, a political adventurer, for a few short weeks. The Assize was long known as the "bloody Assize."

> In Somersetshire, [says Macaulay] on the green of every large village which had furnished Monmouth with soldiers, ironed corpses clattering in the wind, or human heads and quarters stuck on poles poisoned the air, and made the traveller sick with horror. In many parishes the peasantry could not even assemble in God's house without seeing the ghastly face of some neighbour's skull grinning at them on the porch.

In Hampshire, Jeffreys actually sentenced to death a venerable old lady named Lady Lisle, aged above seventy, for no other crime than that of affording temporary shelter to an insurgent; and nothing but the indignant remonstrance of the Winchester clergy prevented her being burned alive. Lord Feversham, the conqueror of Sedgemoor,

---

[1] Exacting vengeance upon Indian mutineers, in 1857–58 British troops shot rebels "from the mouths of cannon, sometimes alive, or their bodies sewn up in the skins of cows and swine" (Winston Churchill, *A History of the English Speaking Peoples*, vol. 4, Barnes and Noble, 1993, p. 87).

[*] I, p. 629.

and Lord Clarendon, the King's brother-in-law, in vain interceded for her. Jeffreys was allowed to work his will, and she was actually beheaded in Winchester marketplace.

For all this abominable cruelty, James II must always be held responsible. The vile agents who shed this blood were his tools, and he had only to speak the word and the work of death would have ceased. Hallam, the historian, expressly says that the King was the author of all this bloodshed, and that Jeffreys afterward declared "he had not been bloody enough for his employer."* But the real secret of the King's savage and detestable conduct was a determination to put down Protestantism by a reign of terror, and deter men from any future movement in its favour. And, after all, the truth must be spoken. James was a bigoted member of a church which for ages has been too often "drunken with the blood of saints and the martyrs of Jesus."[1] He only walked in the steps of the Duke of Alva in the Netherlands;[2] in the steps of Charles IX at the massacre of St. Bartholomew; in the steps of the Duke of Savoy in Piedmont,[3] until Cromwell interfered and obliged him to cease; and in the steps of the hateful Spanish Inquisition. One thing is very certain: there never was a petty insurrection so ruthlessly quenched in blood as Monmouth's rebellion was quenched by James the Papist. Blood makes a great stain. He found to his cost one day that the blood shed by Kirke and Jeffreys with his sanction had cried to heaven, and was not forgotten. When the Prince of Orange landed at Torbay, the western counties joined him to a man and forsook James.

(c) The third black page in the history of James the Second's reign was *his daring attempt to gag the pulpit, and stop the mouths of all*

---

* 3, p. 93.

[1] Revelation 17:6.

[2] Philip II, King of Spain and one time husband of Mary Tudor, commissioned the Duke of Alva to the Netherlands to enforce his father's (Charles V) edicts requiring all convicted heretics to be "burned alive, buried alive, or beheaded." After six years of terror (1567–73), the Duke had executed more than 18,000 men.

[3] In 1655 and again in 1663–64, Charles Emmanuel II, the Duke of Savoy, wrought brutal massacres against the Waldenses. Of their sad plight Milton prayed, "Avenge, O Lord, Thy slaughtered saints; Whose bones lie scattered on the Alpine mountains cold."

who preached against Popery. Preaching in every age of the Church has always been God's chief instrument for setting forward religious truth and checking error. Preaching was one principal agency by which the great work of the Reformation was effected in England. The Church of Rome knows that full well, and, wherever she dares, she has always endeavoured to exalt ceremonials and to depreciate the pulpit. To use old Latimer's quaint words, "Whenever the devil gets into a church, his plan is to cry, 'Up with candles and down with preaching.'" Next to an open and free Bible, the greatest obstacle to the progress of Popery is a free pulpit, and the public exposition of God's Word. That James II, like all thorough-going Papists, knew all this, we cannot doubt for a moment. We need not, therefore, wonder that in 1686 he commenced an attack on the English pulpit. If he could once silence that mighty organ, he hoped to pave the way for the advance of Popery.

> He took on himself, [says Macaulay] to charge the clergy of the Established Church to abstain from touching on controverted points of doctrine in their discourses. Thus, while sermons in defence of the Roman Catholic religion were preached every Sunday and holiday in the Royal Chapel, the Church of the State, the Church of the great majority of the nation, was forbidden to explain and vindicate her own principles.*

William Sherlock, Master of the Temple, was the first to feel the royal displeasure. His pension was stopped, and he was severely reprimanded. John Sharpe, Dean of Norwich, and Rector of St. Giles', gave even greater offence. In reply to an appeal from a parishioner, he delivered an animated discourse against the pretensions of the Church of Rome. Compton, the Bishop of London, was immediately ordered to suspend him, and on his objecting to do so, he was himself suspended from all spiritual functions, and the charge of his diocese was committed to two time-serving prelates named Spratt and Crewe. Compton was already famous for his dislike to Popery. When James came to the throne he had boldly declared in the House of Lords that "the Constitution was in danger." We can well understand that James was anxious to suppress him.†

---

* 2, p. 91.
† Ranke, 4, p. 277.

Singularly enough, this high-handed proceeding worked round for good. For the first time since his accession to the throne, James received a distinct check. The attacks on Sherlock, Sharpe, and Bishop Compton roused the spirit of the whole body of the English clergy. To preach against the errors of Popery was now regarded as a point of honour and duty. The London clergy set an example which was bravely followed all over the country. The King's prohibition to handle controversial subjects was everywhere disregarded. It was impossible to punish an offence which was committed every Sunday by thousands of divines from the Isle of Wight to Berwick-upon-Tweed, and from the Land's End to the North Foreland. Moreover, the spirit of the congregations was thoroughly roused. There were old men living in London whose grandfathers had heard Latimer preach, and had seen John Rogers burnt at Smithfield. There were others whose parents had seen Laud beheaded for trying to Romanize the Church, and prosecuting Protestant churchmen. Such men as these were thoroughly stirred and disgusted by James's movement; and if the clergy had been silent about Popery, they would have resented their silence as unfaithfulness and sin.

The printing presses, besides, both at London, Oxford, and Cambridge, poured forth a constant stream of anti-Popish literature, and supplied all who could read with ample information about every error of the Church of Rome. Tillotson, Stillingfleet, Sherlock, Patrick, Tenison, Wake, Fowler, Clagett, and many others wrote numerous treatises of all kinds to expose Popery, which exist to this day, and which at the time produced an immense effect. Many of these are to be found in the three huge folios called *Gibson's Preservative*, and Macaulay estimates that as many as 20,000 pages of them are to be found in the British Museum.

The whole affair is a striking instance of God's power to bring good out of evil. The very step by which this unhappy Popish monarch thought to silence his strongest foe proved the first step towards his own ruin. Up to this date he seemed to carry everything before him. From this date he began to fall. From the moment he put forth his hand to touch the ark, to interfere with the Word of God, to silence its preachers, he never prospered, and every succeeding step in his reign was in the downward direction. Like

Haman, he had dared to meddle with God's peculiar servants, and like Haman he fell, never to rise again.

(*d*) The fourth black page in the history of James the Second's reign is *his tyrannical invasion of the rights of the two great universities of Oxford and Cambridge in* 1687. The influence of these two venerable bodies in England has always been very great, and I trust they will always be so governed that it will never become less. But it is no exaggeration to say that it never was so great as towards the end of the seventeenth century. Beside them there were no universities or colleges. King's College, London; University College, Durham; St. Aidan's; Highbury; St. Bees, and Cuddesdon did not exist. Oxford and Cambridge stood alone. They were the fountains of all the learning of the day, and the training school of all the ablest divines and lawyers, poets and orators of the land. Even among the Puritans, it would be hard to find any man of ability who had not begun his career and picked up his first knowledge at some college in Oxford or Cambridge. In short, the two universities were the intellectual heart of England, and every pulsation of that heart was felt throughout the kingdom.

All this, we need not doubt, even the dull mind of James II clearly perceived. He saw that he had little chance of Romanizing England until he could get hold of the two universities, and this he resolved to try. He was encouraged, probably, to make the attempt by the notorious loyalty to the House of Stuart which Oxford and Cambridge had always exhibited. Both the universities had suffered heavily for their attachment to the King's side during the unhappy Commonwealth Wars. Many a head of a college had been displaced and his position filled by one of Cromwell's Puritans. Owen had ruled at Christ Church and Goodwin at Magdalen. Many a college plate-chest was sadly empty compared to its state in olden times, having given up its silver to be melted down in aid of Charles I, and to buy arms and ammunition. Ever since the Reformation, the two universities had exhibited the most obsequious subserviency to the Crown, had stoutly maintained the Divine right of kings, and had often approached the throne in addresses full of fulsome adulation. I believe that James flattered himself that they would go on yielding everything to his will, and fondly dreamed that in a few years they would be completely under the Pope's command, and the education of young England would be in the hands of the Church of Rome. It was a grand and intoxicating prospect. But he reckoned without his host. He little knew the spirit that was yet left by the Isis and the Cam.[1]

James opened his campaign and crossed the Rubicon by attacking the University of Cambridge. The law was clear and distinct that no person should be admitted to any degree without taking the Oath of Supremacy,[2] and another oath called the Oath of Obedience. Nevertheless, in February 1687, a royal letter was sent to Cambridge directing that a Benedictine monk, named Alban Francis, should be admitted as Master of Arts.[3] Between reverence for the King and reverence for their own statutes, the academical officers were naturally placed in a most perplexing position. To their infinite credit they took the right course and steadily refused to admit the King's nominee unless he took the oaths. The result was that the Vice-Chancellor of Cambridge was summoned to appear before the New Court of High Commission, presided over by Jeffreys, together with deputies appointed by the Senate. When the day arrived, Dr. Pechell, the Vice-Chancellor, a man of no particular vigour or ability, accompanied by eight distinguished men, of whom the famous Isaac Newton was one, appeared before this formidable tribunal. Their case was as clear as daylight. They offered to prove that they had done nothing contrary to law and practice, and had only carried out the plain meaning of their statutes. But Jeffreys would hear nothing. He treated the whole party with as much vulgar insolence as if they were felons being tried before him at the Old Bailey,[4] and they were thrust out of court without a hearing. They were soon called in and informed that the Commission had determined to deprive Pechell of the vice-chancellorship, and to suspend him from all the

---

[1] Oxford lies along the Upper River Thames, called by Oxonians "the Isis"; Cambridge dwells along the River Cam.

[2] Part of which states: "And I do declare that no foreign person, prelate, state or potentate, hath, or ought to have, any jurisdiction, power, superiority, pre-eminence, or authority, ecclesiastical or spiritual, within this realm, so help me God."

[3] By the end of the sixteenth century, all Benedictines (also known as *Black Friars*) had sworn allegiance to the decrees of the Council of Trent.

[4] The central criminal court in London.

emoluments to which he was entitled as master of a college. "As for you," said Jeffreys to Isaac Newton and his seven companions, with disgusting levity, "I send you home with a text of Scripture, 'Go your way and sin no more, lest a worse thing come upon you.'"[1]

From Cambridge James turned to Oxford. Here, it must be avowed, he began his operations with great advantages. Popery had already effected a lodgment in the citadel, and got allies in the heart of the University. Already a Roman Catholic named Massey had been made Dean of Christ Church by the nomination of the Crown, and the House had submitted. Already University College was little better than a Romish seminary by the perversion of the Master, Obadiah Walker, to Popery. Mass was daily said in both colleges. But this state of things had caused an immense amount of smouldering dissatisfaction throughout Oxford. The undergraduates hooted Walker's congregation and chanted satirical ballads under his windows without the interference of proctors. The burden of one of their songs has been preserved to this day, and you might have heard at night in High Street, near the fine old college, such words as these:

> Here old Obadiah
> Sings Ave Maria.

In short, any careful observer might have foreseen that Oxford feeling towards the King was undergoing a great change, and that it would take very little to create a blaze.

Just at this crisis the President of Magdalen College died, and it became the duty of the fellows, according to their statutes, to elect a successor, either from their own society or from New College. With an astounding mixture of folly and audacity, the King actually recommended the fellows to elect to the vacant place a man named Anthony Farmer, a person of infamous moral character, utterly destitute of any claim to govern a college; a drunkard, a Papist, and a person disqualified by the statutes of Waynflete,[2] as he was neither Fellow of New College nor of Magdalen. To their infinite credit the fellows of Magdalen, by an overwhelming majority, refused to

---

[1] John 5:14.

[2] William Waynflete (c. 1395–1486), English Lord Chancellor, Bishop of Winchester, and founder of Magdalen College, Oxford.

elect the King's nominee, resolved to face his displeasure, and deliberately chose for their president a man named John Hough, a fellow of eminent virtue and prudence. At once they were treated with the utmost violence, injustice, and indignity. The King insisted on their accepting another president of his own selection, and commanded them to take a mean creature of the Court named Parker, Bishop of Oxford. The fellows firmly refused, saying they had lawfully elected Hough, and they would have no other president. In vain they were threatened and insulted, first by the King himself, and then by a special commission sent down from London. They stood firm and would not give way one inch. The Commission finally pronounced Hough an intruder, dismissed him from his presidency, and charged the fellows no longer to recognise his authority, but to assist at the admission of the Bishop of Oxford. It was then that the gallant Hough publicly addressed the following remarkable words to the Commission: "My Lords, you have this day deprived me of my freehold. I hereby protest against all your proceedings as illegal, unjust, and null, and I appeal from you to our sovereign Lord the King in his Courts of Justice." But though thus driven from his office by force, Hough was backed by the general feeling of the whole University and of almost everyone connected with Magdalen. At the installation of his successor (Parker) only two fellows out of forty attended the ceremony. The college porter, Robert Gardner, threw down his keys. The butler refused to scratch Hough's name out of the buttery books. No blacksmith in all the city of Oxford could be found to force the locks of the president's lodge, and the commissioners were obliged to employ their own servants to break open the doors with iron bars.

But the matter did not end here. On the day that Hough was expelled from his presidency and Parker installed, the commissioners invited the Vice-Chancellor of 1687 to dine with them. The Vice-Chancellor that year was Gilbert Ironside, Warden of Wadham, and afterwards Bishop of Hereford. He refused. "My taste," he said, "differs from that of Colonel Kirke's. I cannot eat my meals with appetite under a gallows." The scholars of Magdalen refused to pull off their caps to the new ruler of Magdalen. The demies[1] refused to

---

[1] "Demy," a half-fellow at Magdalen College, Oxford.

perform their academical exercises and attend lectures, saying that they were deprived of their lawful governor, and would submit to no usurped authority. Attempts were made to bribe them by the offer of some of the lucrative fellowships declared vacant. But one undergraduate after another refused, and one who did accept was turned out of the Hall by the rest. The expulsion of the fellows was followed by the expulsion of a crowd of demies. A few weeks after this Parker died, some said of mortification and a broken heart. He was buried in the antechapel of Magdalen; but no stone marks his grave. Then the King's whole plan was carried into effect. The College was turned into a Popish seminary, and Bonaventura Giffard, a Roman Catholic bishop, was made president. In one day twelve Papists were made fellows. The Roman Catholic service was performed in the chapel, and the whole work of violence and spoliation was completed.

Such were the dealings of James II with Oxford and Cambridge. Their gross injustice was only equalled by their gross impolicy. In his furious zeal for Popery, the King completely overreached himself. He alienated the affections of the two most powerful educational institutions in the land, and filled the hearts of thousands of the ablest minds in England with a deep sense of wrong. And when the end came, as it did within eighteen months, he found that no places deserted his cause so readily as the two over which he had ridden roughshod, the two great English universities of Oxford and Cambridge.

(*e*) The fifth dark page in the history of James the Second's reign is his *rash attempt to trample down the English nobility and gentry in the counties*, and substitute for them servile creatures of his own who would help forward his designs. In order to understand this move of the misguided king, it must be remembered that he wanted to get a new House of Commons, a House which would do his bidding and not oppose his Romanizing plans. He knew enough of England to be aware that ever since the days of Simon de Montfort[1] every intelligent Englishman has attached great

---

[1] Earl of Leicester (1208–65), who ruled England for less than a year in 1265. He championed the cause of a limited monarchy ruling through elected councillors and responsible officials, and of parliaments including the great nobles, county knights, and burgesses.

importance to an elected Parliament. He had not entirely forgotten the iron hand of the Long Parliament in his father's days.
He rightly judged that he would never succeed in overthrowing
Protestantism without the sanction of a House of Commons, and
that sanction he resolved to try to obtain.

> Having determined to pack a Parliament, [says Macaulay] James
> set himself energetically and methodically to the work. A proc-
> lamation appeared in the *Gazette* (at the end of 1687) announcing
> that the King had determined to revise the Commissions of Peace
> and of Lieutenancy, and to retain in public employment only such
> gentlemen as would support his policy.

At the same time a committee of seven privy councillors sat at
Whitehall, including Father Petre, an ambitious Jesuit, for the
purpose of "regulating," as it was called, all the municipal corpo-
rations in boroughs:

> The persons on whom James principally relied for assistance,
> [continues Macaulay] were the Lord Lieutenants. Every Lord
> Lieutenant received written orders directing him to go down
> immediately into his county. There he was to summon before him
> all his deputies, and all the Justices of the Peace, and to put to them
> a set of interrogatories framed for the purpose of finding out how
> they would act at a general election. He was to take down their
> answers in writing, and transmit them to the Government. He was
> to furnish a list of such Romanists and Protestant Dissenters as
> were best qualified for commissions as magistrates, and for
> command in the militia. He was also to examine the state of all the
> boroughs in his county, and to make such reports as might be
> needful to guide the London board of regulators. And it was
> intimated to each Lord Lieutenant that he must perform these
> duties himself, and not delegate them to any other person.

The first effect of these audacious and unconstitutional orders
might have opened the eyes of any king of common sense. The
spirit of the old barons who met at Runnymede proved to be not
extinct. Even before this time the Duke of Norfolk had stopped at
the door of Popish chapel which James attended, and when James
remonstrated and said, "Your Grace's father would have gone
farther," had boldly replied, "Your Majesty's father would not have

gone so far." But now it became clear that many other peers beside the Duke of Norfolk were Protestant to the backbone. Half the lord lieutenants in England flatly refused to do the King's dirty work and to stoop to the odious service imposed on them. They were immediately dismissed, and inferior men, of more pliant and supple consciences, were pitchforked into their places.

The list of high-minded noblemen who resisted the King's will on this memorable occasion is even now most remarkable, and deserves to be had in remembrance. One great name follows another in grand succession in Macaulay's pages, until one's breath is almost taken away by the sight of the King's folly. In Essex, the Earl of Oxford; in Staffordshire, the Earl of Shrewsbury; in Sussex, the Earl of Dorset; in Yorkshire, the Duke of Somerset in the East Riding, and Lord Fauconberg in the North Riding; in Shropshire, Lord Newport; in Lancashire, the Earl of Derby; in Wiltshire, the Earl of Pembroke; in Leicestershire, the Earl of Rutland; in Buckinghamshire, the Earl of Bridgwater; in Cumberland, the Earl of Thanet; in Warwickshire, the Earl of Northampton; in Oxfordshire, the Earl of Abingdon; in Derbyshire, the Earl of Scarsdale; and in Hampshire, the Earl of Gainsborough—all were summarily sent to the rightabout; and for what? Simply, as everyone knew, because they preferred a good conscience to Crown favour, principle to place, and Protestantism to Popery. The gallant words of the Earl of Oxford, who was turned out in Essex, when the King demanded an explanation of his refusal to obey, spoke the sentiments of all: "Sir, I will stand by your Majesty against all enemies to the last drop of blood; but this is a matter of conscience, and I cannot comply."

A viler piece of ingratitude than this move of James can hardly be conceived. Most of the noblemen whom he dismissed were the representatives of great families who, in the Commonwealth Wars, made immense sacrifices in his father's cause. Some of them, like the Earl of Derby, could tell of fathers and grandfathers who had died for King Charles. Many of them could show swords and helmets hanging over their Elizabethan fireplaces which had been notched and dented in fighting against the parliamentary forces at Edgehill, Marston Moor, and Naseby. Not a few of them could point to ruined castles and halls, to parks despoiled of their timber, plate-chests emptied of their contents, and properties sadly impoverished in the days when Cavaliers fought against Roundheads. And now, forsooth, the son of the martyred Charles, as they had fondly called him, turned round upon them, trampled on their feelings, and required them to lie down and let him walk over their consciences. Can we wonder that they keenly resented the King's conduct! At one fell swoop he destroyed the affection of half the leading men in the English counties, and from being his friends they became his foes.

In fact, the ingratitude of the King was now only equalled by his folly and impolicy. No sooner was big new machinery for packing a subservient Parliament put in motion, than it broke down and utterly failed. From every corner of the realm there came the tidings of failure. The new lord lieutenants could do nothing. The magistrates and candidates for Parliament evaded inquiries and refused to pledge themselves to do the King's will. Arguments, promises, and threats were alike in vain. A deep-rooted suspicion had got into men's minds that James wanted to subvert Protestantism and reintroduce Popery, and they would not give way. From Norfolk, the Duke of Norfolk reported that out of seventy leading gentlemen in the county, only six held out any hopes of supporting the Court. In Hertfordshire the squires told Lord Rochester that they would send no man to Parliament who would vote for taking away the safeguards of the Protestant religion. The gentry of Bucks, Shropshire, and Wiltshire held the same language. The magistrates and deputy-lieutenants of Cornwall and Devonshire told Lord Bath, without a dissenting voice, that they would sacrifice life and property for the Crown, but that the Protestant religion was dearer to them than either. "And, Sir," said Lord Bath to the King, "if your Majesty dismisses them, their successors would give the same answer." In Lancashire, a very Romish county, the new Lord Lieutenant reported that one-third of the magistrates were opposed to the Court. In Hampshire the whole of the magistrates, excepting five or six, declared they would take no part in the civil or military government of the county while the King was represented there by the Duke of Berwick, a Papist.

The sum of the whole matter is this: The attack of James on the independence of the county gentry and nobility was as completely a failure as his attack on the pulpit and the universities. It was worse than this. It sowed the seeds of disaffection to his person from one end of England to the other, and alienated from him thousands of leading men, who, under other circumstances, would perhaps have stood by him to the last. And the result was that when the Prince of Orange landed at Torbay a year afterwards, he found friends in half the counties in England. By the overruling providence of God and his own judicial blindness, James paved the way to his own ruin, "The Thanes fell from him." The nobility, one after another, forsook him, and he was left friendless and alone.

II. The Closing Scene in King James' Disgraceful Reign

I come now to the closing scene in King James' disgraceful reign, *the prosecution and trial of the Seven Bishops*. The importance of that event is so great, and the consequences which resulted from it were so immense, that I must enter somewhat fully into its details. I do so the more willingly because attempts are sometimes made nowadays to misrepresent this trial, to place the motives of the Bishops in a wrong light, and to obscure the real issues which were at stake. Some men will do anything in these times to mystify the public mind, to pervert history, and to whitewash the Church of Rome. But I have made it my business to search up every authority I can find about this era. I have no doubt whatever what is the true account of the whole affair. And I shall try to set before my readers the "thing as it is."[1]

The origin of the trial of the Seven Bishops was a proclamation put forth by James II, on the 27th of April 1688, called the Declaration of Indulgence. It was a declaration which differed little from one put forth in April 1687. But it was followed by an Order of Council that it was to be read on two successive Sundays, in Divine Service, by all the officiating ministers in all the churches and chapels of the kingdom. In London the reading was to take place on the 20th and 27th of May, and in other parts of England on the 3rd and 10th of June. The bishops were directed to distribute copies of the declaration throughout their respective dioceses. The substance of the declaration was short and simple. It

---

[1] Job 26:3.

suspended all penal laws against Nonconformists. It authorized both Roman Catholics and Protestant Dissenters to perform their worship publicly. It forbade the King's subjects, on pain of his displeasure, to molest any assembly. It abrogated all those Acts of Parliament which imposed any religious test as a qualification for any civil or military office. To us who live in the present century, the declaration may seem very reasonable and harmless. To the England of the seventeenth century it wore a very different aspect! Men know the hand from which it came and saw the latent intention. Under the specious plea of *toleration* and *liberty*, the object of the declaration was to advance Popery and give license and free scope to the Church of Rome, and to all its schemes for reconquering England.

This famous declaration, we can see at a glance, placed the bishops and clergy in a most awkward position. What were they to do? What was the path of duty? They were thoroughly pinned on the horns of a dilemma. If they refused compliance to the King's wishes they would seem intolerant, illiberal, and unkind to the Nonconformists, as well as disloyal, disrespectful, and disobedient to their sovereign. If they yielded to the King's wishes, and read the declaration, they would be assisting the propagation of Popery. The *liberty* James wanted them to proclaim was neither more nor less than *indulgence* to the Jesuits and the whole Church of Rome. In short, they found themselves between Scylla and Charybdis,[1] and could not possibly avoid giving offence. Refusing to sanction the Declaration, they would certainly displease the King and perhaps irritate the Dissenters. Consenting to it, they would infallibly help the Pope. Never, perhaps, were English bishops and clergy placed in such a difficult and perplexing position!

God's ways, however, are not as man's ways, and light often arises out of darkness in quarters where it was not expected. At this critical juncture the Nonconformists, to their eternal honour, came forward and cut the knot and helped the bishops to a right decision. The shrewd sons of the good old Puritans saw clearly what James meant. They saw that under a specious pretence of *liberty*, he

---

[1] Two man-eating monsters in Greek mythology who dwelt on opposite sides of a narrow stretch of water.

wanted a fulcrum for a lever which would turn England upside down and destroy the work of the Reformation. Like the noble-minded Roman ambassador before Pyrrhus, who was shown first a bag of gold, and then an elephant, they refused to be bribed just as they had formerly refused to be intimidated. They would have none of the Royal indulgence, if it could only be purchased at the expense of the nation's Protestantism. Baxter and Bates and Howe and the great bulk of the London Nonconformists entreated the clergy to stand firm, and not to yield one inch to the King. Young Defoe said to his Nonconformist brethren, "I had rather the Church of England should pull our clothes off by fines and forfeitures, than the Papists should fall both upon the Church and the Dissenters, and pull our skins off by fire and faggot."[*]

Oliver Heywood, a famous Nonconformist of the day, says distinctly in his account of the times, "Though the Dissenters had liberty promised, we knew it was not out of love to us, but for another purpose. We heard the King had said he was forced to grant liberty at present to those whom his soul abhorred."[†]

The immediate result was that a meeting of the London clergy was held, and, after much debate in which Tillotson, Sherlock, Patrick, and Stillingfleet took part, it was decided that the Order in Council should not be obeyed. No one contributed to this result more than Dr. Fowler, Vicar of St. Giles, Cripplegate, a well-known broad churchman. While the matter yet hung in the balance, and the final vote seemed doubtful, he rose and said: "I must be plain. The question to my mind is so simple, that argument can throw no new light on it, and can only beget heat. Let every man say 'Yes' or 'No.' But I cannot consent to be bound by the majority. I shall be sorry to cause a breach of unity. But this declaration I cannot read." This bold speech turned the scale. A resolution by which all present pledged themselves not to read the declaration was drawn up and was ultimately signed by eighty-five incumbents in London.

In the meantime the Archbishop of Canterbury, William Sancroft, showed himself not unequal to the emergency. He was

---

[*] C. Knight, *History*, 4, p. 419.
[†] *Heywood's Works*, 1, p. 287.

naturally a cautious, quiet, and somewhat timid man, and the last person to be combative and to quarrel with kings. Nevertheless he came out nobly and well, and rose to the occasion. As soon as the Order in Council appeared, he summoned to Lambeth Palace those few bishops, divines, and layman who happened to be in London and took counsel with them. It was resolved to resist the King and to refuse to read the declaration. The Primate then wrote to all the bishops on the English bench, on whom he could depend, and urged them to come up to London at once, and join him in a formal protest and petition. But time was short. There were no railways in those days. Journeying was slow work. Eighteen bishops, says Burnet,[*] agreed with Sancroft. But with the utmost exertion only six bishops could get to London in time to help the Primate. These six, with the Archbishop at their head, assembled at Lambeth on the 18th of May, only two days before the fatal Sunday when the King's declaration was to be read in London, and before night agreed on a petition or protest to which all affixed their names.

The names of the six bishops who signed this remarkable document, beside Sancroft, deserve to be known and remembered. They were as follows: Lloyd of St. Asaph, Turner of Ely, Lake of Chichester, Ken of Bath and Wells, White of Peterborough, and Sir Jonathan Trelawney of Bristol. It is a curious fact that, with the single exception of Ken, the author of *Morning and Evening Hymns*, not one of the seven men who signed the petition could be called a remarkable man in any way. Not one, beside Ken, has made any mark in the theological world, or lives as a writer or preacher. Not one of the whole seven could be named in the same breath with Parker or Whitgift or Grindal or Jewel or Andrews or Hall. They were probably respectable, worthy, quiet, old-fashioned high churchmen; and that was all. But God loves to be glorified by using weak instruments. Whatever they were in other respects, they were of one mind in seeing the danger which threatened Protestantism, and in determination to stand by it to the death. It was not jealousy of Dissenters but dislike to Popery, be it remembered, which actuated their conduct and knit them together.[†] All honour be to

---

[*] *Own Times*, 3, p. 266.

[†] Ranke, 4, p. 346.

them. They have supplied an unanswerable proof that the real, loyal, honest, old-fashioned high churchmen disliked Popery as much as any school in the Church.

The famous petition which the Seven Bishops drew up and signed on this occasion is a curious document. It is short and tame and cautious and somewhat clumsily composed. But the worthy composers, no doubt, were pressed for time and had no leisure to polish their sentences. Moreover, we know that they acted under the best advice, and were careful not to say too much and give needless offence.

> In substance, [says Macaulay] nothing could be more skilfully framed. All disloyalty, all intolerance, were reverently disclaimed. The King was assured that the Church was still, as ever, faithful to the throne. He was also assured that the bishops, in proper time and place, would, as Lords of Parliament and members of the Upper House of Convocation, show they were by no means wanting in tenderness for the conscientious scruples of Dissenters. The Parliament, both in the late and present reign, had pronounced that the Sovereign was not constitutionally competent to dispense with statutes in matters ecclesiastical. The Declaration was therefore illegal, and the Petitioners could not in prudence, honour, or conscience, be parties to the solemn publication of an illegal Declaration in the House of God, and during the time of Divine Service.

Pointless and tame as the petition may seem to us, we must not allow ourselves to make any mistake as to the latent meaning of the document and the real object of the bishops in refusing to obey the King. We must do them justice. They were thoroughly convinced that the declaration was intended to help Popery, and they were determined to make a stand and resist it. They had no ill-feeling towards Dissenters, and no desire to continue their disabilities. But they saw clearly that the whole cause of Protestantism was in jeopardy, and that, now or never, they must risk everything to defend it. Every historian of any worth acknowledges this, and it is vain to try to take any other view, unless we are prepared to write history anew. A cloud of witnesses agree here. There is an overwhelming mass of evidence to prove that the real reason why the

Seven Bishops resolved to oppose the King was their determination
to maintain the principles of the Reformation and to oppose any
further movement towards Rome. In one word, the cause for
which they boldly nailed their colours to the mast was the good old
cause of Protestantism *versus* Popery. Everyone, churchman or
Dissenter, knew *that* in 1688, and it is a grievous shame that anyone
now should try to deny it. The denial can only be regarded as a
symptom of ignorance or dishonesty.

It was quite late on Friday evening, May 18, when this petition
was finished and signed, and on Sunday morning, the 20th of May,
the royal declaration had to be read in all the churches in London.
There was therefore no time to be lost. Armed with their paper, six
of the Seven Bishops (Sancroft being forbidden to come to court)
proceeded to Whitehall Palace and had an interview with James II,
at ten o'clock at night. The King took the petition and read it with
mingled anger and amazement. He was both deeply displeased and
astonished, and showed it. He never thought that English bishops
would oppose his will. "I did not expect this," he said; "this is
standard of rebellion." In vain Trelawney fell on his knees, saying
"No Trelawney can be a rebel. Remember that my family has
fought for the Crown." In vain Turner said, "We rebel! We are
ready to die at your Majesty's feet." In vain Ken said, "I hope you
will grant us that liberty of conscience which you grant to all
mankind." It was all to no purpose. The King was thoroughly
angry. "You are trumpeters of sedition," he exclaimed. "Go to your
dioceses and see that I am obeyed." "We have two duties to
perform," said noble Ken, "our duty to God and our duty to Your
Majesty. We honour you: but we fear God." The interview ended,
and the Bishops retired from the royal presence, Ken's last words
being "God's will be done."

Before the sun rose on Saturday morning, May 19, the Bishops'
petition was printed as a broadsheet, and hawked through all the
streets of London. By whom this was done is not known to this
day: but the printer is said to have made a thousand pounds by it
in a few hours. The excitement was immense throughout the
metropolis, and when Sunday came, next day, the churches were
thronged with expecting crowds, wondering what the clergy would
do, and whether they would read the King's declaration. They were

not left long in doubt. Out of one hundred parish churches in the City and liberties of London, there were only four in which the Order in Council was obeyed, and in each case, as soon as the first words of the declaration were uttered, the congregation rose as one man and left the church. At Westminster Abbey the scene was long remembered by the boys of Westminster school. As soon as Bishop Spratt, who was then dean, a mean, servile prelate, began to read the declaration, the murmurs and noise of the people crowding out completely drowned his voice. He trembled so that men saw the paper shake in his hand; and long before he had done the abbey was deserted by all but the choristers and the school. Timothy Hall, an infamous clergyman, who read the declaration at St. Matthew's, Friday Street, was rewarded by the King with the vacant bishopric of Oxford. But he bought his mitre very dear. Not one canon of Christ Church attended his installation, and not one graduate would come to him for ordination.

A fortnight passed away, and on the 3rd of June the example of the London clergy was nobly followed in all parts of England. The bishops of Norwich, Gloucester, Salisbury, Winchester, and Exeter, who were unable to reach London in time for the Lambeth Conference, had signed copies of the petition and, of course, refused to order obedience to the declaration. The Bishop of Worcester declined to distribute it. In the great diocese of Chester, including all Lancashire, only three clergymen read it. In the huge diocese of Norwich, the stronghold of Protestantism, it was read in only four parishes out of twelve hundred. In short, it became evident that a spirit was awakened throughout the land which the Court had never expected, and that though the bishops and clergy might be broken, they would not bend. Whether the King could break them remained yet to be proved. On the evening of the 8th of June, all the Seven Bishops, in obedience to a summons from the King, appeared before him in council at Whitehall. They went provided with the best legal advice and acted carefully upon it. They calmly refused to admit anything to criminate themselves, unless forced to do it by the King's express command. They were questioned and interrogated about the meaning of words in their petition, but their answers were so guarded and judicious that the King gained nothing by the examination. They steadily held their ground and would neither withdraw their petition, nor confess they had done wrong, nor recede from their decision about the declaration. At last they were informed that they would be prosecuted for libel in the Court of King's Bench, and refusing, by their lawyers' advice to enter into recognizances for their appearance, they were formally committed to the Tower. A warrant was made out, and a boat was ordered to take them down the river.

Their committal to the Tower was the means of calling out an enthusiastic expression of feeling in London, such as, perhaps, has never been equaled in the history of the metropolis. It was known from an early hour that the Bishops were before the Council, and an anxious crowd had long waited round Whitehall to see what the result would be. But when the Londoners saw the seven aged prelates walking out of the palace under a guard of soldiers, and learned that they were going to prison (practically) in defence of English Protestantism, a scene of excitement ensued which almost baffles description. Hundreds crowded round them as they proceeded to Whitehall stairs, cheering them and expressing their sympathy. Many rushed into the mud and water up to their waists, blessing and asking their blessing. Scores of boats on the river full of people accompanied them down to the Tower with loud demonstrations of feeling. Even the very soldiers on guard in the Tower caught the infection and became zealous admirers of their prisoners. And when Sir E. Hales, the Popish governor, tried to check them, he was told by his subordinates that it was of no use, for his men "were all drinking the health of the Bishops."

The seven prelates were kept in the Tower for a week. Throughout that time the enthusiastic feeling of admiration for them flared higher and higher, and increased more and more every day. They were almost idolized as martyrs who had refused to truckle to a Popish tyrant, like Latimer and Ridley in Mary's days. The Church of England at one bound rose cent. per cent. in public estimation. Episcopacy was never so popular as it was that week. Crowds of people, including many of the nobility, went to the Tower every day to pay their respects to the venerable prisoners. Among them a deputation of ten leading Nonconformist ministers went to express their sympathy, and when the King sent for four of them and upbraided them, they boldly replied that they "thought it a solemn duty to forget past quarrels and stand by the men who stood by the Protestant cause." Even the Scotch Presbyterians were warmed and stirred in favour of the Bishops and sent messages of sympathy and encouragement. From every part of England came daily words of kindness and approbation. As for the men of Cornwall, they were so moved at the idea of their countryman, Trelawney, being in any danger, that a ballad was composed to suit the occasion, and sung over the county, of which the burden is still preserved.*

> And shall Trelawney die? and shall Trelawney die?
> Then twenty thousand Cornish boys shall know the reason why.

Even the miners took up the song and sung it with a variation: "Then thirty thousand underground shall know the reason why."

A king of more common sense than James might well have been staggered by the astounding popularity of the seven episcopal

---

* The following is said to have been the ballad, but it is doubtful whether any part except the chorus is as old as 1688:

> A good sword and a trusty hand,
> A merry heart and true;
> King James' men shall understand
> What Cornish men can do!
> And have they fixed the where and when,
> And shall Trelawney die?
> Then twenty thousand Cornish men
> Will know the reason why.
>   Chorus
> And shall they scorn Tre, Pol, and Pen?
> And shall Trelawney die?
> Here's twenty thousand Cornish men
> Will know the reason why.
> Outspake their Captain, brave and bold—
> A merry wight was he:
> "If London Tower were Michael's Hold,
> We'll set Trelawney free!
> We'll cross the Tamar land to land,
> The Severn is no stay,
> All side by side and hand to hand,
> And who shall bid us nay?"
>   Chorus
> And shall they scorn, &c.

prisoners, and would gladly have found some pretext for dropping further proceedings. But, unhappily for himself, he had not the wisdom to recede and "drove on furiously,"[1] like Jehu, and drove to his own destruction. He decided to go on with the prosecution. On the 15th of June the Seven Bishops were brought from the Tower to the Court of King's Bench and ordered to plead to the information laid against them. Of course they pleaded "not guilty." That day fortnight, the 29th of June, was fixed for their trial, and in the meantime they were allowed to be at liberty on their own recognizances. It was well for the Crown that they did not require bail. Twenty-one peers of the highest rank were ready to give security, three for each defendant, and one of the richest Dissenters in the City had begged, as a special favour, that he might have the honour of being bail for Bishop Ken.

On leaving the court, in order to go to their own lodgings, the Bishops received almost as great an ovation as when they were sent to the Tower. The bells of many churches were set ringing, and many of the lower orders who knew nothing of the forms of law imagined that all was over, and the good cause had triumphed. But whether ignorantly or intelligently, such a crowd assembled round the prelates in Palace Yard, that they found it difficult to force their way through their friends and admirers. Nor could it be said for a moment that the people knew not wherefore they were come together. One common feeling actuated the whole mass, and that feeling was abhorrence of Popery and zeal for Protestantism. How deep that feeling was is evidenced by a simple anecdote supplied by Macaulay.

> Cartwright, Bishop of Chester, a timid sycophant of the Court, was silly and curious enough to mingle with the crowd as his noble-minded brethren came out of the Court. Some person who saw his episcopal dress supposed he was one of the accused, and asked and received his blessing. A bystander cried out, "Do you know who blessed you?" "Surely," said the man, "it was one of the seven." "No!", said the other, "it was the Popish Bishop of Chester." At once the enraged Londoner roared out, "Popish dog, take your blessing back again."

---

[1] 2 Kings 9:20.

At last, on the 29th of June, the ever-memorable trial of the Seven Bishops actually came off, and they were arraigned before a jury of their countrymen in the Court of King's Bench at Westminster. Such a crowd was probably never before or since seen in a court of law. Sixty peers according to Evelyn's diary, thirty-five according to Macaulay, sat near the four judges and testified their interest in the cause. Westminster Hall, Palace Yard, and all the streets adjoining were filled with a multitude of people wound up to the highest pitch of anxious expectation.

Into all the details of that well-fought day I cannot enter. How from morning till sunset the legal battle went on—how the Crown witnesses were cross-examined and worried—how triumphantly Somers, the fourth counsel of the Bishops, showed that the alleged libel was neither false, nor libelous, nor seditious—how even the four judges were divided in opinion, and two of them went so far in their charge to the jury as to admit there was no libel—how the jury retired when it was dark to consider their verdict, and were shut up all night with the servants of the defendants sitting on the stairs to watch the doors and prevent roguery—how at length all the twelve jurymen were for acquittal except Arnold, the King's brewer, and even he gave way when the biggest of the twelve said, "Look at me, I will stay here till I am no bigger than a tobacco pipe before I find the Bishops guilty"—how at six in the morning the jury agreed, and at ten appeared in court, and by the mouth of their foreman, Sir Roger Langley, pronounced the Bishops *Not Guilty*—how at the words coming out of his lips Lord Halifax waved his hat, and at least ten thousand persons outside the court raised such a shout that the roof of old Westminster Hall seemed to crack—how the people in the streets caught up the cheer and passed it on all over London—how many seemed beside themselves with joy, and some laughed and some wept—how guns were fired and bells rung, and horsemen galloped off in all directions to tell the news of a victory over Popery—how the jury could scarcely get out of the Hall, and were forced to shake hands with hundreds crying out "God bless you, you have saved us all today"—how when night came bonfires were lighted, and all London was illuminated and huge figures of the Pope were burnt in effigy—all, all these things are so described in the burning words of Lord Macaulay's pictorial *History* that I shall not attempt to depict them. To go over the field so graphically occupied by that mighty "master of sentences" would be as foolish as to gild refined gold or paint the lily. Suffice it to say that the great battle of Protestantism against Popery was fought at this trial, that a great victory was won, and that to the prosecution and acquittal of the Seven Bishops, James II owed the loss of his crown.

For we must never forget that the consequences of the trial were enormously great, and that results flowed from it of which myriads never dreamed when they shouted and cheered, on the 29th of June:

(i) Within twenty-four hours of the trial a letter left England for Holland, signed by seven leading Englishmen, inviting the Prince of Orange to come over with an army and overthrow the Stuart dynasty. The hour had come at last, and the man was wanted.

(ii) Within four weeks of the trial, Archbishop Sancroft, warmed and softened by the events of May and June, drew up a circular letter to all the bishops of the Church of England, which is one of the most remarkable letters ever penned by an Archbishop of Canterbury, and has never received the attention it deserves. In this letter he solemnly enjoined the bishops and clergy "to have a tender regard to our brethren the Protestant Dissenters, to visit them at their homes, to receive them kindly at their own, and to treat them fairly whenever they meet them." Above all, he charged them "to take all opportunities of assuring the Dissenters that the English bishops are really and sincerely irreconcilable enemies to the errors, superstitions, idolatries, and tyrannies of the Church of Rome." And, lastly, he urged them "to exhort Dissenters to join with us in fervent prayer to the God of peace for the universal blessed union of all reformed churches both at home and abroad." A wonderful pastoral that! Well would it have been for the Church of England if Lambeth had always held similar language, and not cooled down and forgotten the Tower. But it was one of the first results of the famous trial.

(iii) Last, but not least, within six months of the Bishops' acquittal the Great Revolution took place, the Popish monarch lost his crown and left England, and William and Mary were placed on the English throne. But before they were formally placed on the throne the famous Declaration of Rights was solemnly drawn up and signed by both Houses of Parliament. And what was the very first sentence of that declaration? It is an assertion that "the late King James did endeavour to subvert and extirpate the Protestant religion—by assuming a power of dispensing with laws and by committing and prosecuting divers worthy prelates." And what was the last sentence of the declaration? It was the famous Oath of Supremacy, containing these words: "I do declare that no foreign prince, person, prelate, state, or potentate hath, or ought to have, jurisdiction, power, superiority, pre-eminence, or authority, ecclesiastical or spiritual, within this realm. So help me God." Such were the immediate consequences of the trial of the Seven Bishops. They are of unspeakable importance. They stand out to my eyes in the landscape of English history like Tabor in Palestine, and no Englishman ought ever to forget them. To the trial of the Seven Bishops we owe our second deliverance from Popery.

*   *   *

It remains for me to point out three practical lessons which appear to flow naturally out of the whole subject.

1. First and foremost, the reign of James II ought to teach a lesson *about English rulers and statesmen*, whether Whig or Tory. That lesson is the duty of never allowing the Government of this great country to be placed again in the hands of a Papist. If this lesson does not stand out plainly on the face of history, like the handwriting at Belshazzar's feast, I am greatly mistaken. Unless we are men, who having eyes, see not, and having ears, hear not, let us beware of Popish rulers. We know what they were in Queen Mary's days. We tried them a second time under James II. If we love our country, let us never try them again. They cannot possibly be honest, conscientious Papists if they do not labour incessantly to subvert English Protestantism, and turn everything upside down. I yield to no man in abhorrence of intolerance and religious persecution. I have not the slightest desire to put the clock back, and to revive such miserable disabilities as those of the Test and

Corporation Acts.[1] I am quite content with the Constitution as it is, and the laws which forbid the crown of England to be placed on the head of a Papist. But I hope we shall take care these laws are never repealed.

Some may think me an alarmist for saying such things. But I say plainly there is much in the outlook of the day to make a thinking man uncomfortable. I dislike the influence which certain well known Roman Catholic divines are gradually getting among the upper classes. I dislike the growing disposition to make an idol of mere *earnestness*, to forget history, and to suppose that Rome has changed and earnest Papists are as good as any Protestant. I dislike the modern principle, unknown to the good old Puritans, that states have nothing to do with religion, and that it matters not whether the sovereign is Protestant or Papist, Jew, Turk, infidel, or heretic. I see these things floating in the air. I confess they make me uncomfortable. I am sure we have need to stand on our guard, and to resolve that, God helping us, we will never allow the Pope to rule England again. If he does, we may depend upon it, we shall have no more blessing from God. The offended God of the Bible will turn away His face from us, and we shall bid a long farewell to peace at home, influence abroad, comfort in our families, and national prosperity. Once more then, I say, let us move heaven and earth before we sanction a Popish prime minister or a Popish king. On the 28th January 1689, the House of Commons resolved unanimously "that it hath been found by experience inconsistent with the safety and welfare of this Protestant kingdom to be governed by a Popish prince."[*] I pray God that resolution may never be forgotten, and never be canceled or expunged.

2. In the second place, the reign of James II ought to teach us a lesson *about English bishops and clergy*. That lesson is the duty of never forgetting that the true strength of the Established Church of

---

[1] The Test Act (1673) regulated a person's eligibility for public office by their subscription to the Established Church's doctrine of the Lord's Supper. The Corporation Act of 1661 required all persons of local government to renounce the Solemn League and Covenant, take the oath of non-resistance, and receive the sacrament according to the rites of the Church of England.

[*] Hallam, 3, p. 129.

England lies in loyal faithfulness to Protestant principles and hold unflinching opposition to the Church of Rome. Never was the Church of England so unpopular as in the days of Laud, and never so popular as in the days of the Seven Bishops. Never was the Church so hated by Nonconformists as she was when Laud tampered with Rome, never so much beloved by them as when the Seven Bishops went to prison rather than help the Pope. Why was it that when Laud was committed to the Tower few hands were held up in his favour, and few said, "God bless him"? There is only one answer: men did not trust him and thought him half a Papist. Why was it that when Sancroft and his companions were taken to the Tower fifty years afterwards, the heart of London was stirred, and the whole metropolis rose up to do them honour? The answer again is simple. Men loved them and admired them because they stuck to Protestantism and opposed Rome.

3. In the last place, the reign of James II ought to teach a *lesson to all loyal churchmen*. That lesson is the duty of using every reasonable and lawful means to resist the reintroduction of Romanism into the Church of England by the means of extreme ritualism. It is useless to deny that the times demand this, and that there is an organized conspiracy among us for Romanizing the Established Church of this country. Bishops see it and lament it in their charges. Statesmen see it and make no secret of it in public speeches. Dissenters see it and point the finger of scorn. Romanists see it and rejoice. Foreign nations see it and lift up their hands in amazement. Whether this disgraceful apostasy is to prosper and succeed or not remains yet to be proved. But one thing, at any rate, is certain. This is no time to sit still, fold our arms, and go to sleep. The Church of England expects all her sons to do their duty, and much, under God, depends on the action of the laity.

It is false to say, as some of the advocates of extreme ritualism constantly say, that those who oppose them want to narrow the limits of the Church of England, and to make it the exclusive church of one party. I for one indignantly deny the charge. I have always allowed, and do allow, that our church is largely comprehensive, and that there is room for honest high, honest low, and honest broad churchmen within her pale. If any clergyman likes to preach in a surplice, or has the Lord's Supper weekly, or has saints' day services, or daily matins and vespers, I have not the least wish to interfere with him, though I cannot see with his eyes. But I firmly maintain that the comprehensiveness of the Church has limits, and that those limits are the Thirty-nine Articles and the Prayer Book.

Controversy and religious strife, no doubt, are odious things; but there are times when they are a positive necessity. Unity and peace are very delightful; but they are bought too dear if they are bought at the expense of truth. There is a vast amount of maundering, childish, weak talk nowadays in some quarters about unity and peace, which I cannot reconcile with the language of St. Paul. It is a pity, no doubt, that there should be so much controversy; but it is also a pity that human nature should be so bad as it is, and that the devil should be loose in the world. It was a pity that Arius taught error about Christ's person: but it would have been a greater pity if Athanasius had not opposed him. It was a pity Tetzel went about preaching up the Pope's indulgencies: it would have been a far greater pity if Luther had not withstood him. Controversy, in fact, is one of the conditions under which truth in every age has to be defended and maintained, and it is nonsense to ignore it.

Of one thing I am very certain. Whether men will come forward or not to oppose the Romanizing movement of these days, if the Church of England once gives formal legal sanction to the revived Popish Mass and the revived detestable confessional, the people of this land will soon get rid of the Established Church of England. True to the mighty principles of the Reformation, our church will stand and retain its hold on the affections of the country, and no weapon formed against us shall prosper. False to these principles, and readmitting Popery, she will certainly fall, and no amount of histrionic, sensuous ceremonial will prevent her ruin. Like Ephesus which left her first love—like Thyatira which suffered Jezebel to teach—like Laodicea which became lukewarm—her candlestick will be taken away. The glory will depart from her. The pillar of cloud and fire will be removed. The best and most loyal of her children will forsake her in disgust, and like an army whose soldiers have gone away, leaving nothing behind but officers and band, the Church will perish, and perish deservedly, for want of churchmen.

GLOSSARY

act. The result of public deliberation, or the decision of a prince, legislative body, council, court of justice, or magistrate; a decree, edict, law, judgment, resolve, award, determination; as an act of parliament, or of congress. The term is also transferred to the book, record, or writing, containing the laws and determinations.

Act of Uniformity (1662). Act which required from all clergy a declaration of *assent* and *consent* to all and everything contained in the Prayer Book, insisted upon the renouncement of the Solemn League and Covenant, and required the re-ordination of ministers who had not received orders from a bishop.

alderman. A title applied to princes, dukes, earls, senators and presiding magistrates; also to archbishops and bishops, implying superior wisdom or authority.

antinomianism. A belief that under the Gospel dispensation, the law of God is of no use or obligation.

archbishop. A chief bishop; a church dignitary of the first class; a metropolitan bishop, who superintends the conduct of the suffragan bishops in his province, and also exercises episcopal authority.

archdeacon. An ecclesiastical dignitary, next in rank below a bishop, who has jurisdiction either over a part or over the whole diocese.

article. A point of faith; a doctrinal point or proposition in theology.

assembly. A convocation, convention or council of ministers and ruling elders delegated from each presbytery.

Bachelor of Divinity. 1. A bachelor's degree in the liberal arts, usually awarded for studies in the social sciences or humanities. 2. A person having this degree.

bishop. In the Greek, Latin, and some Protestant churches, a prelate, or person consecrated for the spiritual government and direction of a diocese.

Bonner, Edmund. (1500–69), Bishop of London who was Queen Mary's chief henchman during the Marian persecution.

Book of Sports. Issued by James I as the Declaration of Sports, it legalized "May games, Whitsun ales and morris dances, and the setting up of May-poles and other sports" on Sundays. James ordered all clergy to read the declaration from the pulpit, however, after strong opposition he withdrew his command. In 1633 Charles I reissued the declaration ordering all clergy to read it under threat of penalty. After Charles' execution in 1649, the declaration was repealed until the reign of his son, Charles II, in 1660.

bull. A letter, edict or rescript of the Pope, published or transmitted to the churches over which he is head, containing some decree, order or decision.

canon. 1. In ecclesiastical affairs, a law, or rule of doctrine or discipline, enacted by a council and confirmed by the sovereign; a decision of matters in religion, or a regulation of policy or discipline, by a general or provincial council. 2. A dignitary of the church; a person who possesses a prebend or revenue allotted for the performance of divine service in a cathedral or collegiate church.

canon law. A collection of ecclesiastical laws, serving as the rule of church government.

canonry. An ecclesiastical benefice, in a cathedral or collegiate church, which has a prebend or stated allowance out of the revenues of the church commonly annexed to it. The benefice filled by a canon. A prebend may subsist without a canonry; but a canonicate is inseparable from a prebend.

cardinal. An ecclesiastical prince in the Romish church, who has a voice in the conclave at the election of a Pope, who is taken from their number.

cathedral. Pertaining to the church which is the bishop's seat, or head church of a diocese; containing the see of a bishop; as a *cathedral* church; *cathedral* service.

cavalier. The appellation of the party of King Charles I.

chancellor. An officer invested with judicial powers, and particularly with the superintendence of all charters, letters and other official writings of the Crown, that required to be solemnly authenticated. From the Roman Empire, this office passed to the church, and hence every bishop has his chancellor.

chaplain. An ecclesiastic who has a chapel, or who performs service in a chapel. The King of Great Britain has forty-eight chaplains, who attend, four each month, to perform divine service for the royal family. Princes also, and persons of quality have chaplains.

Charles I. (1600–49), King of Great Britain and Ireland (1625–49), whose authoritarian rule and quarrels with Parliament provoked a civil war that led to his execution.

Charles II. (1630–85), King of Great Britain and Ireland (1660–85), who was restored to the throne after years of exile during the Puritan Commonwealth. The years of his reign are known as "the Restoration." In his last hours before his death, he was received into the Roman Catholic Church.

churchman. An Episcopalian, as distinguished from a Presbyterian or Congregationalist &c.

commonwealth. An established form of government, or civil polity; or more generally, a state; a body politic, consisting of a certain portion of men united by compact or tacit agreement, under one form of government and system of laws. A commonwealth is properly a free state; a popular or representative government; a republic.

convocation. An assembly of the clergy, by their representatives, to consult on ecclesiastical affairs. It is held during the session of Parliament, and consists of an upper and lower house.

Cromwell, Oliver. A leading general on the Parliamentary side in the English Civil War against King Charles I, who helped to bring about the overthrow of the Stuart monarchy and was Lord Protector of the republican Commonwealth of England, Scotland, and Ireland from 1653 to 1658.

curate. A clergyman in the Church of England, who is employed to perform divine service in the place of the incumbent, parson or vicar. He must be licensed by the bishop or ordinary, and having no fixed estate in the curacy, he may be removed at pleasure. But some curates are perpetual.

deacon. In the Church of England, the office of deacons is declared to be to assist the priest in administering the holy communion.

dean. 1. An ecclesiastical dignitary in cathedral and collegiate churches, and the head of a chapter; the second dignitary of a diocese. 2. An officer in each college of the universities in England.

deanery. The jurisdiction of a dean.

declaration. A public annunciation; proclamation.

dignitary. An ecclesiastic who holds a dignity, or a benefice which gives him some preeminence over mere priests and canons, as a bishop, dean, archdeacon, prebendary, &c.

diocese. The circuit or extent of a bishop's jurisdiction; an ecclesiastical division of a kingdom or state, subject to the authority of a bishop.

Dissenter. One who separates from, or does not unite with the Church of England.

divine. A minister of the Gospel; a priest; a clergyman.

dragoon. *n.* A soldier or musketeer. *v.* 1. To persecute by abandoning a place to the rage of soldiers. 2. To harass; to persecute; to compel to submit by violent measures; to force

duke. 1. In Great Britain, one of the highest order of nobility; a title of honor nobility next below the princes. 2. In some countries on the Continent, a sovereign prince without the title of *king*; as the Duke of Savoy.

earl. A British title of nobility, or a nobleman, the third in rank, being next below a marquis, and next above a viscount. The title answers to *count* in France, and *graaf* in Germany. The earl formerly had the government of a *shire*, and was called *shireman*. After the conquest, earls were called *counts*, and from them shires have taken the name *counties*.

Edward VI. (1537–53), son of Henry VIII and Jane Seymour (Henry's third wife), was only nine years old when he became king, and died when he was fifteen. He is remembered best for his sweeping Protestant reforms.

episcopal. 1. Belonging to or vested in bishops or prelates; as episcopal jurisdiction; episcopal authority. 2. Governed by bishops; as the Episcopal Church.

esquire. Properly, a shield-bearer or armor-bearer, an attendant on a knight. A title of dignity next in degree below a knight. In England this title is given to the younger sons of noblemen, to officers of the king's courts and of the household, to counselors at law, justices of the peace, while in commission, sheriffs, and other gentlemen.

Establishment. The episcopal form of religion, so called in England.

evangelical. According to the Gospel; consonant to the doctrines and precepts of the Gospel published by Christ and His apostles.

faggot. A bundle of sticks, twigs, or small branches of trees, used for fuel, or for raising batteries, filling ditches, and other purposes in fortification.

fellow. A member of a college that shares its revenues; or a member of any incorporated society; a trustee.

formulary. *n.* 1. A book containing stated and prescribed forms, as of oaths, declarations, prayers and the like; a book of precedents. 2. prescribed form.

friar. An appellation common to the monks of all orders; those who enter religious orders considering themselves as a fraternity or brotherhood. Friars are generally distinguished into four principal branches, *viz.*: 1. Minors, gray friars, or Franciscans; 2. Augustines; 3. Dominicans or black friars; 4. White Friars or Carmelites.

Gardiner, Stephen. (*c.* 1482–1555), English bishop and, in effect, chief minister of the realm during the reign of Mary Tudor. John

Fox describes him as an "enemy of God's word."

gaol. A prison; a place for the confinement of debtors and criminals.

glebe. The land belonging to a parish church or ecclesiastical benefice.

Henry VII. (1457–1509), founder of the Tudor dynasty and was King of England from 1485 to 1509.

Henry VIII. (1491–1547), King of England whose divorce from his first wife, Catherine of Aragon, set in motion the English Reformation.

heretic. A person under any religion, but particularly the Christian, who holds and teaches opinions repugnant to the established faith, or that which is made the standard of orthodoxy.

High Commission. English ecclesiastical court instituted by the Crown in the sixteenth century as a means to enforce the laws of the Reformation settlement and exercise control over the Church. It became a controversial instrument of repression, used against those who refused to acknowledge the authority of the Church of England.

High Mass. A mass celebrated according to the complete rite, in which the liturgy is sung, and not said, by the celebrant, who is attended by a deacon and subdeacon, and which is usually characterized by the use of music and incense.

House of Commons. The lower house of Parliament, consisting of the representative of cities, boroughs and counties, chosen by men possessed of the property or qualification required by law.

House of Lords. The upper house of Parliament consisting of archbishops, bishops holding sees in England, all the dukes, marquesses, earls, viscounts, and barons in the hereditary peerages of England, Scotland, and the rest of the United Kingdom, peeresses, and the judges of the Supreme Court of Judicature.

incumbent. The person who is in present possession of a benefice, or of any office. It is applied to civil officers as well as to ecclesiastical.

James I. (James VI of Scotland, 1566–1625), the only son of Mary, Queen of Scots, became James I of England in 1603. He was a strong advocate of royal absolutism, preferring episcopacy over Presbyterianism.

James II. (1634–85) King of Great Britain, the last Stuart monarch in the direct male line, and avowed member of the Roman Catholic Church. Deposed in 1688, he was replaced by William III and Mary II.

Jewel, John. (1522–71), Bishop of Salisbury who defended Queen Elizabeth's religious policies opposing Roman Catholicism.

Jesuit. One of the society of Jesus, so called, founded by Ignatius Loyola in 1534; a militant order pledged to strict obedience to the Pope and to acting as the Church's instrument for regaining ground lost to Protestantism; a society remarkable for their cunning in propagating their principles.

lecturer. 1. One who reads or pronounces lectures; a professor or an instructor who delivers formal discourses for the instruction of others. 2. A preacher in a church, hired by the parish to assist the rector, vicar, or curate.

litany. A solemn form of supplication, used during public worship.

liturgy. In a general sense, all public ceremonies that belong to divine service; hence, in a restricted sense, among the Romanists, the Mass; and among Protestants, the common prayer, or the formulary of public prayers.

Long Parliament. Session of the English Parliament summoned in 1640 by King Charles I to raise money for the Bishop's War. Duration of the Long Parliament extended either until April 1653, when its remaining members were ejected by the Cromwellian army, or until March 1660, when its members, finally restored, passed an act for its dissolution.

lord. A nobleman; a title of honor in Great Britain given to those who are noble by birth or creation; a peer of the realm, including dukes, marquises, earls, viscounts and barons. Archbishops and bishop also, as members of the House of Lords, are Lords of Parliament. Thus we say, *lords* temporal and spiritual. By courtesy also the title is given to the sons of dukes and marquise, and to the eldest sons of earls.

Lord Chief Justice. In England and Wales, the head of the Queen's (or King's) Bench Division of the High Court of Justice and next in rank to the Lord Chancellor.

martyr. One who, by his death, bears witness to the truth of the Gospel.

Mary Tudor. (Mary I, 1516–58), daughter of Henry VIII and Catherine of Aragon, and the first queen to rule England (1553–58) in her own right. Her persecution of Protestants earned her the unhappy name *Bloody Mary.*

Mary II. (1662–94), Protestant daughter of King James II, wife of King William III, and Queen of England (1689–94), she supported her Dutch husband in becoming co-ruler of England after he overthrew her father's government.

mass. The service of the Romish church; the office or prayers used at the celebration of the eucharist; the consecration of the bread and wine.

master. The director of a school; a teacher; an instructor.

Master of Arts. 1. A master's degree usually in a specific branch of the humanities or social sciences. 2. A person who has been awarded this degree.

May-pole. A long raised pole to dance around in May.

metropolitan. 1. *a.* Belonging to a metropolis, or to the mother church; residing in the chief city. 2. *n.* The bishop of the mother church; an archbishop.

Methodist. One of a sect of Christians so called from the exact regularity of their lives, and the strictness of their principles and rules. They are now a complete denomination.

minister. The pastor of a church, duly authorized or licensed to preach the Gospel and administer the sacraments.

monk. A man who retires from the ordinary temporal concerns of the world, and devotes himself to religion. Monks usually live in monasteries, on entering which they take a vow to observe certain rules. Some however live as hermits in solitude, and others have lived a strolling life without any fixed residence.

Nonconformist. One who neglects or refuses to conform to the rites and mode of worship of an established church.

orator. An officer in the universities of England.

parish. The precinct or territorial jurisdiction of a minister, or the precinct, the inhabitants of which belong to the same church.

Parliament. In Great Britain, the grand assembly of the three estates, the lord spiritual, lords temporal, and the commons; the general council of the nation constituting the legislature, summoned by the king's authority to consult on the affairs of the nation, and to enact and repeal laws. The word is generally used to denote the three estates above named, consisting of two distinct branches, the House of Lords and the House of Commons.

pastor. A minister of the Gospel who has the charge of a church and congregation, whose duty is to watch over the people of his charge, and instruct them in the sacred doctrines of the Christian religion.

Papist. A Roman Catholic; one who adheres to the Church of Rome and the authority of the Pope.

Popery. The religion of the Church of Rome, comprehending doctrines and practices.

Prayer Book. *Book of Common Prayer,* liturgical book used by Church of England. First authorized for use in 1549, it was revised in 1552, with subsequent revisions in 1559 and 1604. The radical revisions to it in 1662 became a point of conflict with the Puritans, ultimately leading to their ejection.

prebend. The stipend or maintenance granted out of the estate of a cathedral or collegiate church.

prebendary. An ecclesiastic who enjoys a prebend; the stipendiary of a cathedral church. A prebendary differs from a canon in this; the prebendary receives his prebend in consideration of his officiating in the church; the canon merely in consequence of his being received into the cathedral or college.

prelate. An ecclesiastic of the higher order, as an archbishop, bishop or patriarch; a dignitary of the church.

Presbyterian. A form of church government by elders (*presbyters*), and a theological system of doctrine.

primate. The chief ecclesiastic in the church; an archbishop.

prior. 1. The superior of a convent of monks, or one next in dignity to an abbot. 2. In some churches, one who presides over others in the same churches.

privy council. The British sovereign's private council.

privy councillor. A member of the privy council.

proctor. 1. In a general sense, one who is employed to manage the affairs of another. 2. Appropriately, a person employed to manage another's cause in a court of civil or ecclesiastical law, as in the court of admiralty, or in a spiritual court. 3. The magistrate of a university.

protector. In England, one who formerly had the care of the kingdom during the king's minority; a regent. Cromwell assumed the title of *Lord Protector.*

protectorate. Government by protector.

Protestant. One of the party who adhered to Luther at the Reformation. This name was afterwards extended to the followers of Calvin. *Protestants* is the denomination now given to all who belong to the Reformed churches.

provost. In a general sense, a person who is appointed to superintend or preside over something; the chief magistrate of a city or town; as the provost of Edinburgh or of Glasgow, answering to the mayor of other cities; the provost of a college answering to the president.

public orator. An officer in the universities of England.

Purgatory. Among Roman Catholics, a supposed place or state after death, in which the souls of persons are purified, or in which they expiate such offenses committed in this life, as do not merit eternal damnation. After this purgation from the impurities of sin, the souls are supposed to be received into heaven.

Puritan. A dissenter from the Church of England. The puritans were so called in derision, on account of their professing to follow the pure word of God, in opposition to all traditions and human constitutions. Hume gives this name to three parties; the *political* puritans, who maintained the highest principles of civil liberty; the puritans in *discipline*, who were averse to the ceremonies and government of the episcopal church; and the *doctrinal* puritans, who rigidly defended the speculative system of the first reformers.

Pusey, E.B. (1800–82), leader in the Tractarian Movement, whose name was used to coin the expressions *Puseyism* and *Puseyite*, obvious references to the movement and its followers.

recorder. An officer of a city who is keeper of the rolls or records, or who is invested with judicial powers.

rector. A clergyman who has the charge and cure of a parish, and has the tithes, &c.; or the parson of an unimpropriated parish.

rectory. A parish church, parsonage or spiritual living, with all its rights, tithes, and glebes.

Reverend. A title of respect given to clergy or ecclesiastics.

Ritualist Movement. Movement beginning in 1859, which held to Romish doctrines and practices. Among other things, ritualism believes in *baptismal regeneration*, the *real presence*, and *apostolical succession*, and advocates the *burning of incense*, the *eastward position*, and *sacrificial dress* within Anglicanism.

Reformation. By way of eminence, the change of the Christian religion from the corruptions of Popery to its primitive purity, begun by Luther, A.D. 1517.

Reformer. One of those who commenced the Reformation of religion from Popish corruption.

regius. Of a professor in a British university holding a chair founded by or dependent on the sovereign.

register. A book in which are recorded the baptisms of children and the marriages and burials of the parish.

Roundhead. A derisive name given to adherents of the Parliamentary Party during the English Civil War.

sacrament. A solemn religious ceremony enjoined by Christ, the Head of the Christian Church, to be observed by His followers, by which their special relation to Him is created, or their obligation to Him renewed and ratified.

sacerdotal. Pertaining to priests or the priesthood; priestly; as *sacerdotal* dignity; *sacerdotal* functions or garments; *sacerdotal* character.

see. 1. The seat of episcopal power; a diocese; the jurisdiction of a bishop. 2. The seat of an archbishop; a province or jurisdiction of an archbishop. 3. The seat, place or office of the Pope or Roman Pontiff; as the Papal *see*.

Sir. The title of a knight or baronet.

Solemn League and Covenant (1643). Agreement between England and Scotland by which the Scots agreed to support the English Parliamentarians in their dispute with the royalists, both countries agreed to extirpate *popery* and *prelacy*, and both countries pledged to work for a civil and religious union of England, Scotland, and Ireland under a presbyterian-parliamentary system.

Star Chamber. In English law, the court made up of judges and privy councillors that grew out of the medieval king's council as a supplement to the regular justice of the common-law courts. The punishments, which were arbitrary, included imprisonment, fine, the pillory, whipping, branding, and mutilation, but never death. It was abolished by the Long Parliament in 1641.

Stuart. Royal house of Scotland from 1371 and of England from 1603. Interrupted in 1649 by the establishment of the Commonwealth, and restored in 1660, it ended in 1714.

surplice. A white garment worn by clergymen of some denominations over their other dress, in their ministrations. It is particularly the habit of the clergy of the Church of England.

synod. A council or meeting of ecclesiastics to consult on matters of religion. Synods are four kinds: 1. *General* or *ecumenical*, which are composed of bishops from different nations. 2. *National*, in which the bishops of one nation only meet, to determine points of doctrine or discipline. 3. *Provincial*, in which the bishops of one province only meet. 4. *Diocesan*

Ten Articles. Anglican statements of doctrine drafted by Henry VIII and Cranmer in 1536. Schaff describes them as "essentially Romish, with the Pope left out in the cold." Fox says they were intended for "weaklings newly weaned from their mother's milk of Rome."

Tracts for the Times. A series of ninety Anglo-Catholic revisionist pamphlets written from 1833 to 1841. Spearheaded by J.H. Newman (1801–90), the Tracts were a doctrinal and historical challenge to the English Reformation. Openly Catholic, their predominant themes were the *Church*, *apostolical succession*, the *sacraments*, and *ritualism*. The propagation of the Tracts became known as the Tractarian Movement.

Tractarian Movement. Nineteenth-century movement that sought a renewal of "catholic," or Roman Catholic, doctrine and practice within the Church of England in opposition to Protestantism. Founded by J.H. Newman, among its members were Froude, Keble, Littledale, and Pusey.

transubstantiation. In Romish theology, the supposed conversion of the bread and wine in the eucharist, into the body and blood of Christ.

Tudor. English royal dynasty of Welsh origin, which gave five sovereigns to England: Henry VII; his son, Henry VIII; and his three children, Edward VI, Mary I, and Elizabeth I.

vestry. A room appendant to a church, in which the sacerdotal vestments and sacred utensils are kept, and where parochial meetings are held.

vicar. In the Canon Law, the priest of a parish, the predial tithes of which are impropriated or appropriated, that is, belong to a chapter or religious house, or to a layman, who receives them, and only allows the vicar the smaller tithes or a salary.

vice-chancellor. An officer in a university of England, a distinguished member, who is annually elected to manage the affairs in the absence of the chancellor.

whig. One of a political party which had its origin in England in the seventeenth century, in the reign of Charles I or II. Those who supported the King in his high claims were called *tories*, and the advocates of popular rights were called *whigs*.

William III. William of Orange (1650–1702) King of Great Britain (1689–1702), reigning jointly with Queen Mary II (until her death in 1694).

yeoman. An officer in the king's household, of a middle rank between a gentleman and a groom; a name or title of certain soldiers.

INDEX

Light From Old Times

Designed by Charles Nolan
Composed by Ruptured Disc Typesetter, Ltd.
in Bembo 11 on 13 point
Line art duplicated by Ruptured Disc Typesetter, Ltd.
Printed by Jostens Printing and Publishing
on 60 lb. Husky Offset
Bound by Jostens Printing and Publishing
in Holliston Roxite C Linen
Dust jacket designed by Evan Wilson
Composed by Trireme d'SIGN

1558 – Elizabeth I crowned
1559 – Parliament restores Act of Supremacy ✦ permits marriage
of clergy ✦ commands destruction of all "Monuments of
feigned miracles, pilgrimages, idolatry, and superstition"
Final edition of Calvin's *Institutes* published
Pope Paul IV establishes *The Index of Forbidden Books*
1560 – "Geneva Bible" published
1563 – Thirty-nine Articles issued
Council of Trent closes ✦ Double *anathema* pronounced
upon all heretics (Protestants)
1564 – John Calvin dies
1568 – "Bishops' Bible" published
1570 – Pope Pius V declares Elizabeth I deposed ✦ absolves English
subjects from allegiance to her ✦ forbids obedience to her
under penalty of excommunication
1572 – St. Bartholomew's Day Massacre (France)
1587 – Mary "Queen of Scots" beheaded
1588 – Royal Navy defeats Spanish Armada

1603 – James I crowned
1607 – Authorised Version of the Bible officially sanctioned
Jamestown founded
1609 – Jacobus Arminius dies
1611 – Authorised Version published
1613 – Galileo affirms Copernicanism
1616 – Galileo condemned for *heresy*
William Shakespeare dies
1619 – Canons of Dort affirm Doctrines of Grace
1620 – "For the glory of God and the advancement of the
Christian faith"—101 Pilgrims sail aboard the *Mayflower*

1625 – Charles I crowned
1633 – Galileo condemned as a *heretic*—again
1639 – Samuel Ward dies
1640 – the Long Parliament commences
1641 – Archbishop Laud imprisoned in the Tower ✦ *thorough* Lord
Strafford beheaded
1642 – English Civil War breaks out
1643 – Westminster Assembly convened ✦ Parliament accepts
Solemn League and Covenant ✦ Directory for the Public
Worship of God released ✦ Westminster Confession begun